BUILT UPON THE ROCK

BUILT UPON THE ROCK

Studies in the Gospel of Matthew

Edited by

Daniel M. Gurtner & John Nolland

WILLIAM B. EERDMANS PUBLISHING COMPANY
GRAND RAPIDS, MICHIGAN / CAMBRIDGE, U.K.

© 2008 William B. Eerdmans Publishing Company
All rights reserved

Published 2008 by
Wm. B. Eerdmans Publishing Co.
2140 Oak Industrial Drive N.E., Grand Rapids, Michigan 49505 /
P.O. Box 163, Cambridge CB3 9PU U.K.

Printed in the United States of America

14 13 12 11 10 09 08   7 6 5 4 3 2 1

Library of Congress Cataloging-in-Publication Data

Built upon the rock: studies in the Gospel of Matthew /
    edited by Daniel M. Gurtner & John Nolland.
      p.   cm.
Includes bibliographical references and indexes.
ISBN 978-0-8028-4563-4 (pbk.: alk. paper)
1. Bible. N.T. Matthew — Criticism, interpretation, etc.
I. Gurtner, Daniel M.   II. Nolland, John.

BS2555.52.B85   2008
226.2′06 — dc22

                          2007042523

www.eerdmans.com

Contents

PREFACE	vii
CONTRIBUTORS	ix
ABBREVIATIONS	xi
Matthew's Sources—Oral or Written? A Rabbinic Analogy and Empirical Insights *Armin D. Baum*	1
How Matthew Tells the Story: A Linguistic Approach to Matthew's Syntax *Stephanie L. Black*	24
Not the Law but the Messiah: Law and Righteousness in the Gospel of Matthew — An Ongoing Debate *Roland Deines*	53
Ἀπό . . . ἕως and Salvation History in Matthew's Gospel *Mervyn Eloff*	85
Matthew and Jerusalem *R. T. France*	108
Matthew's Theology of the Temple and the "Parting of the Ways": Christian Origins and the First Gospel *Daniel M. Gurtner*	128

CONTENTS

Matthew and Anti-Semitism   154
John Nolland

Holiness and Ecclesiology: The Church in Matthew   170
Donald A. Hagner

The Rock on Which to Build: Some Mainly Pauline
Observations about the Sermon on the Mount   187
David Wenham

Balaam-Laban as the Key to the Old Testament
Quotations in Matthew 2   207
David Instone-Brewer

"The Virgin Will Conceive": Typological Fulfillment
in Matthew 1:18-23   228
James M. Hamilton Jr.

The Rhetoric of Hearing: The Use of the Isaianic
Hearing Motif in Matthew 11:2—16:20   248
Jeannine K. Brown

Reflections on the Writing of a Commentary
on the Gospel of Matthew   270
R. T. France and John Nolland

BIBLIOGRAPHY   290

INDEX OF MODERN AUTHORS   313

INDEX OF SUBJECTS   316

INDEX OF ANCIENT SOURCES   318

Preface

The present volume is the product of the 2005 Tyndale Fellowship New Testament Study Group, held at Tyndale House in Cambridge on June 29 through July 1, 2005. It is the link to the Tyndale Fellowship that lies behind the title of this volume: *Built upon the Rock*. For to each of us a personal commitment to Jesus Christ remains the foundation of our scholarly endeavors. Each contributor is part of this confessional and scholarly community, but each is also part of the broader scholarly guild; and it is intended that the papers here presented should also make a contribution to scholarship in its broadest sense.

In *Built upon the Rock: Studies in the Gospel of Matthew*, some of the contributions address issues pertinent to the whole gospel, including a fresh discussion of the nature of Matthew's sources (Baum) and an exploration of the role of grammatical features to mark emphasis (Black). Law and righteousness are classical problem areas given fresh attention (Deines), as is Matthew's portrayal of salvation history (Eloff). Matthew's view of Jerusalem (France) and its Temple (Gurtner) are given comprehensive treatment. The ongoing discussion of anti-Semitism in the first gospel is the subject of a thoughtful and responsible essay (Nolland), as is Matthew's view of the Church (Hagner). The Sermon on the Mount is addressed in relation to the writings of Paul (Wenham). Enigmatic texts in Matthew 2 are illuminated by means of careful attention to Old Testament and Jewish influence (Instone-Brewer). Typological fulfillment is employed to unravel the mystery of the "virgin will conceive" (1:18-23) text (Hamilton). The Isaianic "hearing motif" is traced from a narrative perspective through a significant portion of the gospel (11:2–16:20) (Brown). The volume concludes with the joint reflections on writing commentaries on the first gospel in the twenty-first century by esteemed experts in that field (France and Nolland).

The editors are grateful to the careful guidance of Rev. Dr. David Wenham, who convened the conference on Matthew's gospel and took a keen interest in assembling the papers herein put forth. We are similarly grateful to Dr. Peter Head, secretary of the New Testament group, who executed the administrative duties of putting together our meeting and also offered important input on the papers. We are especially grateful to the staff and readers at Tyndale House for providing an excellent and relaxing atmosphere for stimulating discussion. Particular mention of gratitude goes to Dr. Bruce Winter, Warden of Tyndale House, whose interest in our subject and entrepreneurial spirit were of decisive importance in seeing this project come to print. Finally, thanks also go to Mrs. Gloria Metz for careful attention to formatting these papers, and to Mr. Seth Ehorn for preparing the indexes.

DANIEL M. GURTNER
JOHN NOLLAND

Contributors

Editors

DANIEL M. GURTNER, Ph.D. Assistant Professor of New Testament, Bethel Theological Seminary, St. Paul, MN (U.S.A.)

JOHN NOLLAND, Ph.D. Academic Dean, Vice-Principal, and Lecturer in New Testament Studies, Trinity College, Bristol (U.K.)

Contributors

ARMIN D. BAUM, Dr. theol. Lecturer in New Testament at the Freie Theologische Akademie, Gießen (Germany), and Professor of New Testament at the Evangelical Theological Faculty, Leuven (Belgium). "Matthew's Sources — Oral or Written? A Rabbinic Analogy and Empirical Insights."

STEPHANIE L. BLACK, Ph.D. Ethiopian Graduate School of Theology, Addis Ababa (Ethiopia). "How Matthew Tells the Story: A Linguistic Approach to Matthew's Syntax."

JEANNINE K. BROWN, Ph.D. Associate Professor of New Testament and Associate Academic Dean, Bethel Theological Seminary, St. Paul, MN (U.S.A.). "The Rhetoric of Hearing: The Use of the Isaianic Hearing Motif in Matthew 11:2–16:20."

ROLAND DEINES, Dr.theol.habil., Lecturer in New Testament, University of Nottingham (U.K.). "Not the Law but the Messiah: Law and Righteousness in the Gospel of Matthew — An Ongoing Debate."

CONTRIBUTORS

MERVYN ELOFF, D.Th. Assistant Lecturer at George Whitefield College, Cape Town, and New Testament Research Fellow at the University of Stellenbosch (South Africa). "Ἀπό . . . ἕως and Salvation History in Matthew's Gospel."

R. T. FRANCE, Ph.D. (Retired) Principal of Wycliffe Hall, Oxford. "Matthew and Jerusalem."

DANIEL M. GURTNER, Ph.D. Assistant Professor of New Testament, Bethel Theological Seminary, St. Paul, MN (U.S.A.). "Matthew's Theology of the Temple and the 'Parting of the Ways': Christian Origins and the First Gospel"

DONALD A. HAGNER, Ph.D. George Eldon Ladd Professor Emeritus of New Testament, Fuller Theological Seminary, Pasadena, California (U.S.A.). "Holiness and Ecclesiology: The Church in Matthew."

JAMES M. HAMILTON JR., Ph.D. Assistant Professor of Biblical Studies, Southwestern Baptist Theological Seminary (U.S.A.). "'The Virgin Will Conceive': Typological Fulfillment in Matthew 1:18-23."

DAVID INSTONE-BREWER, Ph.D. Senior Research Fellow in Rabbinics and the New Testament, Tyndale House, Cambridge (U.K.). "Balaam-Laban as the Key to the Old Testament Quotations in Matthew 2."

JOHN NOLLAND, Ph.D. Academic Dean, Vice-Principal, and Lecturer in New Testament Studies, Trinity College, Bristol (U.K.). "Matthew and Anti-Semitism."

DAVID WENHAM, Ph.D. Senior Tutor in New Testament Studies, Trinity College, Bristol (U.K.). "The Rock on Which to Build: Some Mainly Pauline Observations about the Sermon on the Mount."

Abbreviations

I. Journals, Periodicals, Reference Works, and Series

AB	Anchor Bible
ABD	*Anchor Bible Dictionary*
ABRL	Anchor Bible Reference Library
AnBib	Analecta biblica
ANF	*Ante-Nicene Fathers*
ANRW	*Aufstieg und Niedergang der römischen Welt*
ASTI	*Annual of the Swedish Theological Institute*
BBB	Bonner biblische Beiträge
BETL	Bibliotheca ephemeridum theologicarum lovaniensium
Bib	*Biblica*
BJRL	*Bulletin of the John Rylands University Library*
BSW	*Biblical Studies on the Web Journal*
BZ	*Biblische Zeitschrift*
BZNW	Beihefte zur Zeitschrift für die neutestamentliche Wissenschaft
CBQ	*Catholic Biblical Quarterly*
CBQMS	Catholic Biblical Quarterly Monograph Series
CJ	*Classical Journal*
ConBNT	Coniectanea biblica: New Testament Series
CRINT	Compendia rerum iudaicarum ad Novum Testamentum
DSD	*Dead Sea Discoveries*
EKKNT	Evangelisch-katholischer Kommentar zum Neuen Testament
EQ	*Evangelical Quarterly*
ETL	*Ephemerides theologicae lovanienses*
ExpT	*Expository Times*

FRLANT	Forschungen zur Religion und Literatur des Alten und Neuen Testaments
HeyJ	*Heythrop Journal*
HTR	Harvard Theological Review
HUCA	Hebrew Union College Annual
ICC	International Critical Commentary
JBL	*Journal of Biblical Literature*
JETS	*Journal of the Evangelical Theological Society*
JSJSup	Journal for the Study of Judaism: Supplement Series
JSNT	*Journal for the Study of the New Testament*
JSNTSup	Journal for the Study of the New Testament: Supplement Series
JSOT	*Journal for the Study of the Old Testament*
JSOTSup	Journal for the Study of the Old Testament: Supplement Series
JSR	*Journal for the Study of Religion*
JTS	*Journal of Theological Studies*
LCL	Loeb Classical Library
NB	*New Blackfriars*
Neot	*Neotestamentica*
NICNT	New International Commentary on the New Testament
NIGTC	New International Greek Testament Commentary
NovT	*Novum Testamentum*
NovTSup	Novum Testamentum Supplements
NSBT	New Studies in Biblical Theology
NTAbh	New Testament Abhandlungen
NTM	New Testament Message
NTS	*New Testament Studies*
NTTS	New Testament Tools and Studies
OBO	Orbis biblicus et orientalis
OTP	*Old Testament Pseudepigrapha*
P. Gnom.	*Der Gnomen des Idios Logos*
SBLAB	Society of Biblical Literature Academia Biblica
SBLDS	Society of Biblical Literature Dissertation Series
SBLSP	*Society of Biblical Literature Seminar Papers*
SBT	Studies in Biblical Theology
SJLA	Studies in Judaism in Late Antiquity
SJT	*Scottish Journal of Theology*
SNTSMS	Society for New Testament Studies Monograph Series
ST	*Studia theologica*

START	Selected Technical Articles Related to Translation
StrB	Strack, H. L., and P. Billerbeck, *Kommentar zum Neuen Testament aus Talmud und Midrasch*
TDNT	*Theological Dictionary of the New Testament*
TJ	*Trinity Journal*
TLZ	*Theologische Literaturzeitung*
TNTC	Tyndale New Testament Commentaries
TS	*Theological Studies*
TSAJ	Texte und Studien zum antiken Judentum
TynBul	*Tyndale Bulletin*
TZ	*Theologische Zeitschrift*
UPZ	U. Wilcken, *Urkunden der Ptolemäerzeit. I. Papyri aus Unterägypten*
VE	*Vox evangelica*
VT	*Vetus Testamentum*
WBC	Word Biblical Commentary
WMANT	Wissenschaftliche zum Alten und Neuen Testament
WTJ	*Westminster Theological Journal*
WUNT	Wissenschaftliche Untersuchungen zum Neuen Testament
ZNW	*Zeitschrift für die neutestamentliche Wissenschaft*
ZST	*Zeitschrift für systematische Theologie*
ZTK	*Zeitschrift für Theologie und Kirche*

II. Old Testament Pseudepigrapha

Apoc. Elijah	*Apocalypse of Elijah*
Apoc. Mos.	*Apocalypse of Moses*
2 Bar.	*2 Baruch*
Ep. Arist.	*Epistle of Aristeas*
Jos. As.	*Joseph and Asenath*
LAB	*Liber antiquitatum biblicarum*
Liv. Pro.	*Lives of the Prophets*
Mart. Isa.	*Martyrdom of Isaiah*
Pss. Sol.	*Psalms of Solomon*
T. Ash.	*Testament of Asher*
T. Benj.	*Testament of Benjamin*
T. Dan	*Testament of Dan*
T. Iss.	*Testament of Issachar*
T. Jud.	*Testament of Judah*

ABBREVIATIONS

T. Levi — Testament of Levi
T. Naph. — Testament of Naphtali
T. Sol. — Testament of Solomon
T. Zeb. — Testament of Zebulun

III. Apostolic Fathers

Barn. — Barnabas

IV. Jewish Authors

Josephus
    Ant. — Antiquities of the Jews
    C. Ap. — Contra Apionem
    War — Jewish War
Philo
    Legat. — Legatio ad Gaium

V. Mishnaic, Talmudic, Rabbinic, and Targumic Writing

ʿAbod. Zar. — ʿAbodah Zarah
ʾAbot. — ʾAbot
ʾAbot. R. Nat. — ʾAbot de Rabbi Nathan
Ber. — Berakot
ʿErub. — ʿErubin
Exod. Rab. — Exodus Rabbah
Giṭ. — Giṭṭin
Ḥag. — Ḥagigah
Lev. Rab. — Leviticus Rabbah
Num. Rab. — Numbers Rabbah
Pesiq. R. — Pesiqta Rabbati
Sanh. — Sanhedrin
Shab. — Shabbat
Shebuʿ. — Shebuʿot
Sukk. — Sukkah
Taʿan. — Taʿanit
Tg. Isa. — Targum of Isaiah

Tg. Lam.   *Targum of Lamentations*
Tg. Ps.-J.   *Targum Pseudo-Jonathan*
Tg. Neof.   *Targum Neofiti*
Tg. Onq.   *Targum Onqelos*

VI. Greek and Latin Writings

Aristotle
   Rhet.   *Rhetoric*
Cicero
   De or.   *De oratore*
Galen
   Comp. med. gen.   *De compositione medicamentorum per genera*
Eusebius
   Hist. eccl.   *Historia ecclesiastica*
Herodotus
   Hist.   *Historiae*
Jerome
   Comm. in Matt.   *Commentariorum in Matthaeum IV*
Justin
   Dial.   *Dialogus cum Tryphone*
Plato
   Phaedr.   *Phaedrus*
Pliny the Elder
   Nat. Hist.   *Natural History*
Plutarch
   Mor.   *Moralia*
Polybius
   Fr.   *Fragmenta ex incertis libris*
Quintilian
   Inst.   *Institutio oratorio*
Seneca
   Contr.   *Controversiae*
Statius
   Silv.   *Silvae*
Tertullian
   Adv. Marc.   *Adversus Marcionem*
Xenophon
   Apol.   *Apologia Socratis*

Matthew's Sources — Written or Oral?
A Rabbinic Analogy and Empirical Insights

Armin D. Baum

How did the textual similarities and differences between Matthew and Mark and Matthew and Luke develop? The answer to this question has to be well founded. A mere description of the New Testament evidence is not enough. The synoptic data raise a number of preliminary questions, but in themselves they do not provide a reliable answer. In order to solve the Synoptic Problem on the basis of a broader foundation it is necessary to compare the New Testament synoptic data (part I) to the relationship that exists between other parallel texts from antiquity, especially from rabbinic tradition (part II), and to relevant results from experimental psychology and oral poetry research (part III).[1]

Most Gospels scholars have not paid much attention to these analogies to the Synoptic Problem. But of those scholars who took these analogies into account only a minority argued for a simple literary dependence between the New Testament Gospels. Most of them integrated, to varying degrees, an oral factor into their solution to the Synoptic Problem. I would like to develop their approach a step further.

One of my results is that neither the selection of material nor its order is

---

1. For all the details I cannot present in this paper see my monograph *Der mündliche Faktor: Analogien zur synoptischen Frage aus der antiken Literatur, der Experimentalpsychologie, der Oral Poetry-Forschung und dem rabbinischen Traditionswesen* (TANZ; Tübingen: Francke, 2008). Some results of my research on the synoptic problem have already been published: "Experimentalpsychologische Erwägungen zur synoptischen Frage," *BZ* 42 (2000): 37-55; "Die lukanische und chronistische Quellenbenutzung im Vergleich: Eine Teilanalogie zum synoptischen Problem," *ETL* 78 (2002): 340-57; "Oral Poetry und synoptische Frage: Analogien zu Umfang, Variation und Art der synoptischen Wortlautidentität," *TZ* 59 (2003): 17-34; "Bildhaftigkeit als Gedächtnishilfe in der synoptischen Tradition," *TBei* 35 (2004): 4-16; "Der mündliche Faktor: Teilanalogien zu den Minor Agreements aus der Oral Poetry-Forschung und der experimentellen Gedächtnispsychologie," *Bib* 85 (2004): 264-72 (www.bsw.org/project/biblica).

adequate criterion for distinguishing between literary and orally related parallel texts. The verbal agreements and disagreements are much more relevant. But it has turned out to be essential to look not only at the number of verbal agreements (1) but also at their dispersion (2), and at the higher figures in the poetic sections (3), in the words of Jesus (4) and in the Old Testament quotations (5) as well as at the Minor Agreements (6).

I. The Verbal Agreement between Matthew and His Parallels

In this first part of my paper I would like to describe six well-known characteristics of the New Testament synoptic evidence and to formulate six simple questions accordingly. I will try to answer these questions in part III. In part I of my paper I constantly compare the way in which the Chronicler had dealt with the books of Kings.[2] For convenience I choose as my starting point the two-source hypothesis: Matthew used as his main sources a copy of Mark and a copy of Q. Beyond doubt this answer to the Synoptic Question represents the majority view. But it is not without difficulties.

1. *The Average Verbal Agreement*

The average verbal agreement between the synoptic parallel texts amounts to only 40 to 50%. In the material Matthew has in common with Mark and Luke respectively, about 50% of Matthew's words are identical with Mark's and Luke's texts respectively (Appendix 1a).[3] In the Synoptic Gospels the average identity of wording is only half as high as in the Old Testament parallel texts which are definitely connected by a literary relationship. In the passages the Chronicler took over from the books of Kings he copied 80% of its text verbally.

At the same time the content of the common material of the Synoptic Gospels is very similar. And the stylistic improvements of Matthew over against Mark's Gospel have been very moderate.[4] As a result many of the differences

---

2. For the figures related to the synoptic parallels between Kings and Chronicles see Baum, "Die lukanische und chronistische Quellenbenutzung," 340-57.

3. The figures used in this paper come from R. Morgenthaler, *Statistische Synopse* (Zürich: Gotthelf, 1971), and A. M. Honoré, "A Statistical Study of the Synoptic Problem," *NovT* 10 (1968): 59-147; repr. in *The Synoptic Problem and Q: Selected Studies from Novum Testamentum* (ed. D. E. Orton; Leiden: Brill, 1999), 70-122.

4. J. C. Hawkins, *Horae Synopticae: Contributions to the Study of the Synoptic Problem* (2nd ed.; Oxford: Clarendon, 1909; repr. 1968), is still helpful.

between the Synoptic Gospels are relevant neither with regard to content nor with regard to style.

This evidence leads to my first question: *If Matthew only slightly changed the content and style of his two sources Mark and Q, what caused him to change their wording about 50%?* Did other ancient authors treat their sources in a similar way?

2. The Inconsistency of the Verbal Agreement

The amount of verbal agreement in Matthew's different parallel pericopes varies dramatically. The figures for verbal agreement in the single pericopes disperse considerably around the arithmetical mean value of 50%. In some parallel texts only 10% or 20% of the wording is identical, while in other pericopes the verbal agreement amounts to 80% or even 90%.

The dispersion of these figures for the verbal agreement of single pericopes can be expressed mathematically. A relatively high figure for the standard deviation s stands for rather inhomogenous material. If the material is quite homogeneous, the figure for s is low. For the mt-lk double tradition $s = 19.4$ and 18.3 respectively. To what degree the figures for the verbal agreement of the mt-lk parallel pericopes disperse around the arithmetical mean value becomes visible if they are presented in a diagram (Appendix 3a).

For the identical wording of the parallel texts between the books of Kings and the books of Chronicles the standard deviation $s = 9.8$ and 8.0 respectively. In comparison the standard deviation for the synoptic parallel pericopes is relatively high. Evidently, the Chronicler has paraphrased the wording of his written source material much more consistently than has Matthew (Appendix 3b).

This observation raises a second question: *If Matthew copied written sources, why did he not paraphrase the texts of Mark and Q more consistently? What motivated him to change his rewriting style from pericope to pericope?* Do any analogies exist from ancient literature for such a procedure?

3. The Verbal Agreement in the Words of Jesus

The material common to Matthew and Mark consists of narratives and speeches. In the mt-mk double tradition Matthew has copied the narrative material with an average verbal agreement of only 45% and the words of Jesus (and the Baptist) with an average agreement of 56%. In the mt-mk triple tradition the difference between Matthew's treatment of the speech material and the narrative material is even greater. Here the average literary agreement in the narrative parallels is only 43% while the verbal identity in the words of Jesus amounts to 60%. Yet, Matthew did not copy Jesus' speeches with a literary agreement of 100% or even 80%.

The Old Testament parallel texts show no evidence of a similar phenomenon. Therefore I regard it as necessary to ask: *Why did Matthew copy the words of Jesus so much more exactly than the rest of Mark's text (and yet not with a verbal agreement of nearly 100%)? Does ancient literature offer obvious analogies to Matthew's dealing with the speech material of his sources?*

4. The Verbal Agreement in the Poetic Passages

More than half of the words of Jesus are formulated according to the rules of Semitic parallelism *(parallelismus membrorum)* in at least one of its synoptic versions. The mt-lk double tradition (the so-called Q material) contains poetical texts like the Sermon on the Mount and unpoetical pericopae like most of the parables. Matthew's verbal agreement with Luke amounts to 42% in the pericopae without *parallelismus membrorum* and to 54% in the poetical texts. In the mt-mk triple tradition the difference is still greater. Matthew has copied the poetical passages of Mark with an average agreement of 55%, while he has kept only 38% of the wording of his prose material. Since Kings and Chronicles do not contain much Hebrew poetry, they do not offer an analogy to this peculiarity of the New Testament synoptic data.

A fourth question comes to mind immediately: *Why did Matthew copy the wording of the poetic passages of Mark and Q much more exactly than their prose material? And why did he not repeat their poetic texts as closely as possible?* Did any other ancient author deal with his sources in a similar way?

5. The Verbal Agreement in the Old Testament Quotations

In their common Old Testament quotations, the verbal agreement between the Synoptic Gospels is twice as high as in the rest of their parallel material. In the mt-mk double tradition, Matthew copied the Old Testament citations with a verbal agreement of 88% while he copied the rest of Mark's text with a literary agreement of only 48%. The identity of wording in the quotations is 40 percentage points higher. The Chronicler did not deal with his source material in a similar fashion.

Therefore my next question obviously must be: *Why did Matthew quote the*

Old Testament citations twice as closely as the rest of Mark's Gospel, including the words of Jesus? Did other ancient authors paraphrase their written sources in a comparable manner?

6. The Minor Agreements

In the triple tradition Matthew and Luke share about 1850 words with each other and with Mark (the triple agreements). At the same time they have in common against Mark nearly 650 words (the so-called Minor Agreements). This has always been regarded as remarkable and difficult to explain.[5] Hence, the last question I would like to ask does not come as a surprise: *If Matthew and Luke copied Mark's Gospel independently of each other, why do they agree verbally against his text in more than 600 words?* Can any analogies to the synoptic Minor Agreements be found in other parallel texts of ancient literature?

II. The Verbal Agreement between 'Abot de Rabbi Nathan A and B

In the second part of my paper I will deal with this last question. My search for a close analogy to the Synoptic Problem of the New Testament has led me to several different kinds of ancient parallel texts. First, as mentioned already, I analyzed how the Chronicler had dealt with his sources. Next I compared the way in which Josephus had treated the *Letter of Aristeas* with the New Testament evidence. And since Josephus was an Atticist writer, I also took into account, how the writers of the Alexander Romance, an example of ancient folk literature *(Volksliteratur),* used their material. None of these parallel texts provided a more or less complete analogy to the Synoptic Problem.[6]

Finally, I became aware of a promising text of rabbinic literature which exists in two versions, the extracanonical tract 'Abot de Rabbi Nathan A and B. I analyzed synoptically the parallel chapters about the five disciples of Rabbi Jochanan, 'Abot R. Nat. B 28–30 par. A 14–17.[7] Although I am not an expert in this complex and difficult research area, I think my analysis has yielded some important results. I wish to present these in this second part of my paper.

---

5. Cf. the summary of recent scholarship in my article "Der mündliche Faktor," 264-72.
6. For details compare my *Der mündliche Faktor,* chapter B.
7. I used the text edition of S. Schechter (Wien, 1887; repr. Hildesheim: Olms, 1979). Version B has been translated by A. J. Saldarini (SJLA 11; Leiden: Brill, 1975), 19-301; Version A by J. Neusner (BJS 114; Atlanta: Scholars, 1986), 1-258.

1. The Average Verbal Agreement

The verbal agreement between *'Abot R. Nat.* A 14–17 and B 28–30 amounts to only 35% and 36% respectively (Appendix 1b). Obviously, the two parallel versions of *'Abot de Rabbi Nathan* exhibit, like the Synoptic Gospels, a combination of little difference in style and content and great difference in wording (Appendix 2).

2. The Inconsistency of the Verbal Agreement

Secondly, the figures for the verbal agreement of the single pericopes are just as inhomogeneous as in the synoptic parallel texts. For *'Abot de Rabbi Nathan* B par. A the standard deviation $s = 18.4$ and 16.2 respectively. The figures for the verbal agreement of the single pericopes of *'Abot de Rabbi Nathan*. B par. A disperse as much around the arithmetical mean value as do the figures for the mt-lk double tradition. This becomes again apparent when one compares the diagrams for the New Testament and the rabbinic parallel texts (Appendix 3a and 3c). The assumption that *'Abot de Rabbi Nathan* A and B is the closest ancient analogy to the Synoptic Problem of the New Testament can be further substantiated.

3. The Verbal Agreement in the Words of the Rabbis

With regard to the words of Jesus, Matthew and his synoptic parallels exhibit a much higher verbal agreement (by up to 19 percentage points) than in their remaining common material. None of the ancient parallel texts connected by literary dependence is analogous to this aspect of the New Testament Synoptic Problem. Only the two parallel versions of *'Abot de Rabbi Nathan* are very similar in this respect. Just as Matthew reproduced Mark's words of Jesus exceptionally exactly, in *'Abot de Rabbi Nathan* A par. B the statements of the rabbis are in closer agreement than the rest of the common material. The identity of wording is 35 and 40 percentage points higher in the words of the rabbis over against the remaining parallel material (Appendix 4).

4. The Verbal Agreement in the Poetic Passages

In the poetic passages of *'Abot de Rabbi Nathan* A and B, the verbal agreement is higher than in the rest of the common material by 12 and 16 percentage points respectively. This again is very similar to the New Testament synoptic evidence (Appendix 5).

5. The Verbal Agreement in the Old Testament Quotations

The verbal agreement between *'Abot de Rabbi Nathan* A and B in their Old Testament quotations is much higher than in the rest of their parallel material, exactly by 46 and 49 percentage points respectively. The Synoptic Gospels share also this peculiarity with the two versions of *'Abot de Rabbi Nathan* (Appendix 6). Before I turn to the Minor Agreements I would like to summarize the results reached so far in a simple table.

Verbal Agreement in Ancient Parallel Texts

Parallel Texts	Identity	Disp. (s)	Poetry	Speech	Quotations
1 Ki / 2 Chr	74%/78%	9.8/8.0	—	+8/6 Pp	[+7/3 Pp]
mt-lk DT	48%/51%	19.4/18.3	+12/10 Pp	—	+53/42 Pp
mt-mk TT	50%/40%	14.7/13.7	+16/17 Pp	+17/19 Pp	+28/36 Pp
mt-mk DT	49%/40%	11.6/13.1	—	+11/10 Pp	+40/53 Pp
'Ab. R.N. B/A	36%/35%	18.4/16.2	+12/16 Pp	+40/35 Pp	+49/46 Pp

6. The Minor Agreements

Since *'Abot de Rabbi Nathan* is a commentary on the Mishnaic tract *'Abot*, it is possible to compare three versions of this rabbinic tract with each other. Version B takes the place of Matthew and version A the place of Luke. If the three versions of the pericope about "The Good and the Bad Way" (*'Abot R. Nat.* B 29.18-23 par. *m. 'Abot* 2.9 par. *'Abot R. Nat.* A 14.17-31) are analyzed synoptically, the first result is that the three texts display 90 triple agreements. More important for our question is the fact that *'Abot de Rabbi Nathan* A and B have 11 words in common against the text of the Mishnah. These 11 words represent an exact analogy to the Minor Agreements between Matthew and Luke against Mark.

The result reached in this second part has by now become obvious: *'Abot de Rabbi Nathan A par. B offers the closest ancient analogy to the Synoptic Problem of the New Testament.* Probably the New Testament and the rabbinic parallel texts had a similar prehistory. This observation does not in itself answer the Synoptic Question, but it may be a helpful contribution.

III. Characteristics of Human Memory and Oral Tradition

S. Schechter, who published a synopsis of the two versions of 'Abot de Rabbi Nathan in 1887, traced both of them back to a common written original. Later scholars came to the conclusion that versions A and B were literally independent of each other and of written sources. In 1938 L. Finkelstein wrote that the two versions must go back to independent oral tradition and must have been put into writing separately. "The differences between the two versions are such as could hardly arise after the original form had been reduced to writing."[8] As evidence for this thesis, Finkelstein mentioned a number of omissions, word inversions and disagreements in wording. Several years later J. Goldin developed Finkelstein's approach a step further.[9] In the last decades a number of scholars have referred to Finkelstein's thesis without deciding for or against it.[10] Yet, a number of developments in the field of experimental psychology and oral poetry research support Finkelstein's argument and strengthen his main thesis, though Finkelstein was not aware of them. In this last part of my paper I would like to mention at least some of the most important aspects of recent oral poetry and memory research. Of course these aspects are relevant not only to the interpretation of 'Abot de Rabbi Nathan A and B but also to the Synoptic Question of the New Testament.

Before I try to present my six answers to the questions mentioned above (in part I), I would like to make clear that as far as I can see, experimental psychology confirms the conviction that Mark's Gospel was written first. In two-thirds of the cases Mark's version of the common synoptic material is longer than Luke's version and in three-fourths of them it is longer than Matthew's version. Psychological experiments have demonstrated that the human memory is inclined to shorten the material that is committed to memory.[11] In this respect the current research supports Markan priority, although not in the sense of literary dependence.

---

8. L. Finkelstein, "Introductory Study to *Pirke Abot*," *JBL* 57 (1938): 13-50, here 16 and 40.

9. J. Goldin, "The Two Versions of *Abot de Rabbi Nathan*," *HUCA* 19 (1945/46): 97-120.

10. A. J. Saldarini, *The Fathers according to Rabbi Nathan*, 11; M. B. Lerner, "The External Tractates," in *The Literature of the Sages*: vol. 1. *Oral Tora, Halakha, Mishna, Tosefta, Talmud, External Tractates* (CRINT II/3/1; Philadelphia: Fortress, 1987), 367-409; G. Stemberger, *Einleitung in Talmud und Midrasch* (8th ed.; München: Beck, 1992), 225.

11. See B. R. Gomulicki, "Recall as an Abstractive Process," *Acta Psychologica* 12 (1956): 77-94.

1. Low Average of Verbal Agreement

The verbal agreement between Matthew and his sources amounts to about 40 to 50%. '*Abot de Rabbi Nathan* A and B agree literally in 35% of their common material. At the same time the difference in style and content is small in both cases.

As research into oral literature in South Yugoslavia, West Africa and among Native Americans has shown rather low identical wording in parallel texts is a very common result of oral tradition carried by human memory.[12] As we know from cognitive psychology, human memory can recall the content of a statement much better than its exact words (Appendix 7). Therefore, the combination of great content identity and rather low agreement in wording can easily be interpreted as typical of memory activity.[13] Hence, a possible answer to my first question is that *Matthew would have changed the style of Mark and Q only slightly and yet kept only about 50% of their wording, if these two texts reached him orally.*

This observation cannot be demonstrated to be wrong by the widely held assertion[14] that human memory is unable to store and reproduce such a large amount of text as the synoptic tradition with its 30,000 words and an average verbal agreement of 40 to 50%. Rabbinic literature claims that Jewish rabbis have been able to learn by heart not only the Hebrew Old Testament (with its 270,000 words) but also the Babylonian Talmud with close to 2,000,000 words.[15] Scientific evidence supports this claim. Rather high identical wording in long parallel texts cannot only be produced by literary dependence but also by the activity of human memory and oral tradition.

2. Inconsistent Verbal Agreement

The figures for the verbal agreement in the different parallel pericopae of the mt-mk and particularly of the mt-lk double tradition are very inconsistent.

---

12. See Baum, "Oral Poetry und synoptische Frage," 17-34.

13. Examples for verbal agreement in memory reproductions are presented in Appendixes 6 and 7.

14. See, for example, Morgenthaler, *Statistische Synopse*, 281, and J. S. Kloppenborg, *Excavating Q: The History and Setting of the Saying Gospel* (Minneapolis: Fortress, 2000), 29.

15. b. Šebu'. 41b; b. 'Erub. 67a; G. M. Stratton, "The Mnemonic Feat of the 'Shass Pollak,'" *Psychological Review* 24 (1917): 244-47; repr. in *Memory Observed* (ed. U. Neisser; San Francisco: Freeman, 1982), 311-14; compare Y. Elman, "Orality and the Redaction of the Babylonian Talmud," *Oral Tradition* 14 (1999): 52-99.

They disperse considerably around the arithmetical mean value. Matthew also revised the style of his sources from pericope to pericope (and from sentence to sentence) very inconsistently. The same is true for the verbal agreement of *'Abot de Rabbi Nathan* A and B, which also is very inhomogeneous.

It would be difficult to explain such an inconsistent revision as a result of copying. Yet, similar inconsistencies have been shown to be a common outcome of oral tradition.[16] Further, human memory demonstrably works selectively and produces, whether consciously or unconsciously, heterogeneous results. Accordingly, the answer to my second question would be that *Matthew paraphrased the text of Mark and Q so inconsistently because he did not copy it from written sources but, just as Mark had done, drew from a relatively fixed and yet considerably inhomogeneous oral tradition.*

3. Higher Verbal Agreement in Important Material

Matthew reproduced the words of Jesus with a much higher agreement than the narrative parts of his source material. In Jesus' speeches the identity of wording is up to 17 percentage points higher than in the rest of the common tradition of Matthew and Mark, and Matthew and Luke, respectively. In the same way *'Abot de Rabbi Nathan* A and B exhibit a much higher verbal agreement (by up to 40 percentage points) in reproducing the words of the rabbis.

It would be difficult to explain this extraordinary evidence as a normal result of simple literary copying. On the other hand, we know from cognitive psychology that human memory usually stores material regarded as very important much better than material regarded as less important.[17] This had already been observed by ancient authors like Quintilian, who wrote: "There can be no doubt that concentration of mind is the utmost importance in this connexion; it is, in fact, like the eyesight, which turns to, and not away from, the objects which it contemplates."[18]

Of course the disciples of Jesus as well as of the rabbis showed a particularly high respect for the words of their masters. Probably for this reason they have committed their teachers' statements more exactly to memory than the stories about them. This difference can still be detected in the written versions of the texts in question. Hence my third answer is that *Matthew reproduced the*

---

16. See Baum, "Oral Poetry und synoptische Frage," 17-34.
17. E. C. Sanford, "Professor Sanford's Morning Prayer" (1917), in *Memory Observed*, 176-77.
18. *Inst.* 11.2.10 (Butler, LCL); cf. Cicero, *De or.* 2.355.

words of Jesus with a particularly high verbal agreement because in oral tradition they were transmitted more faithfully than the rest of the synoptic material.

4. Higher Verbal Agreement in Poetic Material

In the poetical passages common to the Synoptic Gospels the verbal agreement is considerably higher (by up to 17 percentage points) than in the remaining parallel material. Only rabbinic literature, particularly the two versions of *'Abot de Rabbi Nathan,* proved to be analogous to this peculiar feature of the Gospels.

An explanation for this phenomenon can be deduced from research in cognitive psychology. It has been demonstrated that texts regulated by rhyme (or by meter or parallelism) can be learned by heart better than texts without rhyme. The reason is that every kind of repetition aids memorization. Human memory is able to store poetical texts better than prose texts because it is aided by repetition. As Quintilian put it: "Just as it is easier to learn verse than prose, so it is easier to learn prose when it is artistically constructed than when it has no such organisation."[19]

Therefore the higher incidence of identical wording in the poetical passages also suggests that both the New Testament Gospels and the rabbinic parallel texts draw from an oral tradition carried by human memory. Accordingly, my fourth answer is that *Matthew and Mark display a higher verbal agreement in their common material regulated by* parallelismus membrorum *because both drew their synoptic tradition from a common oral source transmitted by human memory.*

5. Higher Verbal Agreement in Earlier Learned Material

In the common Old Testament quotations of the mt-mk and the mt-lk parallel tradition the verbal agreement is about twice as high as in the rest of the common material. The same phenomenon could be observed in the two parallel versions of *'Abot de Rabbi Nathan.*

In this respect, what we know from ancient sources about Jewish education becomes important. Because of their strong religious education and their regular participation in synagogue life, the later transmitters of both the rabbinic

---

19. Quintilian, *Inst.* 11.2.39 (Butler, LCL); cf. Plato, *Phaedr.* 267a; Aristotle, *Rhet.* 3.9.3; Plutarch, *Mor.* 407f; Galen, *Comp. med. gen.* 5.10; G. H. Bower and L. S. Bolton, "Why Are Rhymes Easy to Learn?" *Journal of Experimental Psychology* 82 (1969): 453-61.

and the synoptic tradition knew central parts of their Holy Scriptures by heart word for word from childhood. Josephus explained: "Should anyone of our nation be questioned about the laws, he would repeat them all more readily than his own name. The result, then, of our thorough grounding in the laws from the first dawn of intelligence is that we have them, as it were, engraven on our souls."[20]

Much later in their lives and under very different conditions the disciples learned the words of Jesus and the stories about him. As we know from ancient sources and from experimental research, human memory is able to reproduce texts learned in early years much better than texts learned later in life. Seneca (Maior) explained about his own memory: "Whatever I entrusted to it as a boy or young man it brings out again without hesitation as though new and just heard. But things I have deposited with it these last years it has lost so entirely that even if they are repeatedly dinned into me, I hear them each time as new."[21]

Irenaeus agreed and spoke about his own experience with the strengths and weaknesses of human memory: "I remember the events of those days more clearly than those which happened recently, for what we learn as children grows up with the soul and is united to it, so that I can speak even of the place in which the blessed Polycarp sat and disputed, how he came in and went out, the character of his life, the appearance of his body, the discourses which he made to the people. . . ."[22]

Therefore, answer number five must be that *Matthew reproduced the Old Testament quotations twice as accurately as the rest of his source material because the oral tradition from which he drew his synoptic material was transmitted by Jews who knew the wording of their Holy Scriptures by heart much better than the words and deeds of Jesus.*

6. Minor Agreements

In the triple tradition Matthew and Luke agree more than 600 times against Mark (Minor Agreements). Such agreements appear also regularly in rabbinic triple traditions.

How did these Minor Agreements develop if Matthew and Luke copied Mark without being literarily related to each other? In this regard it is helpful to

---

20. Josephus, *C. Ap.* 2.178 (Thackeray, LCL); cf. Deut 6:7; Philo, *Legat.* 210; *Lev. Rab.* 7.3.
21. Seneca, *Contr.* 1 pr. 3 (Winterbottom, LCL); cf. Quintilian, *Inst.* 11.2.6.
22. Irenaeus in Eusebius, *Hist. eccl.* 5.20.5-7 (Lake, LCL); cf. D. C. Rubin, S. E. Wetzler, and R. D. Nebes, "Autobiographical Memory across the Lifespan," in *Autobiographical Memory* (ed. D. C. Rubin; Cambridge: Cambridge University Press, 1986), 202-21.

realize that verbal agreements, similar to the Minor Agreements of the synoptic triple tradition, are a natural characteristic of oral versions of the same text. This can be shown from the oral poetry of Yugoslavia and can also be deduced from the results of experimental psychology (Appendix 8).[23]

Ancient texts about human memory activity already sought to explain this phenomenon. Quintilian observed: "that the things we search for frequently refuse to present themselves and then occur to us by chance, or that memory does not always remain with us, but will even sometimes return to us after it has been lost."[24]

Therefore, the assumption that the three Synoptic Gospels are connected orally in similar fashion represents a natural (and the most simple) explanation for the existence of the Minor Agreements. Answer number six therefore is that *Matthew and Luke did not copy the first written Gospel but drew independently of Mark and of each other from the same oral source as he had done*. By this process hundreds of Minor Agreements between Matthew and Luke against Mark emerged in a very natural way.

IV. Results

The six observations summarized in the above section make it highly improbable that the synoptic relationship between the New Testament Gospels may be explained in terms of simple copying. In ancient literature, no literarily dependent parallel texts could be found that exhibited the same characteristic differences and agreements as the Synoptic Gospels. This observation raises the question as to whether the hypothesis of strong literary dependence including the Two-Source Theory really does offer a satisfactory answer to the Synoptic Question (part I).

On the other hand, all these aspects of the Synoptic Question have close analogies in rabbinic parallel texts, particularly in the two versions of '*Abot de Rabbi Nathan* (A par. B). '*Abot R. Nat.* A par. B is the closest ancient analogy to the Synoptic Problem of the New Testament. And this analogy comes from rabbinic literature which has origins that are very different from Graeco-Roman literature (part II).

Results from experimental psychology and oral poetry research suggest that both the New Testament and the rabbinic parallel traditions are connected primarily orally. Every single aspect of the Synoptic Problem may be accounted

---

23. See my "Der mündliche Faktor," 264-72.
24. Quintilian, *Inst.* 11.2.7 (Butler, LCL).

for if Matthew (and Luke) drew their common Markan material from the same oral source as Mark had done before them. As it were, each of our three Synoptic Gospels "froze" a different memory performance of the oral triple tradition by writing it down. This is the reason why all the synoptic parallel texts display a number of characteristic marks of the oral synoptic tradition that would have disappeared through simple copying (part III).

At least in passing, I would like to mention that none of the church fathers before Augustine ever assumed a literary relationship between the Synoptic Gospels. Papias, Justin, Irenaeus and their followers seem to have presupposed that Matthew, Mark and Luke made independent use of the oral Jesus tradition going back to the eyewitnesses.[25] All in all, my results support the hypothesis defended most recently by Bo Reicke (Appendix 9), "that the triple traditions in the Gospels of Matthew and Luke as well as Mark originated in a living, acoustically preserved tradition."[26]

---

25. H. Merkel, "Die Überlieferung der Alten Kirche über das Verhältnis der Evangelien," in *The Interrelation of the Gospels*. A Symposium led by M.-É. Boismard, W. R. Farmer, and F. Neirynck, Jerusalem, 1984 (ed. D. L. Dungan; BETL XCV; Leuven: Leuven University Press, 1990), 566-90.

26. "Die Entstehungsverhältnisse der synoptischen Evangelien," *ANRW* II.25.2 (1984): 1758-91, here 1782; idem, *The Roots of the Synoptic Gospels* (Philadelphia: Fortress, 1986); cf. also A. B. Lord, "The Gospels as Oral Traditional Literature," in *The Relationship among the Gospels: An Interdisciplinary Dialogue* (ed. W. O. Walker; San Antonio: Trinity University Press, 1978), 33-91; J. M. Rist, *On the Independence of Matthew and Mark* (SNTSMS 32; Cambridge: Cambridge University Press, 1978); B. D. Chilton, *Profiles of a Rabbi: Synoptic Opportunities in Reading About Jesus* (BJS 177; Atlanta: Scholars, 1989), passim; J. D. G. Dunn, "Jesus and Oral Memory: The Initial Stages of the Jesus Tradition," *SBLSP* 136 (2000): 287-326; repr. in *Jesus: A Colloquium in the Holy Land* (ed. D. Donnelly; New York: Continuum, 2001), 84-145; idem, "Altering the Default Setting: Re-envisaging the Early Transmission of the Jesus Tradition," *NTS* 49 (2003): 139-75; idem, *Jesus Remembered* (Christianity in the Making 1; Grand Rapids: Eerdmans, 2003), passim; R. McIver, "Implications of New Data Pertaining to the Problem of Synoptic Relationships," *ABR* 45 (1997): 20-39; idem and M. Carroll, "Experiments to Develop Criteria for Determining the Existence of Written Sources, and Their Potential Implications for the Synoptic Problem," *JBL* 121 (2002): 667-87; T. C. Mournet, *Oral Tradition and Literary Dependency: Variability and Stability in the Synoptic Tradition and Q* (WUNT 2/195; Tübingen: Mohr, 2005) and my review in the *TLZ* 131 (2006): 379-82.

Appendices: Diagrams

1. *The Average Verbal Agreement*

a. **The mt-mk Double Tradition**

The mt-mk double tradition

	Matthew	words	%	ident.	%	words	Mark
1	4:18-22	89	61%	54	66%	82	1:16-20
2	13:34	15	27%	4	16%	25	4:33-34
3	13:53-58	107	55%	59	47%	126	6:1-6a
4	14:4-12	117	53%	62	28%	224	6:18-29
5	14:22-33	120	53%	63	45%	139	6:45-52
6	14:34-36	44	66%	29	40%	72	6:53-56
7	15:1-11, 15-20	236	56%	132	37%	359	7:1-23
8	15:21f., 25-28	104	22%	23	18%	130	7:24-30
9	15:29	18	33%	6	30%	20	7:31
10	15:32-39	129	54%	70	48%	146	8:1-10
11	16:7-11	65	32%	21	28%	74	8:16-21
12	16:22-23	40	60%	24	62%	39	8:32-33
13	17:10-13	64	34%	22	42%	52	9:11-13
14	18:8-9	71	49%	35	37%	95	9:43-48
15	19:1-9	151	53%	80	54%	147	10:1-12
16	20:20-23	94	54%	51	46%	112	10:35-40
17	21:10-17	25	28%	7	33%	21	11:11
18	21:18-19	38	45%	17	31%	55	11:12-14
19	21:19ff.; 6:14	76	34%	26	26%	101	11:20-25
20	22:34-40	81	30%	24	31%	78	12:28-31
21	24:23-25	34	71%	24	65%	37	13:21-23
22	24:42	11	64%	7	11%	65	13:33-37
23	26:6-13	109	57%	62	50%	124	14:3-9
24	26:31-32	35	63%	22	81%	27	14:27-28
25	26:59-63	55	56%	31	35%	89	14:55-61a
26	27:27-31	78	42%	33	52%	63	15:16-20a
27	27:46-48	63	43%	27	51%	53	15:34-36
		2,069	49%	1,015	40%	2,555	

15

b. 'Abot de Rabbi Nathan B par. A

'Abot de Rabbi Nathan B 28-30 par. A 14-17

	Version B	words	%	id.	%	words	Version A
1	28.1-5	39	41%	16	44%	36	14.2-4
2	28.12b-13	33	52%	17	44%	39	14.5
3	28.14	29	24%	7	30%	23	14.6-7
4	29.1-12	122	48%	59	47%	125	14.8-16
5	29.13	41	22%	9	41%	22	14.54
6	29.16-17	38	32%	12	50%	24	14.55-56
7	29.18-34	138	73%	101	67%	150	14.17-31
8	29.35-40	62	34%	21	34%	62	15.1-4
9	29.41-100	351	15%	52	19%	271	15.6-36
10	29.101-114	170	28%	47	17%	274	15.53-69
11	29.115-135	177	36%	64	36%	176	15.37ff.
12	29.136	14	79%	11	50%	22	15.73-74
13	30.1-3	27	59%	16	50%	32	16.1.6f.
14	30.6-8	13	23%	3	16%	19	16.50
15	30.9-14	100	27%	27	28%	97	16.57-61
16	30.21-22	28	75%	21	55%	38	17.46-47
17	30.22-25	51	51%	26	48%	54	17.1-4
18	30.26-28	59	39%	23	33%	69	17.6-8
19	30.47-48	28	57%	16	62%	26	17.48
		1,520	36%	548	35%	1,559	

2. 'Abot de Rabbi Nathan A 14 par. B 29

'Abot R. Nathan A 14.8-14

Five / **disciples** / **had** / **he**, / the Rabban / **Johanan** / **ben** / **Zakkai**. /

Each / of them / he called / by name: /
Eliezer / **ben** / **Hyrcanus** / he called / **a plastered** / **cistern** / **which does not** / **lose** / **a drop**, / a pitch-lined / flask / that holds / its / wine. /
Joshua / **ben** / **Hananiah** / he called / him / a three fold / cord, / not / quickly / broken. /
And Jose / **the Priest** / he called / him / **a saint** / in this generation. /
And Simeon / **ben** / **Nathanel** / he called / him / an oasis / in the wilderness, / which holds / **its water**. /
Happy is / the disciple / whose master / praises / him / and testifies / to him. /
And Eleazar / **ben** / **Arakh** / he called / him / an overflowing / stream / **and a surging** / spring, / whose water / overflows, / thus carrying out / what / has been said: / Let your springs / be dispersed / abroad / in the streets / courses / of water.

80 words
24 identical words (30%)

'Abot R. Nathan B 29.1-10

Five / **disciples** / **had** / **he**, / the Rabbi / **Johanan** / **ben** / **Zakkai**, / and who / are they?/
Rabbi / Eliezer / ben / Hyrcanus / and Rabbi / Joshua / ben / Hananiah / and Rabbi / Jose / the Priest / and Rabbi / Simeon / ben / Nathanel / and Rabbi / Eleazar / ben / Arakh. /
Rabbi / Johanan / ben / Zakkai / used / to teach / their virtues / and said: /
Eliezer / **ben** / **Hyrcanus** / - **a plastered** / **cistern** / **which does not** / **lose** / **a drop**. /

Joshua / **ben** / **Hananiah** / - happy is / she / who bore him. /

Rabbi / Jose / **the Priest** / - **a saint** / in his generation. /

Rabbi / Simeon / **ben** / **Nathanel** / - an oasis / which / holds / **its water** / in the wilderness. /

And Rabbi / Eleazar / **ben** / **Arakh** /

- **a surging** / spring.

70 words
24 identical words (34%)

3. The Inconsistency of the Verbal Agreement

a. The mt-lk Double Tradition

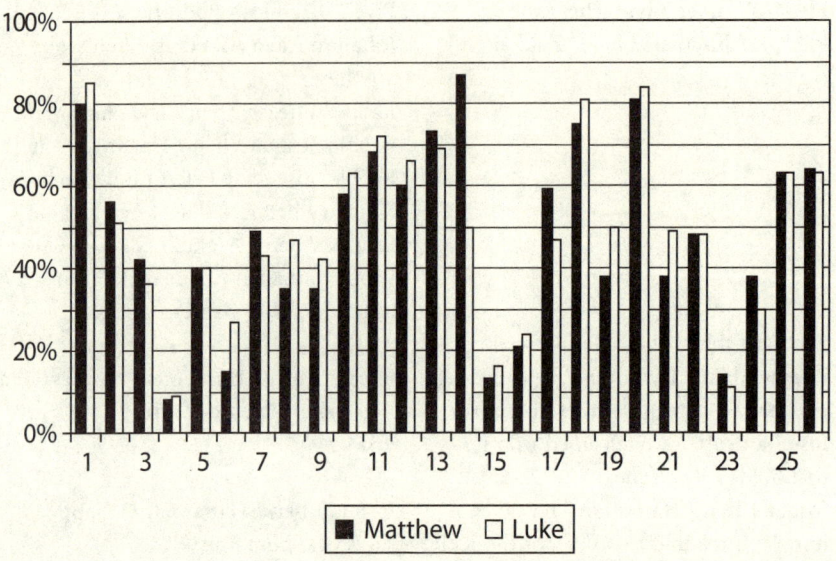

b. 1 Kings 7–10 par. 2 Chronicles 4–9

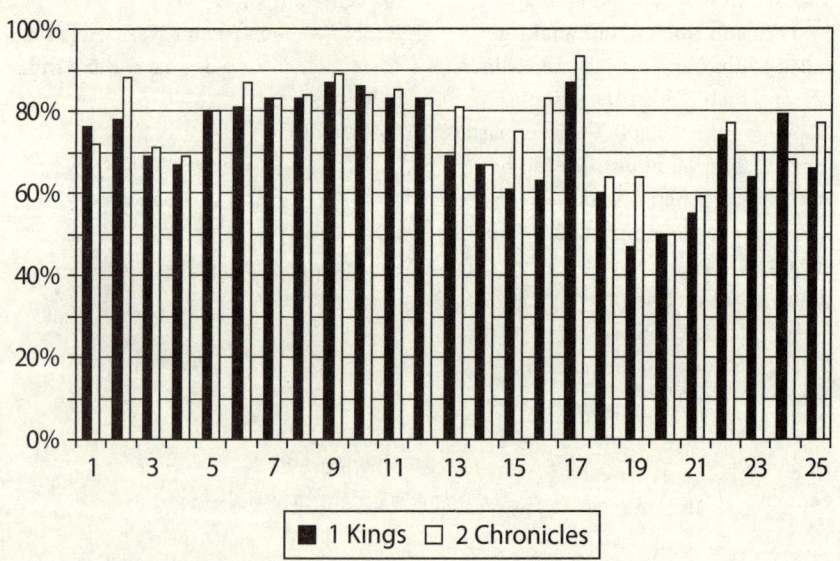

c. *'Abot de Rabbi Nathan* B par. A

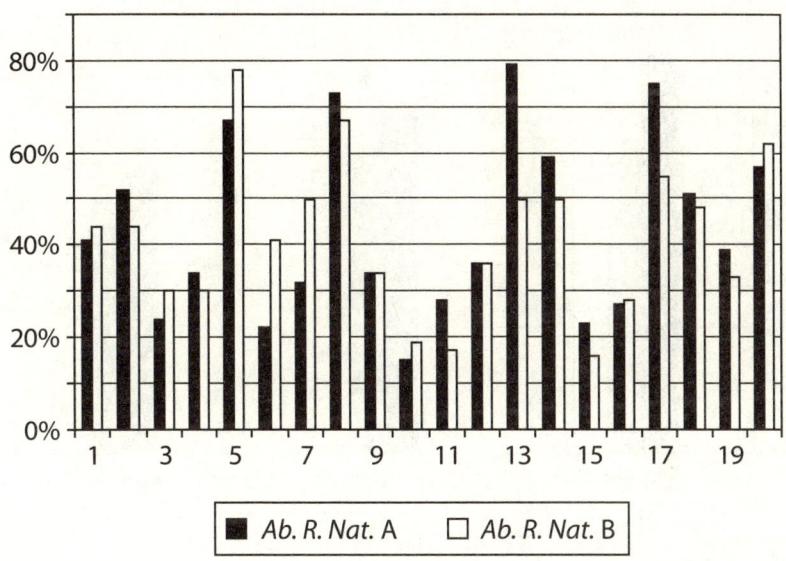

4. *Verbal Agreement in the Speech Material*

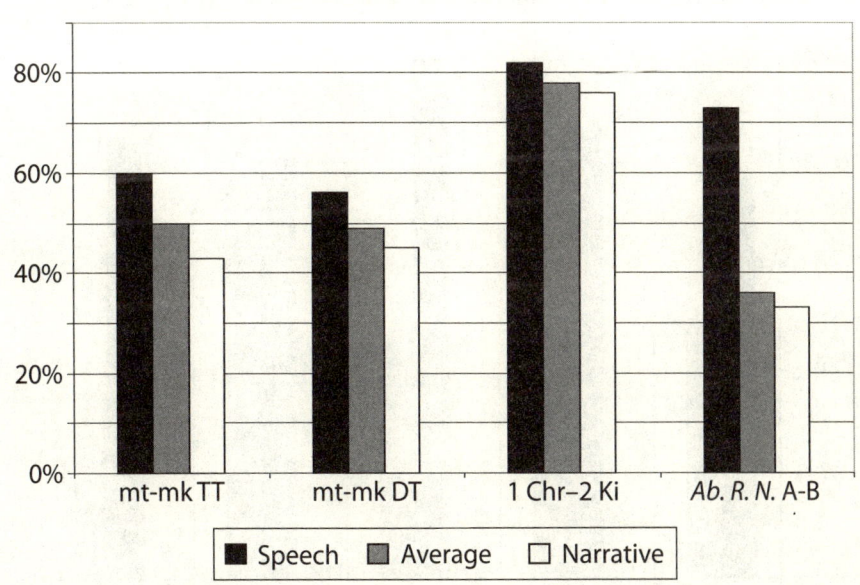

5. Verbal Agreement in the Poetic Passage

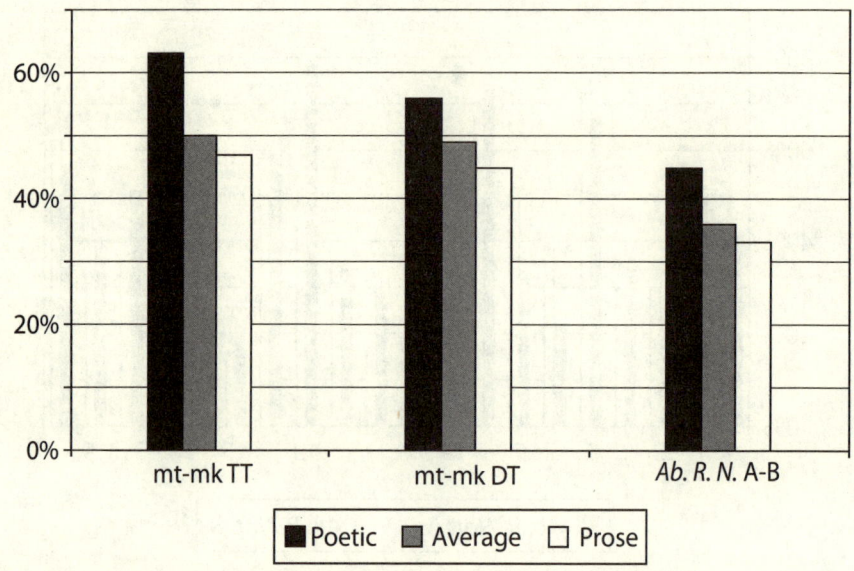

6. Verbal Agreement in the OT Quotations

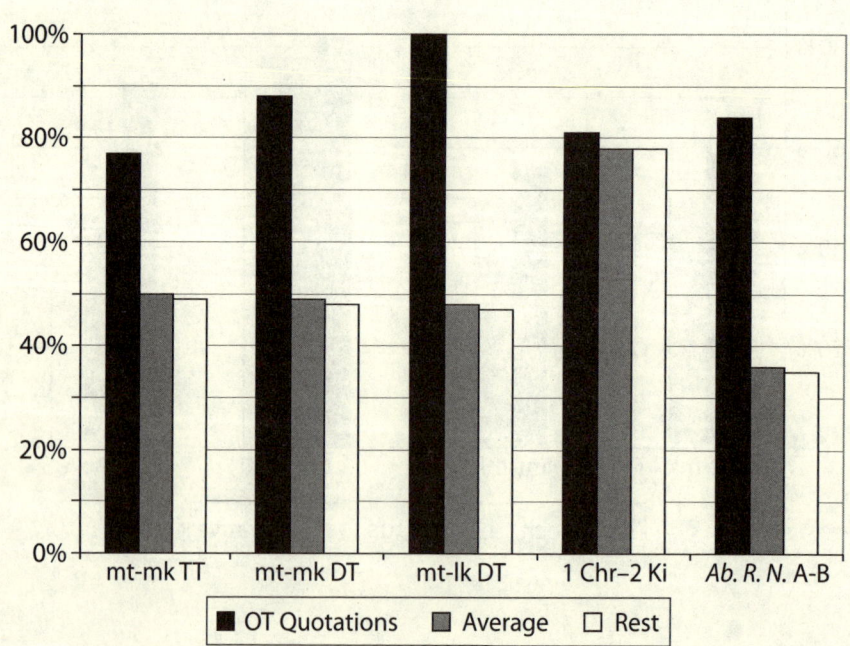

7. Verbal Agreement in Oral Poetry

V. S. Karadzič	M. Parry
	Oj! Mili boze, na svem tebi fala!
	Oj! Dear God, thanks to you for all things!
Vino pije Musa Arbanasa	**Vino pije Musa** Keserdzija
Musa the Albanian is drinking wine	*Musa the highwayman is drinking wine*
U Stambolu, u krčmi bijeloj.	**U Stambolu, u krčmi bijeloj.**
In Istanbul in the white tavern;	*In Istanbul in the white tavern;*
Kad se Musa nakitijo **vina,**	**Kad se Musa** napojijo **vina,**
When Musa had had his fill of wine,	*When Musa had drunk his fill of wine,*
Onda poče pijan besjediti:	**Onda poče pijan** govoriti:
Then, drunk, he began to speak:	*Then, drunk, he began to say:*
	"Mili boze, na svem tebi fala!
	"Dear God, thanks for all things!
"Evo ima **devet** godinica	Ev' imadę **devet** godin' dana
"It is now nine years	*It is now nine years of days*
Kako dvorim cara u Stambolu:	**Kako dvorim cara u Stambolu:**
That I have been serving the sultan in Istanbul:	*That I have been serving the sultan in Istanbul:*
Ni izdvorih konja **ni** oruzja,	Ne izdvori' pare **ni** dinara,
I have not been paid a horse or arms,	*I have not been paid money or dinars,*
Ni dolame **nove ni polovne**:	Nit' aljine **nove ni polovne**.
Nor a coat, new or used:	*Nor clothes, new or used.*
Al' **tako mi** moje vjere tvrde,	A **tako mi** moja vjera tvrda,
But by my firm faith,	*But by my firm faith,*
	I tako me ne rodila majka,
	And may no mother have borne me,
	Ve· kobila neka bedevija,
	But a horse, some bedouin mare,
Odvrć' ću **se u ravno primorje**,	oj! odvrću **se u primorje ravno**,
I shall withdraw to the level coastland,	*O, I shall withdraw to the level coastland,*
Zatvoriću skele oko mora	**Zatvoriću skele oko mora**
I shall close the landing places on the sea	*I shall close the landing places on the sea*
I drumove okolo primorja."	**I drumove okolo primorja."**
And the roads in the coastland."	*And the roads in the coastland."*
63 words	82 words
39 identical words (62%)	39 identical words (48%)

8. Minor Agreement in Experimental Psychology

"The War of the Ghosts"

Version C (after one year)	Version A (after one hour)	Version B (after six weeks)
One day two young men from Egliac went down to the river to hunt seals. While there, it suddenly became very foggy and quiet, and they became scared and rowed ashore and hid behind a log.	One night two young men from Egulac went down to the river to hunt seals. While they were there, it became foggy and calm.	One night, two young men from Egliac went down to the river to hunt seals. While they were there, it became foggy and calm.
	They came ashore quietly and hid behind a log.	
Soon they heard the sound of paddles in the water and canoes approaching.	Soon they heard canoes approaching and the sound of paddling.	Soon they heard the sound of paddles approaching, and they thought: "Maybe it's a war party." They fled ashore and hid behind a log.
One of the canoes, with five men in it, paddled ashore and one of the men said:	One canoe with five men in it came ashore and spoke:	Soon, one of the (unspecified number of) canoes came ashore, with five men in it, and one of them said:
"What do you think? Let us go upriver and make war against the people."	"What do you think? We are going up the river to make war on the people. Come with us." One young man said: "We have no arrows." "There are arrows in the boat," said the war party.	"What do you think? Let us go upriver and make war against the people."
"I cannot go with you," said one of the young men. "My relatives do not know where I have gone. Besides, I might get killed."	"I will not go. I may be killed. My relatives will not know where I have gone."	"I will not go," said one of the young men. "I might be killed. My family does not know where I have gone."
106 words 54 triple agreements 9 C-A agreements 18 C-B agreements	108 words 54 triple agreements 9 C-A agreements 8 A-B agreements	105 words 55 triple agreements 8 A-B agreements 18 C-B agreements

9. The Synoptic Solution of B. Reicke etc.

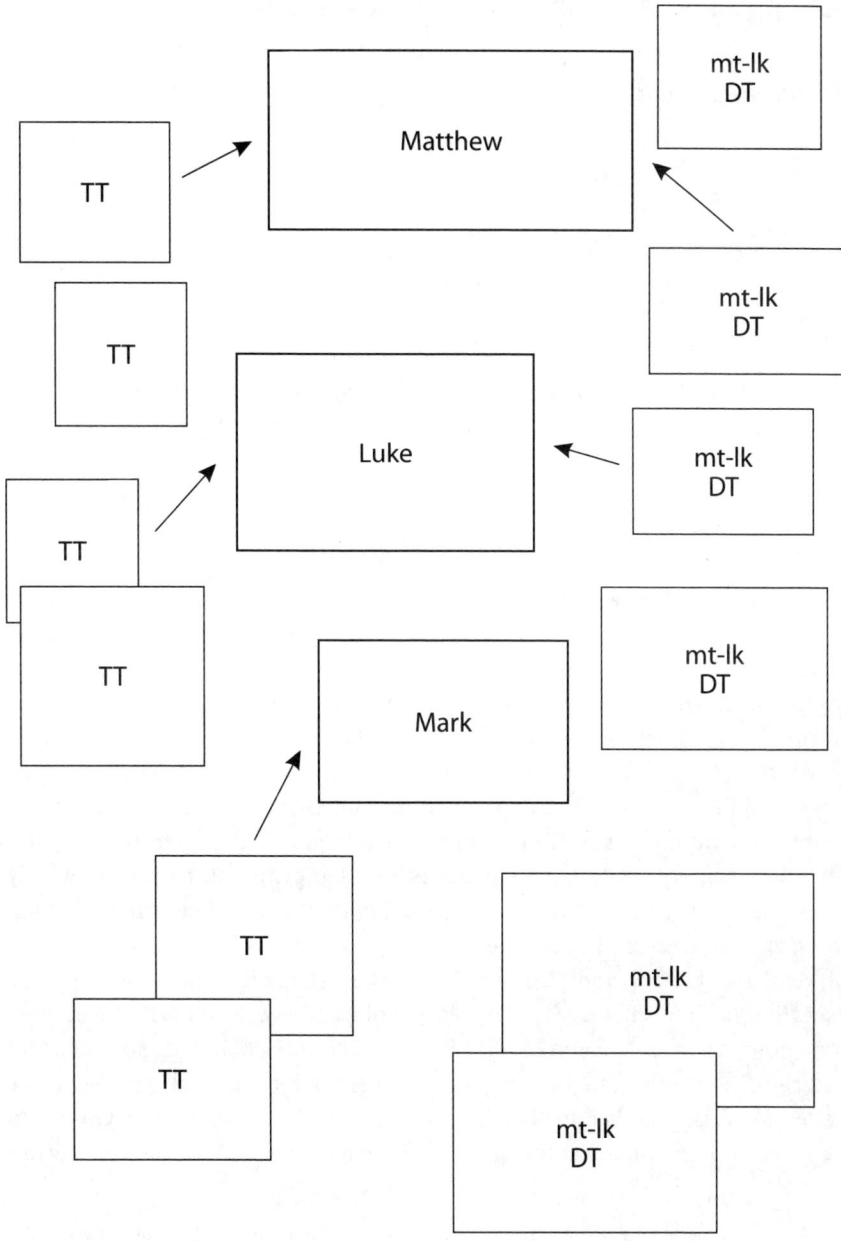

How Matthew Tells the Story:
A Linguistic Approach to Matthew's Narrative Syntax

Stephanie L. Black

> *It is the task and the duty of the N.T. student to apply the results of linguistic research to the Greek of the N.T. But, strange to say, this has not been adequately done.*
>
> A. T. ROBERTSON[1]

New Testament scholars are aware that recent studies in linguistics, pragmatics and cognitive psychology have produced insights into the ways human beings produce and make sense of language. Alongside this, the rise of discourse studies in recent decades has encouraged many biblical scholars to engage texts at the level of paragraphs and larger literary units rather than isolating individual words or even sentences as the locus of meaning. However, a bewildering variety of linguistic models and approaches has emerged to confront the biblical scholar attempting to sift through such research to find the "exegetical payoff" for biblical interpretation. This paper is an attempt to outline several widely used linguistic assumptions, namely *redundancy*, the use of *mental representations*, and *markedness;* to describe certain syntactical features in the Greek text of Matthew's Gospel; and to show what use can be made of these principles in exegeting narrative passages in the Gospel of Matthew. Specifically I will illustrate how interrelated features such as *sentence conjunction* (e.g., καί, δέ, τότε) and *constituent order* (that is, subject-verb, verb-subject or verb-only sentence patterns) work together in the narrative framework of Matthew's Gospel to form a sort of grammatical topography as the narrative progresses.[2] An aware-

---

1. A. T. Robertson, *A Grammar of the Greek New Testament in the Light of Historical Research* (4th ed.; Nashville: Broadman, 1934), 3.

2. For the purposes of this paper, the "narrative framework" of Matthew's Gospel is consid-

ness of these features can help the exegete trace continuity and discontinuity in the narrative, and recognize structural units and special emphases as Matthew tells his story.[3]

Linguistic Principles: Redundancy, Mental Representations, Markedness

Redundancy in Language

The first linguistic principle to be explored here is that *language tends to be highly redundant*. What human beings attempt to convey through language is usually encoded more than once and in more than one way in each sentence or paragraph they produce. Some of the ways a point may be made is through the choice of particular words (lexica), the grammatical forms in which individual words are put (morphology), the order in which the words are arranged in a sentence (syntax), the way sentences are joined and follow on each other (discourse), and the way what is said interacts with the context in which the communication is taking place (pragmatics).[4] In every utterance there may be multiple examples of each type of feature as well — that is, further redundancy. This is why one can be sitting with a friend at a noisy sporting event, miss perhaps as much as a third of what one's companion says, and still follow the conversation reasonably well. One may not hear every word the friend says, but there are likely to be enough redundancies built into his statements that even through the high-decibel noise in the stadium one's mind can collect adequate linguistic data, combined with knowledge of the shared context, to reconstruct much of the intended message.

As I will show in more detail below, Matthew tends to pattern together features from different linguistic "systems," such as certain sentence conjunctions combined with certain constituent orders. These features, while seemingly small when isolated, are among the redundant linguistic signals which are lay-

---

ered to consist of those sentences which convey the action of the narrative — that is, all sentences in Matthew's Gospel excluding exposition attributed to Jesus, reported speech, and Old Testament quotations. Of the approximately 2300 independent clauses in Matthew's Gospel, 720 are identified as forming the "narrative framework."

3. This paper may be taken as a précis and focused application of several concepts from my doctoral thesis, published as *Sentence Conjunctions in the Gospel of Matthew: καί, δέ, τότε, γάρ, οὖν and Asyndeton in Narrative Discourse* (JSNTSup 216; Studies in New Testament Greek 9; London: Sheffield Academic Press, 2002).

4. Additional nonverbal cues would include, of course, indicators such as tone of voice or hand gestures.

ered, one on another on another, as Matthew tells his story. The sum of such choices forms the discourse of Matthew's Gospel and indicates structure and markedness (special emphasis, described below) in the story.

Mental Representations

The second linguistic principle to consider here is that *communication is built on the use of mental representations of discourse.* That is, when human beings communicate with one another they do not tend to remember the exact words and phrases they have heard or read, or they tend to remember them only for a short time. Instead they create what can roughly be called "pictures" in their minds of what another person is conveying. You probably will not remember each specific word you read or hear of this paper, but you are likely to carry away those concepts which you have formed into a coherent mental image.

Early work in artificial intelligence helped linguists become increasingly aware that linguistic comprehension relies strongly on the knowledge of the world a hearer has stored in her memory in integrated "chunks," which various researchers refer to as "scripts," "scenarios," "frames" and so on.[5] These serve as a framework to help her make sense of what she hears or reads. But others, such as Johnson-Laird, have pointed out that even if a hearer or reader has no previous knowledge of a subject or situation, she will create a mental representation based on what she hears or reads. She then carries on, adapts or abandons this mental image on the basis of what she hears or reads next.[6] For example, to borrow an example from a recent New Testament textbook:

The stars will fall from heaven,
    the sun will cease its shining;

---

5. For early studies in this area see, for example, M. Minsky, "A Framework for Representing Knowledge," in *The Psychology of Computer Vision* (ed. P. H. Winston; New York: McGraw-Hill, 1975), 211-77; R. C. Schank and R. P. Abelson, *Scripts, Plans, Goals and Understanding* (Hillsdale, N.J.: Lawrence Erlbaum, 1977). For a brief introduction to the use of scripts in artificial intelligence, see R. Schank and M. Burstein, "Artificial Intelligence: Modeling Memory for Language Understanding," in *Disciplines of Discourse* (vol. 1 in *Handbook of Discourse Analysis;* ed. T. A. van Dijk; London: Academic Press, 1985), 145-66. For more recent linguistic works dependent on representational theory see, for example, Ruth Kempson, Wilfried Meyer-Viol and Dov Gabby, *Dynamic Syntax: The Flow of Language Understanding* (Oxford: Blackwell, 2001), 7-8; William Croft and D. Alan Cruse, *Cognitive Linguistics* (Cambridge: Cambridge University Press, 2004), 1-4, 291-92.

6. See P. N. Johnson-Laird, *Mental Models: Toward a Cognitive Science of Language, Inference, and Consciousness* (Cambridge: Cambridge University Press, 1983), 371.

> the moon will be turned to blood,
>   and fire and hail will fall from heaven.
> The rest of the country will have sunny internals
>   with scattered showers.⁷

The humor in this example lies in the unexpected and forced scrambling of the mental representation the reader has been constructing. When she encounters the final sentence, the reader realizes she has been tricked in the representation she has been in the process of forming.⁸

However, as well-intentioned communicators we usually attempt to create and refine in helpful ways the mental representations our audience is in the process of constructing. Johnson-Laird appeals to Grice's Cooperative Principle and its maxims,⁹ pointing out that communicators tend to be "orderly" in their communication. "In other words, if you construct a mental model on the basis of my discourse, then I am likely to order the information in my description so as to prevent you from going astray. I owe you an account that you can represent in a single model without running into a conflict with information that I only subsequently divulge."¹⁰ Those of us who engage in the cut-and-paste of writing on a computer know that a paragraph moved from one point in a document to another must be reworked in order to present an orderly flow of information to our readers. We will adjust the word order in a sentence, substitute pronouns for proper nouns or vice versa, and provide different sentence conjunctions (for example, "however" rather than "therefore"), once the paragraph is situated in its new location. This has to do with our implicit understanding that our audience is constructing a mental representation of our dis-

---

7. I. Howard Marshall, Stephen Travis and Ian Paul, *A Guide to the Letters & Revelation* (vol. 2 of *Exploring the New Testament*; Downers Grove, Ill.: InterVarsity, 2002), 307.

8. Marshall et al. use this example to show that genre expectations (in this case, apocalyptic) set up certain interpretive frameworks in the reader's mind.

9. See H. P. Grice, "Logic and Conversation," in *Speech Acts* (vol. 3 of *Syntax and Semantics*; eds. P. Cole and J. L. Morgan; New York: Academic Press, 1975), 41-58; also H. P. Grice, *Studies in the Way of Words* (Cambridge, Mass.: Harvard University Press, 1989). Grice was one of the first to suggest that much of the process of making sense of conversation relies on a hearer making a number of pragmatic inferences not about the linguistic (or "logical") content of individual propositions, but about how the speaker intends his or her statements to be taken. Grice argued that both the speaker and the hearer share certain expectations about how conversation should proceed, expectations which he summarized in his Cooperative Principle: Make your conversational contribution such as is required, at the state at which it occurs, by the accepted purpose or direction of the talk exchange in which you are engaged. Within this overarching Cooperative Principle, Grice delineated shared pragmatic assumptions of "quantity," "quality," "relation" and "manner."

10. Johnson-Laird, *Mental Models*, 165.

course as they read, and that as communicators we bear some responsibility for the effectiveness of this process.

In making such changes in a text document, we are not so much changing the propositional content of a paragraph as we are using grammatical and syntactical structures to adjust the flow of information to present it to our audience in a more orderly way. As Givón explains: "Grammar codes, simultaneously, both propositional semantics and discourse coherence (pragmatics). This is indeed one of the most baffling facts about grammar-as-code: Although it is located wholly in the clause, its functional scope is not primarily about the propositional information couched in the clause in which it resides. Rather, grammar is predominantly about the coherence relations between the proposition (clause) and its wider discourse context."[11]

In an earlier work, Givón describes the ways that grammatical features in the narrative help to make such presentations more orderly. He writes, "For the text comprehender, overt grammatical signals — syntactic constructions, morphology, intonation — *cue* the text processor, they *guide* him/her in the construction of a coherent mental representation of the text; and this is a vital cognitive boost."[12] He explains that "one may consider the grammatical signals associated with natural language clauses as the *mental processing instructions* that guide the speech comprehender toward constructing a coherent, structured mental representation of the text."[13]

An important point to note here is that such processing is *linear* rather than hierarchical. Each clause is encountered in turn, and an attempt is made to integrate it into an ongoing mental representation. Processing cues such as sentence conjunctions function primarily locally rather than globally. There is no consistent hierarchical outline structure that can be imposed on a discourse by assigning each sentence conjunction and its related features to a different level in the hierarchy. The combination of sentence conjunction and other features indicates how the *next* clause in a discourse may be related to the previous one in constructing a mental representation, but a given set of features indicating discontinuity, for example, cannot always be equated with breaks at a specific hierarchical level everywhere in the discourse. Other processing cues in the local context form the background against which the relative strength of such indicators of discontinuity are perceived. Givón notes that sentence conjunctions and similar devices "are inherently cataphoric," that is, they look ahead to sub-

---

11. T. Givón, *Syntax: An Introduction* (2 vols.; Amsterdam: John Benjamins, 2001), 1:13.
12. T. Givón, *Functionalism and Grammar* (Amsterdam: John Benjamins, 1995), 343 (his emphasis).
13. Givón, *Functionalism,* 344 (his emphasis).

sequent elements in a text: "The grammatical cue is placed between the two clauses, signalling the degree of thematic continuity of the next clause."[14]

As I will show below, in the Greek of Matthew's Gospel sentence conjunctions and constituent order are two of the features which play this role of indicating continuity or discontinuity as the narrative progresses. Matthew presents his material in a way that facilitates the mental representations his Greek-speaking audience construct of his text. At any point in the narrative, combinations of sentence conjunction and constituent order (along with other grammatical and syntactical features not explored here) help the audience know what to "do" with the next clause they encounter — whether to continue, adjust or discontinue the mental representation they are in the process of constructing. These and other features used in this process form the discourse structure of Matthew's Gospel. A greater awareness of Matthew's habits of use of such features can lead to a more informed reading of the text.[15]

Markedness

The third linguistic principle of interest to biblical scholars is that of *markedness*.[16] Markedness is the notion that where there are two or more choices in a linguistic system — two or more things that could reasonably have been said at a given point, or two or more ways of saying something — it is often the case that one of those choices is thought to be the normal, or default, choice, the more usual choice which carries less interpretive "weight."[17] This is considered

---

14. Givón, *Functionalism*, 373. "Thematic" in this context is a technical term related to the idea of grammatical theme, that is, which syntactical element continues to be "in focus" in an individual sentence, rather than referring to the propositional theme or topic of a larger discourse.

15. This assumes, of course, that what one wants to "do" with the text is in some sense or degree to reconstruct the author's intended meaning. If one is attempting to reconstruct authorial intention, then as Langacker writes, "The ultimate goal of linguistic description is to characterize, in a cognitively realistic fashion, those structures and abilities that constitute a speaker's grasp of linguistic convention. A speaker's linguistic knowledge is procedural rather than declarative..." (Ronald W. Langacker, *Concept, Image, and Symbol: The Cognitive Basis of Grammar* [Cognitive Linguistics Research 1; Berlin: Mouton de Gruyter, 2002], 15).

16. This concept was developed as a language universal by Greenberg: "The concept of the marked and unmarked will be shown to possess a high degree of generality in that it is applicable to the phonological, the grammatical, and the semantic aspects of language..." (J. H. Greenberg, *Language Universals: With Special Reference to Feature Hierarchies* [The Hague: Mouton, 1966], 10-11). Givón notes, however, "Under one guise or another, [the] intellectual roots [of markedness] go back to antiquity..." (Givón, *Syntax*, 37).

17. See B. Comrie, *Aspect: An Introduction to the Study of Verbal Aspect and Related Problems* (Cambridge Textbooks in Linguistics; Cambridge: Cambridge University Press, 1976), 111.

the *unmarked* choice. Against the background of what is considered normal and unremarkable, any other choice is to some degree *marked*. For example, in response to the question, "How are you?," "Fine" (or its local language equivalent) is the unmarked choice in most settings. It is expected as normal and so it conveys little content. The person may or may not in fact be "fine." "Well, I'm here" is a recognizable if less common response. It conveys a bit more meaning — perhaps the responder is tired, or ill, or was simply running late — and may prompt nothing more than a sympathetic smile on the part of the questioner. It can be considered a somewhat more marked response. But if in place of the expected "fine," the responder says "Hideous. Rotten. Horrific, in fact," that communicative choice is highly marked and conveys a great deal more in the context of routine greetings. It is likely (one would hope) to prompt further questions. This example highlights marked words and phrases, but the principle of markedness is similarly represented in marked and unmarked grammatical forms and marked and unmarked syntactical patterns within a discourse.

The challenge for interpreters is that markedness is highly contextual, what Givón describes as "a context-dependent phenomenon par excellence."[18] What is marked in one context may be unmarked in another and vice versa, according to the characteristics of the particular context or the habits of an individual speaker or author. Therefore, the Matthean scholar's task is to determine what are unmarked forms of expression in various contexts in Matthew's Gospel, so that what is more marked in similar settings may be recognized as having more exegetical significance.

Certain universal linguistic tendencies may be used as a starting point in this search. For example, cognitive psychologists working on the ways people make sense of narrative have demonstrated that continuity is the default or unmarked expectation in narrative, rather than discontinuity. Simply put, unless readers are told otherwise, they assume that the events, participants, time and setting of the next sentence are consistent with the one preceding.[19] Segal et al. put forth a "principle of continuity" for narrative which ties this idea to the concept of mental representations discussed above: *"A new sentence in the text is interpreted in terms of an ongoing construction of an integrated component of the narrative's meaning. Unless specifically marked, the new meaning is incorporated into, and regarded as continuous with, the current ongoing con-*

---

18. Givón, *Syntax*, 38. Givón affirms, "One important logical consequence of the context dependence of markedness is that substantive explanations of markedness must be domain-specific" (*Syntax*, 39).

19. As Murray states, "As readers progress through a narrative, they assume that the events will follow in a linear fashion" (J. D. Murray, "Connectives and Narrative Text: The Role of Continuity," *Memory & Cognition* 25 [1997]: 228).

struction."[20] Here "the current ongoing construction" refers to a mental representation of the discourse. Segal et al. explain that "only if there is a textual cue that the new text is discontinuous with the old, or if attempts at continuous integration cannot be maintained, does the reader interpret new information as discontinuous. . . ."[21]

Therefore, an interpreter of Matthew's Gospel can assume that continuity is the unmarked condition in the text, and should be on the lookout for ways Matthew may be signaling any discontinuity in events, participants, time or setting as the Gospel unfolds. As Kroeger explains, "The topic of a sentence, when it is the same as the topic of the preceding sentence, needs no special marking. . . . But in certain contexts the topic may require more elaborate marking. . . ."[22] Certain cues in Matthew's Gospel, such as sentence conjunctions, changes in verb tense or unusual syntactical constructions, are often more significant for their processing role in ordering and adjusting the flow of the discourse than for "logical" or "truth" value within a particular sentence. With discourse continuity as the unmarked condition, the onus is on the interpreter to demonstrate, first, any points of discontinuity in the text, and secondly, the features that serve as cues to that discontinuity.

In addition to universal tendencies like the principle of continuity, specific marked and unmarked forms and structures in Matthew's Gospel can to some extent be identified by careful attention to Matthew's own patterns of use. Statistical frequency can begin to establish this, as unmarked features tend to be more common and marked features tend to be less common, although frequency is not itself a necessary factor in determining markedness.[23] Further-

---

20. E. M. Segal, J. F. Duchan and P. J. Scott, "The Role of Interclausal Connectives in Narrative Structuring: Evidence from Adults' Interpretations of Simple Stories," *Discourse Processes* 14 (1991): 32 (their emphasis). Other cognitive researchers such as Murray, "Role of Continuity," 228, and Y. Bestgen, "Segmentation Markers as Trace and Signal of Discourse Structure," *Journal of Pragmatics* 29 (1998): 775, make use of the "principle of continuity" developed by Segal et al.

21. Segal et al., "Interclausal Connectives," 32.

22. Paul R. Kroeger, *Analyzing Syntax: A Lexical-Functional Approach* (Cambridge: Cambridge University Press, 2004), 136. Kroeger notes that "topic" "is often defined intuitively as the thing which the sentence is 'about.'" He uses the term "focus" for "the essential piece of new information that is carried by a sentence . . . Focus is marked in all languages by intonational prominence (focal stress), but in many languages it is also indicated by word order and/or special particles or clitics" (Kroeger, 136).

23. Linguists tend to agree that no single characteristic, including frequency, automatically identifies a form as marked. A number of factors may come into play, and a cluster of criteria are likely to coincide, such as (to use Givón's schema) structural complexity, frequency of distribution and cognitive complexity. See Givón, *Functionalism,* 28; see also E. L. Battistella, *Markedness: The Evaluative Superstructure of Language* (Albany: State University of New York Press, 1990), 25-26; Comrie, *Aspect,* 111.

more, as Halliday points out in his systemic-functional grammar, linguistic expression actually consists of a series of choices from related systems, that is, sets of meaningful options for every "slot" in a sentence, which also influence the options chosen for other "slots." This combination of variables opens the way for a probabilistic treatment of the interrelated choices which are made.[24]

Building on Halliday's foundation regarding choice and probability, Nesbitt and Plum explain: "What is said is not only interpreted against a background of what could have been said but was not; it is also interpreted against the background of expectancies, against the background of what was more likely and what was less likely to be said. The grammar of a language is not only the grammar of what is possible but also the grammar of what is probable."[25] This idea that "What is said is . . . interpreted against a background of what could have been said but was not" can be seen, for example, in diplomatic language. When a country's leadership issues an official pronouncement, or when a discussion between leaders of two nations is made public, news analysts often comment as much on what was *not* said as on what the participants did say. Analysts realize that the significance of what was actually said is strongly colored by what everyone knows the unused alternatives to have been.

The concept of interpreting an element against the background of other potential choices has been increasingly recognized in biblical studies in lexical semantics, with a move toward "semantic domains" in lexicography, the attempt to establish the range of meaningful choices from which a particular word is selected.[26] It should be noted that this linguistic concept extends to choices of grammatical forms and syntactical relations as well as to choices of lexical items.

Thus, what is marked and unmarked in language is (inversely) proportional to what is expected and unexpected in a given context.[27] Each linguistic feature is part of a system (in Halliday's sense), and each option within that system can be seen as a variable within a set. For example, the system or set of Greek sentence conjunctions in narrative sentences in Matthew's Gospel in-

---

24. See M. A. K. Halliday, *Explorations in the Functions of Language* (London: Edward Arnold, 1973), 115; see also M. A. K. Halliday, *An Introduction to Functional Grammar* (3d ed.; rev. Christian M. I. M. Matthiessen; London: Arnold, 2004), 46-49.

25. C. Nesbitt and G. Plum, "Probabilities in a Systemic-Functional Grammar: The Clause Complex in English," in *Theory and Application* (vol. 2 of *New Developments in Systemic Linguistics*; ed. R. P. Fawcett and D. Young; Open Linguistics Series; London: Pinter, 1988), 9.

26. See, for example, J. P. Louw and E. A. Nida, eds., *Greek-English Lexicon of the New Testament Based on Semantic Domains* (2d ed.; New York: United Bible Societies, 1989).

27. See J. Lyons, *Introduction to Theoretical Linguistics* (Cambridge: Cambridge University Press, 1968), 415.

cludes the variables καί, δέ, οὖν, γάρ, τότε (which is specific to Matthew), and asyndeton (no conjunction) as alternatives within this set.²⁸ Based on the principle of redundancy in language, we would not be surprised to find that this system of sentence conjunctions interacts with other choices made from other systems such as constituent order, which has its own set of choices or variables. What features are expected and unexpected in a given context can, in a large enough database, be estimated on the basis of how frequently they actually appear. In terms of markedness, those features and combinations of features which occur most often can generally be understood as less marked, and those features and combinations of features which occur less frequently are likely to be more marked and therefore of more interpretive significance.

Although not using the terminology of markedness, Halliday is careful to say that quantitative analysis is only one factor in recognizing what features an author is using for special impact. However, as he points out, "A rough indication of frequencies is often just what is needed: enough to suggest why we should accept the writer's assertion" — the assertions made, say, in a particular reading of Matthew's Gospel — "that some feature is prominent in the text, and to allow us to check his statements."²⁹

Putting It All Together: Features of Matthew's Narrative Grammar

Within this theoretical framework, we can begin to see how the principles of redundancy, mental representations and markedness play a role in the attempt to describe Matthew's narrative syntax and the ways it conveys structure and special emphasis in Matthew's Gospel. The principle of redundancy leads us to look for multiple and interrelated signals. The concept of mental representations leads us to look for ways Matthew is using such linguistic features to guide his audience in constructing and modifying their representation of the text — in other words, how he is guiding them through the narrative. The concept of markedness helps us evaluate which of these features are of relative interpretive significance.

These principles shaped a project I undertook to identify and quantify the relationships among features such as sentence conjunctions, constituent order

---

28. There are only four exceptions in Matthew's narrative framework: πάλιν in 4:8 and 26:42, arguably an instance of asyndeton with πάλιν as an adverb; οὐδέ in 22:46, a variation of δέ; and διό in 27:8.

29. Halliday, *Explorations*, 117.

and verb tense as they occur in the narrative framework of Matthew's Gospel. My objective was to identify grammatical and syntactical patterns which occur with some regularity and to explain how they can be understood as relatively unmarked or marked in their use by Matthew. The ultimate goal was to provide data by which readings of discourse features in Matthew's Gospel could be evaluated. Amid a plethora of discourse analyses of Matthew's Gospel, some awareness of these features and their regularities in Matthew's narrative offers at least a modicum of control over what can at times become highly subjective and untestable readings. Thus what is offered here is not another "reading" of Matthew, but evidence for parameters within which such readings may be said to have validity.

In this project I started with sentence conjunctions and introduced other features such as constituent order, verb tense, and whether there was a change in subject from one sentence to the next, but this type of analysis could use any of those features (or some other) as a starting point, or could measure the interactions of such variables without a prescribed starting point. Without going into the statistical approaches and multivariate probabilistic modeling used to evaluate the data, I can offer the following summary of some of these findings.[30]

First, it will not surprise scholars of the Greek text of Matthew that by far the most frequent sentence conjunctions in Matthew's narrative framework are καί and δέ. Either καί or δέ occurs as the sentence conjunction in more than 80% of the sentences in Matthew's narrative framework. What may be less intuitively obvious is that such sentence conjunctions form some prominent syntactical patterns with other sentence features. For example, in Matthew's Gospel καί occurs predominantly with verb-subject or verb-only constituent order (that is, sentences in which a subject follows a finite verb in the main clause or in which there is no expressed subject). At the same time, δέ occurs predominantly with subject-verb constituent order (that is, sentences in which a subject precedes a finite verb in the main clause). Two-thirds (469/720, 65%) of the narrative sentences in Matthew's Gospel consist either of καί with verb-subject or verb-only constituent order (267 sentences), or δέ with subject-verb constituent order (202 sentences). This basic model, with its single related feature of constituent order, accounts for about eight out of every ten occurrences of the sentence conjunctions καί (267/335, 80%) and δέ (202/257, 79%) in Matthew's

---

30. An extensive statistic analysis of the data, including assessments of the strength and significance of the interrelationships among different variables, appears in Black, *Sentence Conjunctions,* especially in the appendix by Elizabeth Allen and Vern Farewell, "Statistical Analysis of the Choice of Conjunction in the Gospel of Matthew."

narrative framework. We can therefore say these combinations are characteristic of Matthew's narrative syntax.[31]

Furthermore, when the following scale of constituent order in Matthew's narrative framework is produced, it becomes clear that the earlier in the sentence an expressed subject occurs, the progressively less likely καί is to appear, while the later in the sentence the subject is placed (with no explicit subject at the far end of the scale), the progressively more likely καί is to appear. Conversely, on the same scale, the earlier in the sentence the subject is placed, the more frequently δέ appears; the later the subject is placed (with no explicit subject considered the least marked choice), the less frequently δέ appears:

	number sentences	number καί	percent καί	number δέ	percent δέ
Subject-verb constituent order					
Subject-verb order, with subject as *first* element in main clause	195	23	12%	155[32]	79%
Subject-verb order (but subject *not* first element in main clause)	99	40	40%	47	47%
Verb(-subject) constituent order					
Verb-subject constituent order	149	69	46%	29	19%
Verb-only constituent order	262	191	73%	25	10%

Why would this be the case? The answer lies in the fact that Matthew tends to pile up unmarked grammatical and syntactical features in unmarked discourse contexts. Καί is most often found with verb-only or verb-subject constituent order, which can be seen as constituting a less marked constituent order in narrative than supplying an explicit subject toward the beginning of a sentence.[33] Similarly, throughout Matthew's narrative framework, καί is most often found with aorist-tense verbs, which constitute the unmarked tense in past-referring narrative.[34] And underscoring the idea that unmarked grammatical

---

31. At present, all that can be said is that these features and combinations of features are characteristic of the Greek of Matthew's Gospel. To my knowledge, there are no similar linguistic studies of other New Testament books or extracanonical writings that would serve as a basis for comparing Matthew's narrative syntax with that of other contemporary writers.

32. This includes 60 instances of the fixed combination of δέ with a pronominal article: ὁ δέ, ἡ δέ, οἱ δέ, αἱ δέ. Even omitting these sentences, there is a correlation between δέ and a constituent order with the grammatical subject as the first element in the sentence. Of the 135 remaining such sentences in Matthew's narrative framework, 95 (70%) have δέ as a sentence conjunction.

33. See Black, *Sentence Conjunctions*, 117-21.

34. See Black, *Sentence Conjunctions*, 114-17.

features correlate with unmarked discourse contexts, καί is also the sentence conjunction found most frequently where the actor — the explicit or understood grammatical subject — is the same as that in the previous narrative sentence (i.e., continuity as the unmarked or expected condition in narrative). At the same time καί occurs *less* frequently with more marked verb tenses in narrative (in particular, with the so-called "historic present"); or with more marked constituent order such as a grammatical subject followed by a verb, especially when the subject is the first element in the sentence; or where there is a change in grammatical subject from one sentence to the next. In other words, the relationships between καί and other unmarked features form redundant syntactical structures conveying continuity, the unmarked condition in discourse.

Similarly, Matthew tends to use the relatively less frequent and somewhat more marked sentence conjunction δέ in contexts where there are additional signals of discourse *dis*continuity, such as subject-verb constituent order, or temporal "shifters" such as prepositional phrases or genitive absolute constructions, and/or with non-aorist verbs, and/or where there is a change in the grammatical subject from the previous narrative sentence. While καί serves as a signal of unmarked continuity in Matthew's narrative framework, δέ indicates low- to mid-level discontinuity. The presence of δέ and its redundant syntactical features cues the audience that some discontinuity is to be incorporated into their mental representation of the discourse, whether that be a change in actor, time or setting, or (closest to the traditional understanding by many of δέ as an adversative particle) a "reversal of expectation" or logical contrast.[35] The presence of such signals is a valuable aid in discourse processing because, as the "principle of continuity" mentioned above posits, "Unless specifically marked, the new meaning is incorporated into, and regarded as continuous with, the current ongoing construction."[36]

Such patterns of relationships among sentence conjunctions and constituent order, plus other features such as verb tense and "subject switch," demonstrate some of the ways choices from different linguistic systems work together in Matthew's Gospel in a linguistic synergy which creates, to use Battistella's phrase, a single superstructure incorporating form and meaning.[37] The sentence conjunctions καί and δέ and their related features function as signals of continuity and discontinuity in Matthew's text, guiding Matthew's readers to maintain or modify their ongoing mental representation of the discourse.

---

35. Thus interpreters should recognize that "adversative" is only one of the semantic contexts in which δέ may be found, and not attempt to force an adversative "logical" or "truth" value on δέ itself.

36. Segal et al., "Interclausal Connectives," 32.

37. See Battistella, *Markedness*, 7.

Where neither καί nor δέ is used, the set of alternatives in Matthew's narrative framework are asyndeton, τότε, γάρ, and οὖν. Each of these last four choices may be understood as to some extent marked in contrast to the vast majority of narrative sentences in Matthew's Gospel in which either καί or δέ occurs. For example, it appears that Matthew uses τότε as a signal of marked continuity, in some ways similar to the use of καί, but often having other marked features associated with it.[38] The fact that καί and τότε are both sentence-initial conjunctions suggests that they share an element of continuity in their function, in contrast to δέ, γάρ and οὖν, all postpositives which express some degree of discontinuity with the ongoing narrative. However, τότε is more likely to be found with present-tense verbs (a more marked form in past-referring narrative) as opposed to καί's association with aorist forms. Discourse contexts in which τότε is commonly used include marking a climactic point within a pericope (especially a pronouncement by Jesus), marking the beginning of paragraphs within an episode (especially when it is combined with subject-verb constituent order and aorist-tense verbs rather than its more usual occurrence with verb-subject order or present-tense forms), and in combination with theologically marked lexical forms such as προσέρχομαι and passive forms of προσφέρω.

Together, the basic καί-δέ model above, and the addition of other, more marked, sentence conjunctions such as τότε with its related features, suggests a topography of narrative syntax in Matthew's Gospel approached from the starting point of sentence conjunctions. Where καί and δέ and their related features occur, Matthew is guiding the audience to incorporate into their representations of the text elements of continuity or discontinuity in the narrative. Where other sentence conjunctions or unexpected combinations of features occur, Matthew may be using these in a more marked manner. The patterning of such syntactical features throughout the narrative creates the narrative's structure and highlights special emphasis.

Exegetical Applications

What do these aspects of linguistic theory — redundancy, mental representations and markedness — and their specific application in terms of sentence conjunctions and related syntactical features in Matthew's narrative suggest for the exegesis of Matthew's Gospel? A brief look at two pericopes in Matt. 8:18-27, about two potential disciples (18-22) and the calming of a storm (23-27), may provide some illustration.

---

38. See Black, *Sentence Conjunctions*, 245-53.

18 Ἰδὼν δὲ ὁ Ἰησοῦς ὄχλον περὶ αὐτὸν ἐκέλευσεν ἀπελθεῖν εἰς τὸ πέραν.	18 Now when Jesus saw great crowds around him, he gave orders to go over to the other side.
19 καὶ προσελθὼν εἷς γραμματεὺς εἶπεν αὐτῷ· διδάσκαλε, ἀκολουθήσω σοι ὅπου ἐὰν ἀπέρχῃ.	19 A scribe then approached and said, "Teacher, I will follow you wherever you go."
20 καὶ λέγει αὐτῷ ὁ Ἰησοῦς· αἱ ἀλώπεκες φωλεοὺς ἔχουσιν καὶ τὰ πετεινὰ τοῦ οὐρανοῦ κατασκηνώσεις, ὁ δὲ υἱὸς τοῦ ἀνθρώπου οὐκ ἔχει ποῦ τὴν κεφαλὴν κλίνῃ.	20 And Jesus said to him, "Foxes have holes, and birds of the air have nests; but the Son of Man has nowhere to lay his head."
21 ἕτερος δὲ τῶν μαθητῶν [αὐτοῦ] εἶπεν αὐτῷ· κύριε, ἐπίστρεψόν μοι πρῶτον ἀπελθεῖν καὶ θάψαι τὸν πατέρα μου.	21 Another of his disciples said to him, "Lord, first let me go and bury my father."
22 ὁ δὲ Ἰησοῦς λέγει αὐτῷ· ἀκολούθει μοι, καὶ ἄφες τοὺς νεκροὺς θάψαι τοὺς ἑαυτῶν νεκρούς.	22 But Jesus said to him, "Follow me, and let the dead bury their own dead."
23 Καὶ ἐμβάντι αὐτῷ εἰς τό πλοῖον, ἠκολούθησαν αὐτῷ οἱ μαθηταὶ αὐτοῦ.	23 And when he got into the boat, his disciples followed him.
24 καὶ ἰδοὺ σεισμὸς μέγας ἐγένετο ἐν τῇ θαλάσσῃ, ὥστε τὸ πλοῖον καλύπτεσθαι ὑπὸ τῶν κυμάτων, αὐτὸς δὲ ἐκάθευδεν.	24 A windstorm arose on the sea, so great that the boat was being swamped by the waves; but he was asleep.
25 καὶ προσελθόντες ἤγειραν αὐτὸν λέγοντες· κύριε, σῶσον, ἀπολλύμεθα.	25 And they went and woke him up, saying, "Lord, save us! We are perishing!"
26 καὶ λέγει αὐτοῖς· τί δειλοί ἐστε, ὀλιγόπιστοι; τότε ἐγερθεὶς ἐπετίμησεν τοῖς ἀνέμοις καὶ τῇ θαλάσσῃ, καὶ ἐγένετο γαλήνη μεγάλη.	26 And he said to them, "Why are you afraid, you of little faith?" Then he got up and rebuked the winds and the sea; and there was a dead calm.
27 οἱ δὲ ἄνθρωποι ἐθαύμασαν λέγοντες· ποταπός ἐστιν οὗτος, ὅτι καὶ οἱ ἄνεμοι καὶ ἡ θάλασσα αὐτῷ ὑπακούουσιν;	27 They were amazed, saying, "What sort of man is this, that even the winds and the sea obey him?" (NRSV)

This passage is located in the "miracle chapters" of Matthew 8–9. The arrangement by which Matthew recounts the events in chapters 8 and 9 varies significantly from that of Mark. Specifically, some of the material in Matt 8:1–22 is also found in a different order in Mark 1:29-45, and Matt. 8:23-34 corresponds to Mark 4:35–5:20. Likewise, although some of the incidents in Matthew 8–9 also appear in Luke's Gospel, Matthew differs from Luke in how he compiles and arranges his account. With respect to the passage above, Matt. 8:23-34 parallels Luke 8:22-39. For these reasons Matt. 8:18-27 can serve as an appropriate exemplar for this investigation: while there are synoptic parallels, this passage represents Matthew's own narrative presentation.

Three exegetical questions will be surveyed here, with an eye to how the linguistic concepts of redundancy, mental representations and markedness may contribute to their solutions: first, the question of whether these two pericopes form part of the same section within chapters 8 and 9, or whether Matt. 8:23 should be seen as beginning a new structural unit; second, Luz's proposal that Matt. 8:1–9:34 exhibits an overall unity that supersedes attempts to further subdivide these two chapters; and third, whether in the calming of the storm, Matthew's emphasis is on Jesus' statements to the fearful disciples or on his power over the storm.

1. Is There a Structural Break Between Matt. 8:18-22 and 23-27?

Although there is a wide consensus among biblical scholars that the collection of ten miracles and healings in chapters 8 and 9 forms a coherent unit within Matthew's Gospel, there is a range of scholarly opinion concerning the internal arrangement of the unit.[39] A small sample of the many commentaries and studies on this passage will serve as examples here.

Held, in his classic study of Matthew's miracle stories, sees in Matt. 8:1–9:34 three major groups of miracles and a final section: 8:1-17, 8:18–9:17 and 9:18-31, with 9:32-34 as the final section.[40] Thompson adopts Held's section divisions for 8:1–9:34,[41] and Burger, while proposing a different overall scheme

---

39. See, for example, H. J. Held, "Matthew as Interpreter of the Miracle Stories," in *Tradition and Interpretation in Matthew* (G. Bornkamm, G. Barth and H. J. Held; trans. P. Scott; London: SCM, 1963), 165-299; W. G. Thompson, "Reflections on the Composition of Mt 8.1–9.34," *CBQ* 33 (1971): 365-88; C. Burger, "Jesu Taten nach Matthäus 8 und 9," *ZTK* 70 (1973): 272-87; J. P. Louw, "The Structure of Mt 8:1–9:35," *Neot* 11 (1977): 91-97; J. D. Kingsbury, "Observations on the 'Miracle Chapters' of Matthew 8–9," *CBQ* 40 (1978): 559-73; G. Theissen, *The Miracle Stories of the Early Christian Tradition* (Philadelphia: Fortress, 1983), 209-11; J. Moiser, "The Structure of Matthew 8–9: A Suggestion," *ZNW* 76 (1985): 117-18; Ulrich Luz, *Mt 8-17* (vol. 2 in *Das Evangelium nach Matthäus*; EKKNT 1.2; Zürich: Benziger Verlag, 1990), 1-73.

40. Held, "Miracle Stories," 248-49.

41. Thompson, "Composition of Mt. 8.1–9.34," 365-66, 368. Gerhardsson also agrees with

for the two chapters, agrees with Held and Thompson in placing a section break between 8:17 and 8:18, so that 8:17 ends a section with the theme of christology while 8:18 begins a new section with the theme of discipleship.[42] Kingsbury agrees with Burger's overall fourfold thematic schema, and likewise places a section break between 8:17 and 8:18.[43] Thus for each of these commentators, the two pericopes in Matt. 8:18-27 are part of the same section, with a focus on discipleship, and there is no significant structural break between 8:22 and 8:23.

Davies and Allison, however, take a different line, viewing the series of healings and other material in Matt. 8:1–9:34 as arranged formally in threes, based on "Matthew's love of the triad, the number of miracle stories in 8-9 (nine), and the fact that the miracle stories appear in three different groups."[44] In their analysis the passage consists of three groups of three stories, interspersed by two units which serve as boundaries.[45] This leads them to treat 8:16-22 as a boundary unit which follows the first three stories in 8:1-15, while 8:23 begins the first in the next series of three stories.[46] Thus in Davies and Allison's schema the calming of the storm in 8:23-27 is the first miracle in a new unit, rather than being more closely tied to Jesus' encounters with two would-be disciples in 8:18-22.

Although Louw's arrangement differs somewhat from that of Davies and Allison, he takes a similar triadic approach, with three sections of healings and/or miracles, each composed of three scenes. He outlines a section of three healings in 8:1-17 (8:1-4, 5-13, 14-17), followed by a section of material on following Jesus in 8:18-22, after which a new section of a miracle and healings begins in 8:23 (8:23-27, 28-34; 9:1-8).[47]

Held's outline (B. Gerhardsson, *The Mighty Acts of Jesus According to Matthew* [Lund: C. W. K. Gleerup, 1979], 39).

42. Burger, "Jesu Taten," 284-87.
43. Kingsbury, "Miracle Chapters," 562.
44. W. D. Davies and D. C. Allison, *Commentary on Matthew VIII-XVIII* (vol. 2 in *A Critical and Exegetical Commentary on the Gospel According to Saint Matthew*; ICC; Edinburgh: T&T Clark, 1991), 3. For others who emphasize a triadic scheme see, for example, W. C. Allen, *A Critical and Exegetical Commentary on the Gospel According to S. Matthew* (3d ed.; ICC; Edinburgh: T&T Clark, 1912), 74; K. Gatzwieler, "Les récits de miracles dans L'Évangile selon Saint Matthieu," in *L'Évangile selon Matthieu: Rédaction et Théologie* (ed. M. Didier; BETL 29; Gembloux: Duculot, 1972), 214; G. H. Twelftree, *Jesus the Miracle Worker* (Downers Grove, Ill.: InterVarsity, 1999), 122.
45. Davies and Allison, *Matthew VIII-XVIII*, 6.
46. W. D. Davies and D. C. Allison, *A Critical and Exegetical Commentary on the Gospel according to Saint Matthew* (3 vols.; ICC; Edinburgh: T&T Clark, 1988-97), 1:67, 102.
47. Louw, "Mt. 8:1–9:34," 91.

Thus there is little unanimity among scholars concerning the points at which Matt. 8:1–9:34 falls into three or four sections, with or without boundary units. Specifically with respect to where 8:18-27 fits into a larger schema, there is difference of opinion about whether the two pericopes are to be taken together as the beginning of one larger unit, or whether 8:18-22 should be seen as in some sense a boundary unit before a new section begins in verse 23. The views of the scholars above can be schematized as follows:

	Held, Thompson, Burger, Kingsbury	Davies and Allison	Louw
8:18-22 A reluctant disciple	Section 2 (on theme of discipleship)	Boundary unit following Section 1 (3 miracles)	On the teaching and preaching of Jesus (on following Jesus)
8:23-27 The calming of a storm	↓	Section 2 (3 miracles)	Section 2 (3 scenes: a miracle and healings)

Held, Thompson, Burger and Kingsbury see a section break at 8:18 which places these two pericopes together into the following section on discipleship, while in the views of Davies and Allison and of Louw the beginning of the next section is delayed until 8:23, separating the pericope of the reluctant disciples from the calming of the great storm.

What can linguistic theory add to this discussion? The concept of mental representations leads us to look for ways Matthew is guiding his audience in constructing and modifying their representation of the narrative as the events in chapters 8 and 9 unfold. This will involve signals of continuity and discontinuity in the way each pericope is presented. The principle of redundancy leads us to look for multiple and interrelated signals — lexical, grammatical and syntactical — which serve as processing cues as the audience constructs its mental representations. The concept of markedness helps us evaluate which of these features are relatively significant in guiding the audience's attention to certain features of the discourse.

Looking at introductory sentence conjunctions and constituent order can help us trace Matthew's presentation of the narrative. In the block of text below other content has been omitted in order to show these features more clearly. We start with Matt. 8:16, the beginning of Allison and Davies' postulated boundary unit in 8:16-22:

	Sentence Conjunction + Constituent Order
16 Ὀψίας δὲ γενομένης προσήνεγκαν . . .	δέ + genitive absolute + verb-only
καὶ ἐξέβαλεν . . .	καί + verb-only
καὶ . . . ἐθεράπευσεν . . .	καί + verb-only
17 ὅπως πληρωθῇ	[subordinate clause]
18 Ἰδὼν δὲ ὁ Ἰησοῦς . . . ἐκέλευσεν	δέ + subject-verb
19 καὶ προσελθὼν εἷς γραμματεὺς εἶπεν . . .	καί + subject-verb
20 καὶ λέγει αὐτῷ ὁ Ἰησοῦς . . .	καί + verb-subject
21 ἕτερος δὲ τῶν μαθητῶν [αὐτοῦ] εἶπεν . . .	δέ + subject-verb
22 ὁ δὲ Ἰησοῦς λέγει . . .	δέ + subject-verb
23 Καὶ ἐμβάντι αὐτῷ εἰς τὸ πλοῖον ἠκολούθησαν αὐτῷ οἱ μαθηταὶ αὐτοῦ . . .	καί + verb-subject
24 καὶ ἰδοὺ σεισμὸς μέγας ἐγένετο . . .	καὶ ἰδού + subject-verb
αὐτὸς δὲ ἐκάθευδεν.	δέ + subject-verb
25 καὶ προσελθόντες ἤγειραν αὐτὸν λέγοντες . . .	καί + verb-only
26 καὶ λέγει αὐτοῖς . . .	καί + verb-only
τότε ἐγερθεὶς ἐπετίμησεν . . .	τότε + verb-only
καὶ ἐγένετο γαλήνη μεγάλη.	καί + verb-subject
27 οἱ δὲ ἄνθρωποι ἐθαύμασαν λέγοντες . . .	δέ + subject-verb

Verse 16 begins with at least two signals of discontinuity, specifically δέ plus a genitive absolute construction, often used by Matthew as a narrative "scene shifter" indicating a temporal shift or new setting in the narrative.[48] The next two clauses in verse 16 exhibit close continuity after the first clause, indi-

---

48. See, for example, Matt. 8:1, 8:5, 8:28, 9:18, 9:32 and 9:33. There is a strong correlation between δέ and genitive absolute participial constructions as mutually redundant signals of discourse discontinuity. Δέ is the sentence conjunction in 23 of the 39 sentences in Matthew's narrative framework in which a genitive absolute construction begins the sentence (59%). In her multivariate statistical analysis of my data, Allen states that "features that have the most noticeable effect on choosing 'δε' as opposed to 'και' appear to be a constituent order of 'subject before verb in first position' . . . , and a topical theme of 'genitive absolute participle'" (Allen, "Greek Syntactical Analysis: An Investigation into the Relationship between Conjunctions and Contextual Variables in the Gospel of Matthew" [M.Sc. thesis, University College London, September 1999], 19-20; see also Allen and Farewell, "Statistical Analysis," in Black, *Sentence Conjunctions*, 361). After adjusting for all other variables and interactions Allen concludes that δέ is about fifty times more likely to be used as the sentence conjunction with a genitive absolute construction than is καί (Allen, "Greek Syntactical Analysis," 26).

cated in each by καί as the sentence conjunction and monolectic verbs (that is, verbs with no expressed subject, the least marked form in Matthew's Greek). Verse 17 then continues with a subordinating conjunction ὅπως connecting the fulfillment of prophecy to the actions in verse 16. Thus 8:16-17 forms a tightly coherent series of clauses.

However, the δέ which begins 8:18, plus the choice to make the subject ὁ Ἰησοῦς explicit and place it before the main verb (subject-verb constituent order), suggests some discontinuity from previous narrative at this point, and offers syntactical justification for the argument made by Held, Thompson, Burger and Kingsbury on other grounds that a segmentation of the narrative occurs here.[49] In terms of mental representations, Matthew provides processing cues which guide readers to make their current representation of the narrative to some degree discontinuous from that which immediately precedes. The sentence conjunction and constituent order are redundant cues. The conjunction δέ is marked relative to the two uses of καί which precede, guiding readers to suspend their expectation of continuity (the unmarked condition) in the narrative.

Again the following two clauses (8:19-20) exhibit continuity, with καί as the sentence conjunction in each and, in 8:20, verb-subject constituent order — the next-to-least marked constituent order in Matthew's Greek as conceived in the scale above. Matt. 8:19 has subject-verb constituent order, but the choice of καί rather than δέ as the sentence conjunction here shows that the author has chosen to portray this clause as more continuous than discontinuous in this context.

The next two clauses (8:21-22) are both of the structure δέ + subject-verb constituent order. None of the commentators argues that these two clauses form separate subunits within the narrative. Given that I have argued above that in 8:18 the combination of δέ and subject-verb constituent order suggests some discontinuity from the previous narrative and in fact begins a new unit, how can these two δέ-clauses be retained within the unit 8:18-22 without recourse to special pleading?

There are four points to consider here. The first is a reminder that discourse processing is *linear* rather than hierarchical. While the combination of sentence conjunction and other features helps guide how the next clause in a discourse will be related to the previous one in the audience's mental representation, the level of discontinuity of a given instance of δέ and subject-verb constituent order is locally determined, rather than indicating a specific level in a global hierarchy. Other processing cues in the local context help the hearer or reader determine the relative strength of such indicators of discontinuity.

---

49. There is also a pre-verbal nominal participle in verse 18. Such participles have not been factored into this study, but further research is needed on their role in discourse structure.

The second point is that in the linear processing of discourse one of the most common low- to mid-level discontinuities encountered is a change in actor or participant, as in both 8:21 (a shift from Jesus to the second inquirer) and 8:22 (a shift from the inquirer back to Jesus). Matthew routinely indicates such changes with δέ + subject-verb constituent order. In narrative sentences overall, καί plus a verb with no expressed subject represents the "default setting" or least marked option, so any deviation from that structure represents an element of choice on the part of the author and is marked to some degree. But the use of δέ + subject-verb constituent order to signal a change in actor would be relatively expected in this context, and therefore seen as relatively unmarked at this point.

The third point is this reminder that markedness is highly contextual. What is marked in one situation may be unmarked in another and vice versa. In this context, Matt. 8:21 and 8:22 are both instances of "speech margins," a term which refers to the syntactical structures used to introduce reported speech, whether conversation or monologue, and to set it into the narrative framework.[50] Matthew frequently uses δέ in speech margins to indicate the alternation between speakers. This is a specific application of the change in actor mentioned above, and again represents a shift not in time, setting or action, but in actor or participant. So again, in this type of context, the audience may look no further for narrative discontinuity than the change from one speaker to another as they attempt to make sense of δέ as a processing cue. In other words, δέ can be less marked for narrative discontinuity in speech margins than in other types of narrative sentences.

Fourthly, and related to the issue of markedness in context, is that δέ may be used within a series of clauses to interrupt continuity in the narrative to mark prominence. In Matt. 8:10, for example, Matthew uses δέ and subject-verb constituent order to introduce Jesus' amazement at the centurion's faith (Matt. 8:10, ἀκούσας δὲ ὁ Ἰησοῦς ἐθαύμασεν . . .). In that pericope 8:10 is the only sentence beginning with δέ in a series of sentences where unmarked καί is the repeated conjunction carrying the scene forward in smooth continuity. At 8:10, δέ and the brief interruption of narrative continuity that it represents mark Jesus' amazement in the face of the surprising statements of the centurion. The contextually marked use of δέ (that is, that Matthew has chosen to insert δέ in a sequence of clauses where he otherwise uses καί) makes the exchange between the centurion and Jesus discontinuous with the smooth flow of the rest of the scene, and indicates the prominence of their interaction in the narrative. Simi-

---

50. Speech margins play a large role in Matthew's narrative framework. Of the 720 narrative sentences in Matthew's Gospel, 299 (42%) function as speech margins, either with or without verbs of speaking like λέγω or φημί.

larly, in Matt. 8:21-22 the use of δέ and subject-verb constituent order as a marked choice on the part of the author, rather than the unmarked default option of καί and verb-only, may not only indicate the change in speaker from the inquirer to Jesus, but may mark as prominent Jesus' interaction with this second disciple and his concluding comment to "let the dead bury their own dead," and thus is potentially significant in the exegesis of these verses.[51]

The audience will look only as far as they need to to make sense of signals of discontinuity,[52] and will continue to maintain as much of the "principle of continuity" as possible. If they can make sense of the text by recognizing that the δέ-clauses in 8:21 and 8:22 indicate a shift from one actor to another, and/or a speech margin with alternating speakers, and/or that one or both point to prominence within the immediate scene, they will likely perceive no need to incorporate a higher-level structural break into the overall mental representation they are constructing of the narrative, and the signals of discontinuity will be seen as only locally relevant.

Having said all that, it is notable than in 8:23, the real focus of this discussion, the signals of discontinuity are muted and signals of continuity prevail. Matt. 8:23 begins with καὶ ἐμβάντι αὐτῷ εἰς τὸ πλοῖον ἠκολούθησαν αὐτῷ οἱ μαθηταὶ αὐτοῦ. . . . Matthew could have used δέ as the sentence conjunction, but he chooses καί; he could have used a genitive absolute "scene shifter" at the beginning of the sentence, but he chooses a dative participle; he could have used subject-verb constituent order, but he chooses verb-subject order. The dative participle in 8:23 is less marked for discontinuity than a genitive absolute would be, and is particularly notable when Matthew shows his willingness in 9:18 to use a genitive absolute construction even with respect to a following dative noun. The redundant elements of continuity are also striking when one

---

51. One can compare the syntax introducing Jesus' statement to the would-be disciple in 8:22, ὁ δὲ Ἰησοῦς λέγει . . . , with that of his statement to the disciples in the boat in 8:26a, καὶ λέγει αὐτοῖς . . . (discussed below). The combination of δέ and subject-verb constituent order in 8:22 is relatively more marked than the combination of καί and a monolectic verb in 8:26a, even though both use present-tense λέγει in the speech margin (an unmarked verb tense for λέγω in speech margins in Matthew's Gospel).

52. This economy of effort is the fundamental assumption of Relevance Theory. See D. Sperber and D. Wilson, *Relevance: Communication and Cognition* (2d ed.; Oxford: Basil Blackwell, 1995). Sperber and Wilson's First (or Cognitive) Principle of Relevance is that human cognition tends to be geared to the maximization of relevance (Sperber and Wilson, *Relevance*, 260). They argue that since there is a cost (in terms of time and effort) in processing communication, hearers pay attention to and process the information which appears to be the most relevant to them at the least cost. One practical outworking of this is that hearers will look to the immediate context first to make sense of what they hear, before spending time and energy searching for larger contexts in which to attempt to make sense of linguistic input.

considers that the material in 8:23-27 is paralleled in differing contexts in Mark and Luke. Assuming that Matthew is making use of an existing story about Jesus, it is all the more notable that he uses such signals of continuity to place it in his own ongoing narrative. In spite of Davies and Allison's tripartite scheme (and Louw's agreement), a section break at 8:23 appears unjustified based on Matthew's choices of narrative syntax here.

The content of the pericope of the calming of the storm (8:23-37) seems at first glance to be distinct from the exchanges about discipleship in 8:18-22. But apparently Matthew intends for the two scenes to be taken as more continuous than discontinuous. The calming of the storm is somehow to be integrated into a mental representation which also incorporates Jesus' statements on discipleship.[53] Here again, an application of linguistic theory offers justification for arguments made by Held, Thompson, Burger and Kingsbury on other grounds to keep the two pericopes together in one larger unit. Exegetes note, for example, the "catchword" connections between 8:23 and the previous pericope in the repetition of ἀκολουθέω (8:19, 22, 23) and μαθηταί (8:21, 23), an example of further redundancies in the text (in this case lexical) which contribute to coherence in the mental representation the audience constructs of the discourse.[54]

2. Narrative Continuity in Matthew 8–9: One Theme or Many?

In contrast to various structural outlines of Matt 8:1–9:34 suggested by commentators, Luz takes a different approach to the flow of Matthew's miracle chapters. Luz argues that 8:1–9:34 is one long unit with a single theme. He notes that Matthew's account of these events conveys a strong sense of continuous movement. As Luz puts is, "[E]vents follow upon one another in quick succession: chapters 8 and 9 convey the impression that Jesus healed the sick without interruption. Each story emerges directly from its predecessor; Matthew offers a narrative thread without a single break in time or place."[55] Luz argues that this

---

53. See G. Bornkamm, "The Stilling of the Storm in Matthew," in Bornkamm, Barth and Held, *Tradition and Interpretation*, 54-55; Held, "Miracle Stories," 202. Bruner treats 8:18-27 together as "The Disciples in the Storm," and suggests that "the 'Disciples-in-the-Storm Miracle (preceded by an introduction to discipleship in the story of the Two Would-Be Disciples) depicts the 'healing' of the storm and of the disciples' 'little faith'" (Frederick Dale Bruner, *The Christbook, Matthew 1–12* [vol. 1 of *Matthew: A Commentary*; revd. and expd. ed.; Grand Rapids: Eerdmans, 2004], 393).

54. See Bornkamm, "Stilling of the Storm," 54; Held, "Miracle Stories," 201-2; Ulrich Luz, *Matthew 8–20* (Hermeneia; Minneapolis: Fortress, 2001), 15.

55. Ulrich Luz, *The Theology of the Gospel of Matthew* (trans. J. B. Robinson; Cambridge: Cambridge University Press, 1995), 63.

is not a collection of miracle stories exemplifying Jesus' deeds, different facets of his teaching, or even the nature of Christian faith, but that in this extended passage Matthew is constructing a single history *(Geschichte)*.[56] For Luz, the organizing principle underlying Matt. 8:1–9:34 is Jesus' conflict with Israel.[57] At its culmination in 9:33-34, the crowds marvel at Jesus while the Pharisees reject him. "Matthew wishes to depict a historical progression culminating in the dual response of the people and Pharisees to Jesus' miracles."[58]

A linguistic approach may not determine whether Luz's claim for the thematic unity of Matt. 8:1–9:34 as conflict between Jesus and Israel is justified, but such an analysis can address the question of narrative continuity in these chapters. In fact, redundant syntactical signals of continuity appear more frequently in this extended unit than they do in Matthew's narrative framework overall. Καί appears as a sentence conjunction in 8:1–9:34 significantly more frequently than it does in narrative sentences in Matthew's Gospel as a whole. Καί is the sentence conjunction in fewer than half of the sentences in the narrative framework outside of 8:1–9:34 (277/634, 44%), but occurs in two-thirds of the narrative sentences in 8:1–9:34 (58/86, 67%). At the same time, δέ, a signal of low- to mid-level discontinuity in narrative, is found less frequently in 8:1–9:34 than in the overall narrative framework. It is used as the sentence conjunction in more than a third of the rest of the sentences in Matthew's narrative framework (236/634, 37%), but it occurs in only about one-fourth of narrative sentences in 8:1–9:34 (21/86, 24%). Overall, there are more uses of καί and fewer uses of δέ in 8:1–9:34 than Matthew tends to use in narrative in general.

Similarly, in Matt. 8:1–9:34 there appears to be an increased use of verb-subject constituent order, a less-marked choice associated with the portrayal of continuity in narrative. There is a corresponding decrease in the number of sentences in which Matthew uses an explicit subject as the first element in the sentence, the most marked constituent order in terms of portraying discontinuity in narrative. Verb-subject constituent order is found in about two out of every ten narrative sentences in the rest of Matthew's Gospel (124/634, 20%), but

---

56. "Es geht Matthäus keineswegs um eine blosse Sammlung von Wundergeschichten, die beispielhaft die Taten des Messias oder gar verschiedene Aspekte seiner Lehre und des christlichen Glaubens erläuten, sondern es geht ihm um eine zusammenhängende Geschichte" (Ulrich Luz, "Die Wundergeschichten von Mt 8–9", in *Tradition and Interpretation in the New Testament* [ed. G. F. Hawthorne and O. Betz; Grand Rapids: Eerdmans, 1987], 152).

57. See Luz, *Theology*, 64-65.

58. Luz, *Theology*, 64. Vledder similarly sees conflict between Jesus and the Jewish leaders as the central issue in chapters 8 and 9. See E.-J. Vledder, *Conflict in the Miracle Stories: A Socio-Exegetical Study of Matthew 8 and 9* (JSNTSup 152; Sheffield: Sheffield Academic Press, 1997), 12-13.

appears in about three out of every ten such sentences in 8:1–9:34 (25/86, 29%). And conversely, while an explicit subject is the first element in nearly 30% of the sentences in the rest of Matthew's narrative framework (179/634, 28%), this is so in less than 20% of the narrative sentences in 8:1–9:34 (16/86, 19%). So it perhaps is not surprising that the events in 8:1–9:34 seem to Luz to follow upon one another in quick succession. Matthew's syntactical choices portray this sequence of events as highly continuous compared to the rest of his narrative framework, as is evidenced in the increased use of καί and of constituent order associated with narrative continuity, and the decreased use of δέ and of constituent order associated with discontinuity. In other words, the mental representation the audience is constructing of this narrative is allowed to continue with relatively few signals of discontinuity to interrupt the assumption of continuity. Of course, this does not mean that Matt 8:1–9:34 cannot also be divided into subunits in some way. But whatever internal arrangement is suggested should be considered in light of the overall portrayal of continuity perceived by Luz.

3. What Is Matthew's Central Focus in the Calming of the Storm?

One question that has received some attention from Matthew intepreters is whether the focus of Matthew's interest in 8:23-27 is on Jesus' statement to his disciples (8:26a) or on the nature miracle as Jesus calms the storm (8:26b).

Again, here is a schema of the narrative clauses in this periocope, with the sentence conjunction and constituent order of each highlighted:

23 Καὶ ἐμβάντι αὐτῷ εἰς τὸ πλοῖον ἠκολούθησαν αὐτῷ οἱ μαθηταὶ αὐτοῦ . . .	καί + verb-subject
24 καὶ ἰδοὺ σεισμὸς μέγας ἐγένετο . . .	καὶ ἰδού + subject-verb
αὐτὸς δὲ ἐκάθευδεν.	δέ + subject-verb
25 καὶ προσελθόντες ἤγειραν αὐτὸν λέγοντες . . .	καί + verb-only
26 καὶ λέγει αὐτοῖς . . .	καί + verb-only
τότε ἐγερθεὶς ἐπετίμησεν . . .	τότε + verb-only
καὶ ἐγένετο γαλήνη μεγάλη.	καί + verb-subject
27 οἱ δὲ ἄνθρωποι ἐθαύμασαν λέγοντες . . .	δέ + subject-verb

The four clauses in 8:25-26 have καί as the sentence conjunction (except for the climactic τότε in 8:26b; see below) and verb-only or verb-subject constituent order. These signals of continuity underline the role of authorial choice in choosing to emphasize continuity over against discontinuity at this point in the narrative. Any of the changes in actor, in 8:25 (from Jesus to the disciples), 8:26a (from the disciples to Jesus) or 8:26c (from Jesus to the impersonal ἐγένετο), could have been portrayed with δέ and a corresponding constituent order. For his own purposes Matthew seems to have chosen to deemphasize the changes in this sequence of clauses and instead to recount this sequence as relatively continuous narrative.

For the first time in chapter 8, in 8:26b Matthew chooses a sentence conjunction other than καί or δέ. I have described τότε elsewhere as a signal of marked continuity, and as such it is not surprising to find it displacing καί, the unmarked signal of continuity.[59] Although none of the lexical or syntactical features which tend to collocate with τότε elsewhere in Matthew's Gospel occurs in the present context — specifically, the so-called "historic present," a finite verb as the first element in the main clause, verb-subject constituent order, or the lexical choice of προσέρχομαι or a passive form of προσφέρω — τότε does appear to mark the high point of 8:25-26. As Buth points out, τότε may appear at "peaks" within a narrative, especially climactic statements by Jesus.[60] In the present context it accompanies not Jesus' words to his disciples decrying their lack of faith, but his rebuke of the storm (a type of statement by Jesus, although the content of his words is not given).

In contrast, Matthew introduces Jesus' statement to his fearful disciples simply by καὶ λέγει αὐτοῖς. . . . Here καί as the sentence conjunction is combined with a common and unmarked "speech margin" (present-tense λέγω) and no explicit subject — all signals of continuity rather than discontinuity or markedness. There are no marked features within this structure; there is nothing in the syntax of this statement to indicate that Matthew is attempting to draw special attention to it.

Some exegetes, observing that Matthew's order is the reverse of Mark's, with Jesus' words to the disciples preceding the calming of the storm rather than following as in Mark's Gospel (Mark 4:39-40), argue that Matthew shows less interest in the miracle itself and directs his attention instead to the interchange between Jesus and the disciples.[61] However, the lexico-grammatical choices displayed here suggest otherwise. Matthew's interest in issues of discipleship is manifest in this pericope; nevertheless, it is not Matthew's habit to use

---

59. See Black, *Sentence Conjunctions*, 248-49.

60. See Randall Buth, "Perspective in Gospel Discourse Studies, with Notes on Euthus, Tote and the Temptation Pericopes," *START* 6 (1982), 8.

61. See, for example, Held, "Miracle Stories," 203-4; R. H. Gundry, *Matthew: A Commentary on His Handbook for a Mixed Church under Persecution* (2d ed.; Grand Rapids: Eerdmans, 1994), 156. Hagner suggests that placing Jesus' question to the disciples before his rebuke of the sea is "in keeping with the discipleship theme and thus heighten[s] its impact" (D. A. Hagner, *Matthew 1–13* [WBC 33A; Dallas: Word, 1993], 222).

τότε to downplay a statement or action in the middle of a paragraph, nor is it his habit to introduce a climactic statement with καί and monolectic λέγει, as in Jesus' rebuke of his disciples' lack of faith in 8:26a. The choices made by the Evangelist in recounting these events indicate that his primary focus in 8:25-26 is on Jesus' authority over the storm.

However, to go further, it is at 8:27 that Matthew next provides signals of relatively marked discontinuity (δέ + subject-verb constituent order), for the first time since 8:24. As in 8:10 and 8:22 described above (and also in 24b, with the use of δέ + subject-verb constituent order to introduce the surprising — and, in light of Jonah 1:5 [LXX], potentially significant — fact that Jesus is asleep), the use of δέ and subject-verb constituent order in Matt 8:27 instead of the unmarked default option of καί and verb-only, is a marked choice on the part of the author at this point in the narrative. In 8:27 such a choice may not only indicate the change in actor from Jesus to the next speaker, but may mark as prominent within this pericope the people's amazed response, "What sort of man is this, that even the winds and the sea obey him?" (cf. Ps. 107:23-32). Thus, there are syntactical indications here that Matthew's ultimate focus in 8:23-27 is not simply on the nature miracle itself but on the reaction of "the people" to Jesus' ability to perform the miracle.[62]

Summary and Conclusion

An ever-increasing variety of linguistic models and approaches competes for the attention of the biblical scholar as she or he searches among linguistic studies for the "exegetical payoff" for biblical interpretation. However, an understanding and application of several established linguistic assumptions — namely *redundancy,* the use of *mental representations* and *markedness* — can be of practical help in the attempt to describe structure and special emphasis in biblical narrative. The principle of redundancy in language leads the biblical interpreter to look for multiple and interrelated linguistic signals in the text. The concept of mental representations in the cognitive processing of language leads one to look for ways authors such as Matthew use such linguistic features to guide their audience in constructing and modifying their mental representations of the text — in other words, in guiding them through the narrative. The

---

62. Luz writes, "With its reference to the 'people' (ἄνθρωποι) this verse leaves the narrative's surface level, since Jesus has already left the people; only the disciples are with him" (Luz, *Matthew 8–20,* 15). Later Luz notes that within the pericope this verse is "decisive for Matthew" and "also emphasizes the christological dimension" (Luz, *Matthew 8–20,* 21).

concept of linguistic markedness helps the exegete evaluate which of these features are of relative interpretive significance. Specifically, in Matthew's Gospel the use of interrelated features such as *sentence conjunction* (e.g., καί, δέ, τότε) and *constituent order* (that is, subject-verb, verb-subject or verb-only sentence patterns) offers an example of how Matthew indicates continuity and discontinuity in the narrative and marks structural boundaries and special emphases as he tells his story.

Three exegetical questions in Matt. 8:18-27 have been surveyed here, demonstrating how the linguistic concepts of redundancy, mental representations and markedness contribute to their solutions. First, with respect to the question of whether the two pericopes in Matt. 8:18-22 and 8:23-27 form part of the same section within chapters 8 and 9, or whether 8:23 should be seen as beginning a new structural unit, the concept of mental representations leads us to look for ways Matthew is guiding his audience in constructing and modifying their representation of the narrative as the events in chapter 8 and 9 unfold. This analysis shows that in 8:23, syntactical signals of discontinuity are muted while signals of continuity are multiplied. While the pericope of the calming of the storm (8:23-37) may seem at first glance to be distinct from the exchanges about discipleship in 8:18-22, Matthew intends the two scenes to be taken together. Jesus' authority over the storm is to be integrated into an ongoing mental representation which incorporates Jesus' statements on discipleship.

Second, addressing Luz's proposal that 8:1–9:34 exhibits an overall thematic unity that is more significant than any attempts to subdivide these two chapters, we have seen that Matthew's syntactical choices portray this sequence of events as highly continuous compared to the rest of his narrative framework. This is evidenced in the increased use of καί and of constituent order associated with narrative continuity, and the decreased use of δέ and of constituent order associated with discontinuity. The mental representation of chapters 8 and 9 which the audience is constructing is allowed to proceed with relatively few signals of discontinuity to interrupt the assumption of continuity. This linguistic analysis supports the portrayal of thematic unity perceived by Luz.

Third, regarding whether Matthew's emphasis is on Jesus' challenge to the fearful disciples in 8:26a, or on his power over the storm in 8:26b, the choices made by the Evangelist in recounting these events indicate that his primary focus in 8:25-26 is on Jesus' authority over the storm. Matthew is not likely to use τότε, a marked signal of continuity found in 8:26b, to downplay a statement or action in the middle of a paragraph, nor is he likely to introduce a climactic statement with καί and monolectic λέγει, as in Jesus' rebuke of his disciples' lack of faith in 8:26a. Moreover, the signals of relatively marked discontinuity (δέ + subject-verb constituent order) Matthew provides in 8:27 appear to mark the people's amazed response, "What sort of man is this, that even the winds and the sea obey him?" as prominent within this pericope. The syntactical choices suggest that Matthew's ultimate focus in 8:23-27 lies in the amazed reaction of "the people" to Jesus' authority over the sea.

However, this analysis of 8:18-27 is not intended primarily as a particular "reading" of Matthew's Gospel, but as an example of linguistic evidence by which various readings of the Gospel may be evaluated in terms of their interpretive validity. My aim here is to identify grammatical and syntactical patterns which occur with observable regularity in Matthew's Gospel, to outline a linguistic rationale for their significance, and to explain how such features can be understood as relatively marked or unmarked in their use by Matthew. It is hoped that an awareness of these features and of their regularities in Matthew's narrative offers a way forward in the application of linguistic theory to New Testament exegesis. With a deeper understanding of the ways human beings produce and make sense of language, New Testament scholars can have a richer understanding of the written communications which form the Christian Scriptures.

Not the Law but the Messiah: Law and Righteousness in the Gospel of Matthew — An Ongoing Debate

Roland Deines

1. Is There a New Consensus?

In his dissertation "Community, Law and Mission in Matthew's Gospel,"[1] Paul Foster designated the already seminal works on Matthew written by Overman, Saldarini, Sim and others (in Germany Vahrenhorst, von Dobbeler)[2] as a "new

---

1. *Community, Law and Mission in Matthew's Gospel* (WUNT 2.177; Tübingen: Mohr Siebeck, 2004).

2. In chronological order: Amy-Jill Levine, *The Social and Ethnic Dimensions of Matthean Salvation History* (Studies in the Bible and Early Christianity 14; Lewiston-Queenstown, Me.: Mellen, 1988); Anthony J. Saldarini, "The Gospel of Matthew and Jewish-Christian Conflict," in *Social History of the Matthean Community: Cross-Disciplinary Approaches* (Minneapolis: Fortress, 1991), 37-61; idem, *Matthew's Christian-Jewish Community* (Chicago: University of Chicago Press, 1994); J. A. Overman, *Matthew's Gospel and Formative Judaism: The Social World of the Matthean Community* (Minneapolis: Fortress, 1990); idem, *Church and Community in Crisis: The Gospel according to Matthew* (Valley Forge, Pa.: Trinity Press International, 1996); David C. Sim, *The Gospel of Matthew and Christian Judaism: The History and Social Setting of the Matthean Community* (Edinburgh: T&T Clark, 1999); Boris Repschinski, *The Controversy Stories in the Gospel of Matthew: Their Redaction, Form and Relevance for the Relationship Between the Matthean Community and Formative Judaism* (FRLANT 189; Göttingen: Vandenhoeck & Ruprecht, 2000); Axel von Dobbeler, "Die Restitution Israels und die Bekehrung der Heiden. Das Verhältnis von Mt 10,5b.6 und Mt 28,18-20. Erwägungen zum Standort des Matthäusevangeliums," *ZNW* 91 (2000): 18-44; Stephanie von Dobbeler, "Auf der Grenze. Ethos und Identität der matthäischen Gemeinde nach Mt 15,1-20," *BZ Neue Folge* 45 (2001): 55-79; Martin Vahrenhorst, *"Ihr sollt überhaupt nicht schwören." Matthäus im halachischen Diskurs*

The paper is an updated summary of my book *Die Gerechtigkeit der Tora im Reich des Messias: Mt 5,13-20 als Schlüsseltext der matthäischen Theologie* (WUNT 177; Tübingen: Mohr Siebeck, 2005). I thank David Wenham for his editing of my English and Matthias Haufe for his help in preparing the first draft of this paper.

consensus" (78) or — perhaps more appropriately — as "an emerging consensus" (253). He speaks of it as an emerging consensus in respect to the social location of the Matthean community "as a deviant movement operating within the orbit of Judaism" (77). In spite of differences in detail, this emerging consensus agrees on the following points:

- The Matthean community in the last third of the first century CE[3] is composed of mainly Jewish believers in Christ.

(WMANT 95; Neukirchen-Vluyn: Neukirchener, 2002); Frederick J. Murphy, "The Jewishness of Matthew: Another Look," in *When Judaism and Christianity Began: Essays in Memory of Anthony J. Saldarini* (ed. A. J. Avery-Peck, D. Harrington and J. Neusner; JSJSup 85; Leiden: Brill, 2004), 2:377-403. A forerunner of this position is Reinhart Hummel, *Die Auseinandersetzung zwischen Kirche und Judentum im Matthäusevangelium* (Beiträge zur evangelischen Theologie 33; München: Chr. Kaiser 1963, 2nd ed. 1966).

3. As far as I see, all authors mentioned in n. 2 agree in dating Matthew in the time after the destruction of the temple and within the historical context of the Jewish people's reorganization after the first revolt. A different approach is taken in the new commentary of John Nolland, *The Gospel of Matthew* (NIGTC; Grand Rapids: Eerdmans; Bletchley: Paternoster, 2005): he tentatively dates Matthew "before the beginnings of the buildup to the Jewish war" (17), which means rather in the fifties or not too late in the sixties. The Matthean community is still *intra muros* and concerned with "all the minutiae of the Mosaic Law" (ibid.), and in his analysis the teaching of "all the requirements of the Law of Moses" is part of the mission command in 28:20 (1270). This would include (see below, n. 6) the obligation for circumcision of Gentile converts, which means they would have to become Jews if they wanted to keep the commandments of Jesus. If the Gospel of Matthew really advocated such a position in the late fifties or early sixties, then it would have been defending a position like that of the Christian Pharisees mentioned in Acts 15:1, 5. But their position is clearly a minority position in Acts and not even shared by James. Against the idea of a uniform entity called Christian Judaism or Jewish Christianity whose adherents were all "zealots for the Law" (Acts 21:20) it is necessary to see the possible variations within Jewish Christianity (as within Judaism!, not every Jew was Law-observant); cf. Donald A. Hagner, "The *Sitz im Leben* of the Gospel of Matthew," in *Treasures New and Old: Recent Contributions to Matthean Studies* (ed. D. R. Bauer and M. A. Powell; SBL Symposium Series 1; Atlanta: Scholars Press, 1996), 50f. The Matthean community can thus be seen as a group which regards itself still as part of the Jewish *ethnos*, but no longer under the (soteriological) obligation to keep the Torah, even if it is held in high esteem and kept voluntarily out of loyalty to the Jewish *ethnos*. The evidence of Josephus about James is often neglected: James, together with some others (Jerusalem "Christians"), was stoned because of transgression of the Law (Josephus, *Ant.* 20.200). In Justin's *Dialogue with Trypho* we get hints that there were Jewish Christians with different attitudes toward the Law, and the more radical wing seems to be the minority (*Dial.* 47.1-5; cf. 16.4). In the *True Word* of the pagan philosopher Celsus, we find a Jew who apparently attacks a group of Jewish Christians for giving up the Law although they claim that they believe in Jesus as the Son of God because the Law and the prophet (which means Moses) prophesied about him (Origen, *Contra Celsum* 2.1-79; cf. Horacio E. Lona, *Die "wahre Lehre" des Kelsos* [Kommentar zu frühchristlichen Apologeten, Ergänzungsband 1; Freiburg: Herder, 2005], 121-77).

- These Christian Jews see no reason to break with their mother religion just because they believe that Jesus is the Messiah, although they are experiencing some pressure in this direction from mainstream Judaism.
- These Christian Jews live according the Law of Moses and its valid halakhic interpretations of their time, with some alterations, softenings or modifications based on the teaching of Jesus.[4] Jesus is seen as a Law-observant Jew, who offered his own individual points of view on some matters and gave his specific interpretations of disputed halakhic rules, but they remained — as Markus Bockmuehl points out — "conversant with contemporary Jewish legal debate and readily accommodated on the spectrum of 'mainstream' first-century Jewish opinion."[5] The Law-critical aspects in the Jesus tradition have to be interpreted within this frame.
- There are differences within this emerging consensus-group about the attitude of the Matthean community toward Gentiles, but the predominant view is that the Matthean community was not significantly involved in reaching out to Gentiles and integrating them into its own Christian-Jewish communities.[6]

This new consensus offers a lot of advantages and solves several problems that Matthean scholarship is confronted with. Its most obvious merits are that it

---

4. The position that the Matthean community is Torah-observant is not restricted to the "consensus-group" and does not necessarily entail placing Matthew *intra muros*; a situation *extra muros* but still living a life according to the Law is represented *inter alia* by Ulrich Luz in his magisterial commentary on Matthew. Andrew Chester sees four different positions in the early Christian movement with respect to the Torah. The first is continuation and intensification of its demands, which he sees represented in Matthew, James and the *Didache*; see his "Messianism, Torah and Early Christian Tradition," in *Tolerance and Intolerance in Early Judaism and Christianity* (ed. G. N. Stanton and G. G. Stroumsa; Cambridge: Cambridge University Press, 1998), 321f., 335f.

5. Markus Bockmuehl, *Jewish Law in Gentile Churches: Halakhah and the Beginning of Christian Public Ethics* (Grand Rapids: Baker, 2000), viiif.

6. Cf. David C. Sim, "The Gospel of Matthew and the Gentiles," *JSNT* 57 (1995): 19-48; idem, *Gospel of Matthew*, 236-47 (he rightly addresses the problem of how a Law-observant Jewish group would be able to evangelize Gentiles without forcing them to convert totally to Judaism); Saldarini, *Matthew's Christian-Jewish Community*, 68-83; Repschinski, *Controversy Stories*, 345-48; Murphy, "Jewishness of Matthew," 379-85: all agree that the Matthean community expects Gentile converts to become circumcised and keep the whole Torah; against the minimizing of Matthew's interest in a Gentile mission see *inter alia* E. C. Park, *The Mission Discourse in Matthew's Interpretation* (WUNT 2.121; Tübingen: Mohr Siebeck, 2000); Florian Wilk, *Jesus und die Völker in der Sicht der Synoptiker* (BZNW 109; Berlin: de Gruyter, 2002), 126-133; Foster, *Community*, 218-52; Deines, *Gerechtigkeit der Tora*, 133f. with n. 103, 223f., 446-51. An important and somehow neglected hint of Matthew's universal outlook is 13:23, 37f.

keeps Jesus within Judaism and that it withstands the long Protestant antilegalistic and supersessionist tradition which is based on a stark antagonism of Law and grace, nurtured by the picture of Judaism as a legalistic religion of deeds. In more recent times a perhaps even more important advantage is that this position allows one to interpret the fierce Matthean polemic against the Jewish leadership, mainly the scribes and Pharisees, as an inner-Jewish struggle for influence.[7] As a result, Matthean studies are no longer confronted with the embarrassment of the supposed anti-Semitism of the gospel.[8] In addition, the positive statements about the Law in the first Gospel can be taken literally, and no exegetical tricks are necessary to avoid what is regarded as the plain meaning of Matt. 5:17-19, namely that these verses "indeed command obedience of the whole Torah."[9] Matthew resembles emerging rabbinic Judaism in this respect, as in the notable verse: "Do what the scribes and Pharisees tell you to do — because they are sitting on the cathedra of Moses" (23:3). Matthew seems to champion a Christianity of deeds, and — as in the famous ring-parable of Gotthold Ephraim Lessing in his play "Nathan the Wise" — he encourages Christians to compete with their Jewish neighbors in doing good — taking care of the needy, clothing the naked, bringing relief to the prisoners. Matthew 25:31-46, the description of the final judgment according to deeds of

---

7. Cf. Anthony J. Saldarini, "Boundaries and Polemics in the Gospel of Matthew," *Biblical Interpretation* 3 (1995): 239-65.

8. Cf. the paper of John Nolland in this volume. That the rebuttal of the alleged Matthean anti-Semitism is one of the motivations of the emerging consensus-group is clearly stated by Anthony J. Saldarini, "Reading Matthew without Anti-Semitism," in *The Gospel of Matthew in Currrent Study* (ed. D. E. Aune; Grand Rapids: Eerdmans, 2001), 166-84; see further Deines, *Gerechtigkeit der Tora*, 19-27. That his message can be understood in this way even from the perspective of a fulfillment-theology is demonstrated by Scot McKnight, "A Loyal Critic: Matthew's Polemic with Judaism in Theological Perspective," in *Anti-Semitism and Early Christianity: Issues of Polemic and Faith* (ed. C. A. Evans and D. A. Hagner; Minneapolis: Fortress, 1993), 55-79.

9. Overman, *Church and Community*, 78; see further Vahrenhorst, "'Ihr sollt überhaupt nicht schwören,'" 234f. How strongly this view is held may be seen in the review of my book (Deines, *Gerechtigkeit*) by Benedict Viviano (*Freiburger Zeitschrift für Philosophie und Theologie* 52 [2005]: 790-94). He accuses me of using "every trick in the exegetical repertoire to avoid the obvious" (790). Many years ago Theodor Zahn similarly complained against the attempts to ignore what he regards as the plain meaning of the verse, namely observing the Law in all its aspects: *Das Evangelium nach Matthäus* (Kommentar zum Neuen Testament 1; Leipzig: Deichert, [4]1922; Ndr. Wuppertal: R. Brockhaus, 1984), 220. I found some consolation in Kari Syreeni's remark that "Matthew not infrequently 'says one thing but means something else'"; see his "Matthew, Luke, and the Law: A Study in Hermeneutical Exegesis," in *The Law in the Bible and in Its Environment* (ed. T. Veijola, SESJ 51 = Publications of the Finnish Exegetical Society 51; Göttingen: Vandenhoeck & Ruprecht, 1990), 137.

mercy, is an important text (not only) for this position.[10] Christology is not a main factor in this emerging consensus, and this is again one of the advantages of this approach, because the downplaying of Christology eases religious dialogue with Judaism and Islam.[11]

But there will hardly ever be a consensus in theological studies without opposing voices. I mentioned the important work of Paul Foster in the beginning, and a long list of others can be added, among them Graham Stanton, Douglas R. A. Hare, and Donald Hagner.[12] Also, my own attempt to interpret Matthew's understanding of the function of the Law can be counted on the opposing side. What I want to do in this article is to explain where I see the points which are to be discussed with the emerging "consensus-group" and how I understand Matt. 5:17-20 in this context. For this at first I will give a short overview of the disputed texts.

---

10. For a recent treatment see Gernot Garbe, *Der Hirte Israels. Eine Untersuchung zur Israeltheologie des Matthäusevangeliums* (WMANT 106; Neukirchen-Vluyn: Neukirchener, 2005), 155-208. Garbe differentiates the scenario of the final judgment in a threefold way: the judgment of the elect (the community), of all people (Matt. 25:31-46), and of Israel (cf. Deines, *Gerechtigkeit*, 116-19, where I proposed a similar solution; see further Graham N. Stanton, *A Gospel for a New People: Studies in Matthew* [Edinburgh: T&T Clark, 1992], 213; David C. Sim, *Apocalyptic Eschatology in the Gospel of Matthew* [SNTSMS 88; Cambridge: Cambridge University Press, 1996], 126f., 227-35). Other scholars speak out against the particularist interpretation of Matt. 25:31-46 and in favor of a universal judgment, where all people, Jews, Christians and pagans alike, are judged according to the Torah (cf., for example, Vahrenhorst, *"Ihr sollt überhaupt nicht schwören,"* 244) or the love commandment (cf., for example, Eduard Schweizer, *Das Evangelium nach Matthäus* (Das Neue Testament Deutsch, vol. 2; Göttingen: Vandenhoeck & Ruprecht, 1973], 313f.; W. D. Davies and D. C. Allison, *The Gospel according to St. Matthew*, vol. 3 [ICC; Edinburgh: T&T Clark 1997], 432f.); Ulrich Luz gives a very helpful summary of the "Auslegungsgeschichte"; he distinguishes three major interpretations: the universal and the particularist as described above, and a third one, which he called the "der klassische Interpretationstyp"; in it the judgment is an inner-Christian one: "all the nations" (25:32) are "all Christians" and the "least of these my brothers" (25:40) are the needy Christians who need the help and solidarity of other Christians; cf. Ulrich Luz, *Das Evangelium nach Matthäus*, vol. I/3: *Mt 18–25* (EKKNT; Zürich: Benziger; Neukirchen-Vluyn: Neukirchener, 1997), 515-44.

11. Cf. Philip A. Cunningham, "Actualizing Matthean Christology in a Post-Supersessionist Church," in *When Judaism and Christianity Began: Essays in Memory of Anthony J. Saldarini* (ed. A. J. Avery-Peck, D. Harrington and J. Neusner; JSJSup 85; Leiden: Brill, 2004), 2:563-75.

12. Donald A. Hagner, "Matthew: Apostate, Reformer, Revolutionary?" *NTS* 49 (2003): 193-209; D. R. A. Hare, "How Jewish Is the Gospel of Matthew?" *CBQ* 62 (2000): 264-77.

2. Yes and No: Two Sets of Texts with Respect to the Torah in Matthew[13]

The First Gospel offers two different sets of texts regarding the Law. The first group seems to support the Law-abiding interpretation, whereas the second can be interpreted as supportive of a new understanding of the Torah and a new place for it in the value hierarchy within the realm of God's kingdom. Matthean scholarship regarding the Law is mainly divided along these lines, weighing either the first or the second set of texts as decisive for the position of the gospel as a whole.

2.1. Texts in Favor of a Law-Abiding Christian-Jewish Community

- 3:8: The call to produce fruits worthy of repentance. Even if this is not specifically linked to Law-keeping, it can be connected with Matt. 7:21ff. and the judgment according to deeds.[14] If the measure of this judgment is found in the Torah (because of ἀνομία in 7:23), then 3:8 might be seen in this context as hinting at the need for obedience to the Law.[15]
- 5:3-10: The beatitudes in Matthew if these are interpreted ethically,[16] an interpretation which may be suggested by the encouragement of deeds of mercy and seeking for peace (although these practices are not specifically linked to the Law in Matthew).
- 8:4: The order to the leper to show himself to the priest and offer the gift that Moses commanded as proof for them has been used since the beginning of Jewish polemical literature as the most obvious evidence that Jesus (or Matthew) encouraged the keeping of the Law.[17] But it is far from clear

---

13. For a similar overview see Roger Mohrlang, *Matthew and Paul: A Comparison of Ethical Perspectives* (SNTSMS 48; Cambridge: Cambridge University Press, 1984, reprint as paperback edition 2004), 7-23; Klyne Snodgrass, "Matthew and the Law," in *Treasures New and Old*, 101-6.

14. Cf. Vahrenhorst, "*Ihr sollt überhaupt nicht schwören*," 302 with n. 458; Ulrich Luz, *Das Evangelium nach Matthäus*, vol. I/1: *Mt 1-7* (EKKNT; 5th rev. ed.; Zürich: Benziger; Neukirchen-Vluyn: Neukirchener, 2002), 206.

15. So Luz, *Matthew*, I/1, 529f.

16. On this see again Luz, *Matthew*, I/1, 267-94; further Hans-Dieter Betz, *The Sermon on the Mount: A Commentary on the Sermon on the Mount, including the Sermon on the Plain (Matthew 5:3–7:27 and Luke 6:20-49)* (Hermeneia; Minneapolis: Fortress, 1995), 130f. (For Betz, as is well known, the Sermon on the Mount does not represent the theology of Matthew, which means that in the Sermon on the Mount "the Torah is the guide on the way to righteousness," whereas for the Evangelist "it is first of all Jesus who through his life and teaching 'fulfilled all righteousness' [Mt 3:15]").

17. Cf. the first (preserved) polemical text against Christianity which uses the New Testament extensively: Daniel J. Lasker and Sarah Stroumsa (eds.), *The Polemic of Nestor the Priest: Qiṣṣat*

of what and to whom this offering shall be a proof. It can be seen, as many would agree, as a reference back to 5:17, that Jesus is "fulfilling" the Law. But it is less obvious if this should be interpreted as a binding rule for the future or as a Christological testimony for the time of fulfillment.[18] Scholars sometimes connect 8:4 with Matt. 5:23f.; 26:17f., which are seen as further attestations of the acceptance of the sacrificial cult in the Matthean community. Against such an understanding of Matt. 8:4 as an encouragement for the continuation of the sacrificial cult one may point to Hos. 6:6 in Matt. 9:13; 12:7[19] and the so-called cleansing of the temple in Matt. 21:12f.[20]

- 9:20; 14:36: Jesus is described as wearing *Zizit* or the tassels the Israelites are commanded to wear on the four corners of their garments (τὸ κράσπεδον, *fringe, tassel, border;* cf. Num. 15:38-39; Deut. 22:12; Zech. 8:23). The function of the tassels, according to Num. 15:40, is remembrance of God's commandment and of Israel's obligation to be holy; so it is appropriate to see in Jesus' dress code a reference to his Law-abiding behavior.[21] In Zech. 8:23 the

---

Mujādalat al-Usquf *and* Sefer Nestor ha-Komer (Introduction, Critical Editions, Annotated Translations and Commentary, 2 vols.; Jerusalem: Ben-Zvi Institute for the Study of Jewish Communities in the East, 1996), § 138 = 2.74, 108, 129 (texts); 2.79 (translation of the Arabic version, which differs from the Hebrew one, cf. ibid., 125, and commentary, 163). For a modern application see again Ulrich Luz, *Das Evangelium nach Matthäus*, vol. I/2: *Mt 8–17* (EKKNT; Zürich: Benziger; Neukirchen-Vluyn: Neukirchener, 1990), 10; Saldarini, *Christian-Jewish Community*, 177f.

18. Cf. the treatment of the phrase in D. A. Hagner, *Matthew 1–13* (WBC 33A; Dallas: Word, 1993), 199f. Some see in this text a further piece of evidence for Jesus as a new Moses; see Dale C. Allison, *The New Moses: A Matthean Typology* (Edinburgh: T&T Clark, 1993), 208f. But then it might be asked: is he not more than Moses? Whereas Moses gave detailed commands for dealing with leprosy (Lev. 13–14), the first miracle of Jesus is the healing of a leper. Admittedly, even Moses healed his sister Miriam from leprosy (Num. 12:13-15), but the difference should not be overlooked. Moses asked God to heal her, and she nevertheless had to stay outside the camp for seven days as a kind of punishment; in Matt. 8:2 the leper addressed Jesus directly and the healing took place in a moment. So "a testimony for them" at least includes a Christological element and is not just a proof that Jesus keeps the Law.

19. That Matt. 9:13 and 12:7 contradict Matt. 8:4 is a fixed point in the Jewish polemical literature; cf. as one example David Berger, *The Jewish-Christian Debate in the High Middle Ages: A Critical Edition of the Nizzahon Vetus, with an Introduction, Translation and Commentary* (Philadelphia: Jewish Publication Society of America, 1979), 182f. = § 171 (for the Hebrew text see p. 120). For a recent discussion see Christoph Landmesser, *Jüngerberufung und Zuwendung zu Gott. Ein exegetischer Beitrag zum Konzept der matthäischen Soteriologie im Anschluß an Mt 9,9-13* (WUNT 133; Tübingen: Mohr Siebeck, 2001); and *"Car c'est l'amour qui me plait, non le sacrifice . . ." Recherches sur Oseé 6:6 et son interprétation juive et chrétienne* (ed. by E. Bons; JSJSup 88; Leiden, Boston: Brill, 2004).

20. Cf. Jostein Ådna, *Jesu Stellung zum Tempel* (WUNT 2.119; Tübingen: Mohr Siebeck, 2000).

21. Luz, *Matthew*, I/2, 53, 413; Saldarini, *Christian-Jewish Community*, 178.

tassels are connected to the eschatological future, when the nations of the world will come to Jerusalem to worship God: "In those days ten men from all languages and nations will take hold of the tassels of a Jew (LXX: καὶ ἐπιλάβωνται τοῦ κρασπέδου ἀνδρὸς Ἰουδαίου), saying, 'Let us go with you, for we have heard that God is with you.'" The unclean woman is praised by Jesus for her faith (9:22), which cannot mean anything other than her firm belief that God is with Jesus and through him with his people (cf. Matt. 1:23: Jesus is called "Emmanuel," which means "God is with us"). So the tassels are not just a hint at the keeping of the Law by Jesus, but they are at the same time an indication of the presence of "those days," when God will be with his people and will reach the nations as well through his people.[22]

- 23:2f.: The disciples and the crowds are told to do what Pharisees and scribes tell them because they are sitting on the seat of Moses. This is one of the most important texts for the assumption of a Law-abiding Matthean community within the context of emerging rabbinic Judaism,[23] but it is contradicted in the Gospel itself (see 15:2, 6-9, 20 [which is clearly not an encouragement to do what scribes and Pharisees tell]; 16:6, 11f.). The commandment to follow their rules is never and nowhere spelled out in practical terms.[24] Or should we imagine that verses 2 and 3 mean that those who

---

22. Both Luz and Saldarini (and many others) fail to mention Zech. 8:23, although the influence of this specific prophet on Matthew's theology is admitted to be high; cf. Craig A. Evans, "Jesus and Zechariah's Messianic Hope," in *Authenticating the Activities of Jesus* (ed. B. Chilton and Craig A. Evans; NTTS 28.2; Leiden: Brill 1999), 373-88, and, more specific, J. T. Cummings, "The Tassel of His Cloak: Mark, Luke, Matthew — and Zechariah," in *Studia Biblica 1978*: II. *Papers on the Gospels 2* (ed. Elizabeth Anne Livingstone; JSNTSup 2; Sheffield: JSOT, 1980), 47-61.

23. Hans-Jürgen Becker, *Auf der Kathedra des Mose. Rabbinisch-theologisches Denken und antirabbinische Polemik in Matthäus 23, 1-12* (Arbeiten zur neutestamentlichen Theologie und Zeitgeschichte 4; Berlin: Institut Kirche und Judentum, 1990), 85-105; Vahrenhorst, *"Ihr sollt überhaupt nicht schwören,"* 8, 306-11; Overman, *Church and Community*, 13, 319f.; Murphy, "Jewishness," 389f.

24. In the late 13th-century polemical treatise *Nizzahon Yashan*, Jesus is blamed because the only place in the New Testament where he directly commanded the observance of a legal prescript from the Torah is in Matt. 8:4: "Moreover, from the time of his birth we don't see that he commanded the observance of any other commandments in the Torah, such as those regarding the Sabbath, circumcision, pork, and the mixing of species, and several others which, in fact, he permitted people to transgress after his advent" (*Nizzahon Vetus* [see above, n. 19], p. 178 = § 166, for the Hebrew text see p. 116). Those Jewish readers of the New Testament obviously do not regard Matt. 23:2f. as a confirmation of the Torah by Jesus, in contrast to Matt. 5:17f., which is the most quoted New Testament reference in this literature. But Matt. 5:17f. is used almost always in the sense: Jesus claimed to preserve the integrity of the Torah, but in reality "he added and diminished (הוא מוסיך וגרע)" from the Law in several places" (ibid., § 157 [translation p. 172, Hebrew text p. 110). Instead, for the "consensus-group" πάντα in Matt. 23:3 is to be con-

want to follow Jesus should use the attacked oath-formulae of 23:16-22?[25] Even the positive comment about tithing herbs (23:23) sounds more like a concession of the sort exemplified in 17:24ff., where the paying of the temple tax is practiced for the reason of μὴ σκανδαλίσωμεν only.[26] The weight of the argument is surely not to support the tithing of herbs, although there is of course nothing wrong with doing so. That tithing is part of the social and religious norms and values of any Jewish society is not disputed, but it is not at all the focus.

- 24:20: "Pray that your flight will not be in winter or on a Sabbath." The mention of the Sabbath is also used as an indication that the Matthean community still sees the Sabbath as a day of rest.[27] It might also be just what Jesus said. The combination of winter and Sabbath suggests at least that the primary point is not Torah observance but more practical reasons. As an isolated sentence it is not very illuminative, so the understanding of this verse depends on the overall picture of the Sabbath conflicts (if they are "conflicts" at all) in the First Gospel. The "consensus-group" interprets them as discussions within the boundaries of acceptable halakhic positions — at least as perceived by the Matthean community, though not necessarily by the Jewish leaders of the time. In all cases, for the "consensus-group" the keeping of Sabbath as a Law is essential for Matthew's understanding of doing the will of Jesus, with only some modifications allowed with respect to charity deeds and merciful acts.[28]

---

nected with πάντα (or πᾶσα respectively) in Matt. 3:15; 5:18d and 28:20, which means that the mission command includes the whole Torah; cf. Becker, *Kathedra*, 88f.; Saldarini, *Christian-Jewish Christianity*, 160-64; Nolland, *Matthew*, 1240 (cf. above, n. 3). I fully agree with Saldarini's comment: "Matthew means for his group to obey fully the demands of the Law as they are understood through Jesus' teaching" (161), but I disagree on the "changing power" of Jesus' teaching with respect to the Torah.

25. Cf. the helpful comments of Luz, *Matthew*, I/3, 301f. According to him it is impossible to assume that Matthew "seine Gemeinde wirklich zum Gehorsam gegen alle Lehren der Schriftgelehrten und Pharisäer aufgefordert hat."

26. Cf. David E. Garland, "The Temple Tax in Matthew 17:24-25 and the Principle of Not Causing Offense," in *Treasures New and Old*, 69-98; Klyne Snodgrass, "Matthew and the Law," 123f.

27. Cf. Overman, *Church and Community*, 334; Saldarini, *Christian-Jewish Community*, 126f.

28. Saldarini, *Christian-Jewish Community*, 126-34; Vahrenhorst, *"Du sollst überhaupt nicht schwören,"* 381-92. For a discussion of the Sabbath pericopae from the position of a fulfillment-theology see Y.-E. Yang, *Jesus and the Sabbath in Matthew's Gospel* (JSNTSup 139; Sheffield: Sheffield University Press, 1997); the best overall treatment is now Lutz Doering, *Schabbat. Sabbathalacha und -praxis im antiken Judentum und Urchristentum* (TSAJ 78; Tübingen: Mohr Siebeck, 1999).

Having offered this *summarizing* list,[29] I believe that it would be helpful to consider some objections. The most important and simple one is that Jesus lived as a Jew in a Jewish-dominated country and society. So it is not surprising that many references in the description of his life and teaching show him exactly as what he was: a Jew. He lived within the boundaries of Judaism, and Matthew highlights this with the restriction of Jesus' and his disciples' mission within Israel during Jesus' lifetime (Matt. 10:5f.; 15:24). In addition, it is necessary to differentiate between the description of specific behavior and the demand for it. Besides the undisputed "ethical" challenges with direct reference to the Torah in 5:21ff.; 7:12 and 22:36-40 (similar, but with important differences in 19:17-19[30]) there remain only 5:18f. and 23:2f., 23 as possible proof-texts for an obligation to live according to the "whole" Law. These verses have to carry the weight against the second set of references, which arguably favor a more revolutionary understanding of the Torah in the presence of God's kingdom, which for the majority of Jewish society would fall outside the legitimate halakhic range of discussion.

This second major position takes the Law-critical aspects as a starting point and sees Jesus (or Matthew) as the one who removed the restriction of God's people to the exclusive Jewish religious-ethnic community. Jesus on this view is regarded as the one who brings the Torah to its goal, end, or fulfillment (cf. Rom. 10:4), replacing it (to use the supersessionist's terminology) or transferring it into a remodeled religious and ethical hierarchy system based on his teaching[31] and oriented toward the universal kingdom of God, which is open to Jews and Gentiles alike. Foster names this process quite illuminatingly as "repriorisation of the status of the Law, which is now made subservient to Jesus' authoritative pronouncements."[32] To some in this camp the so-called antitheses are real antitheses against the Law and against Moses, while others see the confrontation only with some pharisaic or scribal traditions or exaggera-

---

29. It is not exhaustive. One well-worn argument is Matthew's use of ἀνομία (7:23; 13:41; 23:28; 24:12; the word is lacking in the other Gospels; cf. Luz, *Matthäus*, I/1, 529f.), but if the Pharisees can be accused of "Lawlessness" (23:28), it is hardly useful to attack an "antinomian" Christian practice.

30. In this list of decalogue-Laws the Sabbath command is missing, which might be a hint that it was not on top of the agenda of Jesus or the Evangelist.

31. It is obvious that this formulation allows a wide range of possibilities depending on how close the connection is seen between the teaching of Jesus and the Torah. The most obvious difference from the "consensus-group" regarding practical matters is perhaps the function of the Torah in the relation to Gentiles, namely that they can become part of Matthew's Christianity without being obliged to live according to the Law. Where this becomes real in a community, the place and function of the Torah will change (or has already changed) dramatically for the Jewish members of the same group as well.

32. *Community*, 260.

tions.³³ Several books and articles belonging to this tradition are marked with a more or less obvious theological anti-Judaism. This makes it hard to revive their results uncritically in our day, although their main point, namely, that there was something radically new and challenging in the attitude of Jesus toward the Torah which arouses the suspicion and enmity of his fellow Jews is still valid and needs careful consideration.

One result of this fundamental conflict (here indeed the conflicts are seen as such) was that Jesus' Jewish followers were urged to formulate their own identity very early and quickly — first within, and later in a kind of demarcation dispute in opposition to, the Jewish mainstream.³⁴ I see two main reasons for this quest for a new identity: the first arose from the pressure on the "Christians" from the Jewish environment in which they lived; they were more and more being pushed to the margins of Judaism, the clear intent being to dissolve the connections between Jews and Christians.³⁵ The other originates from the teaching of Jesus himself, since he sat loose to the boundary markers within the Jewish society, as well as to those between Jews and Gentiles.³⁶ Even if this was only a minor feature in his ministry — I think it was more than this — the trajectory of his minor gestures toward the sinners and the gentile world nevertheless inspired the Christian transition from an inner-Jewish messianic movement to a new people with a vision for the whole world.³⁷

---

33. But cf. Becker, *Kathedra des Mose*, 80-82, who objects to the possibility of a clear-cut differentiation between written Law and halakhic traditions; similarly, Peter Wick, "Die Antithesen der Bergpredigt als paränetische Rhetorik. Durch scheinbaren Widerspruch zu einem neuen Verständnis," *Judaica* 52 (1996): 158f. A helpful introduction to the topic of the Law and its treatment in the time of Jesus (together with many bibliographical hints) is John P. Meier, "The Historical Jesus and the Historical Law: Some Problems within the Problem," *CBQ* 65 (2003): 52-79.

34. The place of Matthew's Gospel within this development can be seen in its nuanced attitude toward the Jewish crowds and the Jewish leaders. The first are still invited to join the new messianic community, whereas the latter are seen as opponents and false shepherds; cf. Saldarini, *Christian-Jewish Community*, 27-67; J. R. C. Cousland, *The Crowds in the Gospel of Matthew* (NovTSup 102; Leiden: Brill, 2002).

35. Cf. the valuable suggestion of Stephanie von Dobbeler to interpret the attitude of the Pharisees as a well-meant attempt to bring the deviant followers of Jesus back within the accepted realms of Jewish halakhah (63f.). Their interest in Jesus and his disciples is an expression of their "Bemühen . . . , Jesus und seine Jünger in das Heil ermöglichende Judentum pharisäischer Prägung hineinzuholen" ("Grenze," 63).

36. Against the restriction of Matthew's interests to the Jewish world by Sim and others (see above, n. 6) cf. Donald Senior, "Between Two Worlds: Gentiles and Jewish Christians in Matthew's Gospel," *CBQ* 61 (1999): 1-23. Senior himself sees the mixed Matthean community nevertheless as a Law-abiding community (20).

37. See Hare, "How Jewish Is Matthew?" 269, 273, with his emphasis on Matt. 16:18; Levine, *Social and Ethnic Dimensions*, 10f.

2.2. Texts Supporting a New Understanding of the Torah in the Kingdom of God

- 5:21-48: The so-called antitheses: traditionally these have often been seen as a main indication that Matthew is standing outside the bounds of Judaism and is fighting against it and especially against the Law. This interpretation, however, is very doubtful, and the designation "antitheses" is not helpful at all.[38] Jesus does not set his teaching *against* the Torah, but explains through examples how the eschatological righteousness based on his fulfillment of the Law and the prophets (5:17-20) looks. The "antitheses" are therefore to be seen as the guiding norms for the kingdom of God. They do not abrogate the Torah of Moses, but they make it in a way superfluous. Whenever Jesus' followers live according to what is demanded of them, the regulations of the Torah are no longer needed: the laws of retaliation and restoring human relations become superfluous when 5:22-25, 38-42 are kept.[39] The laws about adultery and sexual abuse are superfluous when no transgressions against the sexual integrity of another person are committed (5:28). No divorce regulations are necessary as long as both partners are under the command of Jesus (5:31f.; cf. 19:3-9), though Mat-

---

38. Cf. Davies and Allison, *Matthew*, 2:564-66; Luz, *Matthäus*, I/1, 331f.; Deines, *Gerechtigkeit*, 362 with n. 740.

39. It is again worth looking at the Jewish exegesis of Matt. 5:33ff. in the Middle Ages. Hasdai Crescas in the 14th century, for example, cites Matt. 5:39 as proof for his claim that Jesus added to the Torah and therefore postulated that the Law of Moses was not perfect until his coming. The command for nonretaliation is seen as cruelty because "the ultimate suffering is the absence of revenge." Crescas continues, saying: "God ordered: 'You shall not take vengeance [Lev. 19:18]; you shall not hate your brother [Lev. 19:17]'; but to prepare oneself for degradation and shame is a criminal sin against ordinary love, for every man must love himself (כי כל איש חייבל אהוב את עצמו). [In doing this] he causes his fellow person to sin against him. Causing someone else to sin is a great sin, as is mentioned there [in Mt 5:39]." In Matt. 5:43f., Crescas found "another mistake": "It is clear that the divine Torah does not command hating anyone except the enemies of God, as David, of blessed memory, praised himself, 'Do I not hate them that hate You, O Lord [Ps. 129:21].' [The Torah] prohibits hating anyone other than enemies of God, for he who loves them is wicked. And if [Jesus] commanded to love them, why did the Torah command to hate them, and if [the new Torah] did not command to hate the enemies of God, then this command contained a great mistake (שגגה גדולה)." Text and translation: Daniel J. Lasker, *The Refutation of Christian Principles by Hasdai Crescas* (SUNY Series in Jewish Philosophy; Albany: State University of New York Press, 1992), 73; idem, *R. Uasdai Crescas, Sefer Bittul Iqqarei Ha-Nozrim. Translation of Joseph Ben Shem Tov* (Ramat Gan: Bar-Ilan University Press; Beer-Sheva: Ben-Gurion University of the Negev Press, 1990), 83. This line of interpretation can be seen in Jewish exegesis at least until the 19th century and should perhaps be regarded as an authentic reaction to the "antitheses" from a Torah-oriented Jewish position.

thew is realistic enough to see that personal responsibility ends where the partner is no longer willing to add his or her share to the common task.

- 7:12, the "golden rule," is in itself not decisive with respect to keeping the whole Torah, but in combination with Matt. 22:40 it seems quite obvious that it "is to be understood as synonymous with the love command in Leviticus 19:18."[40] The theological foundation for this behavior is, in 5:45, 48, a kind of *imitatio dei*, as the foregoing verses dealing with God's attitude toward humans show.[41]
- 8:3: The voluntary and unnecessary touching of a leper by Jesus, does not mean any violation of the Torah because it is nowhere forbidden for ordinary people to become unclean. The only point that can be learned from this and some similar references (9:20, 25) is that neither Jesus nor Matthew was concerned about becoming impure. In addition, no interest is shown in how to become pure again after contracting impurity.[42]

---

40. Snodgrass, "Matthew and the Law," 108; cf. Hagner, *Matthew 1–13*, 176f. In opposition to the similar statement of Hillel in *b. Shab.* 31a, Matt. 7:12 and 22:36-40 are all-embracing: "doing this" is doing all that is necessary. There is no room and necessity for further laws; cf. Deines, *Gerechtigkeit*, 392-401. For Hillel, on the other hand, it is the starting point of a proselyte's lifelong learning of the Torah. He dismissed the one who asked him to teach him the whole Torah while standing on one foot with the demand: "Go and learn it."

41. The emphasis on the golden rule and the love command does not necessarily imply the replacement of other laws. A maximalist view in this respect is held by Wick, "Antithesen," 172-74, who sees in Jesus a reformer of neither the Torah nor the halakha (the actual Torah practice is accepted in total), but one who adds with the love command a deeper meaning to the already existing juridical-practical meaning. Love is not enough to be "perfect" (with respect to Matt. 5:45), but only perfect Law-obedience: "Doch anders als bei Paulus, für den die Tora durch die Liebe erfüllt wird (Gal 5,14; Röm 13,8), ist bei Matthäus nicht die Liebe die Matrix der Toraauslegung, sondern die Vollkommenheit im Sinne eines vollkommenen Gesetzesgehorsams (Mt 5,17-20)" (174). This would imply that Matthew totally misleads his readers through 12:14; 15:12-4; 16:12 (cf. also Matt. 5:11f.; 10:16-22, 34-39: how are persecutions in Israel possible, if Jesus and his followers would live strictly according the accepted halakha? And in 15:2 it is clearly stated that the disciples do *not* do what the scribes and Pharisees told the people to do). Wick's view, which adds new meaning to the already existing laws, sounds like new wine in old wineskins (cf. Matt. 9:17). For a better understanding of "old and new in Matthew," see Hagner, "Matthew: Apostate, Reformer, Revolutionary?" 200f.

42. Cf. Josephus, *C. Ap.* 1.281: "anyone who touches or lives under the same roof [with a leper] is regarded as unclean." Matthew has Jesus address the subject of impurity only because the Pharisees forced him to do so (15:2; cf. 23:25-9: here too the practice of purity laws with respect to dishes and graves seems not to be a priority topic for Jesus), but no active interest of Jesus or the Evangelist is discernible in the Gospel. In addition, Matthew avoids any hint of purification rites in connection with Jesus and his disciples. If he really would be interested in promoting a Law-abiding "Christian" community consisting of Jews and Gentiles, why does he transmit only the critical sayings against these practices? Why did he not mention that it is

- 8:22: "Leave the dead to bury their own dead," is one more saying which has been seen with good reasons as contradicting or superseding the Law, in this case not "only" with respect to ritual matters, but connected to the decalogue itself.[43] But here as everywhere the intention of the text is not to act against the Torah (which is not mentioned at all in this paragraph), but to show the unique importance of following Jesus, which qualifies and supersedes all other obligations.
- 9:10f.: Jesus' table fellowship with tax collectors and sinners (cf. 11:19: he is regarded as a friend of tax collectors and sinners, and he pronounces authoritatively that tax collectors and harlots will enter the kingdom of heaven in 21:31f.), though again not *against* any clear law, hints at a hierarchy of values and aims different from that of the Pharisees. This change is connected to the experience of a new era which has come with Jesus. It is the time of the wedding (9:15; cf. 11:19: Jesus accused as a glutton and a drunkard), not of fasting (9:14). Not that Jesus forbade fasting, as is clear from 6:16-8, but the coming of the kingdom means an end of the fasts connected to sins (cf. Zech. 7:3; 8:19; *Ps. Sol.* 3:8). The anointing during fasting (Matt. 6:17) connects it semantically with joy and marriage.
- 11:11-15: The prophets and the Law prophesied till John. These verses contain many exegetical problems, but they are undeniably indicators of a periodization of time. John marks the transition from an era that is passing to a new one. The time is divided between ἕως Ἰωάννου and ἀπὸ δὲ τῶν ἡμερῶν Ἰωάννου τοῦ βαπτιστοῦ.[44]

---

necessary to take a ritual bath after contact with a dead body or before entering the temple precincts?

43. Martin Hengel, *The Charismatic Leader and His Followers* (trans. J. C. G. Greig, ed. by J. Riches, 2nd ed.; Edinburgh: T&T Clark, 1996 [first Eng. ed. 1981, German original 1968]), 11-14. For a defense of the position that Jesus' interpretations of the Torah in this case "as almost always remain well within the range of attested halakhic positions," see Markus Bockmuehl, "'Let the Dead Bury Their Dead': Jesus and the Law Revisited," in idem, *Jewish Law in Gentile Churches* (see above, n. 5), 23-48 (quotation, 47) (originally published under the title: "'Let the Dead Bury Their Dead' (Matt. 8:22/Luke 9:62): Jesus and the Halakhah," *JTS* N.S. 49 [1998]: 553-81). Overman, *Church and Community*, 123f., and Saldarini, *Christian-Jewish Community*, 91, did not take the Law-critical potential of this saying into account at all. Again a look at the Jewish polemical literature might be helpful: In § 106 of the *Qiṣṣa* (see above, n. 17) Matt. 10:37 is quoted as in contradiction to Exod. 20:12; 21:15, 17; in *Nizzahon Vetus* (see above, n. 19) § 172, Matt. 8:22 is part of a list of Jesus' misdeeds.

44. Cf. the comments of Overman, *Church and Community*, 166f., who clearly describes "John's watershed role in the history of the kingdom of God," but does not mention the role of the prophets and the Torah in this changing conditions. Similarly, Saldarini, *Christian-Jewish Community*, 161, mentions this verse just in passing, and in the source-index of Vahrenhorst, *"Ihr sollt überhaupt nicht schwören"* it is totally missing. If and how the verses might have influ-

- 11:28-30: Jesus speaks of *his* own light yoke, which is not the yoke of the Torah and which surely cannot be seen as hinting at a less restrictive halakha taught by Jesus. It might be connected to Jesus' teaching in the Sermon on the Mount and the "least commandments" (5:19).[45] But even more important is the way that Jesus speaks of "my yoke," which is unparalleled in Jewish literature.[46] It is perhaps not by chance that the first Sabbath-conflict story follows immediately after this saying (12:1-8).
- 12:1-8, 9-14: The conflict stories concerning the Sabbath are an intensively discussed topic (cf. above, n. 28), which cannot be treated adequately in this paper. I just want to hint at some points that seemed to me to be decisive. In the first pericope, on plucking grain on the Sabbath, verse 6 contains the main argument, namely that Christology ("something greater than the temple is here") overrides the Sabbath. Even if the disciples have been hungry (12:1), there was surely no threat to life.[47] In the healing scene of the man with a withered hand (12:9-13), the healing does not have to be done on a Sabbath. Even if Jesus offers an analogy from the halakha to ease the understanding of his attitude, the major difference between the pharisaic practice and the one Jesus advocates remains. His practice is oriented

---

enced Matthew's understanding of the function of the Law in the kingdom of God is also not considered at all in Luz, *Matthäus*, I/2, 180; Nolland, *Matthew*, 458f. Hagner, *Matthew 1–13*, 307f., discusses the point but restricts it to the prophetic function of the Law, whereas I think that the four mentions of "Law and Prophets" (5:17; 7:12; 11:13; 22:40) have to be taken as illuminating each other; cf. Deines, *Gerechtigkeit*, 99, 108f.

45. Cf. Becker, *Kathedra des Mose*, 145-61, who downplays too much the differences between the rabbinic texts and Jesus' use of the phrase, which is part of a revelatory, apocalyptic saying (cf. 11:25-27).

46. The closest parallel is Hos. 11:4, where God himself is described as the one "who eases the yoke on their jaws" and gave them rest ("I bend down to them and feed them"). The Targum to Hos. 11:4 substitutes "my word" for "God." In the Old Testament tradition "yoke" is a symbol for foreign (Gen. 27:40; Lev. 26:13; Deut. 28:48; Isa. 47:7; Jer. 27:11; 35:14; Lam. 5:5) or extremely harsh rule (1 Kgs. 12:4-14), and the release of the foreign yoke (Isa. 9:4; 10:27; 14:25; Ezek. 34:27, always initiated by God) means freedom and forgiveness (Lam. 1:14). Also in the Wisdom literature "yoke" bears the mark of pain and labor (Sir. 6:23-26; for the negative imagery of the yoke in Ben Sira see 28:19f.; 33:27; a heavy yoke is a symbol for physical pains in life 40:1), even if the result is joy and blessing (Sir. 6:28-31; cf. vv. 23-27; 51:26). The yoke as a metaphor for the will of God can be found in Jer. 5:5 ("breaking the yoke" as an expression for acting against God's Law); Sir. 6:30 (only in the Hebrew text); 51:26.

47. Only the Matthean version mentions that the disciples were hungry, which is often regarded as a softening of the Markan text and as an adjustment to an accepted halakhic practice (but which might just be taken from Mark 2:25 par. Matt. 12:3). On the other hand, Matthew omits the Markan "as they made their way" (ὁδὸν ποιεῖν, 2:23), which give the scene in Mark a more casual character, whereas in Matthew it looks like real work: ἤρξαντο τίλλειν στάχυας.

toward καλῶς ποιεῖν (12:12),⁴⁸ and theirs toward what is forbidden on the Sabbath (cf. 12:10). It makes sense, therefore, that this healing causes the Law-abiding Jews (Pharisees: 12:14) to take action against Jesus, who is forced to leave the scene for a while (12:15a). In order to understand Matthew at this point, we have to take into consideration how he guides his readers in this story: he inserts verse 11, the halakhic example of a man who has *one* sheep and rescues it when it falls into a pit on the Sabbath. But his use of this example is halakhically not very appropriate because the withered hand is not a one-day emergency-event. Rather, it is a picture taken from a halakhic background to illustrate Jesus as the shepherd who cares about the one lost sheep (18:12-14; cf. 9:36). By using such an halakhic argumentation, Matthew wants to demonstrate that even the Pharisees would have been able to accept Jesus' action if they had been willing. Their rejection of Jesus and their counsel against him is the more sinful because of this. Jesus provided them with a bridge to understand his action, but they refused to use it.⁴⁹

- 15:1-11: The point of departure is the transgression of a pharisaic paradosis, not a biblical law.⁵⁰ But in verse 11 there is an authorial saying, introduced with "hear and understand: Not what goes into the mouth defiles a man [in the sense the purity laws in the Torah regulate it], but what comes out of the mouth, this defiles a man." In nearly all commentaries the view is taken that Matthew has softened Mark's plain comment, "Thus he declared all foods clean" (7:19), to simply "to eat with unwashed hands does not defile a person" (15:20). It is true that Matthew's version sounds less comprehensive, but his message has a much wider range, as when he lets Jesus say twice: "Not what goes into a person defiles him, but what comes out of his heart" (15:11, 17f.). It is not formulated against purity laws; and yet it is unavoidable that such a statement will change the status of purity laws in the course of time. That Matthew understood it in this way is again shown by

---

48. Matthew skipped the Markan dramatization "to save life or to kill" (3:4), although this would have allowed him a halakhically more correct defense of Jesus' behavior, namely that in Judaism a threat to life overrides the Sabbath. The simple καλῶς ποιεῖν seems instead a quite general statement.

49. The same is probably true for 12:5, where Matthew also introduces a halakhic way of argumentation to make his point; see Deines, *Gerechtigkeit*, 485f.

50. In Matthew the conduct of the disciples is described as a παραβαίνειν τὴν παράδοσιν τῶν πρεσβυτέρω (15:2), whereas in Mark it is just a question: "Why do your disciples not live according to the traditions of the elders" (7:5). So it is obvious that Jesus does not expect his disciples to follow the pharisaic rules and even defends them against their accusers. The same is true for Matt. 16:12, where the disciples are clearly told to beware of the *teaching* of the Pharisees and Sadducees. This is often neglected in the interpretation of Matt. 23:3.

the remark of the disciples in verse 12: "Do you know that the Pharisees were offended when they heard this saying?"

- 15:32-39: The next story is about the withdrawal of Jesus into the area of Tyre and Sidon and the move to the eastern shore of the Lake Kinneret, that is, the area of the Decapolis. Matthew gives a healing summary (15:29-31) and continues with the feeding of the four thousand (15:32-38). Without wishing to overinterpret the passage, the suggestion can be made that the feeding creates a kind of table fellowship between Jews and Gentiles, with the disciples serving the tables (cf. Acts 6:2).
- 16:19 (cf. 18:18): The keys to the kingdom of heaven are in the hands of the disciples of Jesus, not in the hands of Moses or the Torah. It is a situation similar to that of 5:13-16, where the disciples are credited with functions normally attributed to the Torah.
- 17:24f.: Jesus paid the temple tax, although "the children are free." Nevertheless, he paid it because he did not want "to give offense to them" (μὴ σκανδαλίσωμεν, 17:27). I think this is one of the most important principles for the attitude toward the Law in the Gospel of Matthew (cf. above, n. 26).
- 18:3: This verse concerns the child as a model for those who want to enter the kingdom of heaven. A child as a child is not under the obligation of the commandments, and judgment is threatened against those who cause children who believe in Jesus to sin (18:6).
- 19:3-9 (cf. 5:31f.): Even if Jesus is in agreement with the school of Shammai here, he is nevertheless critical of the permission given by Moses. That this was not just an acceptable interpretation within Judaism is clear from the reaction of the disciples in 19:10.
- 21:12f.: This is the so-called cleansing of the temple, which fits with Matthew's emphasis on Hosea 6:6. This again is no attack on the Torah, but it is a visible move against the established religious system and — as the reactions of the religious establishment showed — was seen as a serious threat (cf. above, nn. 19f.).
- 21:31f.: Jesus uses his authority and assigns the kingdom of heaven to the tax collectors and harlots (whereas the high priests and the elders are shut out, 21:23); they enter the kingdom because they believe in the way of righteousness that John preached. Again, there is no Torah involved at all.

Summarizing these second set of sources,[51] we again do not get a totally clear picture, but, taken together, there are more hints in the texts which support

---

51. Supportive for this position are, further, Matt. 22:36-40 (the double love commandment as exclusive summary for Law and prophets; cf. below, n. 78); 25:31-46 (the judgment of the na-

the impression that the Law is not (and, taking the Matthean theology of time into consideration, I think it is appropriate to say, *no longer*) central in Matthew's description of Jesus' ministry. What Matthew supports in his gospel is the double love command, deeds of mercy and the avoidance of offenses. Yet the most important demand is discipleship. What counts in this respect is trust and faith in Jesus, and not purity and tithes. The question should be allowed: is it plausible to think that Matthew wrote for the sake of a community (or an ideal community) that wanted the "sinners" whom Jesus called as his followers to become Law-observant in a way that the Pharisees or early rabbis would find acceptable?

Until now I have purposely omitted Matt. 5:17-20 from these two lists, because the pericope forms the cornerstone for both interpretative traditions.[52] It is the first word regarding the Law in Matthew's Gospel — Matthew's first word and Jesus' first word. Because first and last words very often have a specific importance, these verses are appropriately viewed in both camps as a kind of hermeneutical introduction to the Matthean theology of the Law. But Matthew does not start his Gospel with the topic of the Law. Although 5:17-20 is the introduction to his understanding of the Torah, it is not the starting point for his understanding of Jesus. Therefore the following points about the basic concepts of the First Gospel are necessary and will prevent us from focusing on a subject which might not be in the center of Matthew's thoughts.[53]

---

tions has nothing to do with the Torah or any Torah commandments. The judging measure is mercy and nothing else; cf. above, n. 10); 26:26-29 (the new covenant in the blood of Jesus for the forgiveness of sins can be seen as the fulfillment of the promise in 5:6; cf. Deines, *Gerechtigkeit*, 152); 28:20 (the teaching of the commandments of Jesus is the last word in the Gospel. There is no reason to think that this includes the unaltered Mosaic Law, but see above, n. 24).

52. For some recent treatments (besides the commentaries) see Hans-Joachim Eckstein, "Die 'bessere Gerechtigkeit.' Zur Ethik Jesu nach dem Matthäusevangelium," *Theologische Beiträge* 32 (2001): 299-316 (revives the older position that Matthew included in his Gospel with 5:18f. some strict Jewish-Christian sayings, which he tried to mitigate through his overall treatment of the question of the Law); Foster, *Community*, 144-217; Marlis Gielen, *Der Konflikt Jesu mit den religiösen und politischen Autoritäten seines Volkes im Spiegel der matthäischen Jesusgeschichte* (BBB 115; Bodenheim: Philo, 1998), 61-86 (cf. esp. 84f., where she presents a solution similar to Eckstein); Petri Luomanen, *Entering the Kingdom of Heaven: A Study on the Structure of Matthew's View of Salvation* (WUNT 2.101; Tübingen: Mohr Siebeck, 1998), 69-92; Snodgrass, "Matthew and the Law," 111-18; Vahrenhorst, *"Ihr sollt überhaupt nicht schwören,"* 234-49; cf. further Sim, *Gospel of Matthew*, 123-39. For the centrality of this pericope in the ongoing discussion see further Hare, "How Jewish Is Matthew?" 265, 270f.; Hagner, "Matthew: Apostate, Reformer, Revolutionary?" 202f.; McKnight, "A Loyal Critic," 65f.; Murphy, "Jewishness of Matthew," 381, 389f.

53. For my critic Benedikt Viviano (cf. above, n. 9) this will be again a "trick in the exegetical repertoire to avoid the obvious" (790). But I think I have given some reasons why what in his eyes seems obvious (namely, that the Christians have to keep the Torah) is not.

3. The Basic Concepts in the First Gospel as a Framework in which the Law Is to be Understood

(1) Jesus is the offspring of David and the Messiah of Israel (1:1-17). Davidic-messianic expectations are on the agenda of the Gospel from the beginning; Jesus is the Davidic Messiah. The whole Gospel is marked with Davidic motifs (1:20, 23; 2:2-6; 9:27; 12:3f., 23; 15:22; 20:30; 21:9; through 1:1, 16; 22:42, the title Χριστός is connected with the Son of David tradition, and therefore 11:2; 16:16-20; 26:63 as well), which forces the reader to ask: what hopes and expectations are connected with David in scripture?[54]

(2) The main task of Jesus is "to save his people from their sins" (1:21). Matthew connects this with the name of Jesus, *Jehoshua*. The name is programmatic, and the question is to be raised: Why do the people of Israel need a "new" forgiveness for their sins? Is this not right from the beginning of the Gospel at least an indirect hint as to how Matthew understood the Torah and the Messiah's main task? The prominence of the forgiveness motif is visible throughout the whole Gospel (3:6 [only confession of sins, no mentioning of forgiveness as in Mark 1:4, because only Jesus can forgive]; 9:2-6, 13; 12:31; 20:28; 26:28; cf. also Jesus' taking care of the sinners, 9:10f.; 11:19), and it is nowhere connected to the Torah.

(3) The fulfillment of scripture is a prominent and ongoing subject from 1:22 onward through the whole Gospel until the death of Judas in 27:9 (cf. 26:54, 56). The earthly ministry of Jesus until his death is the fulfillment of the prophets and, I would add, of the Law as well. The resurrection of Jesus and the mission command are not under this label. He is dying as "king of Israel" (27:42), but is confessed to be the Son of God only by the centurion under the cross (27:54; cf. 27:43).[55]

(4) The wise men from the east in 2:1-12 form an *inclusio* with the already mentioned centurion under the cross. In both cases foreigners see the signifi-

---

54. Cf. Deines, *Gerechtigkeit*, 469-500 ("§12: Das matthäische Bild des Davidssohnes"), and §13: "Die biblischen Wurzeln der matthäischen Gerechtigkeitstradition" (501-638). Parallel to my own work others emphasized in a similar way the importance of the Davidic-messianic expectations for the first Gospel; see Cousland, *Crowds*, 175-99; Lidija Novakovic, *Messiah, the Healer of the Sick: A Study of Jesus as the Son of David in the Gospel of Matthew* (WUNT 2.170; Tübingen: Mohr Siebeck, 2003); cf. also Saldarini, *Christian-Jewish Community*, 167-71. See also, despite his title, Robert L. Brawley, "Reverberations of Abrahamic Covenant Traditions in the Ethics of Matthew," in *Realia Dei: Essays in Archaeology and Biblical Interpretation* (ed. Prescott H. Williams, Jr. and Theodore Hiebert; Scholars Press Homage Series 23; Atlanta: Scholars Press, 1999), 26-46.

55. Matt. 27:54 contains the last Christological title in the Gospel besides ὁ πλάνος" in 27:63 and perhaps Ἰησοῦς ὁ ἐσταυρωμένος in 28:5.

cance of Jesus more clearly than the respective leaders of Israel. This allows us to interpret the mention of Abraham, who is the most prominent forefather of Jesus next to David, in the first verse of the Gospel as another *inclusio* with the last verses: the Gospel starts and ends with a universal perspective, but at the same time it is deeply and inseparably connected to the people of Israel.

(5) With the message of John the Baptist the ultimate goal is reached, namely the kingdom of God (3:2, cf. 4:17; 10:7).[56] According to John (3:2, 6), repentance and forgiveness of sin are the prerequisites to enter the coming kingdom. With Jesus' overcoming of Satan's temptation to exchange the kingdom of God for "all the kingdoms of the world and their glory" (4:8),[57] Jesus is prepared for his mission as agent of God's kingdom. From the core of the gospel it becomes clear: to enter the kingdom of God (5:20; 7:21; 18:3; 19:23f.) means salvation (cf. 19:25, the reaction of the disciples to Jesus' saying in 19:23f.) and (eternal) life (7:13f.; 18:8f.; 19:17; 25:46; cf. also 25:10, 21, 23). To miss it means to face a future in the Gehenna (5:29f.; 18:8f.). The way to enter into it is through the eschatological righteousness that Jesus has come to impute (3:15; 5:20). Therefore Jesus' message and deeds are characterized as εὐαγγέλιον τῆς βασιλείας (4:23; 9:35). In most of the places where the kingdom of God is mentioned, there is not the slightest reference to the Torah, and nowhere is the Torah the criterion for being saved or not.

Against this position one might point to two possible exceptions: one is the conversation between Jesus and the rich young man in 19:16-22, where the entrance fee for eternal life (the kingdom of God is not mentioned here) seems to be the keeping of the commandments.[58] The second is Matt. 5:19f. Therefore let us concentrate for the rest of the paper on Matt. 5:17-20.[59]

---

56. Cf. Deines, *Gerechtigkeit*, 103-36.

57. Cf. Hans-Christian Kammler, "Sohn Gottes und Kreuz. Die Versuchungsgeschichte Mt 4,1-11 im Kontext des Matthäusevangeliums," *ZTK* 100 (2003): 163-86.

58. I see in this story the failure of Law-keeping: even though the young man can claim to have kept the commandments he still lacks something or, better, *someone*: To be "perfect" (19:21; cf. 5:48) he has to get rid of his wealth and to follow Jesus, if he wants to enter the kingdom of God (19:23f.). The keeping of the commandments seems not to be enough for this ultimate goal; cf. Deines, *Gerechtigkeit*, 388-92; R. F. Collins, "Matthew's *ENTOΛAI*: Towards an Understanding of the Commandments in the First Gospel," in *The Four Gospels 1992* (FS F. Neirynck; 3 vols., ed. F. van Segbroeck et al., BETL 100; Leuven: Leuven University Press, 1992), 2:1325-48, esp. 1326-31.

59. The following outline is a summary of my work mentioned in n. 1, where I discussed the differing positions intensively. This I do not want to repeat but concentrate on the results.

4. Matt. 5:17-20 as a Crucial Text for Understanding Matthew's Concept of Torah and Righteousness

4.1. Why Does Jesus Have to Defend Himself Already at the Beginning of His Career? (5:17)

It is in a way astonishing that Matthew feels it necessary to let Jesus defend himself at this early point of his public appearance. Or should μὴ νομίσατε be understood as a mere introductory phrase without any real background, as many commentators suggest?[60] If not, which of the incidents related in the previous chapters could have aroused the suspicion that Jesus causes a threat to the Law and the prophets? The answer can be found in the verses immediately preceding verse 17. In a twofold way they may give the impression that the Torah as the basic tool for mediation between God and his people is pushed aside.

(1) In the Beatitudes, people are promised participation in the kingdom of God without the Law and the prophets. The keeping of the Law is not mentioned at all. While the goal of the Law and the prophetic hope, namely "righteousness," is mentioned twice (5:6, 10), the traditional and expected way to this goal, namely the keeping of the Law, is not referred to. Also, the addressees are not called the righteous ones, only those who long for righteousness.[61] Nevertheless, they are awarded membership in the kingdom of God. This immediately raises the question (and not only for a Pharisee or scribe): how dare Jesus promise something like that to people without connecting the promise to the keeping of the Law as an expression of God's will and Israel's covenant?

(2) In 5:11-16, the disciples are assigned a position and task comparable to that of the prophets. By calling them the salt and the light of the world, Jesus ascribes features to them that are connected in the Jewish tradition of the time to the Torah, to righteousness, to Israel as a whole, to Jerusalem, to outstanding godly or righteous individuals or to the Messiah.[62] Here again the question arises: how is it possible that Jesus could give such a universal task to such an insignificant group of Galilean fishermen who are not trained scholars? Behind that looms the question: how does this fit in with the Law and the prophets, that is, with the (handed-down) tradition of the Jewish people? In verses 13 to 16 the disciples are engaged and empowered for their task. But the disciples are not

---

60. Cf. Overman, *Church and Community*, 78, who claims that "this reference to the Law and the prophets . . . comes out of the blue" and should be seen as "part of the 'taken for granted' knowledge of the Matthean community." Nolland, *Matthew*, 216f., also sees only a loose connection between verses 16 and 17 and understands 17-20 mainly as an introduction to the following.

61. For my understanding of Matt. 5:6, 10 see *Gerechtigkeit*, 137-81.

62. For references see ibid., 188-233.

expected to fulfill the task they are engaged for by looking at their own potential, but because they are engaged and commanded by Jesus to do what they ought to do. As salt and light they *represent* and *proclaim* the righteousness fulfilled by Jesus (5:10f.; 3:15[63]), but they do not create it themselves.

This understanding of 5:13-16, which has been briefly laid out here, makes sense of the transition from 5:16 to 5:17. The engagement of the disciples and the authority Jesus claimed in this call could have aroused the impression that he sets himself against or above "the prophets and the Law." The position of the Torah is put in question if Jesus speaks of a righteousness which allows the entering of the kingdom of God without any reference to the Torah, and if he puts his disciples in that category of righteousness, and in addition assigns them roles that are traditionally connected to the Torah itself. It is Jesus' Christological authority underlying the sayings in 5:13-16 that impressively dominates the prelude of the Sermon on the Mount. This has to be taken into account in the interpretation of verses 17-20.[64]

4.2. Matt. 5:17: Fulfillment of the Whole Will of God as Jesus' Primary Goal

In the nomistic line of interpretation, righteousness is understood as doing something. To fulfill the Law and the prophets means mainly to keep the whole Torah.[65] According to the proponents of a Law-abiding Matthean community the Evangelist created or used this logion to support his demand for a Law-observant attitude in the Christian communities. Against this I agree with the exegetical tradition that sees πληρῶσαι as an exclusive Christological term, which could in the context of the First Gospel only be understood in the framework of a salvation history which reaches its peak in Jesus.[66] The use of

---

63. The understanding of 3:15 is crucial and therefore, of course, controversial; cf. ibid., 127-32, and the helpful comments in Nolland, *Matthew,* 153f.

64. Viviano, in his review of my book (see above, n. 9), regards my reference to 5:13-16 as a mere strategy for "diverting our attention from the issue of the Law" (790). But was it not Matthew who said first something about Jesus and his disciples, before he spoke about the Law?

65. Cf., for example, Overman, *Church and Community,* 78; Sim, *Gospel of Matthew,* 124f., 207f.; cf. further Allison, *The New Moses,* 182f. It is obvious that the ethical or nomistic interpretation of verse 17 is dominated by the understanding of verses 18 and 19: because they are seen as an admonition to keep every single command of the Law, verse 17 must be read in this way as well, as Luz states in his commentary quite openly (*Matthew,* I/1, 318f., cf. 314). Similarly, Vahrenhorst, *"Ihr sollt überhaupt nicht schwören,"* 244f., cf. 240.

66. A somehow neglected, but helpful, essay for this argument is C. F. D. Moule, "Fulfilment-Words in the New Testament: Use and Abuse," in idem, *Essays in New Testament In-*

the verb as connected to the fulfillment of prophecy is made clear for the reader in 1:22; 2:15, 17, 23; 4:14 (and within this context in 3:15 as well), and it is also accepted in the nomistic exegetical tradition that πληροῦν is usually not the same as ποιεῖν, a verb that Matthew much appreciates in other places. The main argument for Luz to interpret πληροῦν nevertheless in the sense of ποιεῖν is καταλύειν, a verb which he thinks cannot be used in the sense of salvation history, but only as a terminus connected to the breaking of a Law.[67] But in Acts 5:38f. καταλύειν is used in a different way, which comes close to a "heilsgeschichtliches" understanding.[68]

Jesus' fulfillment of the Law and the prophets takes place for Matthew neither only by his deeds nor by his teaching (as the two classic exegetical opinions hold), but through his entire mission that includes his teaching, his deeds and especially his messianic works up to his death and resurrection (cf. the last two references for πληροῦν in 26:54, 56). It is crucial to see that the expression "the Law and the prophets" is understood as a canon- or integrity-formula that summarizes God's revelation that has taken place so far. Parallels from the Jewish literature make clear that affirming the ongoing "integrity" of the canonical writings does not mean the denial of changes, additions and new understandings.[69] The combination of Law *and* prophets, that is, of commandment *and* promise, turns out to be foundational for Matthean theology, with the prophetic element being clearly predominant.

Therefore the first ἦλθον-word in the Gospel claims for Jesus that his mission takes place in the context of God's story with Israel and thus stands at the same time under its claim and promise. As its promises are about to be fulfilled through his coming (a fact that Matthew clearly points out through the fulfillment quotes starting in chapter 2), the claim is also changed by clearly delimiting the time of the kingdom of God from the time of the Law and the prophets that is coming to an end (cf. 11:13).

Because of this, 5:17 may be compared to the preamble of a new treaty that relates what will be in force from now on but based on an existing foundation. There are no hints in the text that indicate that this verse needs to be understood as a demand for a special Law-observant piety.

---

terpretation (Cambridge: Cambridge University Press, 1982 [originally *NTS* 3 (1956): 1ff.]), 3-36, esp. 28-36.

67. *Matthew,* I/1, 310, 313f. For this meaning see, for example, 2 Macc. 2:22; 4:11; 4 Macc. 5:33.

68. Cf. Deines, *Gerechtigkeit,* 271f.

69. The references are in ibid., 281-86. Cf. further Brawley, "Reverberations," 44f., who takes 5:17 as a hint to "a holistic function of the Law and the prophets in anticipating Jesus' fulfillment"; Hare, "How Jewish Is Matthew?" 270.

4.3. Matt. 5:18: Iotas and Jots/Strokes: A Clue to Legal Details or a Confession-Like Formula for the Ongoing Relevance of the Whole Will of God (Abbreviated in the Term nomos)?

The interpretation of 5:17 has to prove itself by also accounting for 5:18, as it is this verse that is understood even more than 5:17 as evidence for the Law-abiding Jewish-Christian position that Matthew is said to have embraced. In order to come to a decision here, it is first necessary to understand the text-pragmatic function of the guarantee that none of the jots and strokes of the Torah will pass away. Against the nearly unanimous view to the contrary, it can be shown that the rabbinic texts that are regularly adduced for the interpretation of 5:18 cannot be used to support the view that Matthew favors a Law-abiding position which lays emphasis on every single detail or on every "small" law (whatever this may be). On the contrary, the everlastingness of each jot and stroke is a confession of the invariability and irreversibility of scripture,[70] and is thus comparable to the way in which Jesus sets himself in relationship with the Law and the prophets in 5:17. In the Matthean context it is thus emphasized that the whole scripture, given to Israel by God, is and remains important. Contrary to Ulrich Luz and many others, verse 18 is not about halakhic observance of the Torah,[71] but is an affirmation of the steadfastness of the revelation of God.

This affirmation became necessary especially because of the engagement of the disciples, related in 5:13-16, that transferred the salvific functions of the Torah to the disciples and consequently evoked the question of what remained of the Torah. Pointing to this background is the verb παρέρχεσθαι in verse 18, which needs to be understood as an apocalyptic *terminus technicus* and cannot be taken exclusively as indicating disregard of the commandments.[72] Because of this, the last part of the verse ἕως ἂν πάντα γένηται (which is, in my view, an original part of the verse and does not represent a Matthean addition) is to be interpreted like πληρῶσαι in 5:17 in a way that takes salvation history and escha-

---

70. As verse 18 is connected to verse 17 by γάρ and ἀπὸ τοῦ νόμου, νόμος in verse 18 can be understood as an all-embracing description of God's revealed will. That here only νόμος is mentioned is not necessarily "the narrowing of focus . . . to the Law" (Nolland, *Matthew*, 219), but might be just an abbreviation, for νόμος is often used for all parts of the scriptures (cf. Rom. 3:19: the quotations given in 3:10-18, all of them taken from the Prophets and the Writings, are summarized with the formula: "what the νόμος says . . ."; in 1 Cor. 14:21 a quotation of Isa. 28:11f. is introduced as "in the Law is written"). That both meanings of the Torah can be used even in one sentence is shown by Midrash Tanchuma B, Yitro 8 (ed. Buber, p. 37a): "The Torah is threefold: Torah, Prophets, and Writings." For further references see Deines, *Gerechtigkeit*, 357, n. 733.

71. Cf. Luz, *Matthew*, I/1, 314f., 319. To the "jots and strokes" he counts the laws about tithing (23:23) and purity of dishes (23:26); similarly Nolland, *Matthew*, 219f.

72. Cf. my discussion in *Gerechtigkeit*, 337f.

tology into account and refers to the messianic mission of Jesus.[73] The next example of this understanding of παρέρχεσθαι in relation to γίνεσθαι can be found in 26:42, where Matthew transmits the prayer of Jesus in Gethsemane. In this decisive moment for the mission of Jesus (with respect to 1:21 and 20:28) both verbs are used to describe what is necessary for salvation: πάτερ μου, εἰ οὐ δύναται τοῦτο *παρελθεῖν* ἐὰν μὴ αὐτὸ πίω, *γενηθήτω* τὸ θέλημά σου (26:42, cf. verse 38). The will of God cannot pass away without realization.

That γίνεσθαι here needs to be understood to mean fulfilling a "heilsgeschichtliche" necessity rather than obeying a specific commandment is obvious from 26:54 and 56. In the first place, Jesus reminds the disciple who wants to fight for him that his heavenly Father is able to provide him with plenty of angelic legions if fighting were part of God's plan. But in this case "the scriptures" would not be fulfilled: πῶς οὖν πληρωθῶσιν αἱ γραφαὶ ὅτι οὕτως δεῖ *γενέσθαι*; ("but how then should the scriptures be fulfilled, that it must be so?" 26:54). What has to happen is obedience to God's plan for salvation. This is repeated in 26:56: whatever happened to Jesus is part of this eschatological fulfillment (τοῦτο δὲ ὅλον *γένενον* ἵνα πληρωθῶσιν αἱ γραφαὶ τῶν προφητῶν. "But all this has taken place that the scriptures of the prophets might be fulfilled"). So nothing from the Law (5:18) and from the prophets remained without fulfillment in the ministry of Jesus. But if "fulfilling" in verse 17 is an exclusively messianic work and verse 18 is to be understood in the same way, then it follows that the Torah and the prophets cannot continue as though this fulfillment, to which the death and resurrection of Jesus and the associated theological convictions are inseparably connected, had never taken place.

4.4. Matt. 5:19: From Christological Fulfillment to Disciples' Obligation

The conditional clause in the third person of verse 19 sets itself apart from the verses 17, 18 and 20, which are directly addressed to the disciples in the second person. This kind of grammatical interruption is found quite frequently in Matthew, as is the pattern of a conditional clause following an authorial statement or rule.[74] In this case, verse 18 is the authorial rule ("Regelsatz"), and verse 19 is one application of this rule in a specific situation. I call this construction which consists of a relative clause with a conditional meaning "Anwendungs-

---

73. For other scholars who hold a similar opinion see ibid., 352f. with n. 721.
74. For details see ibid., 372-74. Good examples are Matt. 12:31f.; 16:24f.; 18:3-6.

bestimmung," that is, an application rule, or better an application guideline, because it is more exemplary than exhaustive.

According to this understanding these two verses belong together very closely; yet a clear hierarchy is discernible from the authorial rule to its application. In our case the transition from verse 18 to 19 is additionally accompanied by a change of perspective: whereas verses 17 and 18 concentrate solely on Jesus and his eschatological task, verses 19 and 20 are describing the consequences for the disciples.[75] Because Jesus is the fulfiller of the Law and the prophets, his disciples are confronted with the consequences that are described in these two verses: verse 19 as a direct outflow of verse 18 in an exemplary and concrete form, verse 20 in a more general way. The horizon of eschatological fulfillment, which marks verses 17 and 18, is in verse 20 envisaged by the mentioning of the kingdom of heaven and its overflowing rich righteousness, which is the direct result of Jesus' fulfillment. Because of the marked change in the perspective from Jesus' task to the obligations of his disciples (who are addressed in verse 19 as teachers), it is plausible to see in τῶν ἐντολῶν τούτων τῶν ἐλαχίστων a forward hint to 5:21ff.[76] What Jesus will teach his disciples in a moment is the outflow of messianic righteousness for the kingdom of God.

I believe that it is possible to argue that the Matthean use of the words ἐντολή and μικρός/ἐλάχιστος hints at the fact that what is meant here is the will of God in the way Jesus proclaimed it for the entrance of the kingdom of God, not the Torah in its previous or traditional shape with its aim to guide Israel to be holy.[77] None of the positive statements of Jesus about an individual com-

---

75. Cf. McKnight, "A Loyal Critic," 65; Yang, *Sabbath*, 115: ". . . in the salvation-history time line the referent of the commandments of v. 19 belongs to the post-fulfilment period, whereas the referent of the Law in vv. 17, 18 evidently belongs to the pre-fulfilment period."

76. That the "least of the commandments" should be understand with respect to 5:21ff. is proposed *inter alia* by Chrysostom (referred to in Zahn, *Matthäus*, 217, n. 80; cited in *Ancient Christian Commentary on Scripture*, New Testament Ia: *Matthew 1–13* [ed. M. Simonetti; Downers Grove, Ill.: InterVarsity Press, 2001], 97); Betz, *Sermon on the Mount*, 186-88; for further references see Deines, *Gerechtigkeit*, 408, n. 862. The majority of scholars see it as a reference to the Mosaic Law and its easiest-to-fulfill laws; cf. Hagner, *Matthew 1–13*, 108; Snodgrass, "Matthew and the Law," 103, 116; Nolland, *Matthew*, 221, who sees the solution preferred here at least as "initially attractive because it takes seriously the way in which v. 17 already anticipates the teaching to come in the antitheses." What mainly persuades Nolland against it is the rupture of "the connection of v. 19 with v. 18," but as I have tried to show, this is the result of a wrong understanding of the jot/stroke-metaphor (cf. next note).

77. Cf. Deines, *Gerechtigkeit*, 383-407. That there is a "thought jump" between verses 18 and 19 is accepted even by those who see in "the least of the commandments" the "smallest parts of the Law in v. 18" (Nolland, *Matthew*, 221). But the "thought jump" might be even bigger than normally assumed, because in the rabbinic tradition, which is cited usually for prooftexts for this reading, the "jot and the stroke" do not mean relatively unimportant or easy laws. On the con-

mandment of the Torah is concerned with a mere continuation of it for its own sake, but all are incorporated into the new reality of the kingdom of God, whose base is the double commandment of love (22:34-40). In the teaching of Jesus the will of God (who is also the "author" of the Law and the prophets) continues to engage the faithful, but there is no way that leads from here to a new casuistry that knows other commandments besides the ones of Jesus.[78] The Sermon on the Mount in its entirety is an exemplary instruction (not a Law) for the ἐντολαί of Jesus, which cannot be considered separately from the missionary and universal horizon of the First Gospel.

Verse 19 is to be understood (like Matt. 5–7 as a whole) on the narrative level as part of the teaching and instruction that Jesus directs mainly at his disciples. From 5:11 onward, he has been speaking to them of their task as *his* messengers (cf. 4:19), that is, as prophets of or for the kingdom of God (cf. 5:12, where the fate of the disciples is paralleled to that of one of the prophets). On the time level *(Zeitebene)* of the Evangelist, verse 19 functions as an instruction for Christian *teachers,* who may be imagined as wandering missionaries whose basic task was to teach all that Jesus has taught them. This comes out in the last word of Jesus in Matt. 28:19f.: because "the Law and the prophets" are fulfilled, only the commandment of Jesus is mentioned for the future.[79] The Torah no longer has a separate function in addition to the commandment of Jesus, not even for the Jewish Christians. What the disciples (and their successors in the churches) are instructed to do is to hand on the commandments of "the only

---

trary, the story about the attempt of Solomon to remove one *yod* out of the scriptures (*y. Sanh.* 2.7 20c and parallels, treated in some detail in my *Gerechtigkeit,* 296-308) is meant as an affirmation of the everlasting existence of God's work. In the answer God gave the Torah complaining about Solomon's attempt to remove an iota he said: "The Holy one, blessed be he, said to it [= the book of the Torah]: Solomon and thousands like him will become null and void, but no word from you will become null and void." The everlastingness of every *yod* in the Torah is at least in the rabbinic literature nowhere connected to a single commandment but has to do with God's confirmation that nobody can change his word and will. This fits very well with verse 17.

78. But as a result of this love one can keep the Law in the way it is presupposed in Matt. 17:24f.; 23:2, 23; cf. further Hagner, "Sitz im Leben," 53f., and Brawley, "Reverberations," 34, with respect to John the Baptist's preaching: "At first glance John's criteria appear to be purely ethical — repentance and the fruits of repentance. But John's proclamation of God's reign is the key to 3:1-10. Those who live under God's reign repent and bear fruit. Here ethics is a matter of the fruit of God's reign." The same is true for Jesus' ethical preaching: what is called for is fruit worthy of God's reign. For helpful observations on the use of ἐντολαί in Matthew see Collins, "Matthew's *ENTOΛAI,*" whose conclusion is: "one must observe and teach the commandments as Jesus had taught them" (1347), in which he includes the whole Law (cf. 1344f.) by subsuming all other commandments besides the double love-commandment under the notion of "the least of the commandments."

79. Cf. the different argumentation referred to above, n. 24.

teacher."[80] The Torah, by contrast, nowhere appears as a binding rule independently of the teaching and interpretation of Jesus. This means that the διδάσκειν of the Christian teachers is defined exclusively Christologically.[81]

4.5. Matt. 5:20: The Implementation of the Eschatological and Exclusive Jesus-Righteousness as the Condition for Entering the Kingdom of God

5:17 refers back clearly to 3:15 with its reference to Jesus' *fulfilling* all righteousness; 5:20 takes up the theme of *righteousness*. The theme is a key one in the Sermon extending from the Beatitudes through to 6:33 (cf. further its concatenation with John the Baptist in 3:15 and 21:32: the first and the last reference for "righteousness" is connected with him, forming an *inclusio* around the five references between 5:6 and 6:33).

Starting from verse 5:17, righteousness, which is at the same time demanded and presupposed in verse 20, means a new reality that is possible through Jesus and — because it is available from now on — also necessary for entering the kingdom of God. Περισσεύειν is an eschatological catchword in the Gospel of Matthew (as it is for Paul) that refers to the fact that the content of what it signifies exists thanks to the working and giving of God.[82] Therefore, a merely quantitative designation of πλεῖον περισσεύειν is to be rejected together with all attempts to find the difference between Judaism and Christianity on the basis of a "better" ethic. What is demanded is a different quality of life according to the kingdom of God that is about to appear. It is the eschatological, overflowingly rich righteousness that Jesus fulfilled and made available to his disciples that from now on alone opens the way into the kingdom of God. Con-

---

80. Samuel Byrskog, *Jesus the Only Teacher: Didactic Authority and Transmission in Ancient Israel, Ancient Judaism and the Matthean Community* (ConBNT 24; Stockholm: Almqvist & Wiksell International, 1994).

81. Cf. McKnight, "A Loyal Critic," 66; Hagner, "Apostate," 203: "There is thus an important shift in Matthew that explains the newness of its perspective of the Law. To be sure, the Law remains significant for these Jewish Christians, but *only as it is taken up in the teaching of Jesus*."

82. Cf. Matt. 13:12; 14:20; 15:37; 25:29; the way Matthew uses περισσεύειν in comparison with the other Evangelists shows his interest in this specific terminology. In the feeding stories τὸ περισσεῦον (14:20; 15:37) describes the abundant surplus of bread after the disciples fed the multitudes of men, women and children. They have enough and even more to give through what is given to them by Jesus (14:19). The multitudes became satisfied, using the same verb χορτάζειν in 14:20; 15:32, 37 as in 5:6. What is true for the eschatological bread is also true for the eschatological righteousness: the disciples can give what they have received. For Paul see 1 Thess. 1:4, 10; 1 Cor. 15:58; 2 Cor. 3:9; 8:2, 7.

sequently, also for this verse the paradigm shift in salvation history that is presupposed with the fulfillment terminology is decisive. Verse 20 is not about *keeping the Law* more or less, but about a radical either-or. In the end, the question is where the foundation for the righteousness that is valid in the kingdom of God lies: in the Torah or in the work and word of the Messiah.[83] Because of that, the righteousness of the scribes and Pharisees misses the goal from now on, for they do not acknowledge Jesus as the one who fulfills the scriptures and who makes the eschatological righteousness that is demanded now, available through his messianic status.

That is why I think that it is appropriate to summarize the Matthean concept of righteousness as Jesus-righteousness. The intention of this phrase is to point out that this righteousness is not possible without Jesus. Those who obey his call to discipleship get a share of this righteousness and thus can be addressed concerning *their* righteousness, as in 5:20 and 6:1. The righteousness of the disciples, however, stays focused on Jesus as its foundation as well as its consequences. As Jesus fulfilled all righteousness, so the disciples should also — as righteous ones — do (their) righteousness (6:1). Jesus does not become righteous by healing the sick, feeding the hungry, driving out demons and proclaiming the kingdom of God, but as the righteous one (cf. 27:19) he did all these things and fulfilled all righteousness.

With this in mind the antitheses should better be called "instructions about the practice of eschatological righteousness" and regarded as exemplary illustration and description: the ("fulfilled") righteousness that Jesus makes possible is supposed to bring forth fruit according to the model of God's own perfection, whose distinctive mark is to do good even to those who are evil (5:45, 48).[84] The disciples prove themselves worthy to the kingdom of God by overcoming enmity, crossing religiously defined (that is, in the Jewish realm: halakhically) and ethnic boundaries with the aim of loving everyone into the presence of God (5:16). The main goal of the Sermon on the Mount is to prepare disciples for their missionary task, which means giving the kingdom of God and his righteousness first place, above (or instead of) all their daily concerns (6:33).[85]

---

83. Helpful thoughts may be found in Robert Morgan, "Towards a Critical Appropriation of the Sermon on the Mount: Christology and Discipleship," in *Christology, Controversy and Community* (Festschrift D. R. Catchpole, ed. D. G. Horrell and C. M. Tuckett, NovTSup 99; Leiden: Brill, 2000), 157-91.

84. For an understanding of the antitheses as "Missionsbefehle" see Fritz Neugebauer, "Die dargebotene Wange und Jesu Gebot der Feindesliebe. Erwägungen zu Lk 6,27-36/Matt. 5,38-48," *TLZ* 110 (1985): 865-76; Deines, *Gerechtigkeit*, 432-34, 443-46.

85. What "his righteousness" in 6:33 means is a matter of dispute and depends on the treatment of the other δικαιοσύνη references in the First Gospel. In the more ethically oriented ex-

Lastly, it should not be overlooked that the verses 5:21-48 are based on the already existing father-child relationship of the disciples to God (cf. 5:16, 45; 6:32). It is necessary to persevere in this relationship but not to create it. Verse 20 can therefore be taken as a summary of what will be commanded from 5:21ff. onward and not just the introduction to it.

5. Conclusions

The following results may be noted: the Torah in its previous function cannot contribute to the now demanded eschatological righteousness, but as an expression of God's will the Torah remains an important part of God's word and revelation, leading and pointing to the ἐντολαί of Jesus (these being based on and inseparably related to this first expression of God's will). Furthermore, the Law will function as a guide to know what sin is (cf. Rom. 3:19) and what it means that God wants the obedience of all humans in all aspects of their personal and social life. But from now on the obedience is oriented toward the kingdom of God, and Jesus is the only one who opens up the way to the universal *basileia*. In view of this the righteousness which is requested and also demanded in the imperative in 5:20; 6:1 is no longer a δικαιοσύνη διὰ νόμου, but it is the δικαιοσύνη that is to be bound to the νόμος Χριστοῦ (Gal. 6:2) or the fulfilled Law, described by Matthew in the shape of the ἐντολαί of the Messiah, that will be *permanent* and *valid for all* from now on (Matt. 24:35).

This sort of yes and no to the Law at the same time explains the difficulties the first Christians have to face.[86] If Jesus is the only teacher, and Jesus lived his

---

planation it is regarded as "the righteousness that God requires of us" (Nolland, *Matthew*, 315). Nolland's argument for this mainly is that an interpretation as "righteousness that comes from God . . . would be to introduce a new thought not encouraged by the main drift of the Sermon or by earlier uses of 'righteousness'" (ibid.), although he admits that 3:15 and 5:6 "come closest to reflecting this." Over against this, I would emphasize the fact that the disciples are already addressed as children of their Father in heaven and as ones who 'have' righteousness (5:20; 6:1). In addition, I do not see the logic in the promise of 6:33 if it is understood in the way described: God promises to take care of the daily needs of the faithful if they stretch themselves out to do the righteousness that God requires from them. Is it not closer to the "drift of the Sermon" to understand the verse as God promising his care to those who on their part are concerned with the spiritual needs of the world (cf. 5:13-6)? With Matt. 1:21; 20:28; 26:28 in mind, I admit that the most pressing need is the missing righteousness that God requires. But the way to get it is not connected to the Law, but to Jesus and his righteousness, which has to be brought to the world by his disciples. Their call is to be "fishers of men" (4:19), and this can mean to have no means of support (cf. 10:9f.) and to be dependent on the heavenly Father.

86. Hagner, *"Sitz im Leben,"* is especially helpful in this respect.

life as a Law-observant Jew who acknowledged Israel's scripture as the word of God, does this mean that his followers have to do the same? I think the answer Matthew (and in different ways the whole New Testament) gave is a clear no. The commandments of Jesus or, to say it in a Pauline way, "the Law of Christ" is what is binding for the disciple of Christ. But the question remains:[87] what does that mean in real life? What belongs to the fulfilled Law or the "Law of Christ": only the double love command? The love command and the Ten Commandments? The Noachitic Laws? The ethical principles of the Old Testament but not the ritual parts of the Law?

In a way this is the question that continues to puzzle us until today — and will endure until Jesus' second coming — and we should not try to solve it with a formal principle. Based upon the understanding of the teaching of Jesus as affirmative fulfillment of Law and prophets, it should be self-evident that both remain the foremost sources for our understanding of what God wants us to do. The ethic of Jesus will always be an ethic based on all of scripture, but from the perspective of the kingdom of God. To handle this question should be the task of a biblical theology which accepts as a theological and "heilsgeschichtliche" necessity that both Old and New Testament are the word of the one living God, but which at the same time takes into full consideration that "the Law and the prophets prophesied until John" (11:13) and that now Jesus is the teacher of the kingdom of heaven. And the kingdom of God has a different dynamic and a different ultimate goal from the Law and the prophets. To express it in a clear but perhaps a little overly simplified way: the task of the Law and the prophets is to keep Israel apart as a chosen people in the world and to champion the will of God *inside* Israel. The ultimate goal of the kingdom of heaven is that all nations live and walk in the light of the Lord. *All* are invited to enter the kingdom of God, and barriers are no longer necessary to keep the pious apart.

The new covenant has its own dynamic, and the Law written in the hearts through the Holy Spirit changes the status of the written Law. The Law remains a witness to the will of God. But its place in the history of God with the world has changed with the appearance of the Messiah. The Messiah paved the way for the eschatological righteousness, and from now on the Torah has only a kind of supportive role. In other words, only as long as the Torah serves the messianic goal is the Torah valid.

87. For the interpretation of this ambiguity as meaningful advice cf. Syreeni, "Matthew, Luke, and the Law," 141-45. He finds the intense hermeneutical interest of Matthew in the question of the Law to be the result of a "progressive distancing from that phenomenon. . . . What was to be taught and obeyed was not the Law, but the words of Jesus. . . . Matthew's final goal was not to defend the Law itself, but to expound Jesus' teaching which — as the antitheses of the great sermon prove — was not simply a duplicate of the Mosaic Law" (144).

The lesson to learn is that fulfillment is neither abrogation nor supersession of the Law but an ongoing transformation for every generation of Christians anew.

Ἀπό . . . ἕως and Salvation History in Matthew's Gospel

Mervyn Eloff

Introduction

The question of salvation history in Matthew's gospel is, at its heart, a theological question, for it primarily concerns the matter of significance. It has been framed in different ways, depending on the particular interests and methodologies of the proponents involved.

The initial application of the concept of salvation history to the study of Matthew occurred in the wake of the broader debate concerning what Cullmann called "fundamental assertions of *New Testament theology* concerning time and history."[1] In particular, redaction critics[2] used the basic concept[3] as an ordering principle and a "hermeneutical key"[4] in terms of which the rele-

---

1. Oscar Cullmann, *Christ and Time* (trans. F. Filson; London: SCM, 1962), 19 (original emphasis).

2. See, e.g., Rolf Walker, *Die Heilsgeschichte im ersten Evangelium* (Göttingen: Vandenhoeck & Ruprecht, 1967); Georg Strecker, *Der Weg der Gerechtigkeit: Untersuchung zur Theologie des Matthäus* (Dritte, durchgesehene und erweiterte Aufl.; Göttingen: Vandenhoeck & Ruprecht, 1971); Hubert Frankemölle, *Jahwebund und Kirche Christi: Studien zur Form- und Traditionsgeschichte des 'Evangeliums' nach Matthäus* (NTAbh 10; Munster: Aschendorff, 1974); John P. Meier, "Salvation History in Matthew: In Search of a Starting Point," *CBQ* 37 (1975): 203-15; idem, *Law and History in Matthew's Gospel* (AnBib 71; Rome: Pontifical Biblical Institute, 1976); Jack Dean Kingsbury, *Matthew: Structure, Christology, Kingdom* (Philadelphia: Fortress, 1975), 25-37.

3. Cullmann, *Christ*, 17-33, raises the question of appropriate nomenclature, opting for "redemptive history" but conceptually preferring *Offenbarungsgeschichte* (revelational history). See further the comment by Donald Senior, *What Are They Saying about Matthew* (rev. and updated ed.; New York: Paulist, 1996), 39, that ". . . the term 'salvation history' is somewhat vague and subject to many interpretations . . . ," as well as the helpful definition of salvation history by John P. Meier, *The Vision of Matthew: Christ, Church and Morality in the First Gospel* (New York: Paulist, 1979), 30.

4. The term is exclusive to Meier (see, e.g., *Law*, 23, 25), but the basic idea of salvation his-

vance of Matthew's gospel for the original recipients could be established. This relevance tended to be seen in relation to a particular "problem area." For Georg Strecker, the problem area was that of *eschatology* and *the delayed parousia*.[5] Rolf Walker, by contrast, saw Matthew's "salvation history" as a "mission history," i.e., a history of God's call *(Berufungsgeschichte)* providing an aetiological justification for the post–AD 70 Gentile mission.[6] John Meier focused on the sociological impact of this Gentile mission on the Matthean communities and described salvation history as ". . . the tool Matthew employs to formulate his higher synthesis, his new vision meant to help a once narrowly Jewish-Christian church over the rough ground of transition."[7]

With the rise of Narrative Criticism, the use of salvation history as a conceptual category for the study of Matthew's gospel not only fell into disuse, but was in fact exposed to significant critique.[8] One example must suffice for our purposes. As part of his study of the narrative rhetoric of Matthew, David Howell[9] evaluates the "theological concept of salvation history" and its value as a "heuristic paradigm for interpreting the inclusive nature of Matthew," i.e., for establishing the significance of Matthew's story of Jesus for readers of the First Gospel. Howell recognizes that the concept of salvation history has connections with the narrative form of Matthew, being "based upon the chronological and configurational dimensions of the text," and that it has *de facto* conceptual similarities to certain aspects of Matthew's *ideological point of view*.[10] But, in the final analysis, he concludes that the use of such a theological-historical framework[11] as a means of inclusion fails because, paradoxically, it ignores "the evangelist's rheto-

---

tory as a conceptual framework in the light of which the gospel material is structured and evaluated is common to all the scholars mentioned above.

5. See Strecker, *Weg*, 45-47; idem, "The Concept of History in Matthew," in *The Interpretation of Matthew* (ed. G. N. Stanton; London: SPCK, 1983), 69-70. Cf. Cullmann, *Christ*, xviii.

6. See Walker, *Heilsgeschichte*, 10-11, 114-20, 145-49. Cf. David R. Bauer, *The Structure of Matthew's Gospel: A Study in Literary Design* (JSNTSup 31; Sheffield: JSOT Press, 1988), 50.

7. See Meier, *Vision*, 29-39.

8. See, in particular, David B. Howell, *Matthew's Inclusive Story: A Study in the Narrative Rhetoric of the First Gospel* (JSNTSup 42; Sheffield: JSOT Press, 1990). See also Bauer, *Structure*; Amy-Jill Levine, *The Social and Ethnic Dimensions of Matthean Salvation History* (Lewiston, Me.: Mellen, 1988); Janice C. Anderson, *Matthew's Narrative Web: Over, and Over, and Over Again* (JSNTSup 91; Sheffield: JSOT Press, 1994).

9. Howell, *Inclusive Story*, 57-90.

10. See Howell, *Inclusive Story*, 56-57, in particular the distinction between "point of view" as a general *Weltanschauung* and "point of view" as "the system of values and beliefs that are operative within the narrative world."

11. It is this perception of salvation history as *external framework* which causes scholars like Kingsbury to discuss salvation history within the broader context of a discussion about the structure of Matthew's gospel. See, e.g., Kingsbury, *Matthew: Structure*, 1-39; Bauer, *Structure*, 45-55.

ric of entanglement." Thus, for narrative critics like Howell, the concept of salvation history had finally to be jettisoned, albeit with faint praises!

Given the growing hegemony of narrative-critical studies of the gospels, it is thus no surprise that Donald Senior, whose earlier survey of the subject in connection with Matthean scholarship was cautiously sympathetic to the idea of salvation history understood as a "faith perspective" in which ". . . the believer looks back at the flow of historical events and detects a pattern which helps shape a religious consciousness of the present . . . ,"[12] has in more recent times expressed some ambivalence about the concept and its value for the study of Matthew's gospel. According to Senior, "attempts to chart Matthew's theology of history have not proven decisive, however, and scholarly interest in them seems to have waned."[13]

The purpose of this essay is neither to discuss the concept of salvation history per se nor to debate in detail the merits or otherwise of its application to the study of Matthew's gospel. I take Howell's warning about the danger of imposing synthetic conceptual frameworks upon the narrative form of the text and thus failing to allow the text to speak in its own terms.[14] And I certainly share the belief that "Matthew's view of *Heilsgeschichte* is less susceptible of neat systematization than some modern scholarship would like."[15] However, it is my opinion that the abuse of the concept does not invalidate the concept itself and that provided we define salvation history as the *temporal-theological* aspects of Matthew's ideological point of view, demonstrable from the text of the gospel itself, its use with regard to Matthew's gospel remains legitimate. Certainly, as even the most cursory reading of the genealogy (Matt. 1:1-17) and birth narratives (Matt. 1:18-25) makes clear, Matthew is interested in connecting *salvation* with *history*, for the one born as a son of Abraham and son of David at a critical moment in the history of Israel (1:17) came "to save his people from their sins" (1:21). My aim is rather simply to reflect upon one important way in which Matthew links history and theology, namely, his use of the characteristically

---

12. Senior, *What Are They Saying?* 38-50.

13. Donald Senior, "Directions in Matthean Studies," in *The Gospel of Matthew in Current Study* (ed. David E. Aune; Grand Rapids: Eerdmans, 2001), 5-21. See also R. T. France, *Matthew: Evangelist and Teacher* (Grand Rapids: Zondervan, 1989), 198-200; W. D. Davies and Dale C. Allison, *A Critical and Exegetical Commentary on the Gospel according to Saint Matthew* (3 vols.; ICC; Edinburgh: T&T Clark, 1988-97), 3:704-7.

14. Howell is quite correct when he points out that temporal categories like "time of Israel," "time of Jesus" and "time of the church" do not actually reflect Matthew's own salvation-historical categories, but rather those of the scholars concerned and the debates about *kerygmatic* and historical theology, the development of doctrine and the relationship between the Testaments in which they were engaged.

15. France, *Evangelist*, 200.

Matthean couplet ἀπό . . . ἕως[16] and to attempt to draw some conclusions regarding Matthew's own purpose in writing his gospel.

1. From Abraham to David to the Exile to the Christ (Matt. 1:17)[17]

The first and, in many ways, the most significant use of the couplet ἀπό . . . ἕως occurs in the triadic formula in Matt. 1:17:

Πᾶσαι οὖν αἱ γενεαὶ
    ἀπὸ Ἀβραὰμ ἕως Δαυὶδ
    γενεαὶ δεκατέσσαρες
καὶ
    ἀπὸ Δαυὶδ ἕως τῆς μετοικεσίας Βαβυλῶνος
    γενεαὶ δεκατέσσαρες
καὶ
    ἀπὸ τῆς μετοικεσίας Βαβυλῶνος ἕως τοῦ Χριστοῦ
    γενεαὶ δεκατέσσαρες

As is clear from the layout above, three successive epochs, centered around four key loci, namely, Ἀβραάμ, Δαυίδ, τῆς μετοικεσίας Βαβυλῶνος and τοῦ Χριστοῦ can be identified. Although each of these epochs has its own inherent significance, it is important to bear in mind that, together, they form a carefully structured whole, serving not only to summarize the genealogy but also to highlight both its symmetrical periodicity and historical progression. Taken as a whole, therefore, the summary statement in 1:17 functions as a vital clue to Matthew's theological intention.

Both the starting point and the terminus of the first epoch is entirely consistent with Matthew's presentation of Jesus as υἱοῦ Ἀβραάμ and υἱοῦ Δαυίδ (1:1). It is striking to note that, outside the genealogy, references to Abraham always occur in contexts which are at best ambivalent about Jewish privilege and which serve to underline Matthew's internationalism.[18] Nevertheless Matthew's

---

16. That this construction is distinctly Matthean can be seen from a comparison with the other synoptics (see Ulrich Luz, *Matthew 1–7: A Commentary* [trans. Wilhelm C. Linss; Edinburgh: T&T Clark, 1989], 55). In the majority of cases the construction has a temporal function — 1:17; 11:12; 23:35 (?); 27:45.

17. For a more detailed discussion of the genealogy see Mervyn Eloff, "Exile, Restoration and Matthew's Genealogy of Jesus ὁ Χριστός," *Neot* 38(1) (2004): 75-87.

18. See Matt. 3:9; 8:11. In both of these references Matthew portrays the notion of inclusion for outsiders, while unbelieving insiders will be excluded. The third postgenealogical ref-

description of Jesus the Christ as a "son of Abraham" must surely also have been made not merely as a biographical fact, but with an eye upon those who were questioning the very *Jewishness* of a group who, though Jewish by birth, had attached themselves as disciples to one whose Messianic status Jewish Orthodoxy had roundly rejected.[19] Similarly, the reference to David as the pivotal point between the first and second epoch, taken in conjunction with the emphatic term τοῦ Χριστοῦ (used here without the personal name Ἰησοῦς and thus clearly titular), the emphatic τὸν βασιλέα in 1:6 and the descriptive ὁ λεγόμενος Χριστός in 1:16, serves to emphasize the *Christological* orientation of the genealogy,[20] stressing in particular the identity of Jesus as *Messiah ben David*.[21]

However, seen in relation to the juxtaposition of the title υἱοῦ Δαυίδ with υἱοῦ Ἀβραάμ in Matt. 1:1, there may well be more to the Abraham / David epoch than meets the eye. The titles υἱοῦ Ἀβραάμ and υἱοῦ Δαυίδ call to mind the promises of Gen. 12:1-3 and 2 Sam. 7:5-16 respectively. According to 2 Sam. 7, the main elements of the promise to David were:

(1) A great name (v. 9).
(2) A place for Israel as a home of their own in which they will be free from oppression (vv. 10-11).
(3) Rest for David, as for Israel (v. 11).
(4) A house, i.e., an offspring for David, the temple builder whose kingdom will be established forever (vv. 11b-16).

---

erence to Abraham occurs in Matt. 22:32 and is directed in a more narrow sense against the teaching of the Sadducees, but the wider context is that of conflict between Jesus and various groups within Judaism (Matt. 21:12–26:14) and contains some of the strongest polemical language in the gospel.

19. I thus concur fully with Stanton's mediating view that the setting of the Matthean communities was that of an *extra muros* dialogue with the Jewish community alongside of which they existed and with regard to which they would inevitably have faced the twin tasks of legitimization and evangelism (see Graham N. Stanton, *A Gospel for a New People: Studies in Matthew* [Edinburgh: T&T Clark, 1992], 124; cf. idem, "The Communities of Matthew," *Int* 46, no. 4 [1992]: 379-91).

20. See Kingsbury, *Matthew: Structure*, 1-39; Brian M. Nolan, *The Royal Son of God: The Christology of Matthew 1–2* (OBO 23; Göttingen: Vandenhoeck & Ruprecht, 1979), 114-240; Luz, *Matthew 1–7*, 108-9.

21. This viewpoint is further emphasized if the number fourteen in Matthew's scheme is indeed a *gematria* on the Hebrew name David, but is not dependent on it — in fact, quite the reverse. See R. T. Hood, "The Genealogies of Jesus," in *Early Christian Origins: FS H. R. Willoughby* (ed. Allen P. Wikgren; Chicago: Quadrangle, 1961), 10; Nolan, *Royal Son*, 59-60; D. A. Carson "Matthew," in *The Expositor's Bible Commentary* (ed. Frank G. Gaebelein; Grand Rapids: Zondervan, 1984), 8:69, and especially Davies and Allison, *Matthew*, 1:161-65.

In Gen 12:1-3 we note the following elements:

(1) A command to leave and the promise of a land (v. 1).
(2) A great nation and a blessing (v. 2a).
(3) A great name and a blessing (v. 2b).
(4) Vindication, protection and mediation (v. 3).

If we further bear in mind that in Gen. 1:1–2:3 the notion of blessing and rest is closely related to God's purpose for creation (see Gen. 1:28; 2:2-3; cf. 2 Sam. 7:28-29), then, despite the differences, the similarities between these two promises are striking indeed. In both the recipient is promised a great name and rest / blessing. In both a place and rest / blessing for Israel is secured, prospectively of course in the case of Abraham. In both the idea of establishment is present, with Abraham in terms of blessing for the nations; with David in terms of God's presence (the temple) and mediated rule (note the conjunction of God's House and David's house in 2 Sam. 7:13). The juxtaposition of the names υἱοῦ Δαυίδ and υἱοῦ Ἀβραάμ in Matt. 1:1 and the lineal relationship between Abraham and David which the summary statement in 1:17 underlines thus suggest that Matthew may well be stressing the relationship between these formative Old Testament promises. Furthermore, although there is clear evidence that Matthew agrees with both the Chronicler and the Deuteronomist in seeing Solomon's reign as the high point of the monarchy,[22] his preference for the title υἱοῦ Δαυίδ means that the first epoch, which extends from patriarchal promise to fulfillment in the Davidic kingdom, ends with David, not Solomon.[23]

---

22. Matt. 1:23; 12:42; 21:12-17; cf. 1 Kgs. 1–10; 2 Chr. 1–10. The key thing to note is that according to Exod. 29:46 the goal of the Exodus was that God should dwell in the midst of his people. According to both Kings and Chronicles, this goal was fulfilled during Solomon's reign when the glory of the Lord filled the temple in Jerusalem (1 Kgs. 8:10-20; 2 Chr. 5:11–6:11). Also note the role of "wisdom" in both form and substance throughout Matthew. Despite the greatness of Solomon, the end of his rule was marked by decline. Jesus, the Son of David, is not equated with Solomon but described as one greater than Solomon, whose wisdom astonished the crowd and silenced his opponents (e.g., Matt. 21:1–22:45).

23. The post-Christian haggadic passage in *Exod. Rab.* 15:26 (196-98; on Exod 12:2) divides the generations from Abraham to the exile into two equal parts according to the pattern of the phases of the moon. It sees Solomon as the high point of the first period, with fifteen generations from Abraham (who "began to shine") to Solomon (when "the disk of the moon was at its fullest"). "Henceforth the kings began to diminish in power" until "with Zedekiah, of whom it is written: 'Moreover, he put out Zedekiah's eyes' [Jer. 29:7], the light of the moon failed entirely" (quoted in Marshall D. Johnson, *The Purpose of the Biblical Genealogies: With Special Reference to the Setting of the Genealogies of Jesus* [2nd ed.; SNTSMS 8; London: Cambridge University Press, 1988], 197-98). If the author of this passage had chosen David and Jehoiachin as loci, we

The second epoch, while beginning with David, has its terminus in the exile. According to Wright,[24] this reference to the exile is "unexpected" in terms of parallel Jewish schemes, but is "crucial" for Matthew. As a whole, the epoch denotes a major reversal of the expectations created by the progression from Abraham to David. Despite God's promise to David, the post-Solomon history of the monarchy was largely a tale of woe until finally, at the time of Jehoiachin and the exile (1:11), the hope of blessing and rest was dashed in the wake of rebellion, division, decline and the ultimate loss of the Promised Land. Thus Matthew's choice of τῆς μετοικεσίας Βαβυλῶνος as the second pivotal point within his triadic structure of Israel's salvation history, while "unexpected" as far as genealogical schemes was concerned, does, as far as the expositional function of the genealogy goes, have a "crucial" role. By highlighting the significance of the exile to Babylon as a *crux historiae* in the story of the nation, Matthew raises questions about the ongoing validity of the promises to Abraham and David. In this way, though it brings the reader to the low point in the history of Israel, it also raises hopes, as far as story time is concerned, concerning the future path of that history.[25] Thus it creates the possibility of restoration from exile as a key aspect for the connection between the story of Jesus and the story of Israel and thus offers promise for a key point in the dialogue between the Matthean communities and their Jewish neighbors.

What is implicit within the first two epochs of Matthew's triadic schema is made explicit within the third epoch, which lasts ἀπὸ τῆς μετοικεσίας Βαβυλῶνος ἕως τοῦ Χριστοῦ. Nineham[26] has pointed out that the pivotal point of each epoch is that associated with ἕως, i.e., the terms Δαυίδ, τῆς μετοικεσίας Βαβυλῶνος and τοῦ Χριστοῦ respectively. I want to suggest that by locating the focal point of this third and final epoch in τοῦ Χριστοῦ, Matthew is stating that the problem of the exile and the consequent nonfulfillment of the promises to the patriarchs, to David, and thus to Israel, are only finally resolved with the coming of Jesus. The phrase μετὰ δὲ τὴν μετοικεσίαν Βαβυλῶνος in 1:12 makes it clear that Matthew is well aware of the historic return to the land under

---

would have had exactly Matthew's 14 generations from Abraham to David, and 14 generations from David to the exile. If Matthew was aware of such a scheme, his answer to the question "Who makes peace for Israel since then?" would be found at the end of the third group of 14 generations — "Jesus who is called the Christ."

24. N. T. Wright, *The New Testament and the People of God: Christian Origins and the Question of God*, vol. 1 (Minneapolis: Fortress, 1992), 385-86.

25. It is striking that in 2 Chr. 6 and 7, both Solomon's prayer at the dedication of the temple and the Lord's response include both the threat of exile and the hope of restoration.

26. D. E. Nineham, "The Genealogy in St Matthew's Gospel and Its Significance for the Study of the Gospel," *BJRL* 58 (1975-76): 421-44.

Zerubbabel. But the sheer obscurity of the names following Zerubbabel in the third table of the genealogy,[27] and the fact that in his summary statement Matthew juxtaposes the exile on the one hand with the coming of the Christ on the other, suggests that it is in the resolution of the problem of the exile that the nature of Jesus' Messiahship finds its first explication, whatever other connotations it may have. Thus in the concluding observations following their discussion of Matthew's genealogy, Davies and Allison note: "Jesus came 'at the right time.' Although the apocalypses of Judaism contain several different outlines of history, Dan. 9:24-27; *1 Enoch* 93:3-10; 91:12-17; and *2 Baruch* 67:1–74:4 are at one in placing the epoch of the exile immediately before the epoch of redemption. This is significant because Matt. 1:2-17 divides history into periods and places the appearance of Jesus at the end of the exilic era. . . .'"[28]

This is expressed even more clearly by Wright when he says: "The genealogy says to Matthew's careful reader that the long story of Abraham's people will come to its fulfillment, its seventh seven, with a new David who will rescue his people from their exile, that is 'save his people from their sins.'"[29] While I disagree with Wright's view that Matthew's intention was for his readers to think of seven sevens rather than as stated three fourteens,[30] I fully concur with his general point. Indeed, it is precisely here that Matthew's carefully crafted, triadic schema comes into its own, for as Nineham points out,

> Whatever the precise background or significance of the number symbolism here — and the question is a much disputed one — Matthew clearly attached great significance to it, and there can be little doubt what, in broad terms, that significance was. I can hardly improve on W. D. Davies'[31] state-

---

27. Johnson, *Purpose*, 179 refers to this third table as "unknown names" between Ζοροβαβέλ and Ἰωσήφ (cf. Davies and Allison, who refer to this list as "postmonarchical Davidids"). The title reflects Johnson's conclusion (1988:180) that although the "names in Matt 1:13-15 are found in the late writings of the OT while three of the ten were used among the Jews in Egypt during NT times. . . . The evidence does not appear to allow a definitive conclusion regarding the currency of the names in Palestine at the time of the writing of Matthew's gospel. Neither can we isolate any general characteristic of the names, although several were priests in the OT text. In short, the names remain Jewish, but otherwise unknown. . . ."

28. Davies and Allison, *Matthew*, 1:187.

29. Wright, *People*, 386.

30. The latter fits with Matthew's propensity to use triads and conveys the idea of symmetry and completion. Cf. Craig A. Evans, "Aspects of Exile and Restoration in the Proclamation of Jesus and the Gospels," in *Exile: Old Testament, Jewish and Christian Conceptions* (ed. J. M. Scott; Leiden: Brill, 1997), 326-27.

31. W. D. Davies, *The Setting of the Sermon on the Mount* (Cambridge: Cambridge University Press, 1964; repr. BJS 31; Atlanta: Scholars Press, 1989), 73. For similar conclusions see Johnson, *Genealogies*, 207-8; Luz, *Matthew 1–7*, 108; Donald A. Hagner, *Matthew 1–13* (Waco, Tex.:

ment of it: "The genealogy is an impressive witness to Matthew's conviction that the birth of Jesus was no unpremeditated accident but occurred in the fulness of time and in the providence of God, who overruled the generations to this end, to inaugurate in Jesus a new order, a time of fulfilment." As Matthew saw it, history was under the direct and detailed control of the divine providence, and in that providential scheme the call of Abraham, the accession of David and the Babylonian exile and the return were pivotal points of great significance. . . .[32]

The linking of Ἀβραάμ, Δαυίδ and τοῦ Χριστοῦ therefore implies that the ancient promise to the Patriarchs will be fulfilled (a key term for Matthew) *only via* the son of David, who is none other than Jesus the Christ. With the addition of the phrase τῆς μετοικεσίας Βαβυλῶνος, what Matthew does is to show that Jesus is the fulfillment of Israel's Messianic hopes precisely *because* he is the one who brings Israel's exile to an end by saving his people from their sins (1:21). It is in this way that Jesus therefore brings hope and rest to the "lost sheep of Israel" (cf. Matt. 10:6).

More must be said, however, for we note that the three epochs listed in 1:17 fall well within the temporal boundaries of Matthew's narrative world. These temporal boundaries range from *creation* (Matt. 25:34; cf. 13:35; 19:4; 24:21) to *consummation* (Matt. 28:20, cf. 24:44; 25:31)[33] neither of which is purely incidental to Matthew's story of Jesus. Thus the time of the consummation is a key component not only in setting the temporal bounds of the disciples' world-wide mission and of Jesus' presence, but also for the ultimate vindication of Jesus as "the Lord" (Matt. 22:44). Similarly, the time of creation, or the beginning (ἀπ' ἀρχῆς) as Matthew sometimes refers to it, is not merely the time at which the ideal pattern for the kingdom is displayed (19:4), but is also the time from which the gift of the kingdom is purposed (25:34). And each of these poles — *creation* and *consummation* — has connections with the first and last of the loci in Matt. 1:17. For the call of Abraham in Gen. 12:1-3 is set against the backdrop of Gen. 1–11 and in particular the loss of the kingdom ideal in the terrible exchange of *blessing* for *curse* and the consequent loss of that *rest in the presence of God* which was God's creation

---

Word, 1993), 7; W. B. Tatum, "The Origin of Jesus Messiah (Matt 1, 18a): Matthew's Use of Infancy Traditions," *JBL* 96 (1977): 528-29.

32. Nineham, *Genealogy*, 429.

33. Cf. Jack A. Kingsbury, *Matthew as Story* (2nd ed., rev. and enl.; Philadelphia: Fortress, 1988), 41. Howell, *Inclusive Story*, 97 states that "the easiest way to determine the temporal boundaries of Matthew's narrative world is to look at the earliest and the latest events referred to in the Gospel." Furthermore, the order within which events are mentioned highlights the importance of certain events for the author.

purpose for humanity (Gen. 2:1-4; cf. Gen. 4:13-14). And there is little doubt, given the aforementioned "international flavor" which Matthew consistently ascribes to Abraham, that it is precisely with this hope of "blessing for the nations" in mind that Matthew ends his gospel in the way he does. But this blessing is of course not independent of God's presence. Thus we find that Matthew ends (28:20) not only with the prospect of the inclusion of the nations, but with the promise of the ongoing presence, until "the end of the ages," of the one who, while both son of Abraham and son of David (1:1), is uniquely God with us (cf. 1:23).

Given this broad sweep of Matthew's concern, how are we to understand the clear emphasis on Abraham, David, exile, Christ, a period which, in terms of Matt. 1:17 at least, does seem to be particularly focused on "the time of Israel"? The answer is surely found in recognizing that both the man Abraham, and his descendants, Isaac, Jacob and "Judah and his brothers" (1:2), are mediators within the unfolding of salvation history of God's creation purposes. What was true for Israel, Abraham's descendants as a nation, becomes in the period of David's reign particularly focused in David and his son. But this mediation of *blessing for the nations* was placed under threat by the fact of the exile. Just as humankind had been excluded from the Garden of God's presence, so Israel was removed from the land. Israel, like Cain, became restless wanderers on the earth (cf. Gen. 4:12-14). Thus it is on reflection not unexpected that Matthew should mention the exile — indeed, given his point of view, it would have been unexpected had he not. Nor is it a surprise that during the course of the narrative we should find Jesus, who has been introduced from the outset as the son of Abraham and the son of David, claiming both a unique filial relationship with God the Father (11:27) and the sole right and ability to restore "rest" (11:28) to *all* who come to him. The precursor to this is Matthew's summary statement that what was promised to Abraham, centered on David, and lost in the exile is ultimately realized through Jesus the Messiah, the son of Abraham, the son of David. Thus Jesus, the son of David, is indeed the true son of Abraham in whom all the families of the earth will be blessed.

2. From the Days of John the Baptist until Now . . . (Matt. 11:1-18)

The offer of spiritual rest that Jesus holds out to all who will come to him (Matt. 11:25-28), and which we noted briefly above, occurs in the midst of a narrative section (Matt. 11:1–12:50) in which Jesus confronts both misunderstanding and apathy with respect to his mission on the one hand (11:1-24) and open, even deadly, hostility on the other (12:1-50). And the reason is not far to seek, for twice in this section Jesus characterizes the "generation" of his day not only as *cynical* (11:16-19), but as *wicked and adulterous* (12:39), designations which prepare the reader for what is to follow in the parable discourse in Matt. 13. Given such a setting, the prospects for the kingdom of heaven, which forms the heart of Jesus' preaching, seem to be very bleak indeed. Jesus' outburst of praise (11:25) and expectant invitation (11:28) therefore come as a great surprise. To what can they be ascribed? The answer comes in Matt. 11:25. Jesus knows that the success of his "preaching and teaching" (11:1) lies ultimately within God's control. It is God who reveals and God who conceals (11:25-26). All that Jesus can do is to go on preaching and urging those who have ears to hear (11:15). It is within this wider context of kingdom proclamation, misunderstanding and hostility that we encounter a second salvation-historical indicator, namely, that found in the notoriously difficult Matt. 11:11-15, particularly verses 12-13.

As may be expected, the passage has been the subject of intense debate[34] in which a number of key questions have been raised and to which the proposed answers appear to be legion.[35] For our present purposes, however, the following points should be noted:

(1) First, despite John's own lack of understanding about Jesus' person and mission (11:3), Jesus is careful to ascribe to John a position of major significance within salvation history.[36] According to Matt. 11:9-14, John's greatness derives from two realities.

---

34. See the discussion and bibliographies in Davies and Allison, *Matthew*, 2:233-65; Hagner, *Matthew 1–13*, 302-11); Ulrich Luz, *Matthew 8–20* (trans. J. E. Crouch; Minneapolis: Fortress, 2001), 129-76. I am particularly indebted to D. A. Carson, "Do the Prophets and the Law Quit Prophesying before John? A Note on Matthew 11:13," in C. A. Evans and R. W. Stegner, *The Gospels and the Scriptures of Israel* (JSNTSup 104; Sheffield: Sheffield Academic Press, 1994), 179-94. I would also like to acknowledge my colleague David Seccombe for his comments and bibliographical notes in an as-yet-unpublished article entitled "The Forceful Who Seize the Kingdom." Of particular interest is his reference to Jacob, who wrestled with God in pursuit of a blessing as the archetypal βιαστής *in bonam partem*.

35. Among others, there are questions regarding: the identity and intention of the βιασταί — are they *in malam partem* or *in bonam partem*? The kingdom of heaven — in what way can it be said to be βιάζεται? The temporal indicators ἀπό and ἕως — are they to be taken as inclusive or exclusive? Finally, of particular importance for our investigation, there is a question about ἄρτι and its particular salvation-historical significance.

36. The immediate context of the statement οὐκ ἐγήγερται ἐν γεννητοῖς γυναικῶν μείζων Ἰωάννου τοῦ βαπτιστοῦ suggests that Jesus may have only prophets in mind. But the broader context of Matthew's story of Jesus as the one who has come to save his people, together with Matthew's distinctive fulfillment theology, suggests that he is referring to the key figures within the history of God's dealing with Israel. Cf Luke 7:28, μείζων ἐν γεννητοῖς γυναικῶν. See Joel B. Green, *The Gospel of Luke* (Grand Rapids: Eerdmans, 1997), 299; see also Carson, "Prophets and the Law," 183; Hagner, *Matthew 1–13*, 306; Craig S. Keener, *A Commentary on the Gospel of Matthew* (Grand Rapids: Eerdmans, 1999), 337-39.

The first of these is the fact that John was *at least* a prophet (11:9), and thus a participant in the prophetic task ascribed to "the prophets and the law" (11:13). In this sense, John belonged to the age of preparation (κατασκευάζω — 11:10) rather than the age of fulfillment, a fact of which John was, by his own confession, well aware (cf. Matt. 3:11-14). Second, John was περισσότερον προφήτου (11:9), which in context refers to the fact that he was τὸν ἄγγελον (11:10), the Elijah-like figure[37] whose prophesied task was to prepare the way for the Coming One. This means that John's greatness was a derived greatness, dependent on the greatness and salvation-historical significance of the one whose forerunner he was.[38] But it also means that, whatever one's conclusion about the inclusive or exclusive function of ἀπό and ἕως respectively,[39] the important point to note from the phrases ἀπὸ δὲ τῶν ἡμερῶν Ἰωάννου τοῦ βαπτιστοῦ (11:12) and ἕως Ἰωάννου is that the ministry of John was a key turning point as far as the revelation and spread of the kingdom are concerned.[40] It is of course true that at the outset and taken at face value, John and Jesus appeared to have the same basic ministry of announcing the nearness of the kingdom and the appropriate response to that nearness (Matt. 3:2; cf. 4:17). But as Carson has pointed out, Jesus and John proclaim the nearness of the kingdom in very different "redactional settings," since "John the Baptist preaches the nearness of the kingdom in the context of being identified as the one who prepares the way for the Lord (3.3) . . . By contrast Jesus preaches repentance and announces the nearness of the kingdom (4.17) in the context of being identified as the one who ful-

---

37. Although both Luke and Mark imply that John the Baptist is *Elijah*, only Matthew makes this identification explicit (see Matt. 11:14; cf. 3:4), the argument of John A. T. Robinson, "Elijah, John and Jesus," *NTS* 4 (1958): 263-81; repr. in *Twelve New Testament Studies* (SBT 34; London: SCM, 1962), 28-52, notwithstanding.

38. The explicit identification of John as the "Elijah who was to come" serves to strengthen the idea of John's salvation-historical importance and, in conjunction with the composite quotation in Matt. 11:10, identifies precisely in what sense he is important. Cf. Robert H. Gundry, *Matthew: A Commentary on His Literary and Theological Art* (Grand Rapids: Eerdmans, 1982), 207-8; John P. Meier, "John the Baptist in Matthew's Gospel," *JBL* 99, no. 3 (1980): 383-405; Carson, "Matthew," 262; Davies and Allison, *Matthew*, 2:249; Keener, *Matthew*, 337-38; Luz, *Matthew 8–20*, 138.

39. For John's so-called inclusion within the kingdom age see, e.g., Walter Wink, *John the Baptist in the Gospel Tradition* (SNTSMS 7; Cambridge: Cambridge University Press, 1968), 33-35; Eduard Schweizer, *The Good News according to Matthew* (trans. David E. Green; London: SPCK, 1976), 259; Gundry, *Matthew*, 209; Hagner, *Matthew 1–13*, 306; Davies and Allison, *Matthew*, 2:253; for exclusion see *inter alia* R. T. France, *The Gospel according to Matthew: An Introduction and Commentary* (TNTC; Leicester: InterVarsity Press, 1985), 194 and esp. Carson, "Prophets and Law," 179-94.

40. See Schweizer, *Matthew*, 263; Hagner, *Matthew 1–13*, 306; Keener, *Matthew*, 338, esp. n. 13.

fills Isaiah 9 by the onset of his ministry in Galilee."[41] It is this transition from prophecy and preparation to fulfillment which marks the "days of John" as significant in salvation-historical terms.

(2) Second, we note that ὁ μικρότερος ἐν τῇ βασιλείᾳ who is described as being "greater than John" should be identified as the disciple who proclaims God's kingdom now present in the person and work of Jesus, rather than its members per se.[42] Although the discourse of Matt. 10 has given way to a narrative section as signaled by Matthew's customary summary statement (11:1; cf., e.g., 7:28-29; 13:53; 19:1), the preceding account of the sending out of the twelve and Jesus' teaching about the mixed reception which his emissaries were to expect still provides the interpretive background against which Jesus' words in 11:11 are to be understood. Though the giving of a cup of water to ἕνα τῶν μικρῶν τούτων is linked to their identity as disciples (10:42), it is also compared with the receiving of both a prophet and a righteous man (i.e., a true prophet), as well as being set in the context of the mission of the disciples to the lost sheep of Israel (10:6). One must not overlook the fact that the disciples are only in need of hospitality, food and water because they are traveling emissaries. Furthermore, we note that the truth that Jesus is indeed the coming one (11:3) and the Son of Man (11:19) has been revealed by the Father to the νήπιοι, which in context must be the disciples themselves. This suggests that the "little ones" of 10:42, the "least in the kingdom" and the "babes" (11:25), are, in fact, the same group, namely, the disciples as missionaries. They are "least in the kingdom" because, as disciples, they have humbled themselves like little children and accepted what the Father has revealed (11:25; cf. 18:1-4); they are greater than John because, having been sent and empowered by Jesus (10:5-8), they proclaim the kingdom as present rather than merely promised! Furthermore, although in the strict sense these little ones who are least in the kingdom have the scope of their ministry restricted to "the lost sheep of Israel" (10:5-6), the proleptic statement in 10:18 and the explicit command in 28:19-20 make it clear that they will in time be greater than John in that there proclamation of the kingdom will extend to the ends of the earth.

(3) Third, we note that the identity of ὁ μικρότερος ἐν τῇ βασιλείᾳ and the missionaries of Matt. 10 casts light on the interpretation of the exceedingly difficult clause ἡ βασιλεία τῶν οὐρανῶν βιάζεται καὶ βιασταὶ ἁρπάζουσιν αὐτήν (11:12). From the beginning of Jesus' ministry in the days of John the Baptist,

---

41. Carson, "Prophets and Law," 184.
42. See Meier, *Vision*, 76; Herman N. Ridderbos, *Matthew* (trans. R. Togtman; Grand Rapids: Zondervan, 1987), 215-16; cf. Carson, "Matthew," 264-65; idem, "Law and the Prophets," 184-86; Keener, *Matthew*, 339.

through the mission to the "lost sheep" and right up to the time within the narrative when Jesus speaks about John to the crowd,[43] the "kingdom of heaven" manifested in the words and works of Jesus and the words of his emissaries has gone forward in triumph (βιάζεται). I thus take βιάζεται as middle, not passive voice,[44] *in bonam partem*, and thus as equivalent in sense to Luke's εὐαγγελίζεται (Luke 16:16). But what are we to make of the next clause? The difficulty arises because each of the two renderings of the clause which I would deem possible in the context is consistent with what Matthew says elsewhere about the kingdom.

Consider *first* the proposal that the construction ἡ βασιλεία τῶν οὐρανῶν βιάζεται καὶ βιασταὶ ἁρπάζουσιν αὐτήν is in fact an "antithetic parallelism" containing a "form of antanclasis (a figure of speech in which the same word is repeated in a different or even contradictory sense), based in this instance not on exactly the same word but on a cognate."[45] In this construction βιάζεται is taken as a middle deponent (as above) and in a positive sense of the forceful advance of the kingdom, but the latter βιασταὶ ἁρπάζουσιν αὐτήν as "conative present tense" with their "normal evil connotations."[46] The kingdom thus advances, but it does so in the context of opposition. This proposal does seem to fit the context, which has in view, not only those who are apathetic to the kingdom present in the words and works of Jesus (11:16-19), but also the Pharisees who are hostile.[47] It also provides an apt answer to John the Baptist's question about the seemingly *ambiguous* nature of the kingdom's presence in Jesus (see below). One possible weak point is that the sense of ἁρπάζουσιν seems to be changed to "opposition" if the kingdom itself is in view and only maintains its meaning of "violent attack" if its object is the "messengers of the kingdom" like the little ones who are Jesus' emissaries (10:16) or Jesus himself (cf. 12:14). Mat-

---

43. I thus take ἕως ἄρτι to be a reference to the "time of Jesus" rather than that of the evangelist. See further below; cf. Howell, *Inclusive Story*, 73.

44. *Contra, inter alia*, W. F. Albright and C. S. Mann, *Matthew: A New Translation with Introduction and Commentary* (New York: Doubleday, 1971), 137-38; France, *Matthew: Evangelist*, 197; Davies and Allison, *Matthew*, 2:256; Hagner, *Matthew 1–13*, 306-7; cf. Carson, "Prophets and the Law," 187; Luz, *Matthew 8–20*, 140-42.

45. Carson, "Matthew," 267; idem, "Prophets and the Law," 187.

46. Carson, *Matthew*, 266-67 points out that the noun βιαστής is "rare in Greek literature (here only in NT), but where it occurs it always has the negative connotations of violence and rapacity," while ἁρπάζουσιν, although fairly common, "almost always has the same evil connotations (a rare exception is Acts 8:39)." This is, in his opinion, conclusive evidence that the second half of the clause should be taken *in malem partem* and the entire clause as antithetical.

47. What is striking is that if this is the sense of βιασται ἁρπάζουσιν αὐτήν, then Jesus, by referring to both the apathetic and the violent opponents as τὴν γενεὰν ταύτην (11:16; 12:45; cf. 12:39 and 23:36), includes both of them as the βιασταί in *malem partem*. Thus by the end of the gospel *both* the crowds *and* the officials are crying out for Jesus' crucifixion.

thew's αὐτήν, which clearly refers to the kingdom, will have to be interpreted as "the kingdom as represented in its messengers so that to attack the latter is to attack the former." However, such a view is by no means impossible and has a number of strengths.

Consider, *second,* the alternative view that Matthew's βιασταί are his equivalent of Luke's πᾶς who βιάζεται into (εἰς) the kingdom. The use of εἰς suggests a positive meaning for βιάζεται in Luke,[48] and, according to this view, Matthew's clause βιασταὶ ἁρπάζουσιν αὐτήν should then be taken *in bonam partem,* rather than that suggested by Carson. But a question remains as to why Luke should use βιάζεται to describe entry into the kingdom. Why should anyone need to "force their way into the kingdom" or, in Matthew's case, why should those entering the kingdom be termed βιασταί *in bonam partem* and their mode of entry as ἁρπάζουσιν αὐτήν?

David Seccombe in an unpublished article[49] has argued that part of the answer lies in an allusion to the figure of Jacob, who is the *archetypal* βιαστής, the one who wrestled with God and prevailed to receive a blessing and the name Israel (cf. Gen. 32:22-30). But while the significance of Jacob would have been great both for Jesus (cf. John 1:47-51) and within Judaism, it is difficult to see the point of such an allusion at this juncture in Matthew's gospel. Furthermore, Matt. 11:25 speaks of God revealing "these things" to little children and 13:11 of the "secrets of the kingdom" being *given,* so that the idea of Jacob's wresting something from God is against the context. It is more likely that the entire clause ἡ βασιλεία τῶν οὐρανῶν βιάζεται καὶ βιασταὶ ἁρπάζουσιν αὐτήν was found in Q and that Matthew, whose purpose and context were different from Luke's, quoted the whole in the sense set out in (1) above. Luke, however, conscious of the βιασταί as violent attackers of those who evangelize the kingdom and thus opponents of those who enter, especially the religious outcasts, depicts the entry of the latter into the kingdom as βιάζεται, because it is the βιασταί that they must overcome. This suggests that the view outlined in (1) above — that the progress of the kingdom takes place within a hostile world and that those who would enter it must do so against opposition — better provides the sense of Matt. 11:12-13.

(4) Fourth, we return briefly to the question of John the Baptist's own misunderstanding of Jesus' ministry. At one level, the misunderstanding is itself quite understandable for John has proclaimed in the person and work of Jesus the coming of the kingdom, the time of *fulfillment* which both he and the entire witness of the "prophets and the law" prophesied. According to John's preaching, this time of fulfillment was to mean both *salvation* and *judgment* (3:12). But

---

48. See inter alia the discussion in Marshall, *Luke,* 628-37.
49. David P. Siccombe, "the Forceful Who Seize the Kingdom" (Cape Town, 2001).

until that time of Jesus' pronouncement (the ἕως ἄρτι in 11:12), although salvation was evident in the pressing forward of the kingdom in the words and works of Jesus, judgment seemed strangely absent — the opponents of the kingdom, the βιασταί, seemed to hold sway. Jesus' answer to John (11:4-6), which, as has frequently been pointed out,[50] excludes the note of judgment which is in fact present in the scriptural texts which Jesus quotes, is both rebuke and warning. John, like Jesus' other hearers, must come to understand the course of salvation history, which is *salvation now, judgment later*, and not stumble over Jesus' agenda.[51] To be scandalized by Jesus' agenda, far from being one of the poor (11:5) who are μακάριος and to whom the kingdom belongs (cf. Matt. 5:3), is in reality to become like the βιασταί who until that time (ἕως ἄρτι) were permitted to oppose the kingdom present in Jesus (11:12).

(5) Fifth, we note that the term ἄρτι in v. 11 coincides with "story NOW," the time of Jesus' own speaking to the crowds rather than the "NOW" of the narrator, i.e., Matthew's time.[52] But we also note that within Matthew's narrative, this *time of Jesus* is itself nuanced by a distinctive temporal and thematic development. It is within the gradual unfolding of Matthew's plot,[53] rather than as formal structural markers[54] marking out a self-conscious literary division of the work, that temporal indicators like the fivefold καὶ ἐγένετο ὅτε ἐτέλεσεν ὁ Ἰησοῦς (Matt. 7:28; 11:1; 13:53; 19:1; 26:1) and the twofold formula Ἀπὸ τότε ἤρχατο ὁ Ἰησοῦς (Matt. 4:17; 16:21) play an important role. Thus by noting

---

50. See, *inter alia*, Gundry, *Matthew*, 206; Carson, "Matthew," 262; Davies and Allison, *Matthew*, 2:244-46; Leon Morris, *The Gospel according to Matthew* (Grand Rapids: Eerdmans, 1992), 275; Hagner, *Matthew 1-13*, 301; Keener, *Matthew*, 335.

51. John's question to Jesus ironically contains the answer. He inquires whether Jesus is indeed the "coming one" (ὁ ἐρχόμενος) or whether he and others must "wait" (προσδοκῶμεν) for another. Hagner, *Matthew 1-13*, 301, points out that the verb προσδοκάω occurs only here and in Matt. 24:50 "in reference to the future parousia of Jesus." For the reader who is aware of Jesus' words in 24:50, the answer to John's question is in retrospect clear. John like others must "wait," not for another one, but for another coming of the one who "until now" allows the βιασταί to continue, but will not do so forever.

52. Howell, *Inclusive Story*, 73; cf. Seymour Chatman, *Story and Discourse: Narrative Structure in Fiction and Film* (London: Cornell University Press, 1978), 63.

53. On the Plot of Matthew's Gospel see Frank J. Matera, "The Plot of Matthew's Gospel," *CBQ* 49 (1987): 233-53; Mark A. Powell, "The Plot and Subplots of Matthew's Gospel," *NTS* 38 (1992): 187-204; Mervyn Eloff, "From the Exile to the Christ: Exile, Restoration and the Interpretation of Matthew's Gospel" (D.Th. diss., University of Stellenbosch, 2002), 4.1–4.52. Cf. Stanton, *Gospel for a New People*, 54-59.

54. *Contra* Edgar Krentz, "The Extent of Matthew's Prologue: Toward a Structure of the First Gospel," *JBL* 83 (1964): 409-14; Kingsbury, *Matthew: Structure*, 7-25. Cf. H. J. B. Combrink, "The Structure of the Gospel of Matthew as Narrative," *TynBul* 34 (1983): 61-59; France, *Matthew: Evangelist*, 141-45; Luz, *Matthew 1-7*, 33-44; Hagner, *Matthew 1-13*, l-liii.

these alongside other narrative rhetorical devices, we recognize that the "advance of the kingdom" (11:12) during the life of Jesus has its own discreet phases and stages such as the limitations placed by Jesus on his own mission (15:24) and that of his disciples (10:6), as well as its own manifestations of *advance* and *opposition* which are likewise experienced both by Jesus' emissaries and by Jesus himself. Such temporal and geographical boundedness (Strecker's so-called historicizing) should not be taken as artificially imposed upon the narrative by Matthew or as inconsistent with what follows later, but rather as necessary stages in the kingdom's advance throughout the lifetime of Jesus, culminating in his death and resurrection. And these events in turn become, as we shall see, the basis of a new beginning and new stage for the advance of the kingdom, one marked by the real, if not corporate, presence of the risen Jesus (see below) and the very real removal of geographical, national or temporal restrictions. Of particular importance here is the fact that as far as Old Testament expectations of the kingdom of God were concerned, the advance of that kingdom to the very ends of the earth was contingent upon the problem of Israel's exile first being resolved. Thus the apparent contradiction between the nationalism of Matt. 10:6 and universalism of Matt. 28:16-20 can be understood as Matthew's expression of what appears to have been a clear understanding of the course of salvation history within the primitive church — salvation is not only "from the Jews" but "for the Jew first, and then for the Gentile" (cf. John 4:22; Rom. 1:16).

To summarize our findings thus far, I take Matt. 11:1-18 to be teaching that it is Jesus, and not John the Baptist, who is the pivotal point in the history of salvation. With the advent of the Baptist, a key stage in the time of preparation had been reached and for that reason he was indeed the most significant figure in that period. But it is with the advent of Jesus during the days of John the forerunner that the time of the kingdom was actually inaugurated.[55] With the coming of Jesus, the time of prophecy gave way to the time of fulfillment, a fulfillment which can be understood in "end of exile" terms. But the nature of this "time of the kingdom" as a time of fulfillment must itself not be misunderstood. It is the time of the advance of the kingdom, but it is also a time during which this advance will be ignored and opposed. Jesus has come to end Israel's exile and to open the way for God's kingdom centered in Jesus to be established and to advance to the ends of the earth. But the reality of these events remains hidden except for the remnant, the "little children" to whom God reveals these things (Matt. 11:25). The full extent of the restoration that Jesus brings for both Jew and Gentile lies in the future.

---

55. I take the formal beginning of Jesus' ministry to be not his public proclamation, but his baptism by John, in which he is publicly anointed by a prophet as the Son of God, Israel's king.

3. From Now until . . . (Matt. 23:39; 24:21)

As we have noted above, the words of Jesus in Matt. 11:12-13 identify two periods within Matthew's portrayal of salvation history. The first of these is the period when "all the prophets and the law prophesy" (11:13). This period lasts, in salvation-historical terms, "until John," who is the most significant character of this period, for it is during his time that "the coming one," i.e., Jesus, actually arrives. The second period is of the "advance of the kingdom," a period initiated by the arrival of Jesus "in the days of John" and lasting, as far as Matt. 11 is concerned, until "now," i.e., the *story now* coincidental with Jesus' words, the "time of Jesus." This period of "kingdom advance" (ἡ βασιλεία τῶν οὐρανῶν βιάζεται) is also a time of opposition and raises questions about the extent to which Jesus ushers in the kingdom of God during his own day. Put in terms of the idea of "restoration from exile," the question remains as to the extent to which the exile is ended and the kingdom of God is established in Jesus. Two key passages in Matthew provide an answer to this question, and it is to these that we now turn in a third and final look at Matthew's use of the couplet ἀπό . . . ἕως as a salvation-historical indicator.

(1) Matthew 23:39 forms the conclusion of a series of denunciations (lit. woes — οὐαί) pronounced by Jesus concerning the teachers of the Law and the Pharisees. N. T. Wright[56] sees these "woes" as the chiastic antithesis of the beatitudes in Matt. 5:3-10, and as related to the series of "blessings" and "curses" in Deut. 27 and 28, thus arguing that Matthew uses his fivefold discourse structure to recall the Pentateuch as *covenant*. However, given Matthew's earlier use of the book of Isaiah,[57] it is preferable to take these woes as an allusion to the language of Isaiah,[58] and, in conjunction with the phrase "this (evil) generation" (Matt. 11:16; 12:45; 23:35),[59] as indicative of the fact that, for Matthew, the nation of Jesus' day, as represented by the religious leaders, was in reality just like the nation described in Isaiah 1–39, a nation under judgment[60] and the threat of ex-

---

56. Wright, *New Testament and the People of God*, 387-88; cf. the observation by Davies and Allison, *Matthew*, 3:285.

57. Matt. 1:22/Isa. 7:14; Matt. 3:3/Isa. 40:3; Matt. 4:14-16/Isa. 9:1-2; Matt. 8:17/Isa. 53:4; Matt. 12:17-21/Isa. 42:1-4; Matt. 13:14-15/Isa. 6:9-10; Matt. 15:8-9/Isa. 29:13; Matt. 21:13/Isa. 56:7.

58. See Keener, *Matthew*, 546-47.

59. *Contra* Davies and Allison, 3:319; cf. Gundry, *Matthew*, 472.

60. See the discussion of οὐαί in David E. Garland, *The Intention of Matthew 23* (NTS 52; Leiden: Brill, 1979), 64-90, especially his observation on p. 87 that in Matt. 23, οὐαί "connotes a powerful and denunciatory judgement akin to a curse." Cf. Ernst Haenchen, "Matthäus 23," *ZTK* 48 (1951): 46; Ulrich Luz, *Das Evangelium nach Mattäus (Mt 18–25)* (Düsseldorf: Benziger; Neukirchen-Vluyn: Neukirchener, 1997), 320-21.

ile because of spiritual obduracy and refusal to hear the word of the Lord. This same threat is echoed in Jesus' plaintive lament over Jerusalem[61] which, in keeping with its long history of rejecting and murdering those whom God had sent to it (Matt. 23:37), had rejected Jesus and would soon become the site of his death also. Uttered within the "temple courts" (Matt. 21:23; cf. 24:1), Jesus' words are stark and echo those of the prophets concerning Jerusalem and its temple — ἀφίεται ὑμῖν ὁ οἶκος ὑμῶν ἔρημος.[62] The parallels between Jesus' words and Isa. 64:10-11 (64:9-10 LXX) are striking indeed. Because of the rejection of God's continually outstretched hands by an obstinate people (cf. Isa. 65:2), the Lord had abandoned his people. The consequence was that "... the sacred cities have become a desert, even Zion is a desert, Jerusalem a desolation ... ," while the "holy and glorious temple" where the fathers had praised "lies in ruins" (Isa. 64:10-11 NIV). But even more striking is Matthew's placement of these words immediately prior to Jesus' departure from the temple (24:1) and his prediction of the temple's destruction. The desolation of the temple by the Babylonians had been preceded by the graphic departure of the *Shekinah* (cf. Ezek 10:1-22). But for Matthew, the "presence of God" has been identified with the presence of Jesus (Matt. 1:23).[63] Thus, from his point of view, and within the context of the narrative as a whole, it is quite appropriate to use a clause as strong as ἀφίεται ὑμῖν ὁ οἶκος ὑμῶν ἔρημος to describe Jesus' *final* departure from the temple.

That this final departure, prompted by the rejection of Jesus, is indeed in view is further substantiated by the words οὐ μή με ἴδητε ἀπ' ἄρτι in Matt. 23:39. I take ἀπ' ἄρτι once again as a reference to story time, i.e., Jesus' present time, not that of the evangelist,[64] but the phrase οὐ μή με ἴδητε implies the absence of Jesus, at least in corporal terms. Thus what is in view is a time be-

---

61. Cf Meier, *Vision*, 166; Garland, *Intention*, 197-204.

62. Davies and Allison, *Matthew*, 3:322 point to the debate regarding whether "your house" in Matt. 23:38 refers to the temple, Jerusalem itself or "the house of Israel." The Matthean context suggests the temple itself, but we should note their point that "... Jewish texts — such as Ezra and 2 Baruch — do not always distinguish between the temple and the capital. Quite often the one implies the other and there are indiscriminate transitions from temple to city and *vice versa* so that one may often speak of their identification." Cf. Garland, *Intention*, 198-200.

63. See, *inter alia*, David D. Kupp, *Matthew's Emmanuel: Divine Presence and God's People in the First Gospel* (SNTSMS 90; Cambridge: Cambridge University Press, 1996), 157-200; Strecker, *Weg*, 213; Garland, *Intention*, 203; Gundry, *Matthew*, 24-25; France, *Matthew*, 79-80; Morris, *Matthew*, 31; Keener, *Matthew*, 455. Contra Kingsbury, *Matthew: Structure*, 69-70.

64. Garland, *Intention*, 205-6, describes the phrase ἀπ' ἄρτι as "peculiar to Matthew's eschatology," added by Matthew to "heighten the saying's predication of a new eschatological situation." Cf. Meier, *Vision*, 166, n. 182. Taking the phrase as a reference to the time of Jesus does not, however, negate its eschatological import.

yond Jesus' impending death and, in the light of 26:29 (see below), probably beyond his subsequent resurrection. Davies and Allison take the statement "you will not see" as a reference to the resurrection of Jesus and as the "antithesis of the parousia," while Meier relates it more generally to "the time of the passion onward."[65] That Jesus was not seen after the resurrection by those designated as "Jerusalem" in 23:39 is quite true, but this is not the case for the disciples who *do see* Jesus after the resurrection, and who are nevertheless included within the audience (cf. Matt. 23:1), albeit on its fringes by the time we get to 23:37-39. It is thus better to take the phrase οὐ μή με ἴδητε as a proleptic reference to the *ascension* of Jesus, which, though not described in either Matthew or Mark, is alluded to in Matt. 24:30, 45-47; 25:14-19, in the reference in 26:29 to Jesus "not drinking of the fruit of the vine" with his disciples ἀπ' ἄρτι until the consummation of the kingdom and the renewal of all things (see below) and implied in the echo of Dan. 7:14 in the words of Jesus in Matt. 28:18.

But what are we to make of ἕως ἂν εἴπητε? The statement εὐλογημένος ὁ ἐρχόμενος ἐν ὀνόματι κυρίου is a quotation from Ps. 118, a psalm that Matthew has already applied to Jesus as the "rejected cornerstone" which will become a cause of destruction on the one hand, and yet the center of something new in God's kingdom on the other (Matt. 21:42-43). And it echoes the words spoken by the crowds and the disciples who accompanied Jesus at the time of the triumphal entry (cf. Matt. 21:9), though, significantly, Matthew distances the city of Jerusalem from this acclaim (21:10). In Ps. 118, the words are spoken in the context of a celebration of the Lord's unfailing love (vv. 1-4, 29) by those who have been rescued from their enemies on God's day of salvation (v. 24) by One who comes in the name of the Lord and who is praised from within the temple. In Matthew they are set in the context of One who has come to save his people from their sins (1:21) approaching first Jerusalem (21:9) and then the temple (21:12, 23) but receiving, not the praise and acclaim of the city and its leaders, but their rejection. In consequence the rejected King will depart and go to his death, thus achieving, ironically, the salvation of "his people." But the city for its part will not see him again and will not only remain "unsaved," but will face what would seem to be an even worse fate than their current condition (cf. Matt. 24:1-51).

According to the words of Jesus in Matt. 23:29, the scenario sketched above is, however, not the end of the story. For the "absence of Jesus" will be only until the words which the city failed to apply to Jesus' *first* appearance are in fact applied to him at his *return*. And it is here that there is some dispute about the

---

65. Davies and Allison, *Matthew*, 3:323; Meier, *Vision*, 166.

sense of Jesus' words.⁶⁶ Are we to take Jesus' εὐλογημένος ὁ ἐρχόμενος ἐν ὀνόματι κυρίου to be the begrudging acknowledgment of a defeated opponent or the glad welcome of one who has come to share in salvation? The context of Ps. 118 and its reference to "unfailing love" implies the latter, but what about Matthew's application of these words in the context of Jerusalem's rejection of Jesus and the impending destruction of the temple? Davies and Allison are worth quoting. Referring to the disputed sense of the words, they point out that "the text means not that when the Messiah comes, his people will bless him, but rather, when his people bless him, the Messiah will come."⁶⁷ This means that although the rejection of Jesus, God's chosen stone, has serious consequences for Israel and its position of privilege within salvation history (Matt. 21:43; cf. Matt. 8:11, 12), these consequences do not preclude hope for those within Israel who in the time of Jesus' physical absence are willing to acknowledge that Jesus is indeed God's chosen cornerstone, the locus of God's blessing and rest. Thus although the command to disciple all nations marks a universalization of a previously restricted mission, it does not imply the abandonment of the mission to the "lost sheep of Israel" or its ultimate failure. Whether we concur with this view or not, what is clear from the above discussion is that Matt. 23:29 designates a third period within Matthew's schema of salvation history, a period which lasts from the ascension of Jesus until his return, a period which, according to Matt. 24 and 25, will also be a time of the kingdom's advance and opposition just as the time of Jesus had been, with the notable exception that the nature of Jesus' presence with his *church militant* will be quite different from what it had been.

(2) A similar perspective emerges from Matthew's use of ἀπό . . . ἕως in Matt. 26:29. This statement by Jesus comes in the context of betrayal and imminent death and looks forward to the period of the consummation of the kingdom of God. Jesus claims that he will once again drink "the fruit of the vine," but that such drinking anew with his disciples (αὐτὸ πίνω μεθ' ὑμῶν καινόν) will be delayed from now (ἀπ' ἄρτι) until *that day* (ἕως τῆς ἡμέρας ἐκείνης). Once again the negative οὐ μὴ πίνω implies *physical absence* so that, although ἄρτι does refer to the story time of Jesus' words, it does look beyond the time of Jesus' physical presence with his disciples.⁶⁸ There are close similarities between Matthew and

---

66. See the discussion and bibliographies in, *inter alia*, Davies and Allison, *Matthew*, 3:323-25; Donald A. Hagner, *Matthew 14–28* (Waco, Tex.: Word, 1995), 678-810 and Carson, "Matthew," 486-88.

67. Davies and Allison, *Matthew*, 3:323; cf. Gundry, *Matthew*, 474, *contra* Garland, *Intention*, 206-7.

68. Indeed, it is the reality of this *impending physical absence* which no doubt required Jesus to underline in Matt. 28:20 that, in the light of his new position of authority, his absence from his disciples would not be absolute but rather only physical.

Mark, although Matthew has his characteristic ἀπ' ἄρτι for Mark's οὐκέτι, τοῦ πατρός μου for Mark's θεοῦ and adds the phrase μεθ' ὑμῶν, a phrase which in 18:20 and 28:20 refers to Jesus' immanence with his disciples, but here in fact points forward to a future presence "on that day." The phrase ἕως τῆς ἡμέρας ἐκείνης is shared by Matthew and Mark (Luke simply has ἕως οὗ ἡ βασιλεία τοῦ θεοῦ ἔλθῃ) and is eschatological in tone. This is clear both from Matthew's use of ἕως τῆς ἡμέρας ἐκείνης elsewhere in his gospel[69] and from the notion of *newness* (καινότης), which I take to be commensurate with the implied newness of the covenant (Matt. 26:28; cf. 5:1–7:29 where Jesus adopts the role of the *royal teacher of the New Covenant*)[70] and the new age of the kingdom, celebrated by eating and drinking in the very presence of God the Father. What Jesus has in mind, then, is the time of the consummation, the time for which he taught his disciples to pray, saying: "Our Father in heaven, hallowed be your name, your kingdom come, your will be done on earth as it is in heaven" (Matt. 6:9-10 NIV).

What is important, then, for our purposes is that both Matt. 23:39 and 26:29 describe the same period, a period lasting *from now* (ἀπ' ἄρτι), which, though it at first glance indicates the time of Jesus' physical presence with his disciples, in fact refers, in the light of the negatives "not see" and "not drink," to the time of his physical departure from them, *until that day* (ἕως τῆς ἡμέρας ἐκείνης), the time of the parousia and the consummation of the kingdom.

Conclusion

Our brief survey of Matthew's use of the temporal expression ἀπό . . . ἕως has led us to identify two schemas of salvation history within Matthew's gospel. The first of these, which is found within the genealogy and summarized as "from Abraham to David, from David to the exile, from the exile to the Christ," provides a *historical-theological backdrop* against which Matthew's story of Jesus is to be read and understood. It places the entire story of Jesus from birth through life, focused in word and deed, to death and resurrection within the context of a bigger story — the story of God's dealings with the human race via Abraham and his descendants, the nation of Israel, most notably the royal line of Judah from whom is descended Jesus, the son of David, the Messiah.

The second schema of salvation history which the reader, alerted to Mat-

---

69. Despite the argument of Kingsbury, *Matthew: Structure*, 28-31, the plural phrase ἐν ἐκείναις ταῖς ἡμέραις often simply means "at that time." But the same is not true for the singular which is used in Matthew as an equivalent for "on the day of judgment." See Matt. 7:21-23; cf. 11:24; 24:36 as opposed to 24:19, 22, 38 (*contra* Davies and Allison, *Matthew*, 1:714).

70. See further Eloff, "From the Exile to the Christ," 5.26–5.32.

thew's historical-theological periodizations and his use of ἀπό . . . ἕως, picks up during the course of reading is the threefold division of salvation history into (1) the period of prophecy, "all the prophets and the law" up till and including the preaching of John the Baptist; (2) the period of the kingdom's advance and conflict from the advent of Jesus in the "days of John" until "now" i.e., the now of Jesus' own story time, what was referred to in more traditional salvation-historical schemas as "the time of Jesus"; (3) the period from the "now" of Jesus' story time, but particularly the end of that time in his departure, until the consummation of the kingdom at the parousia of Jesus.

It is in particular during the latter two periods of salvation history that Matthew's story of Jesus and the coming of the "kingdom of the heavens" unfolds. But it does so against the backdrop of the first period — the *time of prophecy* — a time which in the light of Matt. 1:17 must be seen with particular reference to the promises to Abraham and David, promises which the exile has all but destroyed but which with the coming of Jesus the Messiah are being brought to fulfillment. Nor should the latter two periods, despite their distinction as far as the nature of Jesus' presence, be seen as fundamentally distinct, for they are both part of the *"time of the kingdom,"* a time of the advance of the kingdom in the midst of opposition to it.

Significant within both of these schemas, although largely neglected within the scholarly literature, is the notion of exile and restoration. It is, as we have already noted, explicit in Matt. 1:17. But it occurs again in the other texts — both in terms of the figure of John the Baptist and his role as the voice of Isa. 40 and the Messenger of Mal. 3, and primarily in relation to Jesus as the one who ushers in the time of the kingdom, for talk of the kingdom and the coming of the kingdom did not take place within a vacuum but against the backdrop of an intense eschatological longing that God would finally bring about what the prophets had promised. But the reality of Jesus' rejection by Israel puts an interesting "spin" on the notions of exile and restoration. Matthew presents Jesus as the one who really did usher in the time of the fulfillment of "all that the prophets and the law prophesied." Put in other words, he brought an end to the exile for those who come to him, become his disciples and thus find rest for their souls (cf. Matt. 11:28-30). This restoration opens the door for the worldwide spread of the kingdom, so that, at the consummation of the kingdom, those who share in the kingdom may indeed include people from east and west (cf. Matt. 8:11). But it also implies that those who reject Jesus and the rest he offers must necessarily remain "in exile" — a reality graphically portrayed by Jesus' prediction of another destruction of the temple. And if their rejection of Jesus remains to the end, then it implies a final exile from the kingdom of God, an exile from which there is no return (Matt. 8:12; cf. Isa. 66:24).

Matthew and Jerusalem

R. T. France

Peter Walker's valuable study *Jesus and the Holy City*[1] has highlighted the significance of Jerusalem as a theological issue in early Christian thought and self-understanding. For the Jewish writers of the NT it could hardly be otherwise. It was, in their inherited language, "the holy city" (Matt. 4:5; 27:53), "the city of the great King" (Matt. 5:35). The city, and especially its temple, had been the focus of their national and religious experience and aspirations for a millennium. Yet this was the city where their Messiah had been convicted and executed, at the initiative of its highest authorities. And before that happened, Jesus had wept over the city's failure to respond to his message and had predicted the complete destruction of its temple, to be replaced by "something greater" (Matt. 12:6). So what now was the status of the Jewish capital for those Jews who had decided to follow Jesus? It might be possible for Gentile Christians to shrug off the historical and religious significance of Jerusalem (though it is interesting that one of the most positive accounts of Jerusalem in the NT comes from the Gentile writer Luke), but what about Jewish Christians?

Among those Jewish Christians[2] the evangelist Matthew provides a particularly interesting case-study on this theme. Interpreters regularly note the uncomfortable tension found in his gospel between a strongly Jewish ideology and a substantial body of condemnatory material relating to the Jewish people, especially their leaders, and to the future of their capital and its temple. That so essentially Jewish a writer should be open to the accusation of fostering anti-Jewish prejudice[3] reveals the painful dilemma of its author, for whom Jesus was

---

1. P. W. L. Walker, *Jesus and the Holy City: New Testament Perspectives on Jerusalem* (Grand Rapids: Eerdmans, 1996).

2. See R. T. France, *Matthew: Evangelist and Teacher* (Exeter: Paternoster, 1989), 102-8, against the once popular view that the ultimate author of the First Gospel was a Gentile.

3. For an early discussion of this issue, which has subsequently become central to

the complete fulfillment of the heritage of Israel and yet had been emphatically rejected by Israel's established leadership, and continued to be so rejected by the majority of Jews in Matthew's own day. Matthew speaks of an anti-Christian propaganda campaign among Ἰουδαῖοι (28:15)[4] which probably reflects the experience of Jewish Christians at the time of writing. The resultant delicate balance between a theology of fulfillment and one of replacement, between continuity and discontinuity, forms the basis of Matthew's distinctive theology. It is distinctive in the way it is presented, within the narrative framework of a gospel, but it bears fruitful comparison especially with the differently developed ideology of the Letter to the Hebrews, and indeed with that of many of the other NT writers, notably John, Paul and 1 Peter. In this paper we focus on one aspect of this wider theme of Matthew's theology of fulfillment,[5] namely his attitude to the city of Jerusalem, its temple and its people.

Terminology

Matthew, like Mark and John, uses the "Hellenized" form of the city's name, Ἱεροσόλυμα, rather than the LXX transcription of its Hebrew form, ἡ Ἱερουσαλήμ, which Luke prefers. The only time Matthew uses the LXX form is in Jesus' lament over the city in 23:37, where the shorter form of the name better suits the poetic repetition. The alternative OT name for the city, Σιών, occurs only in Matt. 21:5 in the combined quotation of Zech. 9:9 with Isa. 62:11, where Matthew is constrained by the phrase "daughter Zion" in his LXX originals. The non-Septuagintal form Ἱεροσόλυμα seems, then, to have been the natural way for Matthew and his community to refer to the city, despite his heavy dependence on the LXX in other ways. There is nothing to indicate that he prefers the Hellenized form because of a popular "etymology" from the Greek ἱερός such as Josephus (*Ant.* 7.67; *War* 6.438) and others exploited. When he twice refers to Jerusalem as "the holy city" (4:5; 27:53), he is using traditional OT terminology (cf. Isa. 52:1; Dan. 9:24), not playing on its name; in 27:53 this term may be pre-

---

Matthean studies, see S. Légasse, "L'anti-judaisme' dans l'Évangile selon Matthieu," in M. Didier (ed.), *L'Évangile selon Matthieu: rédaction et théologie* (BETL 29; Gembloux: Duculot, 1972), 417-428.

4. In *The Gospel of Matthew* (NICNT; Grand Rapids: Eerdmans, 2007), I question the common assertion that Matthew here uses Ἰουδαῖοι as in itself a polemical term, as it is in the Fourth Gospel. It lacks the definite article; παρὰ Ἰουδαίοις is better translated "among people in Judea," designating the geographical area within which the rumor was spread as opposed to the Galilean provenance of the gospel which will be emphasized in the following verses.

5. I have explored this theme in my *Matthew: Evangelist*, chapters 5-6.

ferred because it provides an echo of the resurrected "holy people." In 5:35 Jesus describes Jerusalem as "the city of the great King" in order to rebut the casuistry which said that an oath by Jerusalem did not involve God. This too is traditional OT language (Ps. 48:2), and does not in itself require a special ideology beyond conventional OT piety.[6]

The Synoptic Narrative Outline

The Synoptic writers share a narrative outline which has Jesus coming south to Judea only once in the course of his ministry, as opposed to the Johannine pattern of repeated visits to Jerusalem especially in connection with the major festivals. The Johannine pattern seems the more probable historical outline in that, unless Jesus' public ministry lasted only a few months, he and his disciples, as religiously observant Galilean Jews, are likely to have come south to Jerusalem for at least one festival before the final Passover. And there are several features in the Synoptic Jerusalem narratives which suggest that this is not in fact Jesus' first visit to the city. In that case the Synoptic outline is an artificial schematization of Jesus' ministry into two phases, the main period in Galilee (and the surrounding area in the north) and the last week in Jerusalem, with a lengthy journey section in between, which begins with Jesus' announcement at Caesarea Philippi that he must go to Jerusalem to be rejected and killed and to rise again.

The creation of this three-part narrative structure is generally attributed to Mark by those who regard him as the earliest of the Synoptic writers, and it has long been suggested that the geographical scheme of his narrative was deliberately designed to convey also a theological message: Galilee is the place of revelation and response, Jerusalem the place of rejection and death.[7] The overwhelmingly negative portrayal of Jerusalem is focused on its Jewish leadership, the frequently named triumvirate of "the chief priests and the scribes and the elders" (Mark 11:27; cf. in various orders, 8:31; 14:43, 53; 15:1, and without the el-

---

6. Walker, *Jesus* 32-33, suggests that the positive terminology used occasionally for Jerusalem and the temple may be read as "deeply ironic, emphasizing the city's privileged calling and revealing the standard by which she would be judged"; "the holy city" is "an ironic misnomer, (ibid., 34).

7. So classically E. Lohmeyer, *Galiläa und Jerusalem* (Göttingen: Vandenhoeck & Ruprecht, 1936); R. H. Lightfoot, *Locality and Doctrine in the Gospels* (London: Hodder & Stoughton, 1938). See R. T. France, *The Gospel of Mark* (NIGTC; Grand Rapids: Eerdmans, 2002), 11-15, 33-35 and commentary passim; cf. C. Bryan, *A Preface to Mark: Notes on the Gospel in Its Literary and Cultural Settings* (Oxford: Oxford University Press, 1993), 85-125.

ders 10:33; 11:18; 14:1; 15:31), and on the temple which was their power base and which Jesus roundly declares to be ripe for destruction. Two mentions of Jerusalem in the first (Galilean) part of Mark's gospel both identify it as the source of official opposition (3:22; 7:1), while two mentions of Galilee in the third (Jerusalem) part point forward to Galilee as the location of hope for the future (14:28; 16:7). Sensitivity to this "theological geography" has been massively reinforced in recent scholarship by the growing recognition of the political and cultural separation of Galilee from Judea in the first century,[8] a point which may best be made by pointing out that Jesus and his disciples, as Galileans, were conspicuously foreigners in Jerusalem: they were "them" rather than "us," as Mark 14:70; Matt. 26:73 graphically illustrates. In the light of that socio-political divide many incidents in the gospel story can be seen in a fascinating new light, especially in the period after the Galilean prophet and his Galilean entourage come face to face with the people of the southern province. This aspect of Mark's narrative is now too well known to require demonstration. The question to be addressed here, however, is how Matthew has responded to what most scholars assume to have been Mark's innovative scheme.[9]

The first obvious point is that Matthew has adopted the same narrative structure as Mark. There are of course additional elements in Matthew's structural scheme, marked particularly by the discourse-conclusion formula, "And it happened, when Jesus had completed these words" (7:28; 11:1; 13:53; 19:1; 26:1) and by the transitional formula emphasized especially by J. D. Kingsbury,[10] "From that time Jesus began to . . ." (4:17; 16:21). But the latter of these serves merely to underline two of the three turning points already established in the Marcan scheme (the beginning of the Galilean ministry and of the journey to Jerusalem), while the former is more generally regarded these days not as establishing an overall five-part scheme for the gospel such as was famously pro-

---

8. So popularly G. Vermes, *Jesus the Jew: A Historian's Reading of the Gospels* (London: Collins, 1973), 42-57; in more depth S. Freyne, *Galilee from Alexander the Great to Hadrian, 323 B.C.E. to 135 C.E.: A Study of Second Temple Judaism* (Wilmington, Del.: Glazier, 1980); idem, *Galilee, Jesus and the Gospels: Literary Approaches and Historical Investigations* (Dublin: Gill & Macmillan, 1988).

9. I have stated my views on the Synoptic Problem in my *Matthew: Evangelist*, 24-49. While I am not a committed supporter of the classic two-source theory, and in particular of the standard account of Q, I am still less attracted to any of the theories which assume that Matthew wrote first. In this paper, as elsewhere, I work on the assumption that Mark's gospel was completed before that of Matthew, but without presupposing a uniform pattern of literary dependence.

10. J. D. Kingsbury, *Matthew: Structure, Christology, Kingdom* (Philadelphia: Fortress, 1975); cf. D. R. Bauer, *The Structure of Matthew's Gospel: A Study in Literary Design* (JSNTSup 31; Sheffield: Almond, 1988).

posed by B. W. Bacon[11] but simply as marking the end of the distinctively Matthean discourses which are inserted within the Marcan narrative scheme.[12] The essential outline remains that of Mark, with its deliberate movement from a substantial opening ministry in the north, via an extended journey after Caesarea Philippi, to a final week of confrontation in the south.

There is, however, one major modification of this scheme in Matthew, which has important implications for our theme. Whereas Mark's narrative, despite its tantalizing pointers forward to a future meeting in Galilee, finishes still in Jerusalem at the empty tomb, in Matthew those pointers (which are equally emphatically inserted in the Jerusalem narrative at 26:32 and 28:7 and further underlined in 28:10) find their narrative fulfillment in the hills of Galilee in 28:16-20. There is thus in Matthew, unlike Mark, a satisfying rounding off of the story, with a return to the place of original proclamation and response, and a re-launching of the mission of the Galilean Jesus, but now with the vital additional sanction of his conquest of death and his receipt of "all authority in heaven and earth" (28:18). Jerusalem's attempt to silence the Messiah's voice has failed, and Jerusalem has become a backwater in the story of salvation history. God's purpose has moved on, and it is from Galilee that it must move forward.

So appropriate is this ending to the overall scheme of the gospel, and especially to the two explicit forward pointers to Galilee, that it makes it all the more incredible that Mark's narrative should have ended abruptly with the flight of the women from the tomb in 16:8. I have argued elsewhere that Mark surely also intended such an ending, and that in the light of Matthew's close agreement with Mark in the overall plan of the passion narrative it is likely that Matt. 28:16-20 paralleled a corresponding original ending to Mark, now lost.[13] Be that as it may, in Matthew at least the wheel has come full circle, and the mission continues where it began, in the hills of Galilee, while Jerusalem and its leaders are left behind in a sordid attempt to cover up their failure to stifle God's messenger (28:11-15).

Apart from this major enhancement of the Marcan Galilee/Jerusalem scheme, some other additional features in Matthew further underline it. Chapter 2 demonstrates the author's awareness of the significance of geography, as it explains at length and with carefully marshalled OT evidence how the Messiah born in Bethlehem in Judea came eventually in the providence of God to be brought up as a Galilean in Nazareth, and it is not difficult to reconstruct the Judean prejudice which the evangelist is countering when he claims in 2:23 that

---

11. B. W. Bacon, *Studies in Matthew* (London: Constable, 1930).
12. Bauer, *Structure*, especially 27-35, 129-34.
13. France, *Mark*, 670-74.

it was in accordance with what the prophets had declared that he would be "*called* a Nazarene."[14] When Jesus begins his public ministry, not in Nazareth but in Capernaum, Matthew undergirds this also with a formal quotation of the messianic prophecy of Isa. 9:1-2, which identifies "Galilee of the nations" (and specifically that part of it in which Capernaum was located) as the place where the light was to shine (4:12-16); that quotation then forms the launching pad for the programmatic statement of 4:17 which outlines the subject of the first main part of the narrative, Jesus' proclamatory ministry in Galilee. When eventually that northern ministry is over and Jesus at last makes his way to Jerusalem, Matthew tells the story of his arrival in a distinctive way which, as we shall see shortly, underlines the contrast between the Galilean prophet and his followers on the one hand and the uncomprehending and unwelcoming city on the other. It will be in accordance with that perspective that in the story of Peter's denial Matthew will add the incriminating qualification, "You too were with Jesus *the Galilean*" (26:69).

So Matthew has not only adopted the Marcan narrative scheme with its ideological contrast between Galilee and Jerusalem, but has underlined it in several unmistakable ways. His story, even more explicitly than Mark's, is that of a Galilean Messiah, whose mission, despite its initial success in his own province, makes no impression on the entrenched opposition of the Jerusalem authorities. It is only when Jerusalem has been condemned and abandoned that the mission can go ahead — from the hills of Galilee, the place where Isaiah had said the light must shine.

Jerusalem in Chapters 1–20

Unsurprisingly, there are not a large number of mentions of Jerusalem before the narrative brings us outside its walls at the beginning of chapter 21. But some of them are significant for what is to follow.

Matthew is careful to specify that Bethlehem, where Jesus was born, is "in Judea" (2:1, 5, 6), as this is important for the geographical apologetic which this chapter will construct (see above). So it is naturally to Jerusalem that the Magi come to look for the newborn "king of the Judeans" (2:2), a term which will recur only in chapter 27, where it is used only by Romans (the Jewish equivalent

---

14. K. Stendahl, "Quis et Unde? An Analysis of Matthew 1-2," in W. Eltester (ed.), *Judentum, Urchristentum, Kirche: Festschrift für J. Jeremias* (Berlin: Töpelmann, 1960), 94-105; repr. in G. N. Stanton, *The Interpretation of Matthew* (Edinburgh: T&T Clark, 1995), 69-80. See also R. T. France, "The Formula-Quotations of Matthew 2 and the Problem of Communication," *NTS* 27 (1980/1): 237-40, and (on 2:23) 246-49.

in 27:42 is "king of Israel"). The translation of Ἰουδαῖος is controversial. To those outside the Jewish context (such as the Magi and Pilate) it is probably simply a general ethnic term for all those who claim descent from Abraham, but to those in the know it has a more limited geographical sense, and there are some scholars who insist that the default translation should be "Judean" (as opposed to Galilean, Samaritan, etc.), not "Jew."[15] This is a particularly significant issue with regard to the pejorative use of οἱ Ἰουδαῖοι in the Fourth Gospel,[16] and I believe applies also to Matthew's use of Ἰουδαῖοι in 28:15,[17] but it is beyond the scope of this paper to pursue it. It is not only Herod who is disturbed by the inquiry of the Magi but "all Jerusalem with him" (2:3). Historically we might be surprised to find Jerusalem sharing the concern of their increasingly unpopular Idumaean king (unless of course they were disturbed at the thought of what further atrocities this news might provoke from Herod), but for Matthew the city also represents the political power which Jesus will eventually challenge, and the idea will recur when the whole city is "shaken" by the arrival of the Galilean prophet in 21:10. When the Magi bypass Herod, and thus also Jerusalem, after they have worshipped the messianic king (2:12), this is a foretaste of Jesus' future strategy: he will not present his challenge to Judea until the climactic moment has arrived. Until then he, like the Magi, will "withdraw" (a distinctively Matthean word for geographical prudence: 2:12, 14, 22; 4:12; 12:15; 14:13; 15:21) from the place of confrontation.

But before the Messiah declares himself in Galilee there is a preliminary scene still set in the south, in "the wilderness of Judea" (3:1), and the crowds who resort to John are drawn from "Jerusalem and all Judea" (3:5). Judea is thus being prepared for the challenge which Jesus will later throw down to it, and his explicit linking of his mission with that of John in 21:23-27 will make the connection. Jerusalem and Judea have thus already had a chance to respond to the prophetic call, and the fact that they, or at least their leaders, have refused to respond to that call is part of the basis on which Jesus will declare their unfitness for the kingdom of God (21:28-32). That failure is already represented in chapter 3 by the bipartisan delegation of Pharisees and Sadducees whose hypocrisy John unmasks in 3:7-10. But they are not representative of the Judean crowds as a whole, and we will be reminded several times that John was popularly remembered as a true prophet (11:7-11; 16:14; 21:26, 32). Thus already in chapter 3

---

15. Thus R. A. Horsley, *Hearing the Whole Story: The Politics of Plot in Mark's Gospel* (Louisville: Westminster John Knox, 2001), 47, asserts that "the term *Ioudaioi* is a regional (not a religious) reference."

16. M. Lowe, "Who Were the Ioudaioi?" *NovT* 18 (1976): 101-30; E. Schillebeeckx, *Christ: The Christian Experience in the Modern World* (ET, London: SCM, 1980), 335-36, 872-73, n. 36.

17. See above, n. 4.

there is a tension between the reactions of the Judean people and their leaders, which will form the background to a similar tension between the crowd and the leaders in Jerusalem in their response to Jesus in chapters 21–23.

The visionary visit to "the holy city" which forms the basis of Jesus' second temptation in 4:5 does not in itself contribute to our theme: the focus is on the proposed "leap of faith," not on any significance of the city or its temple as such. Similarly, when Jesus refers in the Sermon on the Mount to the temple (5:23-24) and to Jerusalem (5:35), his words simply presuppose the status quo without raising ideological questions.[18] In 12:5-6, however, a new note is sounded, when the authority of the temple which allows its priests to set aside the sabbath rules is taken as a model for Jesus' own authority to dispense with ritual regulations, and the argument is undergirded by the pregnant declaration, "Something greater than the temple is here" (12:6). The issue is not further discussed at this point, though the subsequent references to "something greater than Jonah" and "something greater than Solomon" in 12:41, 42 open up a wider typological perspective which encourages the reader to set Jesus and his ministry against the backcloth of all that was most central to Israel's religious and political tradition and to see his authority as superseding what had gone before. But the specific issue of Jesus and the temple will not recur until he comes to Jerusalem in chapter 21; thereafter, as we shall see, it will be a central issue in his confrontation with the status quo.

Direct mention of Jerusalem in the narrative of the Galilean and journey phases is confined to three types of reference, each of which in a different way points forward to the final section of the story. The "large crowds" who followed Jesus in Galilee were presumably largely made up of the local people. But they are also said in 4:24-25 to include people from Decapolis, from Jerusalem and Judea and from Perea, while reports of his activity had spread through "all Syria." Judea is not here singled out, but is one among many surrounding areas affected by Jesus' ministry. But following on from 3:5 this notice perhaps alerts the reader that Jesus, as John's successor, has already been favorably noticed even in the southern province, so that when he eventually comes to Jerusalem there is some basis for the popular support which he initially enjoys despite the disapproval of the official leadership.

The other side of the coin is found in 15:1, where the dispute on purity is initiated not by local Galilean teachers but by "Pharisees and scribes from Jeru-

---

18. Some commentators, following G. von Rad, find a reference to Jerusalem in the "city set on a hill" (5:14). But nothing in the wording requires this. πόλις does not in itself imply a large settlement (it is used even for Nazareth, 2:23!), and the Galilean setting of the saying makes it more likely that it refers to a local hilltop town. The lack of an article in any case indicates a general proverbial saying, not a specific reference.

salem." It seems then that Jesus' activities in the north have been noticed not only by the enthusiastic crowds of 4:25 but also by the southern authorities who have become concerned at Jesus' apparently cavalier attitude to halakhic rules. Their presence in Galilee does not necessarily indicate that they had come north specifically to investigate Jesus — they could have had many other reasons for being in Galilee — but by specifying where they came from, Matthew gives notice of the controversies which are bound to erupt once Jesus makes a public appearance in Jerusalem. In this, of course, Matthew follows Mark, and it is surprising that he does not also share Mark's observation (Mark 3:22) that the scribes who accused Jesus of demonic activity had also "come down from Jerusalem"; but that was earlier in the narrative, whereas the dispute on purity is the last significant confrontation before Jesus leaves Galilee to travel first north to Caesarea Philippi and then deliberately south toward Jerusalem, so that Matthew may have felt that this was the more appropriate point to draw attention to the hostility building up in the south.

The other references to Jerusalem before chapter 21 are of course in Jesus' predictions of his rejection and suffering in 16:21 and 20:17-18. The listing in the former passage of his opponents as "the elders and the chief priests and the scribes" (the latter two also in 20:18) makes it clear why he must now set off for Jerusalem, because Jerusalem is the seat of the official establishment of the Sanhedrin (whose three chief component groups these are), and it is before the highest authorities of Israel that Israel's Messiah must present his credentials. Matthew, unlike Mark, makes this point explicit by naming Jerusalem as their destination in Jesus' first passion prediction. Thus throughout the journey narrative in 16:21–20:34, as Jesus and his entourage come closer to the southern capital, there will be a growing sense of inevitable confrontation between the official establishment and the Messiah who comes to challenge their authority, between the now discredited temple and the "something greater" which has come to take its place, between Jerusalem's *ancien régime* and the newly proclaimed kingdom of heaven which comes with the arrival of the Galilean prophet.

Jesus Arrives at Jerusalem

The traditional title "The Triumphal Entry" is misleading. Mark and Matthew agree that the enthusiastic welcome by the crowd takes place outside the city, and that it is only afterward that Jesus actually enters Jerusalem (Mark 11:11; Matt. 21:10). The demonstrative actions and the royal acclamation are attributed specifically to "the crowds who were going ahead of him and following him" (Mark 11:9; Matt. 21:9), that same "large crowd" which both evangelists have already described as accompanying Jesus and his disciples on the final approach to the city from Jericho (Mark 10:46; Matt. 20:29). They are presumably, like Jesus, Passover pilgrims coming up to the city for the festival, many no doubt having made the journey from Galilee by the same traditional route avoiding Samaria. In other words, it is unlikely that many of them were Judeans. And they are enthusiasts for Jesus, having witnessed his very public healing of the blind man (men) at Jericho and heard him addressed there as "Son of David," a title which he did not repudiate. Among this pilgrim crowd Jesus and his Galilean disciples would feel at home. And it is this crowd which, taking up his blatant messianic allusion to Zech. 9:9 by riding on the donkey, hail him as the coming Davidic king.

But what about the people of Jerusalem? Mark tells us nothing yet about their reaction to this northern "invasion." But Matthew spells it out in 21:10-11. In striking contrast to the enthusiastic crowds outside the gates "the whole city" was "shaken" and wanted to know "Who is this?" There is no sense here of Jerusalem welcoming its king; it is simply bemused by the sudden appearance of this Galilean pretender. But the crowds leave the city in no doubt of what the demonstration means: "This is the prophet Jesus, from Nazareth in Galilee." It is hard not to hear in these words both a strong sense of ownership, as the predominantly Galilean crowd present Jesus as *their* prophet, and also of challenge to Jerusalem's assumed superiority: he is our prophet, not yours. Jerusalem had better look out. It may not be entirely wide of the mark to compare this scene with the football supporters of a rival town arriving for the local derby match.

So it was not the *entry* to the city which was "triumphal," but rather the approach to the city walls; the entry into the city was more confrontational, and the stage is well set for the power struggle which is to take place over the succeeding days culminating in 27:22-23 in the demand of the Jerusalem crowd (not, *pace* much popular preaching, of the pilgrims who shouted Hosanna outside the walls) that Jesus be eliminated. In what follows we shall try to disentangle the respective roles of the Jerusalem leadership and of the people of the city in this process.

The Jewish Leaders in Jerusalem

"The Jewish leaders" is of course a very imprecise term.[19] Matthew refers to several distinct groups, chief priests, elders, scribes, Pharisees, Sadducees and

---

19. For the extensive debate on Matthew's terminology see my *Matthew: Evangelist,* 219-23.

Herodians. The first three of these were the main component groups of the Sanhedrin, while the terms "Pharisee" and "Sadducee," denoting ideological rather than professional categories, may be expected to overlap with them; Pharisees were already a significant element within the Sanhedrin by this time, though the Sadducean group was still dominant (cf. at a slightly later time Acts 23:6-10). Matthew is clearly aware of the differences between these groups: note the specific groups to whom he attributes the various challenges in 22:15-46. But he seems to view all of them as constituting a sort of coalition opposed to Jesus, which eventually finds its expression in his condemnation by "the chief priests and all the Sanhedrin" (26:59). Matthew's most distinctive contribution is the singling out of "the scribes and Pharisees" to be the butt of Jesus' invective in chapter 23, and many of the points made in that chapter relate especially to the halakhic debates and practices of those groups, but by the end of the chapter they seem to have become a symbol for the failure of the leadership as a whole, with the destruction of the temple (the power base primarily of the priests rather than the scribes) as its inevitable outcome.

The confrontation begins immediately after Jesus' arrival, as "chief priests and scribes" object to his action in the temple (21:15-16) and "chief priests and elders" follow this up by challenging the basis of his authority to act in this way (21:23-27). At this point in Mark's narrative Jesus responds with the single parable of the vineyard, but Matthew sharpens the attack by including here also two other parables. The three parables form a polemical group addressed specifically to the Jerusalem leaders (a resumptive comment in 21:45 identifies the audience as "the chief priests and Pharisees"). All three parables focus on failure to respond appropriately to the divine call and to fulfill the duties placed by God on those he has chosen for positions of responsibility or privilege, and all three talk of a different group who will as a result take over the position of those first chosen. In the parable of the two sons (21:28-32) the contrast is explicitly between "you" and the tax collectors and prostitutes who, unlike "you," accepted John's call to the way of righteousness; so the kingdom of God is for them rather than "you." The parable of the vineyard (which takes up Isaiah's imagery where the vineyard is Israel, Isa. 5:1-7) follows the same pattern as in Mark and Luke, with the ejection of the rebellious tenants in favor of "others," together with the rejected stone quotation from Ps. 118:22. But an additional explanatory comment in Matt. 21:43 raises the stakes considerably: "Therefore I tell you, the kingdom of God will be taken away from you and given to a nation which does produce its fruits." The term "nation," ἔθνος, particularly draws the eye; what sort of "nation" can replace the failed chief priests and Pharisees? The third parable (22:1-14) resembles Luke's parable of the dinner party (Luke 14:16-24), but is escalated by making the meal a royal wedding feast and by including the incongruous motif of the king's revenge attack on those who declined the invitation and his burning of "their city." There is also the curious feature that the replacement guests include "bad as well as good" (cf. the tax collectors and prostitutes of 21:31-32?), and the expulsion of one of them because he is not properly dressed for the wedding.

Among the many exegetical puzzles posed by these parables, it is relevant to our theme to ask how far their replacement motif is intended to extend. The address is specifically to the leaders, and it is easy to recognize them in the disobedient son, the rebellious tenants and the unmannerly guests. But if the message is simply that it is time for a change of leadership, it is surprising that the new regime is expressed not as a new ruling class but as a new "nation"; and if it was simply the first-invited guests who had offended, why did the king feel it appropriate to burn their whole city? It is noteworthy too that all three parables talk about a change which is related to "the kingdom of God/heaven": it is the kingdom of God that the tax collectors and prostitutes will enter "ahead of you"; it is the kingdom of God which will be taken from "you" to be given to the new "nation," and the wedding feast is presented as a parable of "the kingdom of heaven" from which the unworthy are excluded and which others will instead enjoy. The fact that one of the replacement guests is thrown out also suggests that there is some more general principle involved than merely the failure of one group of leaders.

This impression is heightened in chapter 23 where Jesus' exposé of the failings of the scribes and Pharisees develops in 23:29 into an account of Israel's rejection of God's messengers through the ages, a defiance in which surely more than just "scribes and Pharisees" had been and were still involved, the punishment for which is to fall not on a specific group but more generally on "this generation" (v. 36). Jesus' lament in v. 37 is not over the scribes and Pharisees alone but over "Jerusalem," and the devastation of "your house" (v. 38) is more explicitly spelled out in the prediction of 24:2 that the temple would be utterly destroyed. All this is much more far-reaching than a change of leadership in Jerusalem. It is not just the current ruling group but the whole temple establishment and the whole national ideology which it embodies which is declared to be under judgment. The failure and judgment of the leadership is a microcosm of the failure and judgment of Jerusalem as a whole, of which the destruction of the temple, the visible focus of the presence of God among his people, is a potent symbol.

So while it is possible, and profitable, at the narrative level to discuss Matthew's portrayal of the Jerusalem crowd as distinct from their leaders during the period of confrontation in the temple, it is questionable how far this perception modifies the overall sense of condemnation hanging over Jerusalem as a whole.

The Jerusalem Crowd

During Passover time the crowds gathered in Jerusalem would of course be extremely cosmopolitan, including not only the Galilean pilgrims whose arrival we have noted in 21:1-11 but also visitors from all over the Jewish world. The debates of chapters 21–22 are set in the Court of the Gentiles where the crowds would be large, mixed and constantly changing. But it is questionable how far Matthew's various references to "the crowd(s)" in these chapters are intended to reflect that historical context. As far as his presentation is concerned, the setting here is Jerusalem, and the crowds represent the people of Jerusalem. In contrast with the uniformly negative image of the leaders (even the "good scribe" of Mark 12:28-34 is replaced by a lawyer whose motive is described as πειράζων αὐτόν on behalf of the Pharisees, 22:34-35), Matthew speaks of these crowds as at least potentially favorable to Jesus, though the picture is not uniform.

When Jesus first arrives in Jerusalem, it is "the whole city" which reacts with dismay (21:10); Matthew's phrase, echoing the alarm of "all Jerusalem" in 2:3, does not suggest only the leaders. But after Jesus declares his hand in the temple a difference of perspective emerges, with invalids coming to Jesus for healing and children repeating the Hosannas of the Galilean crowd, while the chief priests and scribes try to silence them (21:14-16). Throughout the dialogue with the leaders in chapters 21–22 the crowd remain the silent audience, and twice Matthew mentions that the leaders were afraid to antagonize the crowd who did not share their negative view first of John the Baptist (21:26) and then also of Jesus (21:46; cf. also 26:5). Each was, he tells us, regarded by the crowd "as a prophet." When Jesus has "silenced the Sadducees" by his answer about the resurrection (22:34), the crowd are said to be "astonished at his teaching" (22:33), a verb (ἐκπλήσσομαι) which generally expresses admiration (7:28; 13:54), though it can also express bewilderment (19:25). Then, when Jesus has silenced all his opponents and is left in possession of the field, he launches his attack on the scribes and Pharisees not by direct address at first but by appealing over their heads to the crowd (23:1-12). These verses sound like a deliberate appeal to the people to come over to Jesus' side and to abandon their failed scribal leadership; one has the impression that the crowd, unlike the scribes and Pharisees, is still winnable.

But with the diatribe against the scribes and Pharisees Jesus' public appearances in the Court of the Gentiles come to an end, and from this point we hear no more of the potentially favorable attitude of the crowd: it is "Jerusalem" as a whole, not just its leaders, that Jesus laments over in 23:37-39. It is the city, not just its leaders, that he describes as the one "who kills the prophets and stones those who are sent to her" (23:37). The next mention of a "crowd" will not be a random public gathering but the specific group detailed to arrest Jesus in Gethsemane (26:47), though Jesus reminds them of his temple teaching as if at least some of the same crowd were involved (26:55); if they were, however, they are now decisively on the side of the authorities. And from that time on Jesus is in the hands of his determined opponents, so that the next time we hear of a Jerusalem crowd is outside the governor's palace when Jesus has already been declared guilty by the Sanhedrin. This is the crowd which rejects Pilate's well-meant offer of the release of "Jesus the so-called Messiah" and calls instead for Jesus Barabbas (27:15-23). Any enthusiasm there had been for "the so-called Messiah" has now evaporated, under the pressure of official persuasion (27:20) and also of the more immediate appeal of a "messiah" who, unlike Jesus the Galilean, was prepared to turn his messianic idealism into political action.[20] The cry, "Let him be crucified," represents the final disillusionment of the Jerusalem crowd with the Galilean prophet, whose dramatic arrival at the city had briefly caught their imagination. When Jesus hangs on the cross, it will be not only the chief priests, the scribes and the elders who mock his failed claims, but also the local people in general, "those who passed by" (27:39-44).

It is in this context that Matthew introduces some of the most painfully misunderstood words in his gospel.[21] In response to Pilate's disavowal of responsibility for Jesus' death, "all the people replied, 'his blood is on us and on our children'" (27:24-25). Most English versions make matters worse by gratuitously inserting the language of a wish, "His blood *be* on us and on our children." But there is no verb in the Greek, and in the absence of a verb the normal default rendering is the indicative of the verb "to be." This is no wish. It is a simple acceptance of the statement Pilate has just made, "*I* am not responsible; *you* see to it." . . . "Yes, we accept the responsibility." (Cf. the formula of responsibility for death in, e.g., Lev. 20:9; Deut. 19:10; Josh. 2:19; 2 Sam. 1:16.) That is disturbing enough without turning their simple statement into a blood wish, or, as it has too often been interpreted, as a self-execration.

This is clearly a climactic moment for Matthew. It is presented not simply as the thoughtless words of a few hooligans who happened to be present, not even as the words of "the crowd," but as the declaration of "all the people," using the term λαός which in the LXX and later Jewish use is especially associated with Israel as God's chosen people.[22] This is the voice of a representative group

---

20. For the political choice offered to the crowd by the contrasting agendas of the two Jesuses, see the suggestive "fictional" account by G. Theissen, *The Shadow of the Galilean* (ET, London: SCM, 1987), especially the letter of Barabbas to Andreas, ibid., 177.

21. For an overview of the problem see R. E. Brown, *The Death of the Messiah: A Commentary on the Passion Narratives in the Four Gospels* (New York: Doubleday, 1994), 831-39.

22. See, e.g., D. P. Senior, *The Passion Narrative according to Matthew* (BETL 39; Leuven: Leuven University Press, 1975), 258-59.

of Israel. So the Jerusalem crowds have now decisively cast in their lot with their leaders against the Galilean prophet. They want to be rid of him. "All the people" (or at least all the people of Jerusalem) agree in demanding his death.

The misuse of this text as an excuse for Christian persecution of Jews through the centuries[23] creates a natural embarrassment which makes it difficult to hear what Matthew intended us to hear from it. We may assume that Matthew, as a Jew, was not condemning all Jews for all time. But his choice of the phrase πᾶς ὁ λαός and his inclusion of "our children" suggests that he was thinking of more than the particular group who happened to be in front of the governor's palace at that time. The reference to "our children" may perhaps have been prompted by Matthew's reflection that when the temple was ultimately destroyed it would be a new generation who bore the brunt of it. This statement therefore stands alongside the sustained polemic against the temple as a marker of the fundamental shift in the divine economy which came about with Jerusalem's rejection of Jesus and which is explained in the discourse of chapters 24–25. The kingdom of heaven is no longer to be focused in the λαός, the city and the temple, but in the vindicated and enthroned Son of Man who, after the temple is destroyed, will gather his chosen people from all the corners of the earth (24:29-31). All this will happen within this generation. Jerusalem's rejection of the Son of Man has set the seal on the expulsion of the former tenants from the vineyard, and a new ἔθνος is to take over the tenancy, an ἔθνος made up of those who belong to the Son of Man and so are the continuing members of the kingdom of heaven. As early as 8:11-12 Matthew has given notice of this impending change when he talked of many coming from east and west to share in the banquet of the kingdom of heaven with Abraham, Isaac and Jacob while those who seemed the natural "sons of the kingdom" would be thrown out.

The terrible words uttered by πᾶς ὁ λαός in 27:25 are, I believe, best understood against that overall theology of a new people of God. The people, like their leaders, have rejected the Son sent to them by the owner of the vineyard, and the status of ethnic Israel as the chosen people of God can never be the same again. Together with the city and the temple the people of Jerusalem represent the *ancien régime*. It will be a new ἔθνος which will produce the fruit God requires of his people.

---

23. Against this see especially H. Kosmala, "'His Blood on Us and on Our Children' (The Background of Mat 27,24-25)," *ASTI* 7 (1968/9): 94-126; also J. A. Fitzmyer, "Anti-Semitism and the Cry of 'All the People,'" *TS* 26 (1965): 667-71.

The Replacement of the Temple

Why did the Jerusalem crowd, initially apparently open to consider Jesus' claims, eventually side so decisively with his opponents? Twenty years ago E. P. Sanders[24] argued convincingly that from a historical point of view the principal issue which united different strands of Judaism against Jesus was his perceived attitude to the temple. To speak against the temple had always been a risky business, as Jeremiah and Uriah had found out (Jer. 26) and as another Jesus, son of Hananiah, would show a generation later (Josephus, *War* 6.300-305), and the charge against Stephen shows that this aspect of Jesus' message remained a potent cause of offense (Acts 6:13-14). The temple for a Jew, and especially for a Jerusalem Jew, was much more than just a religious building; it was the focus of national identity and ideology, the visible symbol that Israel was the chosen people of Yahweh, and Jerusalem his holy city. You could hardly take up the stance of an anti-temple prophet and expect to remain a favorite in Jerusalem.

And Matthew leaves no doubt of the significance of this theme for Jesus' message. Was it for this reason that, as Matthew alone tells us, people compared Jesus with Jeremiah (Matt. 16:14)? As early as 12:6 we meet the theme of "something greater than the temple" being present in the ministry of Jesus, and on Jesus' arrival in Jerusalem his first action is to declare his messianic repudiation of the temple's current role in the life of Israel; it has become, in words which ominously echo Jeremiah's anti-temple polemic, "a bandits' hideout" (21:12-13). A study of the significance of Jesus' temple demonstration would require a separate paper,[25] but it is widely accepted that his concern was more fundamental than simply any unfair trading practices on the part of the merchants, and that the issue, as the subsequent challenge from the chief priests and their allies demonstrates, was essentially one of authority, the authority of the Messiah over against that of the priestly group who had authorized the use of the temple to which Jesus objected. Most commentators agree that, even though Matthew does not make the connection as clear as Mark, his juxtaposition of the cursing of the fig tree (21:18-19) with the demonstration in the temple is intended to symbolize the fruitlessness of the temple and its readiness for destruction.

From that point on "the temple" (in reality presumably the Court of the Gentiles, but Matthew does not differentiate the areas within the temple complex) becomes the location for Jesus' confrontation with its ruling authorities. It is a highly symbolic setting for the struggle over who now represents the true

---

24. E. P. Sanders, *Jesus and Judaism* (London: SCM, 1985), especially 61-90, 301-5.
25. E.g., C. A. Evans, "Jesus' Action in the Temple: Cleansing or Portrait of Destruction?" *CBQ* 51 (1989): 237-70.

people of God. But in the end Jesus breaks off the dialogue and declares the coming devastation of "your house" (23:38). When he goes out from the temple and then takes his seat on the Mount of Olives (24:1-3), the reader is likely to recall the vision of Ezek. 10:18-19; 11:22-23 where God's abandonment of his temple is visualized in the ascent of the chariot of his presence from inside the temple courts, out by the east gate until it comes to rest "on the mountain east of the city." As he goes Jesus declares explicitly the coming total destruction of the temple (24:2), and in the discourse which follows as he sits opposite the temple on the Mount of Olives he explains to his disciples in the language of the OT prophets that the lights are going out for Jerusalem and that the new regime of the vindicated Son of Man will shortly take the place of the old order with its focus on Jerusalem and its temple (24:29-31).[26]

If any of this subversive ideology had found its way to the ears of the high priest (and it is not unlikely that part of Judas's role was as an inside informer on the less public teaching of Jesus), it would explain why Jesus' alleged threat to destroy and replace the temple played such a prominent role at his trial (26:61-63; note that Matthew, unlike Mark, describes this charge as supported by two witnesses and therefore legally valid) and in subsequent popular scorn for the Galilean upstart (27:40); it was not just a threat to a sacred building, but the manifesto of a whole new regime. Anyone who makes such claims cannot be allowed to go on, and Jesus' ringing claim that "from now on you will see the Son of Man seated at the right hand of power and coming with the clouds of heaven" (26:64) unapologetically underlines his challenge to the status quo.

Against such a background the reader is well prepared to grasp the symbolic significance of what happens when Jesus dies on the cross: the temple curtain is torn apart from top to bottom, a mark both of the coming destruction of the building and of the opening of the access to the presence of God which its rituals have hitherto obstructed. From this point on, as the Letter to the Hebrews so memorably explains, the earthly sanctuary in Jerusalem has passed its sell-by date, and it is only a matter of time before it will be physically removed by the troops of Titus. But by then it has ceased to matter, since already with the coming of Jesus "something greater than the temple is here," and the kingdom of the Son of Man has been established in the calling of a new people of God from all corners of the earth.

---

26. I have argued for this exegesis of the so-called "eschatological discourse" (in Mark as well as in Matthew) in several places. See, e.g., my *The Gospel according to Matthew* (TNTC 1; Leicester: InterVarsity Press, 1985), 333-36, 343-46 and more fully (with reference to the Mark parallel) my *Mark*, 500-505, 530-40. I have now presented the argument in relation to the Matthew version more fully and with fuller documentation in *The Gospel of Matthew* (NICNT; Grand Rapids: Eerdmans, 2007), especially pp. 889-901 and 919-28.

A Future for Jerusalem?

All this sounds entirely negative with regard to Jerusalem, its temple, and its people. Has Jesus then washed his hands of "the holy city"? Is there no room for Jerusalem to play a part in the future reconstituted people of God? A hint of such a hope is often found in the enigmatic words with which Jesus concludes his public teaching in the temple courtyard: "I tell you, from now on you will never see me until you say, 'Blessed is he who comes in the name of the Lord'" (23:39). Following on the wistful tone of his appeal to "Jerusalem, Jerusalem," whom he had longed to embrace as a bird gathers her chicks under her wings (23:37), surely here is at least a potential ground for hope, if only Jerusalem will change its mind? The words of welcome are those, drawn from Ps. 118:26, with which the Galilean pilgrims had escorted their Messiah to the city in 21:9; might Jerusalem then one day come to share the Galileans' enthusiasm?

But there are grounds for caution in drawing this conclusion, both in the wording of the saying and in the context in which it is set. The wording consists of an emphatic negative, οὐ μή με ἴδητε followed by a temporal clause which is in effect a condition expressed in the indefinite form, ἕως ἂν εἴπητε. This construction does not mean "You will see me when you say . . . ," or even "You would see me, if you were to say. . . ." It is less optimistic than that, despite the surprising assumption of many commentators[27] that Jesus here *predicts* a future welcome by Jerusalem. He sets out the condition on which Jerusalem might see him again, but in a way which expresses doubt over whether it will be met, and the fact that the main clause is emphatically negative tilts the meaning strongly in the direction of a condition most unlikely to be fulfilled. To paraphrase it crudely: "The only condition on which you might see me again would be if you were to say . . . but that is unlikely to happen." The fact that the crucial words are those of the Galilean crowd which had so disturbed the people of Jerusalem a few days earlier makes the possibility even more remote.

And the context is hardly more sanguine. Jesus has just declared the "devastation" of "your house," and will immediately go on to declare as a matter of fact, not of conditional possibility, that not one stone of the temple will be left on another. The judgment is not only threatened, but will actually happen. And those to whom Jesus addressed these words will soon be heard declaring the very opposite of the messianic welcome of Ps. 118:26: both leaders and people

---

27. E.g., G. R. Beasley-Murray, *Jesus and the Kingdom of God* (Grand Rapids: Eerdmans, 1986), 305-7; G. N. Stanton, *A Gospel for a New People: Studies in Matthew* (Edinburgh: T&T Clark, 1992), 248-50.

will demand his blood. The leaders will indeed see him again (26:64), but that will not be as their acclaimed sovereign but as their vindicated judge.

So, despite the best efforts of commentators, Matt. 23:39 remains at best extremely discouraging for those who wish to find any future for Jerusalem in Matthew's perspective.[28] It does not say that Jerusalem will ever welcome him, and both the wording and the context strongly suggest that the condition he lays down is one they are unlikely ever to fulfill.[29] The final portrayal of Jerusalem in 28:11-15, licking its wounds and trying to arrange a cover-up after Jesus' resurrection, does not inspire hope. It is to Galilee that the disciples must go, and it is there in Galilee that the mission to all nations will be launched. Jerusalem has been left behind.

Conclusion

The negative view of Jerusalem which is implied by the Marcan dichotomy between Galilee and Jerusalem is adopted and strongly reinforced by Matthew. Jerusalem — the city, its leaders, its people and its temple — represents for him the opposition. Once Jesus came down from Galilee to present his claim in Jerusalem, two fundamentally incompatible ideologies came into confrontation. A choice had to be made, and Jerusalem made the wrong choice. Its leaders opposed Jesus from the beginning, while its people apparently came more gradually to the view that Jesus had to be eliminated as a threat to the status quo, prompted in large measure by Jesus' radical attitude to the temple. Jerusalem for Matthew thus embodies the old order, now superseded by the kingdom of heaven in which Jesus the Son of Man holds kingly authority, and membership of which depends on one's response to and relationship with Jesus rather than on belonging to a particular ethnic or political community. The vineyard has been taken away from its long-standing tenants, and given to a new "nation" which will produce its fruits. But this is a new type of "nation," not a simple substitution of Gentiles for Jews, but a new and potentially all-inclusive community under the kingship of the Son of Man, whose representatives are sent out from the hills of Galilee to "make disciples of all the nations." That is how the kingdom of heaven is to be achieved.

Matthew expresses this theology in his own way, but it is not difficult to see its likeness in other parts of the NT, particularly in the "supersessionist" theol-

---

28. D. E. Garland, *The Intention of Matthew 23* (NTSup 52; Leiden: Brill, 1979), 204-9.

29. See further my *Matthew: Evangelist,* 237-39; D. C. Allison, "Matt. 23:39 = Luke 13:35b as a Conditional Prophecy," *JSNT* 18 (1983): 75-84.

ogy of the Letter to the Hebrews, with its vision of a heavenly Mount Zion as the counterpart to the terrors of Mount Sinai (Heb. 12:18-24), in Paul's vision of a new, inclusive Israel, an olive tree with wild olive grafts (Rom. 11:17-26), and of a "Jerusalem above" which, unlike "the present Jerusalem," is "the mother of us all" (Gal. 4:25-26), and in Peter's metaphor of a temple made up of the "living stones" of his predominantly Gentile readers who now constitute the "chosen race," who once were no people, but now are the people of God (1 Pet. 2:4-10). This is of a piece with the general pattern of NT reference to the nation, the land, the city and the temple, whereby their former literal place in the purposes of God is transcended by a new Jesus-centered perspective, within which the people becomes a community of all nations, the land becomes a symbol for the kingdom of God, the earthly city is overshadowed by the heavenly Jerusalem, and the physical temple gives way to a temple not made with hands.[30]

In this radically new NT perspective, which owes its origin to the vision and teaching of Jesus of Nazareth, Matthew's gospel takes its place as a far-sighted if sometimes uncomfortable reminder that God cannot be confined within the walls of even the most holy city. We began with reference to Peter Walker's study *Jesus and the Holy City*. It is appropriate in conclusion to note his summary of Matthew's theology of Jerusalem as it relates to the OT prophecies of the restoration of the city. "Matthew's readers were not to hanker after a restoration of Jerusalem, a resumption of the previous *status quo* (or even something far better). Instead they were to focus upon Jesus, the one who through his death and resurrection had brought about the restoration predicted by Jeremiah and the prophets. God had now transferred onto Jesus the future restoration promises which previously had related to Jerusalem; no physical restoration of the city was therefore to be expected. . . . Jerusalem has effectively, through the coming of Jesus, been left behind. Jesus is the new Zion."[31]

---

30. This remarkably consistent orientation may be traced through what I like to think of as a "trilogy" of works of NT scholarship, even though they were written quite independently of each other and over a period of a quarter of a century: R. J. McKelvey, *The New Temple: The Church in the New Testament* (Oxford: Oxford University Press, 1969); W. D. Davies, *The Gospel and the Land* (Berkeley: University of California Press, 1974); Walker, *Jesus and the Holy City*.

31. Walker, *Jesus and the Holy City*, 47, 41.

Matthew's Theology of the Temple and the "Parting of the Ways": Christian Origins and the First Gospel

Daniel M. Gurtner

Introduction: Matthew's Relationship with Judaism

In the discussion of Matthew's gospel it is fashionable to speak of his "anti-Jewish polemic." Yet scholars have sometimes unwittingly grouped together all of Matthew's negative statements toward the Jewish crowds and leaders of his day with the institution of Judaism and its identifying markers — Jerusalem, the Temple, even the Sabbath, etc. — without giving due credence to his understanding of the institution of Judaism portrayed in Matthew by his characterization of defining components of Judaism itself. Lohmeyer asserts that Matthew is anti-Temple[1] while Andreoli argues that Matthew is against the Temple because it represents the "old order."[2] Scholars have long recognized the affirmation afforded to Judaism by the first evangelist by his uniquely positive statement about the Law in 5:17: "Think not that I have come to abolish the law and the prophets; I have come not to abolish them but to fulfil them" (RSV). This crucial text underscores Matthew's value for one of the pillar institutions of Judaism. Richard Bauckham, challenging the now popular notion of referring to first-century Judaisms (in the plural rather than the singular), rightly points

---

1. E. Lohmeyer, *Das Evangelium des Matthäus* (4th ed.; Göttingen: Vandenhoeck & Ruprecht, 1967), 184.
2. D. Andreoli, "Il velo squarciato nel Vangelo di Matteo," *BSW* 1 (1998): 35-40.

Earlier drafts of this paper were presented at the Tyndale Fellowship New Testament Study Group (Cambridge; 30 June 2005) and subsequently at the Society of Biblical Literature's Annual Meeting, Matthew Section (Philadelphia; 20 November 2005). Many thanks to the conveners for the offer to present this paper and to all participants who contributed to my thinking on this subject. Excerpts from *The Torn Veil: Matthew's Exposition of the Death of Jesus,* by Daniel M. Gurtner. Copyright © Daniel M. Gurtner 2007. Reprinted with the permission of Cambridge University Press.

out that for all its diversity, Judaism retained three central pillars that both defined and unified it in its first-century context. These are the importance of the Torah, the observance of the Sabbath, and the centrality of the Temple. Indeed, for Bauckham the Temple was "central" to "Jewish self-identity."[3]

It seems to me that if Bauckham is correct, and we are able to define the Jerusalem Temple as a distinguishing characteristic of what can broadly be called Judaism in the first century, it is worth considering the role of the Jerusalem Temple in Matthew's gospel in order to discern the first evangelist's understanding of, for example, his relationship to first-century Judaism and other related issues. Therefore I will examine all Matthean texts which may or may not reflect Matthew's notion of the Temple and its cult. I will focus on Matthew's redactional use of his Markan material and some interest in its role in the gospel narrative as a whole. This will provide a sufficient profile of what I find to be a comprehensive and consistent portrayal of the Temple throughout the Gospel of Matthew.

Contradictory Views of the Temple in Matthew?

The most striking obstacle we face is that, as is the case with Matthew's Christology, it is difficult to reconstruct a clear portrait of the Temple,[4] for though statements *about* the Temple are present and important, they are scant. They must, then, be pieced together with the evangelist's compositional portrayal of the Temple to arrive at a coherent picture. At a surface level, however, Matthew could be seen to present somewhat contradictory views of the Temple. Is it a place to be "cleansed" and preserved for prayer (21:13)? Or is it a place to be left desolate (23:38) and ultimately destroyed (24:2)? Some contend that Matthew's Jesus seems to replace the function of the Jerusalem Temple[5] as he immediately

---

3. R. J. Bauckham, "The Parting of the Ways: What Happened and Why," *ST* 47 (1993): 141.

4. R. T. France, *Matthew: Evangelist and Teacher* (Downers Grove, Ill.: InterVarsity Press, 1989), 279. Cf. F. W. Barnett, "Characterization and Christology in Matthew: Jesus in the Gospel of Matthew," *SBLSP* 28 (1989): 588-603.

5. J. D. Kingsbury (*Matthew as Story* [2d ed.; Philadelphia: Fortress, 1988], 30) declares, ". . . Jesus himself supplants the temple as the 'place' where God mediates salvation to people." Cf. D. A. Carson, "Matthew," in *Expositor's Bible Commentary* (ed. F. Gaebelein; Grand Rapids: Zondervan, 1984), 580; R. Thysman, *Communauté et directives éthiques: La catéchèse de Matthieu* (Gembloux: J. Duculot, 1974), 43, n. 1; H. L. Chronis, "The Torn Veil: Cultus and Christology in Mark 15:37-39," *JBL* 101 (1982): 111; W. Carter, *Matthew: Storyteller, Interpreter, Evangelist* (Peabody, Mass.: Hendrickson, 1996), 221; H. L. Kessler, "Through the Veil: The Holy Image in Judaism and Christianity," *Kairos* 32 (1990): 67; esp. M. Knowles, *Jeremiah in Matthew's Gospel: The Rejected-Prophet Motif in Matthean Redaction* (JSNTSup 68; Sheffield: JSOT Press, 1993), 175; P. Luomanen, *Entering the Kingdom of Heaven* (WUNT 2.101; Tübingen: Mohr Siebeck, 1998), 228.

provides healing for the lame and blind within its courts (21:14). Others have claimed that this "cleansing" text illustrates that the Herodian Temple was "judged inadequate as the place of God's presence and authentic worship."[6] But it was *also* an appropriate place for Jesus to teach (21:23; 26:55) as well as *still* a place to offer sacrifices (5:23-24; 8:4), though Jesus remained superior to it (12:6). Addressing these tensions may lead us to a more comprehensive picture of Matthew's understanding of the Temple. In light of Matthew's infamous "anti-Jewish polemic," scholars frequently conjecture that he is likewise anti-Temple. We will see, however, that the first evangelist has a remarkably consistent and positive portrayal of the Temple. No negative word is uttered by either the evangelist or his Jesus about the Temple *itself*. Indeed, Matthean redaction seems to stifle texts where Mark's Jesus could be understood as anti-Temple, and Matthean negative statements about it, such as its impending (or past?) destruction, are centered on confrontations with the religious leaders who mismanage it. Allusions and statements about the destruction of the Temple also resonate with language and theodicy found in Jeremiah, where God's displeasure with those managing the Solomonic Temple finds expression in judgment executed against the Temple itself.[7] The fault lies with *them*, and, as in Jeremiah's time, the Temple, so to speak, took the fall.

Matthew's Temple Language

This evangelist, as is common in the NT, can use any of four terms for the Temple: οἶκος, οἰκία, ἱερόν, or ναός. His use of οἶκος is rather straightforward (9 times). Naturally, it refers to a private home (9:6, 7), the "house" of Israel (10:6; 15:24) and a king's "palace" (11:8). In a parable it refers to a "house" vacated by an evil spirit (12:44). In reference to the Temple, οἶκος is used only in allusions to or citations from the OT without necessarily any further intention than to connote the Semitic circumlocution of God from his OT source.[8] Mat-

---

6. J. P. Heil, *The Death and Resurrection of Jesus: A Narrative-Critical Reading of Matthew 26–28* (Minneapolis: Fortress, 1991), 85.

7. B. W. Longenecker ("Rome's Victory and God's Honour: The Jerusalem Temple and the Spirit of God in Lukan Theodicy" [in G. N. Stanton, B. W. Longenecker, and S. C. Barton, eds. *The Spirit and Christian Origins* {Grand Rapids: Eerdmans, 2004}, 93]) defines this as "theodicy," in which "God is said to have permitted disasters to fall on [his] people as a means of disciplining them, since [he] had grown dissatisfied with their infidelity as a covenant people."

8. 12:4 (1 Sam. 21:7). No Temple term is used here in the LXX, only references to ἐκ προσώπου κυρίου (21:7) and ἐνώπιον κυρίου (21:8); 21:13 (Isa. 56:7; 60:7, using οἶκος); 23:38 for "house" of Jerusalem (Ps. 118:26, using οἶκος).

thew uses οἰκία similarly (25 times). It is likewise used of a private home (2:11; 8:6, 14; 9:10, 23, 28; 10:12, 13, 14; 13:1, 36; 17:25; 19:29; 26:6) or a hometown (13:57). Οἰκία is also used in parables or illustrations, such as reference to a light shining to everyone in a house (5:15) or to a man building his house upon the stability of a rock (7:24, 25, 26, 27), or to a "household" divided among itself (12:25). Matthew also uses it in a similar context with reference to robbing a man's house (12:29) or not going onto the roof of one's house or taking things out of the house while awaiting the *parousia* (24:17; cf. 24:43). Yet the possibility of οἰκία referring to the Temple is only remotely present in the "house upon a rock" analogy (7:24-27).

Τὸ ἱερόν typically refers to the general structure of a Temple and its courts in extracanonical texts.[9] Yet in the LXX it is almost exclusively reserved for pagan shrines (Ezek. 45:9; 1 Chr. 29:4; 2 Chr. 6:13), perhaps emphasizing the particularity of Israel's sanctuary.[10] It is the extracanonical use that seems to be more prevalent in the NT, where τὸ ἱερόν most frequently refers to the Temple, generally (cf. Matt. 12:6; Acts 24:6; 1 Cor. 9:13), and Matthew seems to favor using the term for the general Temple complex, including its courts and sanctuary (ναός). Jesus is placed upon the highest point of the Temple (ἱερόν) when tempted by Satan (4:1-11), and its courts are the location of his confrontation with the priests on a Sabbath controversy (12:5). Jesus is said to be greater than the ἱερόν (12:6), and from there he drove out "all who were buying and selling" (21:12). Here he also heals the blind and lame (12:14), and here he evokes the acclamation of the children who shouted, "Hosanna to the Son of David" (21:15), an act about which the chief priests and teachers were indignant. He was teaching in the Temple (ἱερόν) when the chief priests and elders challenged the origin of his "authority" (τὴν ἐξουσίαν; 21:23). And only after leaving the Temple (ἱερόν) and having his attention called to its buildings (24:1) does Jesus predict that every one of its stones will be thrown down (24:2). Finally, Jesus is arrested in Gethsemane even though he sat teaching in the Temple (ἱερόν) daily (26:55). Within the Temple (ἱερόν), Jesus was not to be touched, a point raised by Jesus himself at his arrest (26:55), which may indicate the generally positive relationship Matthew's Jesus has with the Temple, as we will see.

Ναός in classical Greek was long known to refer to an "abode of the gods" with respect to a Temple[11] or the innermost shrine in which the deity dwells.[12]

---

9. Herodotus, *Histories* 1.183; 2.63; Polybius, *Fr.* 16.39.4; Josephus, *Ant.* 6.374; *War* 7.123; 1 Macc. 10:84; 11:4.

10. G. Schenk, "τὸ ἱερόν," *TDNT*, 3:235.

11. Cf. O. Michel, "ναός," *TDNT*, 4:880.

12. Herodotus, *Hist.* 1.183; 6.19; Xenophon, *Apol.* 15; *UPZ* 1.c; *P. Gnom.* 79; Liddell and Scott, *Lexicon*, 1160. Cf. J. H. Moulton and G. Milligan, *Vocabulary of the Greek Testament* (Peabody,

Though the LXX can use the term to translate אולם (also אילם; "vestibule" or "porch"),[13] it overwhelmingly translates היכל ("Temple" or "main room of a Temple").[14] This refers to the Temple, holy place and holy of holies, within the precincts of the ἱερόν. Dalman's claim that this distinction holds firm in the gospels seems likely.[15] The term ναός does not occur in Matthew's gospel until the "woes" chapter (23), where Jesus rebukes "blind guides" for their oaths "by the Temple" or "the gold of the Temple" (23:16). Yet Jesus affirms that it is the Temple (ναός) that makes the gold "sacred" (ὁ ἁγιάσας; 23:17). He further affirms that the importance of swearing by the Temple is compounded by the presence of "one who dwells in it" (ἐν τῷ κατοικοῦντι αὐτόν; 23:21). The curious event of the murder of Zechariah son of Berekiah occurred just outside the ναός: "between the Temple (ναός) and the altar" (23:35).[16] Testimonies, clearly said to be false, accuse Jesus of claiming he will destroy the Temple (ναός; 26:61; 27:40), and Judas throws his money into the ναός prior to going away and hanging himself (27:5). But the fact that the ναός included both the holy place and the holy of holies still precludes our using the term to discern which veil Matthew had in view. Indeed, Matthew's Temple language is helpful in discerning how he uses terms, but does not provide apparent indications of his view of the Temple and its cult in general. For that we must cast our nets more broadly to examine how the evangelist portrays the Temple generally both in his redactional use of Temple language and pericopae and in his depiction of it and its cult in the narrative as a whole.

Mass.: Hendrickson, 1997), 422; repr. of *Vocabulary of the Greek Testament* (London: Hodder & Stoughton, 1930).

13. 1 Chr. 28:11; 2 Chr. 8:12; 15:8; 29:7, 17.

14. W. L. Holladay, *A Concise Hebrew and Aramaic Lexicon of the Old Testament: Based upon the Lexical Work of Ludwig Koehler and Walter Baumgartner* (Leiden: Brill, 1988), 79. Cf. Lust, *Lexicon*, 2:313. LXX 1 Sam. 1:9; 3:3 [A οἴκῳ κυρίου]; 2 Sam. 22:7; 1 Kgs. 6:3, 5, 17 [τψβ and A add οἶκος], 33, 36; 7:21, 50 [A adds τοῦ οἴκου; cf. τψβ]; 2 Kgs. 18:16; 23:4; 24:13; 2 Chr. 3:17; 4:7, 8, 22; 26:16; 27:2; 36:7; Ezra 5:14; 6:5; Pss. 5:7; 10:5; 17:6; 26:4; 27:2; 28:9; 44:15; 64:4; 67:29; 78:1; 137:2; 143:12; Amos 8:3; Joel 3:5; Jonah 2:5, 8; Hab. 2:20; Hag. 2:16, 19; Zech. 8:9; Mal. 3:1; Isa. 66:6; Jer. 7:4; 24:1; Ezek. 8:16; 41:1, 4, 15, 21, 23, 25; Dan. 4:26; 5:2, 3. Cf. Michel, *TDNT*, 4:882, nn. 6, 7.

15. G. Dalman, *Orte und Wege Jesu* (3d ed.; Gütersloh: C. Bertelsmann, 1924), 301. Cf. Michel, *TDNT*, 4:882, n. 8.

16. C. Deutsch ("Wisdom in Matthew: Transformation of a Symbol," *NovT* 32 [1990]: 43-44) contends that this pericope (23:35f.) has Matthew's Jesus place himself among the tradition of rejected prophets, wise men and scribes from Israel's past, which was later transferred to Wisdom's history (cf. Wis. Sol. 7:27; 10:1–11:14; 1 Kgs. 18:1-16; 2 Chr. 24:17-23; *Mart. Isa.* 5.1-16; *Liv. Pro.* 2.1; 3.18; 6.2; 7.1-3; D. E. Aune, *Prophecy in Early Christianity and the Ancient Mediterranean World* (Grand Rapids: Eerdmans, 1983), 158f.

The Temple and Its Cult (Matt. 1–11)

At the beginning of his gospel, Matthew shows no knowledge of Luke's introduction of the "Temple of the Lord" in the Zechariah episode nor with reference to a sacrifice (as in Mark), but in his "temptation" narrative (4:1-11), where the devil (ὁ διάβολος) takes Jesus into the "holy city" and places Jesus "on the highest point of the Temple" (ἐπὶ τὸ πτερύγιον τοῦ ἱεροῦ; 4:5), a feature absent from Mark and appearing a bit later in Luke (4:9). Though it is difficult to say with any certainty, that Matthew introduces readers to the Temple in this confrontation scene may begin to indicate Matthew's developing notion of authority confrontations that occur in the ἱερόν.

Readers are given a more revealing glimpse of the evangelist's view of the Temple by his presentation of the Temple cult in 5:23-24, a text perhaps loosely related to Mark 11:25. Here the worshipper brings his gift (προσφέρω + δῶρα; 8:4; 2:11)[17] upon the altar (τὸ θυσιαστήριον, probably the altar of burnt offering in Jerusalem[18]) and is to be reconciled with his brother prior to offering it. That the gift is given at all seems to presume the validity of this sacrifice. Yet Matthew's favor toward the cult is subservient to reconciliation, which must occur first (πρῶτον; 5:24); then the gift is given (5:24). Though elsewhere no such injunction is proposed, it is apparent that here at least "participation in the sacrificial system," far from being replaced or mooted, is "presupposed."[19]

Further indirect reference to the Temple by virtue of its cult is found in Matt. 8:1-4 (Mark 1:40-45; Luke 5:12-16), which Matthew has removed from the Markan introductory material to place the reference immediately after the Sermon on the Mount and at the head of his section concerning miraculous healings, etc. (Matt. 8:1–9:34). In this scene Matthew takes Mark's account of the healing of a leper, which reads "the leprosy left him and he was cleansed" (Mark 1:42; ἀπῆλθεν ἀπ' αὐτοῦ ἡ λέπρα, καὶ ἐκαθαρίσθη), and simply asserts that the man was "cleansed of his leprosy" (ἐκαθαρίσθη αὐτοῦ ἡ λέπρα). Immediately (καὶ εὐθέως)[20] Jesus tells the man to tell no one of his healing but to go to the high priest (omitting Mark's "concerning your cleansing," Mark 1:44; also Luke 5:14). As in 5:24, Matthew alone records that the man is to offer a "gift" (8:4; τὸ δῶρον) *after* the cleansing, again presuming the legitimacy of offering the appropriate sacrifice. Though Mark (1:44-45) and Luke (5:15-16) have more of the

---

17. This is a favorite Matthean combination. So W. D. Davies and D. C. Allison, *Matthew* (3 vols.; ICC; Edinburgh: T&T Clark, 1988, 1991, 1997), 1:248, 517.

18. Davies and Allison, *Matthew*, 1:517.

19. Davies and Allison, *Matthew*, 1:518.

20. Here Matthew is uncharacteristically preserving this from Mark. U. Luz, *Matthew 8–20* (Hermeneia; Minneapolis: Fortress, 2001), 6.

story, Matthew ends it rather abruptly here, perhaps content to finish his narrative with Jesus insisting on the man's offering the gift that Moses commanded.[21]

It seems curious that though Matthew affirms the validity of sacrifices, he elsewhere asserts that God desires "mercy and not sacrifice" (ἔλεος θέλω καὶ οὐ θυσίαν; 9:13; also 12:7; cf. Hos. 6:6). The first citation is a direct response by Jesus to criticisms by the Pharisees that Jesus is eating with "tax collectors and sinners" (τῶν τελωνῶν καὶ ἁμαρτωλῶν; 9:11). This citation is unique to Matthew among the synoptics (Mark 2:17 reads οὐκ ἦλθον καλέσαι δικαίους ἀλλὰ ἁμαρτωλούς) and matches precisely with Aquila's version of the LXX of Hos. 6:6.[22] It is largely accepted that Matthew's καὶ οὐ is not a starkly contrastive assertion but a Hebraic idiom of "dialectical negation" meaning "I desire mercy *more* than sacrifice."[23] Luz further asserts that this understanding "was clearly the understanding of Hosea himself, the Targum, and contemporary Jewish exegesis. It also best fits the thought of Matthew himself, who did not abolish the cultic law but made it inferior to the love command (5:18-19; 5:23-24; 23:23-28)."[24] The affirmation of this reading of the Hosea citation is seen in 12:7 in a Sabbath controversy. Here Matthew, again in a text unique to his gospel, quotes the Hosea text immediately following his declaration that Jesus was greater than the Temple (12:6).[25] Matthew provides the same meaning in a differing context. Indeed, that Matthew's Jesus did not intend to abolish the sacrificial laws is affirmed by his argument based upon them in the immediate context (12:5-6).[26] He thus makes the same point that "unless informed by a spirit of mercy, observance of the Torah can become uninformed slavery to the traditions of men."[27]

Matthew's Temple in Relation to Jesus (Matt. 12–20)

More explicit discussion of the Temple is found in 12:5-6, unique to Matthew, where Jesus demonstrates his lordship over the Sabbath (12:1-14). This text is an insertion into the Markan pericope (Mark 2:23-28) concerning the action of

---

21. Luz, *Matthew 8–20*, 6.
22. Davies and Allison, *Matthew*, 2:104.
23. Luz, *Matthew 8–20*, 34. Pace G. Strecker, *Der Weg der Gerechtigkeit: Untersuchung zur Theologie des Matthäus* (Göttingen: Vandenhoeck & Ruprecht, 1962), 32; J. P. Meier, *Matthew* (NTM 3; Wilmington, Del.: Michael Glazier, 1981), 94.
24. Luz, *Matthew 8–20*, 34; Davies and Allison, *Matthew*, 2:104-5.
25. Presumably in both cases "sacrifice" stands for mere obedience to Torah requirements of outward action.
26. Luz, *Matthew 8–20*, 182.
27. Davies and Allison, *Matthew*, 2:105; cf. D. J. Moo, "Jesus and the Mosaic Law," *JSNT* 20 (1984): 10.

David in the Temple and asserts that "the priests in the Temple desecrate the day [Sabbath] and yet are innocent" (12:5). Jesus then asserts that "one greater than the Temple is here" (τοῦ ἱεροῦ μεῖζόν ἐστιν ὧδε; 12:6). While the identity of the "one greater" than the Temple (ἱερόν; 12:6) has been disputed, surely the saying is associated with Jesus himself, and what is greater (μεῖζόν) than the Temple is likely Jesus.[28] Mark's "greater than" statements have nothing to do with the Temple.[29] Yet though Matthew adopts Mark's use of the "greater than" formula elsewhere,[30] he uses it with respect to the Temple three times: here Jesus is greater than the Temple, later the Temple is greater than its gold (23:17), and finally the altar is greater than the gift given on it (23:19). With respect to Jesus, Matthew affirms that he is greater than the Temple (12:6), than Jonah (πλεῖον, 12:41) and than Solomon (πλεῖον, 12:42).[31] Matthew also uses "greater" expressions in the escalated shouts of Hosanna (Matt. 20:31), the greater righteousness Jesus demanded (πλεῖον, 5:20), and to underscore the importance of nonmaterial things (6:25; cf. 20:10). Matthew seems to have perhaps adapted Mark's and "Q"'s (or perhaps extending a "Q" pattern) "greater than" statements to elevate first Jesus (12:6, 41, 42 ["Q" 11:31, 32])[32] and then the Temple (23:17, 19). Yet the first of these uses (12:6) puts things in perspective: the former (Jesus) is greater than the latter (the Temple).[33] It seems that Matthew, in his affirmation of the Temple and its cult elsewhere, is careful in these statements to put it in its place with respect to Jesus. It is a valid place to offer sacrifices and (later) to pray, but ultimately it is secondary (as a means of a relationship with God) to Jesus. The Markan Sabbath healings (2:23–3:6), other than mentioning priests in the house of God, have nothing to do with the Temple.

These are the only explicit references to sacrifices in Matthew (though per-

---

28. R. H. Gundry, *Matthew: A Commentary on His Handbook for a Mixed Church under Persecution* (Grand Rapids: Eerdmans, 1994), 223; so also Davies and Allison, *Matthew*, 2:314; France, *Matthew: Evangelist and Teacher*, 215; D. C. Kupp, *Matthew's Emmanuel: Divine Presence and God's People in the First Gospel* (SNTSMS 90; Cambridge: Cambridge University Press, 1996), 75-76.

29. They are simply made with respect to the mustard plant (4:32), the priority of the disciples (9:34), the greatest commandment (12:31) and the significance of a poor widow's offering (12:43).

30. He uses it with respect to the mustard seed (Matt. 13:32) and the disciples (18:1, 4; 23:11; cf. 11:1). Cf. O. L. Cope, *Matthew: A Scribe Trained for the Kingdom of Heaven* (CBQMS 5; Washington: Catholic Biblical Association of America, 1976), 35.

31. Cf. Cope, *Scribe*, 43.

32. Cf. J. M. Robinson et al., *The Critical Edition of Q* (Hermeneia; Minneapolis: Fortress, 2000), 252-55.

33. Cf. R. Beaton, *Isaiah's Christ in Matthew's Gospel* (SNTSMS 123; Cambridge: Cambridge University Press, 2002), 184.

haps implicit in Matt. 8). However, in Mark (1:44; Luke 5:14; cf. Luke 2:24), the healed leper is commanded to offer sacrifices for his cleansing, and loving God and one's neighbor is "more important than all burnt offerings and sacrifices" (12:33). That this is omitted by Matthew may indicate that he viewed the statement as potentially nullifying the sacrifices that he has elsewhere affirmed. Though, for Matthew, God desires mercy *more than* sacrifices (just as Jesus is *more than* [greater than] the Temple), he nonetheless affirms the validity of the sacrifice being offered.

Some have suggested a Temple allusion in 16:18, where Peter is called the "rock." This argument reads Matthew's "my church" statement in light of 2 Sam. 7, and presumes the church to constitute a new Temple, noting that "in Jewish tradition the rock at the base of the Temple on Zion, the so-called *'eben šětîyyâ*, is at the centre of the world."[34] While this is congruent with other groups in Judaism and early Christianity conceiving of people as a Temple,[35] Matthew does not here make a clear transition from identifying the Temple as a legitimate cultic enterprise in itself to identifying it as a group of people.[36] A stronger argument could be in the evangelist's use of οἰκοδομέω with respect to the church, a term that it is used elsewhere with respect to accusations against Jesus in both 26:61 (from Mark 14:58) and 27:40 (from Mark 15:29), regarding his apparent threat to tear down the Temple (ναός) and raise it up (οἰκοδομέω).[37] From Mark 14:58, Davies and Allison contend that the reference here to a ναός "not made with hands" is to the church.[38] Yet the Markan account bears no more evidence of an ecclesiastical reading than does Matthew's. Moreover, they argue that the Davidic motifs in Matt. 16:13-20 suggest that 2 Sam. 7 and 1 Chr. 17 are in view, which evokes a Temple imagery.[39] Yet even if such contexts were in view, it does not necessarily follow that the Temple images present in the OT texts are brought to the Matthean pericope, let alone that they apply to the newly formed church. We cannot say for certain that Matthew identified his church with the Temple.

Matthew again alludes to the Temple in the account of the Temple tax

---

34. W. D. Davies and D. C. Allison, *A Critical and Exegetical Commentary on the Gospel according to Saint Matthew* (3 vols.; ICC; Edinburgh: T&T Clark, 1988-97), 3:627-28.

35. Cf. Davies and Allison, *Matthew*, 3:627, n. 86; B. Gärtner, *The Temple and the Community in Qumran and the New Testament: A Comparative Study in the Temple Symbolism of Qumran Texts and the New Testament* (Cambridge: Cambridge University Press, 1965).

36. Davies and Allison, *Matthew*, 3:627 claim that an allusion to 2 Sam. 7 "evokes the idea of a temple," which seems a rather weak basis to claim that the people *are* the Temple. They also say that the notion of the church being the Temple is here "implicit."

37. Davies and Allison, *Matthew*, 3:627.

38. Davies and Allison, *Matthew*, 3:627; cf. n. 89; 3:335, n. 54; Donald Juel, *Messiah and Temple: The Trial of Jesus in the Gospel of Mark* (SBLDS 31; Missoula: Scholars Press, 1977), 144-57.

39. Davies and Allison, *Matthew*, 2:603.

(17:24-29), which is entirely unique to his gospel. In this scene, Jesus declares his exemption from the Temple tax but nonetheless pays his and Peter's taxes by invoking a miraculous provision of the funds from the mouth of a fish (17:27). He pays it not out of obligation, but "so that we may not offend them" (17:27). Davies and Allison, following Bauckham,[40] comment that here Matthew affirms the Temple cult but questions "the idea that taxation is the appropriate means of maintaining that divine institution."[41] This verdict is underscored by the conclusion that Jesus gives Peter instructions to pay the tax (17:27). Yet why is Matthew here concerned that his Jesus not offend people, when only a few chapters later such concerns are by no means obvious? Luz suggests the concern is to "compromise for the sake of peace and love" on matters that are not fundamental to faithfulness to the Torah.[42] Davies and Allison, however, capture more of Matthew's view of the Temple when they assert that "Voluntary payment should be made in order to prevent others from inferring that Peter or Jesus has rejected the Temple cult."[43]

The "Triumphal Entry" and the "Cleansing" of the Temple (Matt. 21)

The Temple setting is important, for though Matthew (21:9), Mark (11:9-10) and John (12:13) all record Jesus' "triumphal entry," only the First Evangelist explicitly states that the children's praises of "Hosanna," apparently in response to Jesus' healing, likewise occurred *in the Temple* (ἱερόν, 21:15).[44] Davies and Allison suggest that the locus is a portent, and that a Temple, as the locus of special revelations, joined with a (frequently oracular) acclaim of children, forcefully confirms "God's approval of Jesus."[45] From here, Jesus departs from the Temple to spend the night in Bethany (21:17; Mark 11:11), only to return "early in the morning" (πρωΐ), whereas Mark has "on the next day" (τῇ ἐπαύριον; 11:12).[46] The Markan Jesus' departure from the Temple (cf. 11:28-30)[47] has been seen as con-

---

40. R. J. Bauckham, "The Coin in the Fish's Mouth," in *Gospel Perspectives 6: The Miracles of Jesus* (ed. D. Wenham and C. Blomberg; Sheffield: JSOT Press, 1986), 219-52.
41. Davies and Allison, *Matthew*, 2:745.
42. Luz, *Matthew 8–20*, 418.
43. Davies and Allison, *Matthew*, 2:746.
44. David Daube, *New Testament and Rabbinic Judaism* (London: Athlone, 1956), 20-21; Cf. Knowles, *Jeremiah in Matthew's Gospel*, 234-35, n. 4.
45. Davies and Allison, *Matthew*, 3:141.
46. It is possible here to recognize Matthew's identification of Jesus with Wisdom, as he does more explicitly in 11:19, 25-30. Cf. Deutsch, "Wisdom in Matthew," 33-39.
47. Cf. M. J. Suggs, *Wisdom, Christology, and Law in Matthew's Gospel* (Cambridge, Mass.: Harvard University Press, 1970), 77-98.

tributing to his Wisdom Christology, whereby Jesus is depicted as the personification of Wisdom, who departs in judgment because one is unwilling to heed the wisdom conveyed.[48] Apparently Matthew's adjustment intends to lend narrative continuity with the previous pericope, though typically such urgency depicted by action is expected in Mark.

The Temple itself (τὸ ἱερόν)[49] first appears in Mark's gospel in 11:11, a pivotal point in that gospel to introduce the Second Evangelist's Passion Narrative.[50] In this climactic scene in Matthew's gospel (21:1-27), Jesus enters Jerusalem (21:1-11) and the Temple (ἱερόν; 21:12), where he performs his notorious "cleansing." Carter, to name but one scholar, insists that Jesus' actions here demonstrate the completion of the necessity of the Temple's sacrificial system, and that Jesus now replaces the Temple and is the location where "God's presence and atonement were experienced."[51] Yet this contention seems to violate the plain sense of the pericope. For, as Bauckham contends, by his insistence on the Temple's being a house of prayer, accompanied by his actions, Jesus is not rejecting or downplaying the sacrificial cult.[52] Instead he looks for it to be "the expression of the prayer of those who came to the Temple to worship." That Matthew's Jesus asserts that the Temple "will be called" (κληθήσεται) a house of prayer (a reading found in neither the Isa. 56:7 nor Isa. 60:7 texts to which he alludes) seems to affirm the legitimacy of its function and a desire on the part of Matthew to see that function restored: that is, it has a future.[53] Though κληθήσεται may be simply a "prophetic" future and may not indicate a future in this sense in the Matthean context, surely the contrastive element (21:13; ὑμεῖς δὲ αὐτὸν ποιεῖτε σπήλαιον λῃστῶν) serves to underscore the culpability of the

---

48. For a discussion of Wisdom in Matt. 11:25-30, cf. C. Deutsch, *Hidden Wisdom and the Easy Yoke: Wisdom, Torah and Discipleship in Mt 11, 25-30* (JSNTSup 18; Sheffield: Academic Press, 1987); T. Arvedson, *Das Mysterium Christi: Eine Studie zu Mt. 11.25-30* (Leipzig: Alfred Lorentz, 1937); H. D. Betz, "The Logion of the Easy Yoke and of Rest (Mt. 11:28-30)," *JBL* 86 (1967): 10-24. For Wisdom in Matt. 23:34-36, 37-39, cf. F. Burnett, *The Testament of Jesus-Sophia: A Redaction-Critical Study of the Eschatological Discourse in Matthew* (Washington, D.C.: University Press of America, 1979).

49. Cf. Longenecker, "Rome's Victory and God's Honour," 95.

50. M. Kähler (*The So-Called Historical Jesus and the Historic Biblical Christ* [Philadelphia: Fortress, 1964], 80, n. 11) has suggested that the gospels could be called "passion narratives with extended introductions."

51. Carter, *Matthew*, 221.

52. While Bauckham's analysis seems to attend more to issues relating to the historical Jesus, his conclusions are congruent with the theological interests of the First Evangelist.

53. Though it is possible to see this reference as being to the future of the church (cf. Gundry, *Matthew*, 413), again we find no clear evidence that the church is equated with, let alone supplanting, the Temple in Matthew's gospel.

Temple management. That is, the intended function of the Temple was being frustrated by corruption and exploitation within the Temple precincts,[54] and Jesus, as messianic king, comes to the Temple "to purge it of practices that mocked its divinely intended purpose."[55]

Immediately upon entering Jerusalem (21:12-13), Matthew has Jesus entering the Temple (ἱερόν; 21:12), whereas Mark claims Jesus entered the next day (11:12). Though such urgency is typically associated with Mark (his καὶ εὐθύς statements), Matthew seems particularly concerned with Jesus' location *in the Temple*.[56] After he entered the Temple, the "blind and lame" (τυφλοὶ καὶ χωλοί) came to Jesus, and he healed them *there* (ἱερόν; 21:14),[57] presumably in the outer courts, where they were permitted, and where Jesus also found the merchants and tax collectors (21:12). However, each of Mark's healings of the blind occurs not only outside the Temple, but outside the city (Mark 8:22-23; 10:46, 49, 51). Matthew knows that the "blind and lame" (τυφλοὶ καὶ χωλοί) were to keep their distance from the house of the Lord.[58] Why does Matthew seem to diverge, partly by means of relocation, from Mark's account? Moreover, why does he bring the unfortunate people within the Temple's outer courts when he is so concerned about "fulfilling" the law (5:17)? The reader may be intended to recall Jesus' claim to superiority over the Temple and therefore, presumably, the authority to "trump" legal matters pertaining to it, but Gerhardsson has offered a more tenable solution.[59] He proposes that Matthew's Jesus is not violating the Law by acknowledging these outcasts in the Temple but upholding it. Jesus does this by removing the quality which forbade them entrance in the first place: he heals their disabilities "so that they may then enter."[60] So it seems possible that

---

54. R. J. Bauckham, "Jesus' Demonstration in the Temple," in *Law and Religion: Essays on the Place of the Law in Israel and Early Christianity* (ed. B. Lindars; Cambridge: James Clarke, 1988), 84.

55. D. A. Hagner, *Matthew* (2 vols.; WBC 33A-B; Dallas: Word, 1993, 1995), 2:598; cf. Beaton, *Isaiah's Christ*, 183.

56. Cf. France, "Chronological Aspects," 38.

57. He has seen them before in Matthew and healed them (15:30), apparently in ironic contrast to the "blind" Pharisees who refuse to be healed and whom Jesus commands his disciples to leave (15:14). Cf. Knowles, *Jeremiah in Matthew's Gospel*, 234-35, who associates this text with the Davidic Messiahship of Jesus.

58. And so Matthew presumably means that they were in the court around the Temple (the "court of the gentiles"). 2 Sam. 5:8 forbids the blind and lame to enter εἰς οἶκον κυρίου. Cf. Lev. 21:18-19; 1QSa 2:5-22; CD 15:15-17; m. Ḥag. 1.1; 1QM 7:4-6; 12:7-9. Cf. Strecker, *Der Weg der Gerechtigkeit*, 19, n. 1.

59. Hagner (*Matthew*, 2:601) seems to suggest this is an ironic narrative device intended to show the kingdom blessings which transformed the Temple precincts "from a commercial center to a place of healing."

60. Cf. Gerhardsson, *Mighty Acts of Jesus*, 30, cf. n. 16; cf. especially Gerhardsson's contri-

Matthew is presuming that the healed person is then permitted to go offer the sacrifice after he is healed, as Jesus encourages the leper to do. Sacrifices, on at least one occasion in Matthew, followed healings (cf. 8:4). Surely Matthew in this pericope is concerned that Jesus restore the Temple to its intended function by making it a "house of prayer,"[61] which we must see as the driving thesis of the pericope, and this pericope seems best understood in that light, to prepare the unfortunate man to participate in its worship by healing him.[62]

Along the way Jesus causes the fig tree to wither explicitly to demonstrate the power of faith (21:21-22). This subject has been discussed in some detail by W. R. Telford's work on Matthean redaction of the account.[63] Telford's work demonstrates that Matthean redaction of the Markan pericope lays emphasis on the power of Jesus and resulting faith,[64] as is common in Matthean redaction of Markan miracles,[65] *rather than associating the miracle of the cursed fig tree with the Temple.* With "Jesus' miracles of healing in the Temple (21.4), the cursing of the fig-tree no longer stands out as it does in Mark as the *only* miracle performed by Jesus in Jerusalem. . . . The story has been removed from the sphere of judgment and eschatology, and is treated as if it were a normal miracle story."[66] France asserts that in this pericope Matthew has subordinated strict chronology to a more dramatic presentation of the incident in order to draw out more powerfully what he understands to be its theological implication."[67] Matthew has removed "practically all" elements from Mark that suggest the account was primarily symbolic.[68] Thus the saying regarding the throwing of the mountain into

---

bution in C. H. Martling and S. E. Staxäng, eds., *Kommentar till evangelieboken, Högmässotexterna* (Part 3; Stockholm: Uppsala, 1964), 484-86.

61. Cf. Davies and Allison, *Matthew*, 3:132.

62. Beaton (*Isaiah's Christ*, 183-85) asserts that particularly during Hezekiah's restoration of the Temple (2 Chr. 29:3-7) the "cleansing of the temple and healings therein point to motifs of purification and wholeness." Cf. "Son of David" in *Pss. Sol.* 17.30; Davies and Allison, *Matthew*, 3:139.

63. This is the lengthy subtitle of the work, the full title of which is *The Barren Temple and the Withered Tree: A Redaction-Critical Analysis of the Cursing of the Fig-Tree Pericope in Mark's Gospel and Its Relation to the Cleansing of the Temple Tradition* (JSNTSS 1; Sheffield: JSOT, 1980).

64. Cf. Telford, *Barren Temple*, 81.

65. Telford, *Barren Temple*, 81.

66. Telford, *Barren Temple*, 80.

67. R. T. France, "Chronological Aspects of 'Gospel Harmony,'" *VE* 16 (1986): 38.

68. Telford (*Barren Temple*, 81) notes that Matthew has removed or altered Mark's account with respect to "Jesus' survey of the Temple (11.1), his disappointed search for fruit, the show of leaves, the curious 'for it was not the season for figs,' the delay in the effect of the curese. . . . The strange position of the story before and after the cleansing episode has been altered. . . . The position of the story in Mt. 21, while derivative of Mark, appears logically unrelated to the surrounding material, despite Matthew's attempt to provide closer contextual links."

the sea (Mark 11:23; Matt. 21:21) is no longer suggestive of the Temple Mount, as it is in Mark.[69] We find, then, that Matthew, while clearly escalating Mark's polemic against the Jewish leaders, softens his polemic against the Temple.

Immediately after this event Jesus once again enters the Temple courts (ἱερόν, 21:23), an account found likewise in Mark (11:27) and Luke (20:1). Yet whereas Mark says that again Jesus went into Jerusalem and entered the Temple, and Luke casually mentions Jesus' being in the Temple teaching the people, Matthew's account may emphasize the Temple (ἱερόν) by placing it earlier in the sentence than it appears in the other synoptic accounts and making it the first noun in that sentence. A conflict arises *here*, of all places, with the chief priests and elders of the people regarding Jesus' "authority" (ἐξουσίᾳ) to do "these things" (ταῦτα):[70] both by what authority he does these things and who gave him such authority.[71] Thus Matthew seems to provide a wording that emphasizes that the conflict here concerns authority, with the context of Jesus' priestly critics, a theme we have found consistently throughout.

Another possible allusion to the Temple is found in 21:33-46.[72] This, the "parable of the Wicked Tenants," seems to be a thinly veiled illustration of the Jews' rejection of Jesus. Scholars have recognized that v. 33b is clearly dependent upon the LXX of Isa. 5:2, and that in the *Targum* of that text (*Tg. Isa.* 5:1b-2, 5) the tower becomes the Temple, and the wine vat the altar (cf. *t. Suk.* 3.15; *t. Me'il.* 1.16), and "the song as a whole has become a prediction of the Temple's destruction."[73] Here Jesus responds to the self-condemning words of his listen-

---

69. Telford, *Barren Temple*, 79.

70. Hagner (*Matthew*, 2:609) says that it refers to the events of the preceding day, while Davies and Allison (*Matthew*, 3:159) presume it to include everything in chapter 21 (save the withering of the fig tree). Cf. John T. Carroll and Joel B. Green, *The Death of Jesus in Early Christianity* (Peabody, Mass.: Hendrickson, 1995), 54.

71. Cf. Beaton, *Isaiah's Christ*, 185.

72. Cf. Wesley G. Olmstead, *Matthew's Trilogy of Parables: The Nation, the Nations and the Reader in Matthew 21.28–22.14* (SNTSMS 127; Cambridge: Cambridge University Press, 2003); R. J. Bauckham, "Synoptic Parousia Parables Again," *NTS* 29 (1983): 129-34.

73. Olmstead, *Trilogy*, 110; cf. 113-16; 116 n. 95. Though there is some discussion about the dating of the Isaiah Targum, C. Evans and G. Brooke have found similar tower/Temple allusions in *1 Enoch* 89 (cf. *1 Enoch* 89.3, 56, 66b-67; *Barn.* 16.1-2, 4, 5) and 4Q500 respectively, both of which predate the NT (cf. Olmstead, *Trilogy*, 110-11 and nn. 67-69, citing C. A. Evans, "God's Vineyard Parables of Isaiah 5 and Mark 12," *BZ* 28 [1984]: 82-85; B. Chilton, *A Galilean Rabbi and His Bible: Jesus' Own Interpretation of Isaiah* [London: SPCK, 1984], 111-14; idem, "God's Vineyard and Its Caretakers," in *Jesus and His Contemporaries* [Leiden: Brill, 1995], 401; G. J. Brooke, "4Q500 1 and the Use of Scripture in the Parable of the Vineyard," *DSD* 2 [1995]: 279-85, 87-89, 293; W. J. C. Weren, "The Use of Isaiah 5, 1-7 in the Parable of the Tenants [Mark 12, 1-12; Matthew 21, 33-46]," *Bib* 79 [1998]: 15-17; E. Lohmeyer, "Das Gleichnis von de bösen Weingärtnern," *ZST* 18 [1941]: 242-59; M. Black, "The Christological Use of the Old Testament in the New Testa-

ers (21:41) by citing Ps. 118:22. This indicates that they have, in fact, rejected the "cap stone" (κεφαλὴν γωνίας; cf. Isa. 28:16). Though this stone likely refers to the "keystone" or "capstone" at the top of a doorway,[74] *T. Sol.* 22–23 suggests that this refers to the stone that completed Solomon's Temple.[75] It is possible that, as Jesus "fulfills" the law (5:17), he is here depicted as "completing" the Temple — that is, providing what is presently lacking: communion with God embodied in Matthew's "God with us" Christology. This is difficult to substantiate, however, because it is not clear that Jesus is here associating himself with the stone that completes the Temple, which would indicate that they have rejected what makes the Temple complete.

Matthew's Temple and Escalating Judgment (Matt. 22–25)

A potential allusion to the Temple is found in the parable of the Wedding Banquet (22:1-14). Here is a description of the "kingdom of heaven" (22:2), in which a king was enraged by the mistreatment of his servants and rejection of his invitation (22:3-7a). As a result, "He sent his army and destroyed those murderers and burned their city" (22:7). McNeile, to name but one scholar, insists this text refers to the fall of Jerusalem and thus uses it as a basis for dating the First Gospel after the tragedy of 70 C.E.[76] Yet scholars such as Gundry contend that the allusion is rather to Isa. 5:24-25, a context behind Matt. 21:33 (cf. Isa. 5:1-7), suggesting that Matthew edited his parable, borrowed from a previous tradition, to conform to the Isaiah text. Thus he insists that the reference is not to the fall of Jerusalem in 70 C.E.[77] For Davies and Allison *both* the Isa. 5 text *and* the events

---

ment," *NTS* 18 [1971]: 12-14, and K. Snodgrass, *The Parable of the Wicked Tenants: An Inquiry into Parable Interpretation* [Tübingen: Mohr Siebeck, 1983], 63-64, 113-18).

74. Hagner, *Matthew*, 2:622.

75. Davies and Allison, *Matthew*, 3:185-86.

76. A. H. McNeile, *The Gospel according to St Matthew* (London: Macmillan, 1915), xxvii. Cf. Hagner, *Matthew*, 2:630; Longenecker, "Rome's Victory and God's Honour," 93-95; Olmstead, *Trilogy*, 119, n. 115.

77. Gundry, *Matthew*, 436-37. Cf. C. H. Dodd, *The Parables of the Kingdom* (London: Nisbet, 1935), 61-65; C. A. Evans, "Predictions of the Destruction of the Herodian Temple in the Pseudepigrapha, Qumran Scrolls, and Related Texts," *JSP* 10 (1992): 89-147; S. J. D. Cohen, "The Destruction: From Scripture to Midrash," *Prooftexts* 2 (1982): 18-39; R. Goldenberg, "Early Rabbinic Explanations to the Destruction of Jerusalem," *SBLSP* 21 (1982): 517-25 and A. J. Saldarini, "Varieties of Rabbinic Response to the Destruction of the Temple," *SBLSP* 2 (1982): 437-58. For the view that there may be no reference to the 70 C.E. events, see R. J. Bauckham, "The Parable of the Royal Wedding Feast (Matthew 22:1-14) and the Parable of the Lame Man and the Blind Man *(Apocryphon of Ezekiel),*" *JBL* 115 (1996): 447-64.

of 70 C.E. are in view.⁷⁸ Regardless of whether before or after, conspicuously absent in this statement about the Temple is any statement which could be read negatively against the Temple itself. Instead we find that the siege was upon the city (22:7) because the invited guests abused the king's servants. The city (and its Temple?) had done nothing wrong though it was destroyed as an act of judgment against those who refused the king's invitation to the banquet.⁷⁹

The Temple is a prominent feature in Matthew's "seven woes" section (chap. 23). In this unique Matthean material, Jesus chastises the "blind guides" for thinking that swearing by the Temple (ναός) means nothing, but swearing by the gold of the Temple (ναός) is binding (23:16). They are criticized for making distinctions between oaths taken "by the Temple" (ἐν τῷ ναῷ) and "by the gold of the Temple" (ἐν τῷ χρυσῷ τοῦ ναοῦ) on the one hand, and "by the altar" (ἐν τῷ θυσιαστηρίῳ) and "by the gift upon it" (ἐν τῷ δώρῳ τῷ ἐπάνω αὐτοῦ; cf. 5:23) on the other.⁸⁰ Both the gold and the gift, he states, have significance because of the altar with which they are associated.⁸¹ Furthermore, Jesus insists that the value of such gold is found in the *Temple* (ναός; 23:17), and swearing by this Temple (ναός) is the same as swearing by the one who dwells in it (23:21, 22). Though the subject here is surely the use of oaths, Matthew explicitly cites the Pharisees' misappropriation of their oaths *with respect to the Temple and its sacrifices*. This observation, as we have seen throughout, underscores Matthew's concern to portray the Temple as being misused by those in charge of it.⁸² Moreover, Matthew brings this woe to a climax by first *presuming* God still to be present within the Temple (23:21; ἐν τῷ κατοικοῦντι αὐτόν)⁸³ and adding to it a new charge of swearing by heaven and acknowledging God's presence there (23:22).

Moreover, "between the Temple (ναός) and the altar" is the location of Matthew's curious account of the murder of Zechariah, son of Berechiah (23:35), apparently a "Q" text ("Q" 11:50),⁸⁴ providing details absent from the Lukan version (11:50).⁸⁵ Moreover, Matthew has changed the reading as found

---

78. Davies and Allison, *Matthew*, 1:132.

79. Gundry, *Matthew*, 436.

80. Hagner, *Matthew*, 2:669.

81. Davies and Allison, *Matthew*, 3:292. Cf. U. Luz, *Das Evangelium nach Matthäus* (EKKNT; 4 vols.; Zürich: Benziger, 1985-2002), 3:326-28.

82. Davies and Allison (*Matthew*, 3:292-93) rightly observe that they are chastised precisely for disobeying the *cultic* law.

83. On potential implications for the dating of the gospel in light of this observation, cf. Davies and Allison, *Matthew*, 3:293; France, *Matthew: Evangelist and Teacher*, 88.

84. Robinson et al., *The Critical Edition of Q*, 286-88.

85. For a helpful survey of the issue, cf. Hagner, *Matthew*, 2:676-78, where he takes the position that the Zechariah referred to here is that of 2 Chr. 24:20-22, who was stoned to death in

in Luke 11:49 (which reads "wisdom of God sends you prophets") to "I send you prophets" (cf. "Q" 11:50), clearly ascribing a Wisdom identity to his Jesus.[86] Although which Zechariah is in view has been disputed, it seems probable that the one in 2 Chr. 24:20-22, who was stoned to death in the courtyard of the Temple, is the best choice. If this is so, then Matthew changed his source.[87] The LXX of this account (24:21) reads that the murder occurred ἐν αὐλῇ οἴκου κυρίου (so also Luke 11:51; MT = בחצר בית יהוה), yet Matthew changes it to ναός. Why Matthew changes οἴκου κυρίου to ναός here, as he does in 27:5, is not immediately apparent. It may be, as we will see below, that Matthew's aversion to speaking negatively against the Temple is heightened even further when it is associated with God (κύριος). That is, when Matthew speaks negatively of the Temple, he avoids associating it with God. His point of contention, as we have seen before and will revisit, in typical prophetic (Jeremiah) fashion, is misuse of the Temple.[88]

The pericope culminates in two further "judgment" texts. The first (23:38) recounts Jesus' declaration: "Look, your house is left to you desolate (ἔρημος)." Traditionally, scholars have seen this as a reference to God's abandonment of his own Temple, resonating with the language of his abandonment of the First Tem-

---

the courtyard of the Temple (ἐν αὐλῇ οἴκου κυρίου; 24:21), interpreting "from the blood of Abel to the blood of Zechariah" to mean from the beginning to the end of the Hebrew Bible. Cf. R. Beckwith, *The Old Testament Canon of the New Testament and Its Background in Early Judaism* (Grand Rapids: Eerdmans, 1985), 211-22; Str-B 1:422-23; Cf. Hans Jürgen Becker, "Die Zerstörung Jerusalems bei Matthäus und den Rabbinen," *NTS* 44 (1998): 59-73.

86. Deutsch, "Wisdom in Matthew," 41. Cf. Aune, *Prophecy*, 237; E. Schweizer, *Matthäus und seine Gemeinde* (Stuttgart: K. B. W. Verlag, 1974), 283; Suggs, *Wisdom*, 59f.; U. Wilckens, *Weisheit und Torheit: Eine exegetisch-religionsgeschichtliche Untersuchung zu 1. Kor. 1 und 2* (Tübingen: Mohr Siebeck, 1959), 197.

87. Robinson et al., *The Critical Edition of Q*, 286-88. Knowles (*Jeremiah in Matthew's Gospel*, 107) notes that the slaying of this Zechariah is often associated with the fall of Jerusalem (2 Chr. 24:21-22; *Tg. Lam.* 1.19; 2.20; 5.11, 13; *y. Ta'an.* 4.9 [69ab]; *b. Giṭ.* 57b; *b. Sanh.* 96a; *Pesiq. Rab. Kah.* 15.7; *Lam. Rab.* Proem 23; 1.16.51; 2.20.23; *Eccl. Rab.* 3.16 [86b]; cf. *b. Yoma* 38b; S. H. Blank, "Death of Zechariah in Rabbinic Literature," *HUCA* 13 [1938]: 327-46; Becker, "Die Zerstörung Jerusalems," 59-73). The destruction of Jerusalem is also associated with Israel's rejection of Jesus, the Jeremiah-like prophet (*2 Bar.* 2.1; *Par. Jer.* 1.1-3; Knowles, *Jeremiah in Matthew's Gospel*, 142).

88. This point is most explicitly seen in Matthew's allusion to Jer. 7:11 (Matt. 21:13; cf. Isa. 56:7; Knowles, *Jeremiah in Matthew's Gospel*, 188). It may be possible that Matthew chooses ναός, the holiest portion of the Temple complex, to heighten the sense of sacrilege produced by the deeds. That is, the offense is done not just against the Temple, but against the holiest part of the Temple. Yet this option seems less likely because it fails to account for Matthew's dissociation of the Temple from God. If the evangelist were simply heightening the degree of sacrilege involved, would he not *preserve* the name of God, the presence of whom is what makes the Temple holy (Matt. 23:21)?

ple just prior to its destruction (Ezek. 8:6, 12; 9:3, 9; 11:23; cf. Bar. 4:12)[89] and perhaps looking back to the departure of the *Shekinah* from the Temple (cf. 1 Kgs. 9:6-9; Isa. 64:10-11).[90] While Knowles is correct that these texts describe God's *departure* from the Temple, not its destruction, the departure of God's presence from the Temple was surely a prelude to the city's destruction (Josephus, *War* 5.412-13; 6.295-300; Tacitus, *Histories* 5.13; *2 Bar.* 8.2; 64.6-7; *Par. Jer.* 4.1). But the destruction of the Temple was seen as subsequent to God's departure, both of which were inescapably the result of the sins of God's people. This is apparent in a similar use of Matthew's "desolation" (ἔρημος) saying, which occurs in *T. Levi* 15.1, announcing that "the sanctuary which the Lord chose shall become desolate through your uncleanness, and you shall be captives in all the nations."[91] Similarly, Josephus says, "God himself... turned away from our city... because he deemed the Temple to be no longer a clean dwelling place for Him" (*Ant.* 20.166; cf. *War* 5.19).[92] This view is underscored by the departure of Jesus' presence, which Matthew has already identified with the Shekinah (Matt. 18:20; cf. *m. 'Abot* 3.2),[93] from the Temple (ἱερόν), in prophetic fashion going toward the Mount of Olives (24:1; cf. Zech. 14:4).[94] This is significant, Knowles contends,

---

89. Hagner, *Matthew*, 2:681. France (*Matthew: Evangelist and Teacher*, 215-16) sees this text as the "first explicit prediction of the future desolation of the Temple," which is strategically located at "the climax of the extended denunciation of the scribes and Pharisees in chapter 23." It is particularly related, he contends, to "the statement that the sins of the fathers have culminated in 'this generation', upon whom punishment is now at last to fall. Jesus' last, earnest appeal to Jerusalem has met with no response (23:37)." As we have shown in the Introduction, many ancient scholars associated this verse, along with the rending of the veil, with the destruction of Jerusalem.

90. Davies and Allison, *Matthew*, 3:321.

91. *OTP* 1:793. Knowles (*Jeremiah in Matthew's Gospel*, 101) indicates that, in true Jeremiah fashion, rejection of the words of God's prophets and of the just are among the other sins leading to the Temple's destruction (cf. *T. Jud.* 23.1-5; *T. Iss.* 6.1-4; *T. Zeb.* 9.5-8; *T. Dan* 5.7-9; *T. Naph.* 4.1-5; *T. Ash.* 7.2-7; *Pesiq. R.* 31 (146a); *Exod. Rab.* 31:16; *Pesiq. R.* 29 (138a); O. H. Steck, *Israel und das gewaltsame Geschick der Propheten: Untersuchungen zur Überlieferung des deuteronomistischen Geschichtsbildes im Alten Testament, Spätjudentum, und Urchristentum* (WMANT 23; Neukirchen-Vluyn: Neukirchener, 1967), 147-62; M. A. Knibb, "The Exile in the Literature of the Intertestamental Period," *HeyJ* 17 (1976): 264-66. Knowles also is careful to note that the destruction of the Temple in 70 C.E. is the product of a Deuteronomistic cycle of people's rejection of God (*Jeremiah in Matthew's Gospel*, 115-16; cf. Ezra 3:30; 5:28; *b. Yoma* 9b: "Why was the first Sanctuary destroyed? Because of three things which prevailed there: idolatry, immorality, and bloodshed").

92. Longenecker, "Rome's Victory and God's Honour," 94.

93. Knowles, *Jeremiah in Matthew's Gospel*, 144. For more discussion of Matthew's identification of Jesus with the *Shekinah*, cf. Davies and Allison, *Matthew*, 2:789-90.

94. Cf. France, *Matthew: Evangelist and Teacher*, 215; Luomanen, *Entering the Kingdom of Heaven*, 227-28.

because God's presence in that shrine was an affirmation of Israel's election, sanctification and protection. Yet the realities of 586 B.C.E. indicate "that the covenantal sanction afforded by God's 'presence' was not inviolable."[95] It would seem natural, then, for a first-century Jewish reader to see Jesus' departure as a similar act of abandonment[96] and, perhaps, the removal of the mark of Israel's identity as the people of God. Again, though, fault lies with the misuse and corruption of an otherwise perfectly legitimate Temple.

The second judgment text in this pericope is related to the first. Immediately, Jesus' disciples marvel at the structure, yet Jesus emphatically predicts, in a tradition found in each synoptic account, that "not one stone here will be left on another; every one will be thrown down" (24:2; cf. Mark 13:1; Luke 21:5).[97] Though the evangelist provides no immediate explanation of this saying, the fact that it is placed right after Jesus' statement about his return (23:39, citing Ps. 118:26) and before his extended monologue regarding signs of the end of the age (24:3–25:46) strongly suggests that his prediction of the Temple's destruction is an integral factor in Matthew's eschatology[98] and bears defining characteristics of divine judgment.[99] Yet Jesus' implicit and explicit statements regarding the destruction of the Temple do not themselves "question the legitimacy of the cult," as some seem to presume.[100] Instead, as is the case in other prophetic foretellings of the destruction of Jerusalem and its Temple,[101] destruction is the

---

95. Knowles, *Jeremiah in Matthew's Gospel*, 267. Yet in the Herodian Temple, Knowles shows, some rabbis held the Shekinah was never present (*b. Yoma* 21b; *Num. Rab.* 15.10), or at least "not as helpful" as before (cf. *2 Bar.* 68.5-6). God was thought to dwell with Israel in Zion, his holy mountain (Joel 2.27; 4[3].16-17). Knowles notes that "the security of both the city and the Temple constituted a sign of divine favor and covenant faithfulness. . . ." With the destruction of the Temple, acts of piety (prayer and obedience to the Torah) replaced Temple sacrifices (1QS 9:3-6; cf. Gärtner, *The Temple and the Community in Qumran and the New Testament*, 15, 20-21, 44-46; J. Neusner, "Judaism in a Time of Crisis: Four Responses to the Destruction of the Second Temple," *Judaism* 21 (1972): 318; A. J. Saldarini, "Varieties of Rabbinic Responses to the Destruction of the Temple," *SBLSP* 21 (1982): 437-58; Knowles, *Jeremiah in Matthew's Gospel*, 270. Cf. G. I. Davies, "The Presence of God in the Second Temple and Rabbinic Doctrine," in *Templum Amicitiae: Essays on the Second Temple Presented to Ernst Bammel* (ed. W. Horbury; JSNTSup 48; Sheffield: JSOT Press, 1991), 32-36.

96. Kupp, *Matthew's Emmanuel*, 93-94; Davies and Allison, *Matthew*, 3:333.

97. Olmstead (*Matthew's Trilogy of Parables*), arguing for the collective guilt of all Israel for the sins against Jesus rather than just her leaders, asserts that this is how one should read Matt. 27:25, that Jesus' blood should "be on us and on our children."

98. Cf. Knowles, *Jeremiah in Matthew's Gospel*, 188-89.

99. France, *Matthew: Evangelist and Teacher*, 216.

100. See Davies and Allison, *Matthew*, 3:334.

101. Davies and Allison, *Matthew* 3:335, citing Micah (Mic. 3:12), Jeremiah (Jer. 7:8-15; 9:10-11; 26:6, 18) and Jesus bar Ananias (Josephus, *War* 6.300ff.).

direct and immediate consequence of the sins of Israel's leadership in mismanaging the Temple. This is culminated when Jesus goes to the Mount of Olives (24:3), where he sees the Temple which will be destroyed, and indicates a return to the Mount of Olives (cf. 27:53; Acts 1:9, 12).[102] This resonates with Zech. 14:4, which asserts that the Lord will stand on the Mount of Olives at the great day of judgment upon Jerusalem (14:1-21). The prophetic judgment is announced.

Among the signs of the end of the age (Matt. 24) the evangelist includes a reference from Daniel, speaking of "the abomination that causes desolation" (τὸ βδέλυγμα τῆς ἐρημώσεως) standing in the holy place (24:15). The citation is taken from Daniel (9:27; 11:31; 12:11; and partially via Mark 13:14), where it refers to a pagan altar or image of Zeus set up in the Jerusalem Temple by Antiochus IV Epiphanes (167 B.C.E.; cf. *T. Levi* 15:1; *Apoc. Elijah* 2:41; 4:21).[103] The referent in this saying is uncertain, though it may allude to the attempted desecration by Caligula (40 C.E.), to the destruction of the Temple itself (as in Luke 21:20) or to a future "eschatological defilement" associated with the antichrist.[104] Regardless of the precise referent, Matthew seems to identify the defilement of the Temple with some eschatological "sign." Olmstead contends that this "signals God's judgment on rebellious Israel for the rejection of his servants which spans her history," for which the 70 C.E. tragedy is a "precursor."[105] We see, then, that this abandonment and impending destruction are the *consequences* of Israel's failed leadership.

A further allusion to the Temple with respect to the leaders' (mismanaged) stewardship of it is found in 24:45, where Jesus refers to a servant "whom the master has put in charge of the servants in his household" and who is expected to be found faithful upon the master's return (24:46-51). This is part of a parable given privately to the disciples regarding the end of the age (24:3). The symbolism again refers to the leaders of Israel, though the "household" may simply refer to their leadership in general over the "house" of Israel, including their management of the Temple.

Matthew's Portrayal of the Temple (Matt. 26–28)

Chapter 26 begins Matthew's Passion Narrative, in which Jesus is arrested, protesting that "Every day I sat in the Temple courts (ἱερόν) teaching, and you did not arrest me" (26:55). Though this complaint is mentioned in each of the ca-

---

102. Davies and Allison, *Matthew*, 3:347.
103. Davies and Allison, *Matthew*, 3:345.
104. Davies and Allison, *Matthew*, 3:345-46.
105. Olmstead, *Trilogy*, 116.

nonical gospels (Mark 14:49; Luke 22:53; John 18:20), in Matthew's narrative it seems to point back to the events in 21:1-27. Matthew takes this pericope from Mark, and though he condenses it to a degree, he edits points where the Temple (ναός) is soon to become a central issue of controversy. First, Mark's "this manmade Temple" (τὸν ναὸν τοῦτον τὸν χειροποίητον; Mark 14:58) becomes "God's Temple" (τὸν ναὸν τοῦ θεοῦ; Matt. 26:61). This is a strange redaction, since, as we have seen previously, Matthew seems careful to avoid identifying the Temple with God where it is spoken against. Yet since these charges are explicitly said to be false (26:59-60), perhaps Matthew was emphasizing the illegitimacy of accusations that Jesus betrayed animosity toward the divinely instituted Temple. Next Jesus is accused of saying, "I am able to destroy the Temple (ναός) of God and rebuild it in three days" (26:61), whereas Mark's accuser says that Jesus claimed that he *will* destroy the Temple (καταλύσω; 14:58). Explanations for Matthean redaction have been various, with some suggesting that it is inappropriate for Matthew to preserve Mark's "will destroy" after 70 C.E. But it would seem just as inappropriate for Matthew's Jesus to tell people to offer sacrifices (5:23-24; 8:4) and presume that God is still in the Temple (23:21) when it was already destroyed. It seems more plausible that Matthew is trying to mute Mark's polemic against the Temple with respect to Jesus. That is, perhaps Matthew is concerned that, though his Jesus speaks against the mismanagement of the Temple and of its imminent destruction, Jesus not speak directly against it.[106] Though both accusations are clearly said to be "false witnesses" (ψευδομαρτύρων; Matt. 26:60; cf. Mark 14:56, 57), Matthew seems to emphasize Jesus' ability, while identifying the Temple as God's (τοῦ θεοῦ; cf. 26:61). Matthew stresses the *power* of Jesus, but not his instrumentality in the destruction of the Temple. Moreover, Matthew's Jesus speaks of the destruction of the ἱερόν (cf. 24:1-2), while the false accusations insinuate that he spoke against the ναός. Some scholars believe that the Temple "not made with hands" refers to the church, suggesting that Matthew was concerned that his Jesus founded the church after his resurrection.[107] This cannot be the case, for Matthew clearly depicts the founding of the church during Jesus' ministry.[108] Davies and Allison believe that the Temple reference is to Jesus himself, so "I am able to destroy the Temple of God" = "I am able to lay down my life."[109] Yet this is not entirely satis-

---

106. Telford, *Barren Temple*, 83.

107. Cf. Davies and Allison, *Matthew*, 3:526; Lohmeyer, *Matthäus*, 367-68; Luz, *Matthäus*, 4:176.

108. Cf. Davies and Allison, *Matthew*, 2:628.

109. Davies and Allison, *Matthew*, 3:526 and n. 38, citing Gundry (*Matthew*, 543), who observes that Matthew's "I am able" statement harmonizes with the voluntary nature of Jesus' death in that gospel. Cf. Luz, *Matthäus*, 4:176, n. 20.

factory, since Matthew's Jesus emphasizes not his *ability* to lay down his life but the fact that, in each of his passion predictions, he *will*. Instead, perhaps Matthew is concerned to emphasize the power of Jesus over the Temple to affirm his superiority to it (12:6), yet still recognizes it as belonging to God. Moreover, Luz suggests that Jesus' ability to destroy the Temple underscores his power as the Son of God (4:3, 6; 26:53; 27:40-42) to do so, but his obedience as the Son of God not to (cf. 27:43).[110]

We next come across the Temple in 27:5, where Judas throws his ill-gained money into the Temple (ναός) and leaves to hang himself. The early Christians understood Judas's suicide, found only in Matthew among the gospels, as an act of judgment (Acts 1:18). Scholars are widely agreed that the gesture is symbolic of the priests' guilt accompanying that of Judas.[111] This pericope (Matt. 27:3-10) is a redactional addition between Mark 15:1 and 15:2 (cf. Acts 1:15-20; Jerome, *Com. in Matt.* 27:9). Here the temporal sequence of his narrative is clearly broken, as 27:2 leaves the priests and elders leading Jesus to Pilate, while 27:3-10 places them in the Temple sanctuary.[112] The account itself is apparently a Matthean redaction of the OT, for his source (LXX Zech. 11:13) says that the money will be "thrown" (ἐμβάλλω)[113] "into the house of the Lord" (εἰς τὸν οἶκον κυρίου).[114] Yet Matthew asserts that it was "cast" (ῥίπτειν) "into the Temple" (εἰς τὸν ναόν).

The ναός is almost surely referring to the inner sanctuary of the Temple complex,[115] accessible only to the priests, and quite a long distance to throw a handful of coins from the outer court into which Judas would be permitted.[116] Judas could enter the court of the Israelites, which was adjacent to the court of the priests. If the latter is loosely designated ναός (properly the sanctuary build-

---

110. Luz, *Matthäus*, 4:176.
111. Davies and Allison, *Matthew*, 3:564-65.
112. Raymond E. Brown, *The Death of the Messiah: A Commentary on the Passion Narratives in the Four Gospels* (2 vols.; New York: Doubleday, 1994), 1:637.
113. Though Aquila and Symmachus use ῥίπτειν. For a discussion of the textual variations in the Zechariah text, cf. C. C. Torrey, "The Foundry of the Second Temple at Jerusalem," *JBL* 55 (1936): 247-60.
114. Cf. Knowles, *Jeremiah in Matthew's Gospel*, 56-57. Josephus refers to the allusion to Zechariah as τὸν ἱερὸν θησαυρόν, καλεῖται δὲ κορβωνᾶς (*War* 2.175). Cf. also R. Gundry, *The Use of the Old Testament in St. Matthew's Gospel: With Special Reference to the Messianic Hope* (NovTSup 18; Leiden: E. J. Brill, 1967), 124; J. A. Upton, "The Potter's Field and the Death of Judas," *CJ* 8 (1982): 214-16; P. Benoit, "La mort de Judas," in *Exégèse et théologie* (Paris: Cerf, 1961), 1:341-59.
115. This is usually the case in Matthew. Davies and Allison, *Matthew*, 3:564.
116. Scholars conjecture, then, that the money was thrown over a wall or through a gate. Cf. Hagner, *Matthew*, 2:812.

ing), then he does not have to throw far. Apparently, though, Matthew does presume a long distance because he intensifies Zechariah's term "throw" (ἐμβάλλω) to "cast" (ῥίπτειν), perhaps to compensate for a longer distance. That is, he seems to have first changed the destination of the throwing (into the sanctuary), and then modified the verb accordingly. Why, however, is he so concerned to read ναός for τὸν οἶκον κυρίου? Brown suggests that the emphasis upon the ναός here is to "communicate the horror of profanation,"[117] that is, to emphasize the degree of sacrilege involved. But why could Matthew not do that by retaining τὸν οἶκον κυρίου, particularly given his tendency to retain οἶκος from an OT source when alluding to it, as he is doing here (Matt. 12:4 [1 Sam. 21:7]; 21:13 [Isa. 56:7; 60:7]; 23:38 [Ps. 118:26])? The uniqueness of this pericope may supply the answer, for in two of the other texts where Matthew retains the LXX οἶκος reading (Matt. 12:4 [1 Sam. 21:7]; 21:13 [Isa. 56:7; 60:7]) nothing negative is said about the Temple. And it is only *after* Jesus' lament over Jerusalem's lack of repentance that he will speak a negative word toward the οἶκος when alluding to OT texts (Matt. 23:38 [Ps. 118:26]). Then, perhaps, there is nothing negative to say about the Temple, a divinely instituted enterprise established in the OT (cf. 5:17), until after Jesus has lamented the lack of repentance of its leaders. *Then* its destruction, despite its legitimacy, is depicted using OT οἶκος language. Perhaps more plausibly: if, as is sometimes recognized, this gesture is in part a demonstration that the priests bear some of the blame for Judas's betrayal,[118] Matthew may have been concerned to remove κύριος from association with it.[119]

Perhaps that it was cast into the ναός depicts that the guilt incurred by Judas is to be shared with those who conduct services therein, for which οἶκος κύριου would be too general. That the guilt is in some way intended to be shared with the priests is supported by the fact that immediately the priests are on the scene. They take the money away from the Temple treasury and purchase a field (27:7), literally "the field of the potter" (τὸν ἀγρὸν τοῦ κεραμέως). It was used to buy a field called "Field of Blood," and Matthew justifies it in characteristic fashion by citing the OT,[120] likely a combination of texts from Zechariah and Jeremiah, in-

---

117. Brown, *Death*, 1:642.
118. Davies and Allison, *Matthew*, 3:564-65.
119. Yet another reading is worthy of consideration. It could be that, as Judas is first said to recognize his error (27:4-5; ἥμαρτον is a standard term for "confession," Davies and Allison, *Matthew*, 3:263 and n. 22), throwing his money into the inner sanctum could be understood as an attempt to make a sin offering. Previously we have seen that Matthew is concerned that one first make reconciliation, then offer his gift on the altar (5:23-24), and, though it is difficult to be certain, it would not be surprising if he were indicating a similar scenario with Judas.
120. Though Matthew says his citation comes from Jeremiah (19:1-13; 32:6-9), it more closely fits with the LXX of Zech. 11:12, 13. Cf. Brown, *Death*, 1:648-51.

Matthew's Theology of the Temple and the "Parting of the Ways"

dicating that even this was within God's sovereign control.[121] The ναός continues to be a point of contention even on the cross, where passersby, apparently hearing and believing the (false) accusations against Jesus, mock him by saying, "You who are going to destroy the Temple (ναός) and build it in three days, save yourself! Come down from the cross, if you are the Son of God!" (27:40; cf. Mark 15:29-30). Again, it is important to recognize that accusations of Jesus' polemic against the Temple itself are said to be false. For the present, I will suspend judgment on the Temple (ναός) reference in 27:51 until I can profile a more decisive view of Jesus' death in Matthew's gospel in general.

The ναός continues to be a point of contention even on the cross, where passersby, apparently hearing and believing the (false) accusations against Jesus, mock him by saying, "You who are going to destroy the Temple (ναός) and build it in three days, save yourself! Come down from the cross, if you are the Son of God!" (27:40; cf. Mark 15:29-30). Again, it is important to recognize that accusations of Jesus' polemic against the Temple itself are said to be false. The final reference to the Temple pertains to the tearing of its veil at the death of Jesus. While it is surely likely that a reader of Matthew's gospel would associate the rending of the veil with the calamities of 70 C.E., it is an oversimplification, in my view, simply to equate the rending of the veil with the destruction of the Temple as a *primary* meaning of the event. For that to be the case, the veil would have to be understood to in some way represent the Temple as a whole, which it does in only two obscure references (the Greek of Sir. 50.5 and *Vis. Paul* 12.10-13), only one of which is certain to predate 70 C.E. Instead, it seems much more plausible to bring together the uniquely positive view Matthew has of the Temple with the unquestionably atoning significance of Jesus' death to propose that the event, in part, indicates the accessibility of God accomplished by the death of Jesus and congruent with Matthew's Emmanuel Christology lens through which the entire gospel is to be read.[122]

Conclusion: Matthew's Temple from Beginning to "End" — An *Intra Muros* Issue

In this sketch we have seen that frequently Matthew is deliberate about his choice of location and issues surrounding the Temple and its cult. Telford has

---

121. Brown, *Death*, 1:652.
122. See Daniel M. Gurtner, "The *Velum Scissum*: Matthew's Exposition of the Death of Jesus" (Ph.D. thesis, University of St Andrews, 2005); forthcoming as *The Torn Veil: Matthew's Exposition of the Death of Jesus* (SNTSMS; Cambridge: Cambridge University Press, 2007).

also made this observation in his analysis of Matthew's redaction of the Markan fig-tree pericope examined above. Yet he adds that such a conclusion is supported by what Matthew omitted from Mark, including Mark 11:16, which seems to allude to Jesus' obstruction of sacrificial worship, and Mark 12:32-35, which could be taken to disparage the Temple cult. Matthew retains but modifies Mark's account of Jesus' prediction of the destruction of the Temple, as I showed above. Yet where he retains Mark's prophecy concerning the destruction of the Temple (Matt. 27:1-2; Mark 13:1-2), "he does precede it by the Lament over Jerusalem (23.37-39), which shows Jesus' attitude to be one of regret over the imminent demise of the city and its Temple. . . . For Matthew (5.17), Jesus is one who has come to fulfill (πληρῶσαι) rather than to destroy (καταλῦσαι)."[123] On this point Davies and Allison concur: "Matthew, writing after A.D. 70, had no need to attack the Jerusalem Temple, nor did he. Rather did he assume its propriety, that is, its foundation in the Torah, and its one-time sanctity: God intended the Temple to be a house of prayer (21.13), a place for offering of sacrifices (5.23-4), and a holy site sanctifying the objects within it (23.16-22). If the Temple had ceased to be these things, and then ceased to be altogether, the explanation was simply that God's judgment had come upon Jerusalem: the corruption of the priests and others (21.13; 23.35) and the rejection of Jesus (21.42-43; 22.7) brought divinely ordained destruction."[124]

The assertions by Lohmeyer that Matthew is anti-Temple fail to distinguish between the Temple and the leaders responsible for it.[125] Andreoli's argument that Matthew is against the Temple because it represents the "old order" fails to account for Matthean redaction of Markan texts or for positive statements about the Temple's cult.[126] Instead, Matthew is an author "emphasizing the sovereignty of Jesus over the Temple rather than one reflecting an antagonism towards it."[127] Matthew's references to its destruction are made only following a lament over the unwillingness of its leaders to repent. The lament, found only

---

123. Telford, *Barren Temple*, 83.

124. Davies and Allison, *Matthew*, 3:143, cf. n. 64; 2 Kgs. 21:10-15. In all this (Davies and Allison, *Matthew*, 3:143, cf. nn. 65-67), Matthew falls in line with late first-century Jewish thought. 4 Ezra, 2 Baruch and the *Apocalypse of Abraham*, for instance, likewise attribute Jerusalem's tragic demise and the leveling of its sanctuary to Jewish failing. Cf. G. W. E. Nickelsburg, *Jewish Literature between the Bible and the Mishnah: A Historical and Literary Introduction* (London: SCM, 1981), 294-99; J. Z. Smith, "The Temple and the Magician," in *God's Christ and His People: Studies in Honour of Nils Alstrup Dahl* (ed. J. Jervell and W. A. Meeks; Oslo: Universitetsforleget, 1977), 233-47.

125. Telford, *Barren Temple*, 83, n. 106; Lohmeyer, *Matthäus*, 184.

126. Andreoli, "Il velo squarciato nel Vangelo di Matteo," 35-40.

127. R. A. McConnell, "Law and Prophecy in Matthew's Gospel" (Ph.D. diss., University of Basel, 1964), 72-75, esp. 75; Telford, *Barren Temple*, 83-84.

in Matt. 23:37-39 and Luke 13:34-35 (cf. "Q" 13:34-35), is nearly identical in each text, with Matthew apparently preserving the original.[128] A similar lament was pronounced by Jeremiah (Jer. 2:30; cf. Neh. 9:26), and that the destruction of Jerusalem is depicted on the heels of this account leads us to conclude that the destruction is necessitated not because of fault with the Temple but because of the unrepentance of the Jewish leaders.[129]

That the data seem so consistent suggests a concerted perspective on the part of the First Evangelist toward the Jerusalem Temple. The strikingly positive redactional and narrative portrayal of the temple raises important questions regarding Matthew's relationship to first-century Judaism. He stresses the authority of Scripture, acknowledges the importance of the Sabbath (though through Christological lenses) and now is in favor of the existence of the Temple, God's presence in it, and the legitimacy of its sacrifices. According to Bauckham's reckoning, Matthew fits broadly within the common elements of first-century Judaism. Indeed, Matthean redaction could be seen to curb Mark's rather blunt statements against the Temple, carefully walking a razor's edge between legitimacy on one hand and judgment on the other. Ultimately, the Temple will face an unfortunate end. Yet Matthew is careful that its end, in Jeremiah-like, prophetic fashion, is a consequence of failed leadership and appropriation of it. Its destruction follows a lament.[130] If these data are valid, then scholars must reconsider Matthew's place within Judaism. For not only does Matthew affirm one of the pillars of Judaism — the Temple — but even his discussion of its destruction is rooted within Jewish tradition resonating with the language of Jeremiah. Matthew's Temple is surely an *intra muros* issue.

---

128. Cf. Robinson et al., *The Critical Edition of Q,* 420.

129. Cf. Davies and Allison, *Matthew,* 3:324; cf. Olmstead, *Trilogy,* 83; D. C. Allison, "Matt. 23.39 = Lk 13.35b as a Conditional Prophecy," *JSNT* 18 (1983): 75-84; C. Deutsch, "Wisdom in Matthew," 13-47. Such a reading would depict the incarnate wisdom departing as a pronouncement of judgment on those who reject wisdom (cf. Prov. 1:20-33; Matt. 11:16-19, 20-24; R. J. Miller, "The Rejection of the Prophets in Q," *JBL* 107 (1988): 225-40; Steck, *Israel und das gewaltsame Geschick der Propheten,* 280-97.

130. For other evidence that Matthew's discussion of the destruction of the Temple is an *intra muros* issue, see David M. Moffitt, "Righteous Bloodshed, Matthew's Passion Narrative and the Temple's Destruction: Lamentations as a Matthean Intertext," *JBL* 125.2 (2006): 299-320.

The Gospel of Matthew and Anti-Semitism

John Nolland

Introduction

What I want to look at is Matthew's contribution to anti-Semitism. At its most extreme there are those who are convinced that it is Matthew who is ultimately responsible for the Holocaust and that, therefore, we can lay at his feet the root responsibility for the deaths of more than six million Jewish men, women and children in the 20th century alone. It is not hard to find a dark streak of anti-Semitism in the history of the church. And it is not hard to find the use of texts from Matthew in support of anti-Semitism.[1]

From the beginning I will want to make a distinction between unintended consequences and consequences for which a writer might reasonably be considered responsible. I am well aware that in practice it is often quite difficult to draw a hard-and-fast distinction between these two options. If unintended consequences result from a failure to exercise a duty of care in reflecting on the possible effects of an action, then we would all be inclined to hold a person responsible for those effects, at least to some degree. Similarly, if the unintended consequences represent no more than a taking further of the logic of what were already the intended consequences, then a measure of responsibility can hardly be evaded. Again, if the consequences align with what is likely to be an unconscious intention of a writer, then we can hardly spare the writer a measure of responsibility for the consequences. Nonetheless, despite all caveats, the distinction I am drawing, with its setting off of unintended consequences, still

---

1. F. Frankemölle has addressed this question in "Antijudaismus im Matthäusevangelium? Reflexionen zu einer angemessenen Auslegung," in *Studien zum jüdischen Kontext neutestamentlicher Theologien*, FS J. Gnilka (Stuttgarter Biblische Aufzatzbände Neues Testament 37; Stuttgart: Katholisches Bibelwerk, 2005), 168-98.

remains serviceable. And in the name of it I will, in the first instance, spare Matthew immediate responsibility for the uses of Matthean texts in the service of anti-Semitism through the centuries. It might be that the responsibility for these may have to be given back to him again, but a decision about this must turn on our investigation of the Gospel itself, and not simply on the fact of its anti-Semitic use. For that reason I do not intend to provide any survey of the history of anti-Semitic use of the Gospel of Matthew.

I am well aware that my approach here does not engage with the contemporary focus on the importance of the *Wirkungsgeschichte*. I am quite happy to believe that the history of the effects of something can offer important windows onto the substance of that with which one is dealing. But I also believe that *Wirkungsgeschichte* is a very blunt instrument. And it seems to me that much of the time what is offered as *Wirkungsgeschichte* has its significance in connection with the history of thought and culture rather than in connection with the original item that is being interpreted. So I am happy, for the present, to leave *Wirkungsgeschichte* to one side.[2]

There are two places in Matthew that are most heavily implicated in the discussion of anti-Semitism.[3] The first is Matt. 23, with its set of woes against the scribes and Pharisees, and the other is in the role given to the Jewish crowds in the trial of Jesus before Pilate in Matt. 27. In Matt. 23 the issue under discussion is pervasive, but some selected verses will highlight the issues. "[The scribes and Pharisees] bind up heavy burdens and place them on the shoulders of the people, but they themselves are not willing to move them with a finger" (v. 4); "They do all their deeds to be seen by people" (v. 5); "Woe to you, scribes and Pharisees, hypocrites, because you shut the kingdom of heaven in the face of people" (v. 13); ". . . because you cover sea and land to make one proselyte, and when it happens, you make them full twice as much a child of Gehenna as yourselves" (v. 15); ". . . because you tithe mint, dill and cummin, and have abandoned the weightier matters of the Law, justice and mercy and faith" (v. 23). In Matt. 27 the point of sharpest focus is v. 25: "All the people responded, 'His blood [be] upon us and upon our children.'"

I think that it is not only issues of anti-Semitism that make these texts difficult for us. A culture of tolerance has been a very important part of the formation of most of us. So much is the importance of tolerance emphasized in many

---

2. The *Wirkungsgeschichte* of Matt. 27:25 in the Latin Church up to Leo the Great is explored by R. Kampling in *Das Blut Christi und die Juden. Mt 27,25 bei den lateinischsprachigen christliche Autoren bis zu Leo dem Grossen* (NTAbh 16; Münster: Aschendorff, 1984).

3. Various other texts could be included in a discussion of Matthew and anti-Semitism, but other texts are either less significant or lend themselves to be considered in an analogous manner to that which is adopted here.

of our settings that for many tolerance has been elevated to being the chief virtue of our times. Part of the background for this in Britain has been reflection on the history of Christian persecution of Christians in earlier generations; and then more recently a further impetus in this direction has been provided by living in a Britain that has become increasingly religiously, ethnically and culturally pluralist. We also live in a postmodern context in which suspicion is automatically cast on every kind of absolute. Where there are no absolutes, there must be room for every kind of person and for people with any and every kind of personal conviction. It has become one of those self-evident truths that everybody deserves respect and tolerance; and increasingly tolerance is being redefined as equal affirmation of all the options to which people are committed. And Matthew's language sounds anything but tolerant, and even more intolerant in relation to the new definition of tolerance.

I do not plan to address the issue of toleration as such, but just to alert us to the fact that when we discuss anti-Semitism issues of tolerance are likely to add their own unseen weight to the discussion. I am sufficiently of my age to think that tolerance is a matter of considerable importance in our world today. But I would want to make one point here. Christianity arose in a context that was religiously pluralist and by and large religiously tolerant. But the NT has not a single reference to toleration or tolerance. The closest we get is "bearing-with" or "putting-up-with" language (ἀνέχομαι; e.g., Col. 3:13; 1 Cor. 4:12; 2 Cor. 11:20; Eph. 4:12). This putting up with has a certain relationship to tolerance, and may at times produce quite similar behavior, but it is really quite different from the larger understanding of things that undergirds modern tolerance. However, beyond pointing out that questions of tolerance inevitably sit in the background as we discuss anti-Semitism, we will stay with anti-Semitism for this paper.

Matthew 23: "Woe to You, Scribes and Pharisees"

Some people have no difficulty with taking simply at face value the criticism of the scribes and Pharisees in Matt. 23. The use of critical language may not strike home so much when the people involved are a long way away, either way back in the past or, if in the present, well removed from us. There is always a certain reality test involved in the situation where one is called upon to say something about another person face to face. We cannot do that here, but I think we can engage better imaginatively here if we ask ourselves questions like the following. What do you think the wife of one of these scribes or Pharisees would have made of these things being said of (among others) her husband? Would their friends have recognized their friend in this description? To what extent would those addressed have recognized themselves in the critical words of Matt. 23? What would those who looked to them for advice and direction make of such statements?

Because of the unfortunate caricature of first-century Pharisaism to which the material of Matt. 23 has contributed, most scholars are not prepared to trace much of it to the historical Jesus. But though these matters need to be addressed on their own terms (but not here), I doubt whether this is where the real problem with Matt. 23 lies. I think it is that what was originally formulated in one context is being related to in quite another context.

There is all the difference in the world between viewing Matt. 23 as something which is addressed *to a group of people* or is comment about a group of people addressed *to those who know these people well,* and reading it as providing a description *of a group of people for those who have no other link to these people.* Criticism of some of the Pharisees some of the time, or even of aspects of the Pharisaic movement in general, is easily turned into a general portrait of all of the Pharisees all of the time. And whereas those who listened to the historical Jesus criticizing the Pharisees and even, at least to a considerable degree, those who read Matthew as its original readers (see below) could interpret Jesus' criticism of the Pharisees in relation to a reality that they had their own experience of, independent of what Jesus was saying, we are not in that position.

In their original context the criticisms of Matt. 23 set up a dialectic. Without the presumed second source of knowledge we are in danger of taking Jesus' words much too literally. A passionate prophetic consciousness will catch attention and challenge in ways that involve the exaggeration involved in hyperbole and the imaginative presentation of what are only partial perspectives. When one is talking to the actual people involved or talking about people that those hearing already know about for themselves, then it is not too hard to realize that what is being said is not claiming to be everything that could be said. It is simply claiming to be what needs to be heard at that particular moment. We all exaggerate to get a point across. Sometimes this is unhelpful and inflammatory. But it also has a proper place in any rhetoric which is concerned to get a point across forcefully. The exaggeration used is a known part of the rules of the game, and is understood for what it is by speakers and hearers alike. But it is all too easy for us to make the mistake of taking these things out of their rhetorical contexts and using them in a far more descriptive and analytical context.

Going on from this reflection on the kind of rhetoric involved, it is also important to set the material into the cultural context of ancient conventions of polemic and not modern conventions of politeness. L. T. Johnson's article "The New Testament's Anti-Jewish Slander and Conventions of Ancient Rhetoric" is very helpful in this area.[4] We have become supersensitive, and words have an impact on us that they did not necessarily have on our forebears. They played hardball with each other in ways that are hardly imaginable today. But it is we who are out of step historically. Throughout most of history people have spoken much more sharply and directly with each other than most of us are comfortable with. It is interesting that Weinfeld has been able to show that most of accusations of Matt. 23 can be paralleled in rabbinic sources as accusations against either particular Pharisees, or particular kinds of Pharisees or even at times Pharisees in general.[5]

The problem with materials like Matt. 23 is that in the ongoing conflict between emerging church and Jewish leadership Christians were increasingly further removed from normal Jewish life. And so when Christians made use of these materials in a polemical context, and did so with some justification, there was, nonetheless, a real danger of distortion. They were at times throwing stones from a safe distance and therefore not really aware all too often of the whole identity of the people they were vilifying. Once Christianity had become the established religion and the power realities were totally inverted, the issues change again. What has been said in relation to powerful opponents to challenge them or to seek to lessen their influence (seen as harmful) on others is not necessarily what one ought to be saying to these same people when they have become a marginalized and disempowered group.

A key question here is: how far removed from normal Jewish life were Matthew and those to whom he addresses himself? This is not a matter that can be properly addressed here, but I draw attention to conclusions for which I have argued elsewhere.[6] First, I think it very likely that Matthew's Gospel was written before the buildup to the Jewish War that resulted in the destruction of Jerusalem in AD 70. If I am right about such an early date for the work, then no matter what the level of hostility between Matthew and his readers and wider Jewish life, there is no denying a living awareness on their part of that wider Jewish life. This judgment finds further support from a consideration of the provenance of the Gospel. As I see it, Matthew writes for a constituency that consists of Jewish Christians and to churches of Jewish Christians that appear not to have had any significant Gentile membership and not to have much natural social interaction with non-Jews.

---

4. L. T. Johnson, "The New Testament's Anti-Jewish Slander and Conventions of Ancient Rhetoric," *JBL* 108 (1989): 419-41.

5. M. Weinfeld, "The Charge of Hypocrisy in Matthew 23 and in Jewish Sources," *Immanuel* 24/25 (1990): 52-58.

6. See the introduction to Nolland, *The Gospel of Matthew* (NIGTC; Grand Rapids: Eerdmans, 2005), esp. 14-18.

It might be that it is too much to claim that the words of Matt. 23:2-3 ("the scribes and Pharisees sit on Moses' seat . . . do whatever they teach you") directly reflects the situation of Matthew's community, but they represent an idea with which Matthew's community is at home. And though the sense of these verses is much disputed, I take them to reflect a recognition that Christian disciples were in practical terms dependent on these Jewish religious leaders for their access to the Law. What the religious leaders did with it might be suspect, but not their knowledge of it. The scribes and Pharisees could and should be relied upon to report the Law of Moses with care and accuracy.[7] These opening verses in a very clear way, and other material through the chapter in more subtle ways, involve a general endorsement of the Pharisaic system. As Mason has already seen, it is against this background and only this background that the Matthean Jesus can press his accusation of hypocrisy.[8] It is from such a perspective of proximity that the criticisms of the scribes and Pharisees are being made.

Jesus could be very critical of individuals, groups and even the culture of the whole of his people. But his criticism always took place in a context of openness to the other person. In an important sense people may have become his enemies, but Jesus insisted on love of enemies. So even in his most radical criticism he was invested in seeking the welfare of those he addressed. In the critical stances we have adopted as Christians we have not always been as ready for an open engagement with others and invested in seeking their welfare. We readily retreat into our comfortable ghetto and use our critical remarks to place boundaries around ourselves. And here we part company from Jesus.

The question is: Do we part company not only from Jesus but also from Matthew? It is a matter of debate whether Matthew's use of the Matt. 23 material means that he is speaking from and for a disaffected group within the wider Jewish culture. It is certainly true that sociologically there is much here that reminds one of how disaffected groups speak about the dominant culture in relation to which they have become disaffected.[9] But I think that at the end of the day there remains an openness within Matthew's approach that makes it, for all the likeness, different in important respects.

---

7. Cf. M. A. Powell, "Do and Keep What Moses Says (Matthew 23:2-7)," *JBL* 114 (1995): 419-35 (here 424): "Since Jesus' disciples do not themselves have copies of the Torah, they will be dependent on the scribes and the Pharisees to know what Moses said. . . . In light of such dependence, Jesus advises his disciples to heed the words that the scribes and Pharisees speak when they sit on the seat of Moses, that is, when they pass on the words of the Torah itself."

8. See S. Mason, "Pharisaic Dominance Before 70 CE and the Gospels' Hypocrisy Charge (Matt. 23:2-3)," *HTR* 83 (1990): 363-81.

9. See Mason, "Pharisaic Dominance"; A. J. Saldarini, "Delegitimation of Leaders in Matthew 23," *CBQ* 54 (1992): 659-80.

It is to Matthew that we are indebted for the most careful articulation of Jesus' vision for love of enemies. The degree to which Matthew is reproducing blocks of preformed material in the Sermon on the Mount is disputed. But, however this might be judged, one must assume that what Matthew offers is something to which he would intend to be personally committed. Whatever the relationship of Matthew's editing to traditional blocks in the Sermon on the Mount, when it comes to Matt. 26:52 ("All who take the sword will perish by the sword") a distinctive Matthean investment seems clear. For "Return your sword to its place" Matthew shares a tradition base with John 18:11, but the vocabulary is almost entirely different.[10] For the rest of Jesus' words here Matthew stands alone. Matt. 26:52 has widely been recognized as echoing Matt. 5:38-39. Elsewhere I have drawn attention to *Joseph and Asenath* 29:3-4.[11] Verse 4 has "return your sword to its place" in words identical to Matthew's, apart from the choice of a different Greek word for "sword."[12] In addition, v. 3 says, "It does not befit a man who worships God to repay evil for evil," which must have some relationship to the fifth antithesis. Matthew seems to be deliberately echoing a body of Jewish tradition which also sits in the background of *Jos. As.* 29:3-4.[13] Matthew seems intent on encouraging his readers to set Jesus' teaching on love of enemies, and in particular its application in "all who take the sword shall perish by the sword," into the context of a tradition of Jewish moral reflection: the implicit message is that Jesus' teaching is to be seen as sharing the general approach of an existing strand of Jewish moral reflection, but as representing it in a radical form.[14] Here at least Matthew is not simply reproducing Jesus materials, but reflecting on them and interpreting them into his own situation. Matthew has reflected carefully on the challenge to love of enemies.

The family likeness of Matthew's heavy-handed criticism of the scribes and Pharisees to how disaffected groups speak about the dominant culture in relation to which they have become disaffected is not to be denied, but it is also important to realize that Matthew is not just castigating those who have become the enemy. He is much more involved in articulating an ethic to which Christians are to con-

---

10. The extent of common vocabulary in Greek is τὴν μάχαιραν and εἰς.
11. J. Nolland, "The Mandate: Love of Enemies. Matt. 5:43-48," *Anvil* 21 (2004) 23-33 (here 31).
12. ῥομφαίαν is used instead of μάχαιραν.
13. The use of "your" in *Jos. As.* 29:4 provides a clue that "return your sword to its place" there is meant to be recognized as a quotation: Benjamin, who is being addressed here, has no sword of his own, but has drawn the sword that is in his hand from the sheath strapped to the prostrate form of the son of Pharaoh whom he intends to kill. The language is likely to have come originally from 1 Chr. 21:27 (cf. Jer. 47:6), but it has come to both Matthew and the author of *Joseph and Asenath* via some Jewish tradition of ethical reflection.
14. For more detail see Nolland, "Mandate."

sider themselves answerable. For Matthew it is not just a "they" who are to be judged, but just as much a "we/you" who will be judged. For Matthew it is not good enough to be a Christian rather than a scribe or a Pharisee; what counts is that there should be an abundance of righteousness, outclassing anything on offer from the scribes and Pharisees (Matt. 5:20). The point is not to label others hypocrites, but to avoid being one oneself (6:1-18). "The Son of Man is to come with his angels in the glory of his Father, and then he will repay *everyone* for what *they* have done" (16:27). The clear capacity for Christian self-criticism which is evident keeps Matthew's criticism of the scribes and Pharisees from simply being reflex criticism indulged in by a member of a disaffected group.

If there is a feature of Matt. 23 at the beginning that was important for gaining a balanced perspective on the criticism leveled, there is another at the end of the chapter. Matthew is quite convinced that the destruction of Jerusalem and the temple, a replay of the Babylonian Exile, was in prospect for the Jewish people, once they have rejected Jesus. But it is also clear that Matthew does not just leaves the non-Christian Jews to their fate. Though the claim is made from time to time, there is no turning in 28:19 from the Jews and to the Gentiles; it is, rather, a widening of scope which is in view, after the restricted focus on Israel of 10:5. Matthew uses ἔθνη *alone* when referring to the Gentiles, but when he speaks of "all the ἔθνη" he is no longer using ἔθνη to distinguish Gentiles from Jews but rather making reference to the whole of humanity.[15] There is judgment, but for him there is also hope. For him mission is to be to all the nations, including the Jews (28:19). And from the language at the end of Matt. 23 we may judge that he expected a day in which Jewish people, who had rejected the claims of Jesus, would change their minds and finally say, "Blessed is he who comes in the name of the Lord" (23:38b). At least this is the case if I have rightly understood the force of v. 38, since these words have been understood in various ways.

The precise force of οὐ μή . . . ἕως ἄν ("will certainly not [see me] until") is disputed. The syntax choice is between (a) taking οὐ μή . . . ἕως ἄν as indicating that seeing will resume at an indicated future moment and (b) understanding the form conditionally as indicating that a future seeing is dependent on meeting a specified condition.[16]

---

15. Matt. 4:15; 6:32; 10:5; 10:18; 12:18, 21; 20:19, 25; vs. 24:9, 14; 25:32; 28:19. Matthew's sense for "all the ἔθνη" and his universal perspective are well matched by the vision of Ps. 96 (LXX 95) where to the call in v. 3 to "declare his glory among the nations, his marvellous works among all the peoples" (and cf. v. 10) corresponds in vv. 7-9 the call to the "families of the peoples" to "ascribe to Yahweh/the Lord the glory due to his name" and to "bring an offering and come into his courts."

16. K. H. Tan, *The Zion Traditions and the Aims of Jesus* (SNTSMS 91; Cambridge: Cambridge University Press, 1997), 115-16, helpfully identifies three of the four options considered here, but tries too hard to correlate each with a syntax consideration.

The sense that (a) produces depends on how "Blessed is the one who comes in the name of the Lord" is to be understood. The words clearly represent some kind of acknowledgment of something that is happening, namely a fresh coming of Jesus. Something like the coming of the Son of Man of Matt. 10:23; 16:27-28 is clearly in mind.[17] But what of the attitude of those who utter the words? The view that the fragment from Ps. 118:26 used here is to be uttered by those facing judgment is to be rejected. Blessing belongs to welcoming and celebrating, not to fear and despair.[18] The one who says, "Blessed is the one who comes in the name of the Lord" is involved in joyful welcome of one whose significance is appreciated. It is in effect an abbreviated form of the shout of the welcoming crowds in 21:9. But something is still missing here. There has clearly been a major change of heart. There are two possible ways of finding a place for such a change of heart. It could be the visible arrival of Jesus that provokes a change of heart and produces a hearty welcome. But this is difficult to square with the strong association in Matthew between the coming of the Son of Man and judgment (see 16:27). Or it could be that the material is prophetic of a change of heart that will come during the period of the church's mission. The Gospel seems to reflect a quite negative experience of mission to Israel, but that would not preclude such a prophetic hope.

What, however, if we take the syntax as representing a condition, as in (b) above? The obvious understanding to emerge along these lines involves the coming of the Son of Man being delayed until such time as there will be a proper reception for him in Jerusalem. Jesus will wait in heaven until the circumstances are right.[19] Despite the formal attractions of this view, it is not easy to imagine the Matthean Jesus quite saying: "You were not ready for me at this point. Never mind. I will go off and wait quietly in heaven until you are ready."

The best option seems to be to understand the material as prophetic of a change of heart that will come during the period of the church's mission: despite all the difficulties and all the hostility, the Matthean church expected that a significant Jewish turning to Christ would come. This is a mark of a fundamental ongoing openness to the very people Matthew feels so free to criticize.

---

17. The coming of the Son of Man will again be in view in Matt. 24:27, 30, 37, 39, 44; 25:31; 26:64; and cf. 24:5, 42, 50; 25:10.

18. Cf. W. D. Davies and D. C. Allison, *A Critical and Exegetical Commentary on the Gospel according to Saint Matthew* (ICC; Edinburgh: Clark, 1988-97), 3:323. (Exceptionally in *1 Enoch* 62:6, 9-10; 63:1-12 the wicked bless God as a ploy in an attempt to evade judgment.)

19. This view is well defended by D. C. Allison, "Matt. 23.39 = Luke 13.35b as a Conditional Prophecy," *JSNT* 18 (1983): 75-84; and cf. H. van der Kwaak, "Die Klage über Jerusalem (Matth. xxiii 37-39)," *NovT* 8 (1966): 156-70.

From various angles we have sought to look at the question of whether the material of Matt. 23 should be adjudged anti-Semitic. My answer has been that these materials for all their sharp criticism are not to be thought of as anti-Semitic. At the general level, we should distinguish between intended and unintended consequence, and we need to be careful that the recent redefinition of tolerance should not be allowed to distort the discussion. Specifically in connection with Matt. 23, we need to see these materials as intending to set up a dialectic, for those with other acquaintance with those criticized, between what is being now said and what they themselves know. The dialectic allows the hyperbole and incompleteness to emerge clearly for what it is. We also need to correlate the rhetoric involved in Matt. 23 with the sharpness involved in ancient conventions of polemic and not with modern conventions of politeness. Moreover, the Matthew who gives us chap. 23 also gives us the clearest window onto Jesus' vision of love of enemies, which is clearly something Matthew has reflected deeply on, not simply reproduced traditions about. He is committed to a fundamental openness to the hostile other. What is more, as critical as Matthew can be of the scribes and Pharisees, he is just as critical of kindred attitudes within the church. And finally Matthew does not just leave the non-Christian Jews whom he criticizes to their fate: despite the fact that the Gospel reflects quite a negative experience of mission to Israel, the task goes on, and Matthew has good hopes of a happy outcome: Jewish people ready to welcome Jesus as the one who comes in the name of the Lord.

Matthew 27:25: "His Blood Be on Us and on Our Children!"

Now we need to turn our attention to the second text. For most people this has been the more troubling. Matt. 23 deals with scribes and Pharisees, not with Jewish people in general, but Matt. 27:25 refers to the Jewish people in general. Matt. 27:25 has traditionally been read as laying the blame for Jesus' death upon the whole Jewish people (not Pilate because he wanted to release Jesus, and not just the Jewish leaders, but all the Jewish people). And it has been used as a basis for holding as responsible for Jesus' death, not just the Jews of Jesus' generation, but also the Jews of every subsequent generation. On the basis of this verse Christians have over the centuries been inclined to write Jews off as "God-killers," and often treated them with contempt and burdened each individual Jew with the guilt of the execution of Jesus.

The question for us is: is this fair to how Matt. 27:25 functions in Matthew's telling of the story? There can be no doubt that a very unflattering image of the Jewish crowds emerges in Matt. 27:25, but is the long history of anti-Semitic use of the verse fair to Matthew? A lot is at stake here, and we need to read Matthew's text with considerable care.

Let me take you through the main aspects of Matthew's setting for 27:25, starting from v. 15. First vv. 15-18. The dynamic of the story works best if we are to understand that Barabbas was the already known choice of the people, but that the arrest of Jesus has potentially changed the situation.[20] What makes best sense of the Gospel materials is that the agreed candidate for release was Barabbas, and that what should have been expected in the Gospel scene was a ritualized request for his release. But a late complication had arisen with the arrest of Jesus, a complication that has potentially changed the situation in a major way. Barabbas was the already known choice of the people, but that was before the arrest of Jesus. Pilate is offering a last-minute renegotiation. The choice between Barabbas and Jesus would have been a choice between the one already pre-indicated as the one who would be chosen and a newly arrested prisoner who had known great popularity. A possible last-minute change of choice is what Pilate has is mind. He clearly hopes that the crowd will choose Jesus. If we look closely we will see just how manipulative Pilate is trying to be here. Through vv. 15-21 he is portrayed as wanting everybody to assume that he intended to go along with the wishes of the chief priests and elders, and therefore that Jesus was already as good as condemned, and that only the Paschal pardon could save his life. (Only this makes sense of putting Barabbas and Jesus up as alternatives.) But Matthew's Pilate had not at all decided on his verdict. (This becomes clear in vv. 24-25.) And if the crowd would but choose Jesus for release, then Pilate would be spared a difficult decision. If his plan had worked, he would have avoided a major confrontation with the Jewish leaders with whom

---

20. Because we know of it only through the Gospel accounts, little can be said about the details of how the Paschal pardon operated. Did the people have a totally free choice, or was a process of bargaining involved in which both the governor and the people would have to be satisfied, or did Pilate unilaterally dictate the options? The middle option seems intrinsically likely. Both Mark and Matthew emphasize the people's choice (Mark has ὃν παρῃτοῦντο, Matthew has ὃν ἤθελεν), but then have Pilate offer only two names. How do we put these two features together? It is unlikely that justice can be done to the Gospel language with a choice limited to one or other candidate from a short list of two drawn up unilaterally by Pilate.

What is most likely is that we are not actually dealing with a short list created by Pilate. Mark's version of the status of Barabbas may help us a little here. It is notable that Barabbas is not the leader of the insurrection, but only a popular figure who had taken life in the name of the cause. Barabbas is a "big enough fish" to satisfy the people, but not such a "big fish" that Pilate could not consider, with whatever reluctance, letting him go. The choice of Barabbas fits well with a process of bargaining in which there would have been explicit or implicit ground rules that constrained the people's choice. But the bargaining over choice is not what is taking place in the scene reported in the Gospels; that must be understood to have taken place earlier.

he needed to work, kept Barabbas in his hands, and released a popular Jesus back to his public — a Jesus whom Pilate really considered innocent (v. 24; cf. v. 19) despite Jesus' unwillingness to defend himself (vv. 12-14). Pilate had it worked out that it was out of envy or jealousy that the leaders had acted against Jesus (v. 18). He knew that it was actually Jesus' popularity with the crowds that motivated the Jewish leaders. It is this divide between people and leaders that Pilate seeks to make use of.

We can pass over the message from Pilate's wife and move on to v. 20, which reports the surprising development in the story. The change in the attitude of the ordinary people to Jesus is as much of a surprise to a reader as it is to Pilate. Matthew has some hints of the possibility of a negative attitude to Jesus that went beyond the named leadership groups.[21] But the main impression is of great popularity.[22] It seems to me that the most likely key to the sharp turn-around involves an appeal to nationalism.[23] As long as the choice was between their own flawed leaders and an exciting prophetic figure who had newly come upon the scene, then it was not too hard for the people to side with the prophet over against their own leaders. But now a choice between Barabbas and Jesus was a choice between Jesus and a Jewish nationalist who had the glamor of a freedom fighter; and it was at the same time a choice between Pilate and their own Jewish leaders. It was one thing to choose Jesus over their own natural

---

21. On the negative side there is "and all Jerusalem with [Herod]" in his fear in Matt. 2:3; the anticipation of persecution (and not only from official leaders) that is prominent in the mission instructions in chap. 10 (and cf. 24:9); the description of the response of "this generation" to John the Baptist and to Jesus in 11:16-19; the woes in 11:20-24 upon Chorazin and Bethsaida in their failure to repent; the explanation in 13:11 of Jesus' use of parables in speaking to the crowds; Jesus' reception in his hometown in 13:54-58; Jesus' words against "this generation" (which is represented by the disciples!) in 17:17; and the lament over Jerusalem in 23:37. But none of this allows for an easy explanation of how it is that the people could be persuaded so quickly and so thoroughly.

22. See pervasively the role of the crowds in Matthew and then esp. 21:8-11, 46; 26:5 and cf. 27:18.

23. The Paschal pardon is intrinsically all about appeasing Jewish nationalism inasmuch as it is a concession to popular Jewish sentiment at a point where the Jewish view and that of the Roman governor were sharply at variance. Matthew does not, however, immediately help his readers here with his abbreviation of the Markan information about Barabbas. Matthew repeats "a prisoner" (δέσμιον) from 27:16 rather than explain, as in Mark, the larger group to which Barabbas belonged. Ἐπίσημον replaces Mark's description of the man's crime. The breadth of the word ἐπίσημον is probably useful to Matthew. Its basic meaning is "significant." The form of significance is quite open: one could be significant as being "conspicuous," "well known," "outstanding" or even "notorious." Matthew probably wants to say nothing more precise than that Barabbas is a "big fish," but he may intend to indicate with this word the popularity which made Barabbas a prime candidate for the Paschal pardon.

leaders; it would be quite another thing to choose Pilate's candidate over that favored by their leaders and who had, moreover, been their own favorite before ever Jesus came into the equation. All of a sudden Jesus seems to be identified with the Romans, over against a Barabbas who represented the most committed form of Jewish nationalism. The driving force here had little to do with Jesus and a lot to do with the loyalties of a confused nationalism. But notice that for Matthew responsibility for leading the people astray is laid squarely at the feet of the leadership groups (v. 20). The people are doing only what they have been led to do.

I think the NRSV translation of the opening words of v. 24 is somewhat misleading. "When Pilate saw that he could do nothing" tends to make it sound like he is powerless in the face of the fury of the crowd. But the words are ὅτι οὐδὲν ὠφελεῖ. They are a comment on the failure of Pilate's strategy, not a statement of impotence. I would want to translate "[seeing] that he was achieving nothing." Pilate's attempt at manipulating the situation has failed; and the Jewish leaders have regained control over the people.

What is Pilate to do now? His wife has begged him to have nothing to do with Jesus. As he saw things, that is what Pilate now tries to do. In v. 21 the crowd has asked for Barabbas. The responsibility for what is to be done with Jesus is now sitting squarely back on Pilate's shoulders. Vv. 22-24 are the account of how Pilate seeks to evade this responsibility. Pilate is not a man trying to save Jesus' life here, as is sometimes claimed; Pilate is a man who is trying to "pass the buck." Why ask the crowd what to do with Jesus? That is Pilate's responsibility. The crowd is eager for Jesus' blood. But Pilate is eager to duck responsibility. In an extraordinary abdication of responsibility Pilate makes the crowd "judge and jury" in his place. He says "I am innocent of this man's blood," but the hand washing is only a charade.[24] In Pilate's action we are probably meant to see a parody of what is prescribed in Deut. 21:1-9 (where the elders of the town near-

---

24. Matthew does not use the word for "wash" (νίπτειν) here that he has uses earlier and which is the common word for wash in the rest of the NT and in the LXX. Instead he uses ἀπονίπτειν, which is not found elsewhere in the NT and which is found just three times in the LXX, in each case with negative overtones, and especially in the two cases which use middle forms as here. (In 3 Kgdms. 22:38 it the blood of Jehoshaphat, which had drained to the bottom of the chariot as he stood propped up but fatally wounded through the rest of the battle, which is being washed out of the chariot in which he died. In the LXX of Prov. 30:12 "the evil grandchild judges himself to be righteous, but does not wash [off] his ἔξοδον (lit. "departure," but perhaps referring to death as a judgment)." The LXX of Prov. 30:20 has, "This is the way of the adulterous woman, who when she does [it], after having a wash says, 'I have done nothing wrong.'" The latter two use the middle as in Matt. 27:24, and in neither of these is the washing effective, except as an act of self-deception.) Matthew may intend to carry into his text something of these negative overtones.

est to the site of a murder by person or persons unknown wash their hands and declare their innocence).[25] Pilate wants to be considered innocent. He has in mind his wife's message. He knows that innocent blood is going to be shed,[26] but he does not want the resulting ritual impurity to contaminate him (there is an analogous concern on the part of the chief priests in Matt. 27:6 in connection with the blood money). The ritual washing of the hands is meant as a kind of prophylactic. Jesus dies because Pilate does not have the courage to stand up to the pressure brought to bear by the Jewish leaders and the intimidating behavior of the crowd.

Pilate's eagerness to pass responsibility is matched by the people's readiness to take responsibility.[27] If that is what it takes to achieve their goal, then the people are ready for it. Whatever it takes, Jesus must be done away with. On the lips of the people the words are a statement of readiness to take responsibility, not a confession of guilt. By this stage in the story they will share the view expressed at the conclusion of the Sanhedrin hearing in 26:66: "he deserves death." But Matthew chooses the "blood . . . upon" (αἷμα ἐπί) language to echo 23:35. And since, as far as Matthew is concerned, it is innocent blood that the people take upon themselves, the overtones of bloodguilt and of punishment which the OT links provide for 23:35 carry over now to 27:25. "And on our children" is not intended to pass responsibility down through the generations. To involve one's children as well as oneself betokens a deeper level of commitment and seriousness. And since for Matthew judgment is to fall within the generation (23:36), inevitably those who are now children will also fall victim to its coming.

Matthew paints quite a nasty picture of the crowds baying for Jesus' blood.

---

25. Cf. Pss. 26 (LXX 25):6; 73 (LXX 72):13, which have "wash/washed my hands in innocence," which seem to merge notions of moral innocence and ritual purity: on the basis of existing moral innocence ritual purity is achieved by the washing of hands. Cf. further "clean hands and a pure heart" in Ps. 24:4 and the full phrase in Ps. 73:13: "I have kept my heart clean and washed my hands in innocence." Pss. 26 (LXX 25):6; 73 (LXX 72):13 seem to have generated the practice in *Ep. Arist.* 305-6 of washing hands during prayer as an assertion that one has done no evil.

26. The textual witness for Matt. 27:24 is finely balanced over whether the reading should be τούτου ("of this [person]") or τοῦ δικαίου τούτου ("of this righteous [person]"). The presence of "righteous" makes the link back to Matt. 27:19 explicit. If "righteous" is not original, it is an accurate gloss on Matthew's intended sense. But on balance its addition is easier to explain than its loss.

27. There is some similarity here to the scene played out in 2 Sam. 14:4-11, where, to gain the king's support for the sparing of the life of her one son who had killed the other son in a fight, the woman of Tekoa says in v. 9, "On me be the guilt . . . and on my father's house; let the king and his throne be guiltless" (LXX has ἀθῷος as in Matt. 27:24).

But in the larger shape of Matthew's story, the important thing for us is that by this stage in his story the landscape is littered with people who have a share in the responsibility for Jesus' death. There are some, like Judas and the people, who readily own responsibility (vv. 3-5, 25); there are some, like Pilate and the chief priests and the elders, who prefer to see the responsibility as falling elsewhere (vv. 24, 4, 6-7); and there are some, like the disciples and especially Peter, whose part has simply been to deny and to abandon Jesus (26:31, 56, 69-75).[28] All are guilty, and the judgment heralded in 23:35-36 will certainly fall, but for all as well the possibility of forgiveness and restoration remains. The cross reveals the guilt of all, but in turn it offers forgiveness to all.[29] If complicity in the death of Jesus is a barrier to benefiting from the ransom paid (20:28) and from the blood poured out for the forgiveness of sins (26:28), then the giving of the bread and wine at the Last Supper (26:26-29) is an empty gesture, and this is certainly not what Matthew thinks.

Matthew treads a careful path in his allocation of guilt for the death of Jesus and highlights the ways in which the responsibility of each links with that of the others. The cry of the people in 27:25 marks a dramatic high point in the story, but behind it stands the role in persuasion of the chief priests and the elders (v. 20). While the people are not to be spared their own responsibility, it is the leaders who are responsible for turning the people against Jesus. The Jewish leadership has been marked by long-standing hostility to Jesus and a growing desire to destroy him (12:14; 26:4). In turn the Jewish leadership is given its opportunity by the role of a betrayer within Jesus' closest group of followers (vv. 14-16, 47-50), and the other disciples are not so different from Judas in their failure to stand in solidarity with Jesus once the threat of arrest becomes immediate. But given the Roman control over capital punishment, none of this would have led to Jesus' execution without the role of Pilate. In Matthew's telling it is not just that Pilate sanctions what the Jewish leadership is pressing upon him.

---

28. The only group that seems to be spared complicity in the death of Jesus is the group of women who had followed from Galilee (Matt. 27:55-56). Where Mark is content to say of the women that "they also were looking [on] from afar," Matthew with his simple addition of ἐκεῖ ("there") emphasizes first and foremost that they were *there*. The contrast is with 26:56, "then all the disciples left him and fled," and then more particularly with Peter in v. 58, whose "following [Jesus] from afar" . . . "to see the end" had proved so disastrously abortive. The women were still there.

29. T. B. Cargal, "'His Blood Be upon Us and upon Our Children': A Matthean Double Entendre?" *NTS* 37 (1991): 101-12 (here, 110-11), and others argue for a double entendre in "his blood be upon us": responsibility and guilt on the one hand; covered by the "blood . . . poured out for the forgiveness of many" (Matt. 26:28). But I do not think the case for this double entendre has been successfully made, nor the case for taking 27:25 in only a redemptive sense (e.g., D. Sullivan, "New Insights into Matthew 27:24-25," *NB* 73 [1992]: 453-57).

Pilate, failing to own the responsibility that was his, sends to his death a man whom he believes to be innocent. There is a lot of finger pointing going on here, but the inclusion of Pilate and of the disciples and in particular Judas indicates that it does not have an anti-Semitic nature.

Christian history is full of readings of 27:25 that fail to pay sufficient attention to its role as embedded in Matthew's story. The consequence has been a most un-Christian hatred and persecution of the Jews. But I do not think we should be holding Matthew responsible for this abuse of his text.

Conclusion

If Matthew could have anticipated that his Gospel would become the church's Gospel for the dominant Gentile church of the later centuries, no doubt he would have expressed himself more judiciously than he did. But he wrote in a Jewish-Christian context and spoke to his own peers. As the church lost a living connection to its Jewish roots, so its capacity to read faithfully this Jewish and Christian text was diminished. Christianity cannot give away the scandal of particularity and be true to itself. And the particularity of Christianity, by definition, makes claims which involve a stringent criticism of all that resists the saving initiative of God in Jesus Christ. But anti-Semitism as classically understood is something that, while the church has been far from free of it, the Gospel of Matthew does not, so far as I can see, fall into. In our context, however, and given the past misuse of Matthew to anti-Semitic ends, we need to be particularly judicious in our use of this Gospel and in particular of its heavy-handed criticisms of the Jewish leaders and people of Jesus' day.

Holiness and Ecclesiology:
The Church in Matthew

Donald A. Hagner

For a challenging call to a high standard of holiness it would be hard to top the Gospel of Matthew. The Sermon on the Mount (chaps. 5–7) presents an idealism so daunting that it has often been regarded as a kind of foil for the gospel — the exceptionally high standard of the law, as interpreted by Jesus, being intended to drive us to the necessity of grace. Indeed, so insistent is Matthew's call to this new level of righteousness that it is easy to misread him as arguing for salvation by works. But this would be to ignore the main affirmation that Matthew makes, namely the announcement of "the gospel of the kingdom (τὸ εὐαγγέλιον τῆς βασιλείας)," a phrase unique to Matthew (4:23; 9:35; 24:14; cf. 26:13). The dawning of the kingdom in the historical figure of Jesus is purely a matter of grace. It comes to the unworthy, as something to be received rather than earned.

With the coming of the eschatological reality of the kingdom, however, it is equally clear that a new standard of righteousness comes into effect: the righteousness expected of those who belong to the dawning kingdom. The connection between righteousness and the kingdom is vital. This essay explores the interconnection between the gospel of the kingdom of God, the new eschatological community, and the call to a new form of righteousness. In the process we hope to gain some insight into the dynamic of righteousness among the earliest disciples of Jesus and to draw lessons for the contemporary church.

The Gospel of the Kingdom

One of the unique and most conspicuous features of the Gospel of Matthew is found in the five discourses (chaps. 5–7; 10; 13; 18; and 24–25). These provide an incomparable compendium of the teaching of Jesus. While this emphasis on the teaching of Jesus is one of the distinctives of the Gospel, the teaching presupposes and relies upon the more important fact of the announcement of the kingdom. Although the phrase "the gospel of the kingdom" is found only once in the five discourses (24:14), the word "kingdom" (βασιλεία) occurs frequently there and throughout the gospel (55x total; Mark: 20x; Luke 46x). The kingdom serves as the prior, determining fact in the narrative, including the teaching sections. Matthew, like the other Synoptics and John too, describes the dawning of an eschatological reality. This is the fundamental, governing fact that controls the narratives. All that Jesus says and does is in one way or another related to the dawning of the kingdom of God.

The point is, as Matthew likes so much to stress, that with the coming of Jesus we have arrived at the fulfillment of the promises of scripture. One sees this throughout Matthew's narrative, as, for example, at the very beginning in the genealogies, with their stress on Abraham and David. Both the Abrahamic and Davidic covenants find their realization in Jesus. At the beginning of the Sermon on the Mount, the Beatitudes affirm the reality of the kingdom in the present (see 5:3, 10), and not merely something to be expected in the future. John the Baptist's doubt about whether Jesus was the Messiah, the One who would bring the kingdom, is answered by Jesus with words pointing to apocalyptic fulfillment (11:4-5). Jesus identifies John as fulfilling the role of Elijah (11:14; 17:12), the one preparing the way for the promised One, adding "For all the prophets and the law prophesied until John" (11:13). John is therefore at the pivotal point of the turning from the age of prophecy to the age of fulfillment. Just as the healings are signs of the presence of the kingdom of God, according to 11:4-5, so too the exorcism of demons points to that same reality: "But if it is by the Spirit of God that I cast out demons, then the kingdom of God has come upon you" (12:28). In the parables discourse, Jesus stresses the fulfillment he brings: "But blessed are your eyes, for they see, and your ears, for they hear. Truly I say to you, many prophets and righteous people longed to see what you see, and did not see it, and to hear what you hear, and did not hear it" (13:16-17). As the narrative approaches its climax, Jesus accepts Peter's confession of him as Messiah (16:16), and as he enters Jerusalem as messianic king (note Matthew's quotation of Zech. 9:9) he does not turn away the shouts of "Hosanna to the Son of David!" (21:9; cf. 21:15-16).

At the same time, it is clear that even with all of the realized eschatology in Matthew, the kingdom also awaits a future manifestation. The kingdom comes *into* the present age without bringing it to an end. Currently the kingdom is present in a paradoxical form. Jesus admits as much when he says to the disciples: "To you it has been given to know the secrets (τὰ μυστήρια) of the kingdom" (13:11). One of the mysteries of the kingdom revealed in the parables discourse of chapter 13 is the surprise that the kingdom arrives without bringing judgment upon the wicked. Judgment is delayed. Indeed, as the parables of the mustard seed, the leaven, the hidden treasure and the pearl reveal (13:31-33, 44-46), the kingdom first comes in a small, inconspicuous way, without overwhelming the world (as it eventually will). The greatest of surprises, of course, is the fate of the Messiah, who comes not triumphantly, but humbly, not to ascend the throne of David, but to die (16:21). And then too comes further surprising teaching: the disciples of Jesus must also be prepared to suffer, take up their cross and follow after him (16:24-27). The reality of the kingdom is to be lived out here and now, in this still very imperfect world, in advance of the time of the parousia of the Son of Man.

What needs to be stressed here is that a new eschatological reality has arrived with, in, and through Jesus, and that together with that reality comes a new standard of righteousness and a new pattern of obedience.[1] One cannot talk of righteousness and obedience without giving attention to the new reality of the kingdom. "The king of whom Matthew's gospel speaks is Jesus. The kingdom into which he invites his readers is the kingdom of heaven. Matthean spirituality springs out of encounter with that king and involves entry into that kingdom."[2]

The New Eschatological People of God

Among the Synoptic Gospels it is in Matthew that the emergence of a new community is most explicit. As is well known, the word ἐκκλησία ("church") occurs in the four Gospels only in Matthew (16:18; 18:17). Of course, speaking in Aramaic, Jesus would not have used the Greek word ἐκκλησία, but an Aramaic word for "community."[3] Nevertheless, by the time of the writing of the Gospel, the evangelist would have been prepared to understand the Greek word in the explicit meaning of "church," the meaning it has elsewhere throughout the NT. The new community founded by Jesus is nothing other than the "church."

As the community of the kingdom, this is a new eschatological people. While on the one hand there is an obvious and inevitable discontinuity with Israel, on the other hand this community regards itself as the initial fulfillment of God's promises to Israel. Although the language is lacking, it is a kind of new Israel, or, better, the true Israel. Jesus says, "I tell you, you are Peter (Πέτρος), and

---

1. Stephen C. Barton, "Dislocating and Relocating Holiness: A New Testament Study," in *Holiness: Past and Present* (ed. Stephen C. Barton; London: T&T Clark, 2003), 198-200.
2. Stephen C. Barton, *The Spirituality of the Gospels* (London: SPCK, 1992), 10.
3. Probably *qahal*, but also possible are *'edah* (= Greek συναγωγή) or *kenishta*.

on this rock (πέτρα)⁴ I will build my church" (16:18). Very significant here is Jesus' reference to "my church," where the pronoun, preceding the noun in the Greek, is emphatic: μου τὴν ἐκκλησίαν ("*my* church"). The church is the community *of Jesus*, a designation that stands in remarkable contrast to the phrase *qahal YHWH*, "community of the Lord" (LXX: ἐκκλησία κυρίου, e.g., Deut. 23:1-2; 1 Chr. 28:8; Mic. 2:5; cf. Neh. 13:1; Lam. 1:10). The community of Jesus as the community of the Messiah is the eschatological counterpart to Israel — or, better, the eschatological manifestation of Israel.

A few scholars have argued in recent years that Matthew's community is to be understood as a sect within Judaism rather than an actual manifestation of Christianity.⁵ Although they have rightly emphasized the Jewishness of Matthew's Gospel, in my opinion they seriously underestimate the degree of newness and the discontinuity with Israel that is found repeatedly in Matthew.⁶ This eschatological community — the community of the kingdom — represents the fulfilled expression of Israel. It is in continuity with Israel but it is also a new people. Very important is the fact that it centers no longer on Torah, but on Jesus (cf. 10:32-33, 37-39). It is this community that will enjoy his presence wherever two or three are gathered in his name (18:20);⁷ it is this community that Jesus promises he will be with "always, to the close of the age (τῆς συντελείας τοῦ αἰῶνος)" (28:20).

This community of the kingdom is called to faithfulness to the Torah (cf. 5:17-19) but, as we will see, in a unique way. Jesus does not call the community to follow the Torah directly, but to follow *his* teaching (cf. 7:24-27). For it is the Messiah's teaching that represents the true interpretation of the Torah (cf. 23:8,

---

4. The word play on "Peter" and "rock" is effective in the Greek, but would have been even clearer in the Aramaic where both words would have been exactly the same: *Kepha'*.

5. Andrew Overman, *Matthew's Gospel and Formative Judaism: The Social World of the Matthean Community* (Minneapolis: Fortress, 1990); idem, *Church and Community in Crisis: The Gospel According to Matthew, The New Testament in Context* (Valley Forge, PA: Trinity Press International, 1996); Anthony J. Saldarini, *Matthew's Christian-Jewish Community* (Chicago and London: University of Chicago Press, 1994); "The Gospel of Matthew and Jewish-Christian Conflict," in *Social History of the Matthean Community: Cross-Disciplinary Approaches* (ed. David L. Balch; Minneapolis: Fortress, 1991), 38-61. David Sim, *The Gospel of Matthew and Christian Judaism: The History and Social Setting of the Matthean Community* (Edinburgh: T&T Clark, 1998); idem, "Christianity and Ethnicity in the Gospel of Matthew," in *Ethnicity and the Bible* (Biblical Interpretation Series 19; ed. Mark G. Brett; Leiden: Brill, 1996), 171-95; idem, "The Gospel of Matthew and the Gentiles," *JSNT* 57 (1995): 19-48.

6. See my "Matthew: Apostate, Reformer, Revolutionary?" *NTS* 49 (2003): 193-209; and "New Things from the Scribe's Treasure Box (Mt 13:52)," *ExpT* 109 (1998): 329-34.

7. Cf. the parallel rabbinic saying that the *Shekinah* glory is present where two or three gather to study Torah (*m. 'Abot* 3:2; *b. Sanh.* 39a; *b. Ber.* 5b).

10). To follow the teaching of Jesus is in effect to be faithful to the Torah. The great commission thus includes the words "teaching them to observe all that I have commanded you" (28:20).

Righteousness in Matthew

The ἅγιος ("holy") word group is not prominent in Matthew. The verb ἁγιάζω ("sanctify") occurs only in 6:9, "hallowed be thy name," and in 23:17, 19, where it refers to the gold of the temple which the temple "makes sacred," and a gift that the altar "makes sacred." The noun ἁγιασμός ("holiness") does not occur. The word ἅγιος ("holy") occurs mainly as an adjective modifying "Spirit" and "city," and once the holy "place," i.e., the inner sanctuary of the temple (24:15). It occurs twice as a noun, "what is holy" (7:6), and, in plural form, "the saints who had fallen asleep" (27:52).

Matthew's word for the conduct of believers is not "holiness," but δικαιοσύνη, "righteousness." Among the Synoptic Gospels, the word occurs only in Matthew, except for its single occurrence in Zechariah's prophecy in Luke 1:75. Matthean scholarship has tended to follow the conclusion of Benno Przybylski that all seven occurrences of the word in Matthew refer to ethical conduct.[8] This seems true in most of the instances, but not, in my opinion, for all of them. I find exceptions in the two references outside the Sermon on the Mount. In 3:15 and 21:32 the righteousness in view can be understood as the righteousness of God, i.e., God's saving activity (as, e.g., in Paul [!], in Rom 1:17), rather than human righteousness. In view in both references is John the Baptist as the forerunner of the messianic salvation brought by Jesus. Furthermore, it also seems unlikely that δικαιοσύνην in 5:6 refers to ethical righteousness. Instead, in keeping with the context of the other beatitudes, the hunger in view is for eschatological *justice*, for the realization of God's rule on earth (in accord with the point of the future tenses of vv. 4, 5, 7, 8, and 9).[9]

---

8. Benno Przybylski, *Righteousness in Matthew and His World of Thought* (SNTSMS 41; Cambridge: Cambridge University Press, 1982). Oddly enough, Przybylski denies that "righteousness" is of any great importance to Matthew, regarding it as "essentially a Jewish concept" (pp. 115, 123).

9. I am well aware of the danger of "Paulinizing" Matthew. For a defense of these conclusions, see my "Righteousness in Matthew's Theology," in *Worship, Theology and Ministry in the Early Church: Essays in Honor of Ralph P. Martin* (ed. M. J. Wilkins and T. Paige; Sheffield: JSOT, 1992), 101-20; and "Balancing the Old and the New: The Law of Moses in Matthew and Paul," *Interpretation* 51 (1997): 20-30. An excellent treatment of the subject can be found in J. Reumann, "Righteousness" in the New Testament: "Justification" in the United States Lutheran–Roman Catholic Dialogue (Philadelphia/New York: Fortress/Paulist, 1982), 125-35.

The four remaining occurrences of the word do have ethical righteousness in view, and to these we now turn our attention. The beatitude of 5:10, "Blessed are those who are persecuted for righteousness' sake," has in view the ethical righteousness of those who follow Jesus. The allusion to this logion in 1 Pet. 3:14 also points to this understanding. The parallelism between 5:10 and 5:11 is striking, where ἕνεκεν δικαιοσύνης ("on account of righteousness") parallels ἕνεκεν ἐμοῦ ("on account of me"). Righteousness is associated with relationship to Jesus. Clearly ethical righteousness is also in view in 5:20: "For I tell you, unless your righteousness exceeds that of the scribes and Pharisees, you will never enter the kingdom of heaven." The difference in righteousness here is not quantitative, but qualitative. Although the language here sounds quantitative (lit. "abound more than"), the contrast is really qualitative, as the great difference between the ethical teaching of Jesus in the Gospels and the oral tradition of the Pharisees indicates (note too the reference to the "heavy burdens" imposed by the Pharisees in 23:4, and the contrast to the "easy yoke" and "light burden" of Jesus in 11:30). It is thus not a matter of increasing the legal stipulations, building a higher fence around the Torah than the Pharisees did, but rather of exhibiting the new righteousness associated with the kingdom as its resultant fulfillment.

"Righteousness" in 6:1 (RSV: "piety") refers merely to the concrete practices of almsgiving, prayer, and fasting (6:1-18). The avoidance of hypocrisy (see vv. 2, 5, 16) is clearly important in the pattern of righteousness taught by Jesus.

The reference in 6:33, however, is one of the most illuminating: "But seek first his kingdom and his righteousness, and all these things shall be yours as well." In this exhortation we are confronted directly with the connection between the kingdom and righteousness. Jesus here calls his disciples to make the kingdom their priority: they are to put it "first." To make a priority of living under the sovereign rule of God, his kingdom, is at the same time to seek God's righteousness. The second phrase, "his righteousness," is epexegetical of the first, "his kingdom." That is, to prioritize the first is in effect also to prioritize the second.

The call to righteousness is therefore inseparable from the gift of the kingdom. It is this fact that conditions all references to righteousness in the Gospel, enabling us to speak of righteousness not only as demand, but as gift at the same time. And this is why the righteousness of the disciples is qualitatively different from the righteousness, for example, of the Pharisees. The imperative is preceded by an indicative; the demand is preceded by the gift. That was true, of course, for the OT era too, where the giving of the law is preceded by a statement of the already existing covenant relationship between YHWH and Israel. But now a new era of fulfillment has arrived. The reality of the dawning kingdom makes possible not merely a correct exegesis and new definition of the law in the teaching of Jesus, but also brings to the recipients of the kingdom a new ability to live according to the will of God.

The ethical teaching of Matthew is thus directed to those who have received the kingdom. These are particularly kingdom ethics, applicable to those who belong to the kingdom. They cannot successfully be separated from this context, in which alone they make sense. The Sermon on the Mount is understood correctly only when it is seen in the context of the whole Gospel.[10]

The Righteousness of the New Community

Eschatology has begun with the arrival of the kingdom brought by Jesus. This turning point in the ages entails the creation of a new community of God's people, the church. Matthew calls that new community to righteousness. We have seen that this demand of righteousness presupposes the gift of the kingdom. But now we must explore further the nature of this righteousness. More exactly, what does discipleship look like in concrete, lived-out terms?

To begin with, the obedience of discipleship is now centered not upon the commandments, but upon Jesus and his teaching. "The law is no longer the center of gravity; Jesus is."[11] Although the righteousness of the Torah is still in view, the call is not to obey the commandments per se, but to obey the teaching of Jesus. It is *his* interpretation of the law that is definitive: "You have heard it said . . . but *I* [emphatic in the Greek] say to you" (5:22, 28, 32, 34, 39, 44). It is *his* words that will not pass away (24:35). In the commission that ends the Gospel, those who are discipled are "to observe all that *I* have commanded you" (28:20). Since he is the "one teacher" (23:8) of the community, it is *his* teaching that is to provide the rule of the community.

This does not, however, involve a new nomism, i.e., a centering on the commandments of Jesus parallel to the way contemporary Judaism centered on the Mosaic commandments. If there is an intended parallel between Jesus and Moses going up a mountain to deliver the law of God,[12] it would be a mistake to suppose that it is simply a matter of replacing the law of Moses with the new law

---

10. *Pace* Hans-Dieter Betz, who attempts to isolate the Sermon on the Mount from the Gospel and to deal with it independently as an entity with self-standing, universal relevance. See his *The Sermon on the Mount* (Hermeneia; Minneapolis: Fortress, 1995), and G. N. Stanton's critique of Betz in *A Gospel for a New People: Studies in Matthew* (Edinburgh: T&T Clark, 1992), 307-25.

11. K. Snodgrass, "Matthew and the Law," in *Treasures New and Old: Contributions to Matthean Studies* (ed. D. R. Bauer and M. A. Powell; Atlanta: Scholars Press, 1996), 126.

12. See D. C. Allison, Jr., *The New Moses: A Matthean Typology* (Minneapolis: Fortress, 1993), 172-80.

of Jesus, all else remaining essentially the same. Because, as we have seen, the teaching of Jesus occurs in the context of eschatological fulfillment, an entirely different dynamic is at work. For the same reason, while Moses was significant only as a mediator of the law, Jesus is the focal figure of the new covenant. Discipleship revolves around him (10:37-38) rather than around the law. The key issue is following Jesus rather than obeying the law. Of course, for Matthew, to follow the teaching of Jesus is at the same time in effect to be faithful to the entirety of the law properly understood (even hyperbolically down to the smallest letter and the smallest mark; 5:18). In no way does Matthew regard Jesus as being disloyal to or undermining the righteousness of the Torah. Rather, Matthew's Jesus upholds it and defines it (5:17).

The words "disciple" and "follow" are regularly used in connection with following Jesus. The first, "disciple" (μαθητής), occurs far more frequently in Matthew (73x) than in Mark (46x) or Luke (37x).[13] The second, "to follow" (ἀκολουθεῖν), is also more frequent in Matthew (25x) than in the other Synoptic Gospels (Mark, 18x; Luke, 17x). A disciple is one who is in special relationship with Jesus, as a learner in relation to a teacher (10:24-25), and as one who will eventually become a teacher.[14] Jesus, the Messiah, is the "one teacher" of the community (23:8-10). When Jesus sits down to teach — the typical position of one who teaches — "his disciples" come to him (5:1). The word is commonly used specifically to refer to the twelve, though it can refer to, and often implies, a wider circle. The "disciple" is preeminently one who "learns" — the root meaning of the word. What is learned are the mysteries of the kingdom (13:51-52) — its dawning and its present, unobtrusive form — as well as the righteousness appropriate to the kingdom (chaps. 5–7; cf. 11:1). But the disciples must also learn the strange necessity of Jesus' death (16:21; 20:17), together with the disturbing fact that they must follow in his footsteps, taking up their own cross (16:24). What is finally most important, however, is that disciples are those who do the will of the Father as explicated by Jesus (7:21; 12:50; 21:31).[15]

---

13. The word occurs twenty-eight times in Acts, but nowhere else in the NT. The cognate verb μαθητεύειν, "to make disciples," occurs three times in Matthew, and in the remainder of the NT only once, in Acts 14:21. The verb μανθάνειν, "to learn," occurs three times in Matthew, and only once in Mark. For a full study, see Michael J. Wilkins, *Discipleship in the Ancient World and Matthew's Gospel* (2nd ed.; Grand Rapids: Baker, 1995); cf. too, by the same author, *Following the Master: Discipleship in the Steps of Jesus* (Grand Rapids: Zondervan, 1992).

14. A. T. Lincoln, "Matthew — A Story for Teachers?" in *The Bible in Three Dimensions* (ed. D. J. A. Clines et al.; Sheffield: JSOT, 1990), 103-26. P. S. Minear, *Matthew: The Teacher's Gospel* (New York: Pilgrim, 1982).

15. Matthew would have agreed fully with the statement made by Jesus in John 8:31: "If you continue in my word, you are truly my disciples."

The verb ποιεῖν, "to do," is very important in Matthew.[16] It is not just a matter of hearing the words of Jesus, but of doing them. Matthew would be in full accord with James (cf. Jas. 1:25) — well, and for that matter, Paul too! (Rom. 2:13). "Everyone who hears these words of mine and does them will be like the wise person. . . ." "Everyone who hears these words of mine and does not do them will be like a foolish person . . ." (7:24-27). "The Son of man is to come with his angels in the glory of the Father, and then he will repay every person for what he or she has done" (16:27). The stress upon doing is found throughout the Gospel (cf. also 19:16-22; 24:26; 25:40, 45).

The disciples are those who "follow" Jesus. Indeed, the essence of discipleship is following Jesus (4:19-22; 8:22; 9:9; 19:21, 27-30). In view is learning from Jesus, doing what Jesus teaches and in this way manifesting the righteousness of the Torah. Equally important is following Jesus in self-giving obedience to the will of the Father, even to the point of dying to self (16:24-28; cf. 10:38).

Jesus, as we have noted, fulfills the law in the sense of bringing it to its intended meaning (5:17). In the Sermon on the Mount, Jesus radicalizes the law, focusing not merely on actions but even on the thoughts that underlie the actions.[17] What should especially be noted, however, is that Jesus does not get bogged down in what might be called nomistic detail. He does not multiply the commandments or engage in any casuistry. (This in itself suggests that it is a mistake to approach every specific command of the Sermon in a flat-footed, simplistic and absolute literalism.[18]) Instead, in his sovereign authority Jesus is able to cut through to the very essence of the law. He defines the weightier matters of the law as "justice, mercy and faithfulness" (23:23), sounding very much like an Old Testament prophet. The essence of the law, however, is found in the striking twofold love commandment. It is here that the ethical teaching of the law finds its root. "You shall love the Lord your God with all your heart, and with all your soul, and with all your mind" and "You shall love your neighbor as yourself." "On these two commandments," Jesus concludes, "hang all the law and the prophets" (22:40). This is the heart of the law for Jesus, and these two commandments accordingly provide a hermeneutic for the understanding of all the other commandments.[19] In a similar way, the Golden Rule points to

---

16. It is worth noting that while Matthew uses περιπατεῖν, "to walk," in its literal sense, he avoids using it as the equivalent to the Hebrew verb *halach*, though we might have expected him to do so. Does he deliberately want to avoid any suggestion of a parallel between Jesus' teaching and the Pharisees' *halacha*? Cf. R. T. France, *Matthew: Evangelist and Teacher* (Grand Rapids: Zondervan, 1989), 257-60.

17. See K. E. Brower, "Jesus and the Lustful Eye: Matthew 5:28," *EQ* 76 (2004): 291-309.

18. See my "Ethics and the Sermon on the Mount," *ST* 51 (1997): 55.

19. See B. Gerhardsson, "The Hermeneutic Program in Matthew 22:37-40," in *Jews, Greeks*

what is to be regarded as the essence of the law: "In everything do to others as you would have them do to you; for this is the law and the prophets" (7:12). Here is the center of Matthew's call to righteousness; nothing is more basic than this. "The greatest holiness to which the disciples are called is a life of faith in Jesus, manifested by love for others. All laws are secondary to and must be interpreted in light of this commandment of love."[20] Brower too finds the double love commandment central to holiness: "Single-minded devotion to God and love of neighbor, flowing from the people of God in loving relationship with the holy God through Jesus Messiah by the Spirit, is the motivational center of Christian holiness."[21] Stephen Barton's conclusion seems justified: "It seems fair to say, then, that the double command to love God and neighbor expresses in a nutshell what practical spirituality is about according to Matthew."[22]

The righteousness of the new community is of a radical character. The Sermon on the Mount is its blueprint. Those who will manifest it are described as "the salt of the earth" and "the light of the world" (5:13). They are learning to deal not merely with their actions, as basically important as that is, but also with their thoughts, with their heart, with their innermost being. They are faithful; their word is as good as gold. Far from being vengeful, they are loving and good, even toward their enemies. They are not hypocrites, playacting, pretending to be something they are not. Their piety is more private than public. They are forgiving of others, just as they have experienced God's forgiveness. They are not materialistic. They are not anxious, but place their trust in God's provision for them. They make the kingdom of God and the righteousness associated with that kingdom their priority. They are not judgmental. They act toward others as they would like others to act toward them. They are serious about the call to righteousness.

This comprehensive picture of righteousness in the Sermon on the Mount contains virtually all of the ethical teaching that can be found in the remainder of the Gospel, implicitly if not explicitly. It is this pattern of righteousness that is in view when Jesus commissions his disciples to make other disciples, "teaching them to observe all that I have commanded you" (28:20). Ritual purity, so important to contemporary Judaism, plays no role in the teaching of Jesus. "Holiness, in the view of Jesus, was not maintained by ritual purity — clean

---

and Christians: Religious Cultures in Late Antiquity, Essays in Honor of William David Davies (ed. R. Hamerton-Kelly and R. Scroggs; Leiden: Brill, 1976), 129-50, and T. L. Donaldson, "The Law that Hangs (Matthew 22:40): Rabbinic Formulation and Matthean Social World," *CBQ* 57 (1995): 689-709.

20. Leonard Doohan, *Matthew: Spirituality for the 80's and 90's* (Santa Fe: Bear, 1985), 22.
21. K. Brower, *Holiness in the Gospels* (Kansas City: Beacon Hill, 2005), 126.
22. Barton, *Spirituality*, 22.

hands — but by the integrity of being that identified wholly and unreservedly with the purposes of God in compassion and redemption for His lost and dying world."[23]

The Dynamic of the New Righteousness

If we have a grasp of the "what," the content of the righteousness of the kingdom, what can be said of the "how," that is, the implementation of that righteousness? Matthew does not speak directly concerning this, but there are some things that can be said from what Matthew does provide. Here the interrelationship of ideas mentioned earlier becomes all-important.

(1) First and foremost is the fact of a new eschatological reality in the presence of the kingdom now, in and through Jesus, in advance of its fullest coming, in the Eschaton. This is the fundamental basis, the underlying predication, upon which the call to righteousness rests. We have entered an unprecedented era of fulfillment, and with it comes *a new potentiality*.

> The Sermon as it lies before us now in Matthew represents the design for Christian living which the apostolic Church gave its catechumens — that is, it was preceded by the preaching of the Gospel and conversion. But what is true of the Sermon as a whole is true also of the separate sayings which make it up. Originally they were all preceded by something else — the proclamation of the glad news of God's inbreaking Reign and the new relationship with God which it made possible.[24]

The gift of the kingdom speaks of grace with clarity. The ability to live in the manner laid out by the Sermon on the Mount depends upon the new empowering of God's grace now available to us. With the dawning of a new era, new things are possible (cf. 13:52). The Beatitudes that stand at the beginning of the Sermon on the Mount affirm the blessed status of those who are the recipients of the kingdom. The kingdom is theirs *now* (5:3, 10) and the fullness of eschatological blessing will be theirs at the consummation of the age, as the future tense verbs indicate.[25] But the emphasis is on the first part of each beatitude, the present blessedness that is ascribed to the disciples. The possibility of a rad-

---

23. K. Brower, *Holiness in the Gospels*, 115.
24. A. M. Hunter, *A Pattern for Life: An Exposition of the Sermon on the Mount, Its Making, Its Exegesis and Its Meaning* (rev. ed.; Philadelphia: Westminster, 1965), 104.
25. As we have noted above, the beatitude of 5:6 refers probably to those who hunger and thirst for justice, not personal righteousness, and thus is not relevant to our discussion here.

ical transformation of the disciples must start here. The ethical teachings that follow depend on this present reality brought by Jesus. The disciples do not start empty-handed in their quest for righteousness. Far from it. Jesus refers to the treasury from which they may draw: "The good person out of his or her good treasure [Luke (6:45) adds "of the heart"] brings forth good" (12:35). It is fully in keeping with the thrust of the Gospel to conclude that the "good treasure" is rightly understood as the fruit of the grace of the newly dawning kingdom and reception of it.

(2) A further new reality that is essential to living as disciples is the relationship with Jesus. We have already noted that following Jesus is practically a definition of discipleship. The acceptance of Jesus as Messianic Teacher and Lord is obviously a *sine qua non* so far as righteousness is concerned. The disciples were "learners" by virtue of their being with Jesus. During the course of his ministry they were in the process of being formed by him. Personal commitment to him meant everything (10:32-33, 37-39). But can Jesus be a resource to later disciples who do not have the privilege of his bodily presence? Matthew supplies the later church with a superb compendium of the teaching of Jesus. But more than that, he implies that Jesus himself remains a resource for later disciples. "Where two or three are gathered in my name, there am I in the midst of them" (18:20). But the most impressive promise here is found in the final words of the Gospel: "and lo, I am with you always, to the close of the age" (28:20). And, it must be noted, these words follow immediately after the commission "teaching them to observe all that I have commanded you." The continuing presence of Jesus with his disciples through the centuries is part of the realized eschatology of the present kingdom and remains an important factor in personal transformation and the practice of righteousness. The invitation of 11:28-30 is applicable to all who would be disciples of Jesus — not just the twelve, not just the disciples in Matthew's church, but all the disciples of Jesus throughout the history of the church: "Come to me, all who labor and are heavy laden, and I will give you rest. Take my yoke upon you, and learn from me; for I am gentle and lowly in heart, and you will find rest for your souls. For my yoke is easy and my burden is light." Jesus is the ultimate resource for discipleship.

(3) The church, the new community of faith created by Jesus, constitutes a family for disciples and an environment in which righteousness can be encouraged. This new community, analogous to Israel, is called to obedience. It is "part of a holy fellowship — a fellowship marked by submission and obedience to Jesus' words about the divine reign, cost what it may."[26] Fictive kinship be-

---

26. B. Gerhardsson, *The Ethos of the Bible* (trans. Stephen Westerholm; Philadelphia: Fortress, 1981), 62.

comes an important factor.²⁷ Matthew alone among the Synoptics specifies the "disciples" in the following statement: "And stretching out his hand toward his disciples, he said, 'Here are my mother and brothers! For whoever does the will of my Father in heaven is my brother, and sister, and mother'" (12:49-50). The members of the new community, the ἐκκλησία, constitute a new family that does the will of the Father, i.e., that lives righteously. This family has an enabling role; its members provide a significant resource for the achievement of righteousness. An example of this can be seen in the discourse of chapter 18. Here, among other things, we find warnings concerning the gravity of causing "one of these little ones [= disciples]" to stumble (18:6-7). But the helping role of the community of brothers and sisters is most strikingly apparent in the example of dealing with one member of the community who sins against another (18:15-17). Here it is the larger church that finally holds the individual accountable. Matthew only begins to speak of the potentiality of the community for the life of the disciple. It is left more to Paul and others to draw out more of the rich resources of the church, now described as "the body of Christ," for discipleship.

(4) It is the Holy Spirit who applies the reality of the present kingdom to the Christian in everyday life. Anything that anyone ever experiences of the reality of God is due to the agency of the Holy Spirit. The outpouring of the Spirit at Pentecost not only constitutes the formal birthday of the church; it also provides the church with the supernatural power to live out its identity. What does Matthew have to say about the Holy Spirit?

With the other evangelists, Matthew sees the exceptional activity of the Spirit in the story of Jesus as a mark of its eschatological character. Jesus is conceived by the Holy Spirit (1:18, 20), and anointed by the Holy Spirit at his baptism (3:16; cf. 12:18). More important for our purposes, however, is the promise that Jesus would baptize others with the Holy Spirit (3:11). It is also important to note that when the disciples make disciples of others, they are to baptize them "in the name of the Father and of the Son and of the Holy Spirit" (28:19). The Holy Spirit is self-evidently important to discipleship. Matthew knows that disciples will be empowered with the Spirit. The Spirit will have an important role to play in very practical matters. Speaking of the time in the future when persecution comes upon the disciples, Jesus exhorts them not to be anxious, because what they are to say "will be given in that hour; for it is not you who speak, but the Spirit of your Father speaking through you" (10:19-20). Although Matthew does not talk about the Holy Spirit specifically in connection with righteousness, it seems a safe inference to conclude that the Spirit, as the identifying

---

27. See David deSilva, *Honor, Patronage, Kinship, and Purity: Unlocking New Testament Culture* (Downers Grove, IL: InterVarsity Press, 2000), 157-239.

mark of the reality of present eschatology, is at the same time a central factor in the disciple's pursuit of living in accord with the will of the Father.

Righteousness for Today?

Several questions remain about the contemporary relevance of the teaching in Matthew concerning discipleship. Is that material applicable today? To all Christians? Is it practicable?

To begin with, there has been considerable debate about whether Matthew's description of the disciples is to be regarded as "historicizing" or as involving "transparency."[28] The issue is whether the disciples are thought of as strictly historical, in an unrepeatable past, and therefore that what is said of the disciples refers only to them ("historicizing"), or whether what is said of them applies equally to disciples in the church of Matthew's time and later ("transparency"). Are the commands of Jesus valid only for the Twelve, or do they apply to later Christians equally?

It is clear that there is a sense in which the original circle of twelve disciples was and remains unique. There are, furthermore, points in the narrative where we have the unrepeatable. A case in point would be the sending out of the Twelve and the accompanying discourse (10:1-15). Some of this material is necessarily limited to the time of the historical Twelve — the only time, for example, when the restriction of the gospel of the kingdom to "the lost sheep of the house of Israel" (10:5-6) would have been permissible. Already in Matthew's day the gospel was proclaimed to the Gentiles (24:14; 28:19). The same thing is true, for example, concerning portions of the discourse on the Mount of Olives (chaps. 24–25), e.g., 24:15-28, where the exhortation to those in Judea to "flee to the mountains" (24:16) is necessarily limited to the original situation of the first century. Thus we sometimes encounter material of a mixed nature, some applying to the historical Twelve exclusively, some to the disciples of later times.

Luz concludes that there is not "a thorough-going historicizing in the understanding of the disciples in Matthew's Gospel. At only one point is Matthew consistent: discipleship is always related to the teaching of the historical Jesus ... It is as pupils of the historical Jesus that the disciples become transparent and are models of what it means to be a Christian."[29] Matthew's church and the church throughout history has always rightly understood itself as addressed by

---

28. See U. Luz, "The Disciples in the Gospel according to Matthew," in *The Interpretation of Matthew* (ed. Graham Stanton; Philadelphia/London: Fortress/SPCK, 1983), 98-128.

29. Luz, "The Disciples in the Gospel," p. 105.

the call to discipleship in this Gospel. Much or most of what Jesus spoke to the disciples is applied more broadly than to the Twelve.

If we assume the extensive transparency of the disciples, we are still left with further complicating questions of applicability. Besides the kind of historical limitedness we have noted in connection with the Twelve, it is clear that not all instructions about discipleship apply to all Christians. Thus, for example, not all are called to celibacy (19:10-12) or to sell all that they have as a part of their discipleship (19:21). Practical instructions provided in the missionary discourse (e.g., 10:8-14) would perhaps be generally applicable, but even then only to those who are called to leave secular professions for full-time evangelism. Thus some of Matthew's instructions concerning discipleship may need to be taken to apply only to a special group within the church, the so-to-speak religious professionals, rather than also to its "ordinary" members. At the same time, however, the ethical stipulations of the Sermon apply across the board to all believers. Every Christian without exception is called to exhibit the higher righteousness of the kingdom.

Even commandments that are pertinent to all in the church can raise the question of whether they are to be applied to the personal or societal level. To cite a famous example, are we to turn our other cheek to one who strikes us only in personal relationships, or can the commandment be taken as a justification for pacifism? What about forgiveness, not resisting evil, and so forth? This is a well-known problem in the ethical appropriation of the Sermon on the Mount. Although this is not the place to go into the problem fully, I may simply indicate that my impression is that the primary level of application is to the individual, but that there are also often implications for the societal level that should be heard.[30]

The final problem to be dealt with here is the absolute nature of this call to righteousness and the issue of practicality. What are we to say concerning the idealism of the discipleship that Matthew puts before us? Discipleship calls for total commitment (13:44-46). It calls for death to the self, the losing of one's own life for the sake of Christ (16:24-26). In terms of holiness or righteousness, it calls us to perfection. "You, therefore, must be perfect, as your heavenly Father is perfect" (5:48). The Sermon on the Mount is precisely a call to perfection because it is meant to reflect the present reality of the kingdom. The idea that τέλειος here refers to "maturity" rather than perfection is, in my opinion, not correct. "Perfection" here points to a quality of life marked by the kind of righteousness described in the antitheses — behavior that manifests an inner orientation dominated by the priority of the kingdom (cf. 6:33). The challenge

---

30. See my "Ethics and the Sermon on the Mount," *ST* 51 (1997): 44-59.

here is indeed startling. It is analogous to the call in 1 Peter to be *holy,* as the Lord is holy (1 Pet. 1:15-16, quoting Lev. 11:44-5). What is within our reach at present, however, is a pattern of life (not to be undervalued) rather than any absolute achievement of righteousness. This is evident from the fact that the Sermon implicitly acknowledges that perfection understood as sinlessness is an impossibility under present circumstances, i.e., in the present age. Thus in the middle of the Sermon, the disciples are taught to pray, "Forgive us our debts (ὀφειλήματα)," i.e., "shortcomings" (6:12; cf. the Lukan parallel, 11:4, "sins"). The fact that we are to pray regularly for such forgiveness indicates that, at least for the present, sin unfortunately will remain a reality in the life of the disciples.[31] A similar concessive note is sounded in 26:41, "Watch and pray that you may not enter into temptation; the spirit indeed is willing, but the flesh is weak." We encounter here an instance of the familiar tension between realized and future eschatology: we are called to a perfection already in the present, which will be fully ours only in the future.

The idealism of the discipleship to which Matthew calls us is therefore a perpetual reminder of the necessity of grace. To strive after a high goal beyond our reach should make us humble, but it should not defeat us. With the resources available to us, we can do more and better than we have. For what we do we are fully dependent upon God's enabling; for what we cannot do we are dependent upon God's forgiveness.

Matthew's Challenge to the Contemporary Church

The Gospel of Matthew calls disciples of Jesus — disciples of the present — to be "the salt of the earth" and "the light of the world" (5:13-16). The more one contemplates Matthew's call to righteousness, the more one realizes the impact that the church could make upon the world if it were to make a more significant attempt to exhibit that righteousness. It is for this reason that Jesus exhorts his followers with these words: "Let your light so shine before others, that they may see your good works and give glory to your Father who is in heaven" (5:16).

The radical pattern of righteousness that emerges in Matthew is striking, as we have seen. It repeatedly does nothing less than turn the standards and values of the world on their head. To pick just one stunning example, the world thinks

---

31. "The fuller righteousness which Jesus asks of the disciple is not his as a possession permanently at his disposal, as a something which he can *have*; it is his only as God's perpetually renewed gift." Martin H. Franzmann, *Follow Me: Discipleship According to Saint Matthew* (St. Louis: Concordia, 1961), 55.

that greatness consists in being served, whereas Jesus teaches the opposite: "It shall not be so among you; but whoever would be great among you must be your servant, and whoever would be first among you must be your slave; even as the Son of man came not to be served but to serve, and to give his life as a ransom for many" (20:26-28). Not pride, but humility is to be the way of the disciple who would follow Jesus (18:3-4).

Matthew's pattern of righteousness may be called "prophetic" in the classical sense: as going directly against the prevailing conduct of the secular world. Jesus calls his disciples to a discipleship that counts, that makes a difference. This is to be a discipleship of more than words — a serious discipleship of action and deeds. "Not everyone who says to me, 'Lord, Lord,' shall enter the kingdom of heaven, but the one who does the will of my Father who is in heaven" (7:21). The potential impact of this kind of discipleship is incalculable.

But this challenge — to realize this kind of discipleship, to live out the righteousness of the Sermon on the Mount — seems hopelessly impossible, does it not? If we look at this challenge solely in terms of human potentiality, the answer must be that no one is adequate. Here, however, the words of Jesus concerning the difficulty of a rich man being saved may be relevant: "With human beings this is impossible, but with God all things are possible" (19:26). It remains for the church to act in faith and for the disciples of Jesus to press on toward the goal.[32]

---

32. This essay was originally written for a volume honoring Alex Deasley (a longtime member of the Tyndale Fellowship), entitled *Holiness and Ecclesiology in the New Testament* (ed. Kent Brower and Andy Johnson; Grand Rapids: Eerdmans, 2007). It appears here by permission of the editors and publisher.

The Rock on Which to Build: Some Mainly Pauline Observations about the Sermon on the Mount

David Wenham

"Christian churches across the theological and confessional spectrum, and Christian ethics as an academic discipline that serves the churches, are often guilty of evading Jesus, the cornerstone and center of the Christian faith. Specifically, *the teachings and practices of Jesus* — especially the largest block of his teachings, the Sermon on the Mount — are routinely ignored or misinterpreted in the preaching and teaching ministry of the churches and in Christian scholarship in ethics. This evasion of the concrete teachings of Jesus has seriously malformed Christian moral practices, moral beliefs and moral witness. Jesus taught that the test of our discipleship is whether we act on his teaching, whether we 'put into practice' his words. This is what it means to 'build our house on rock' (Mt. 7:24)." So say Glen Stassen and David Gushee in their useful book *Kingdom Ethics*.[1] They go on to warn that "when Jesus' way of discipleship is thinned down, marginalized or avoided, then churches and Christians lose their antibodies against infection by secular ideologies that manipulate Christians into serving the purposes of some other lord. We fear that kind of idolatry now" (p. 11).

If the Sermon on the Mount has been so seriously neglected in the modern period, what has led to this neglect? Two factors (among others) have been influential, and will be considered in this article. One is critical questioning about the Sermon's origins: many scholars have argued that the Sermon as we find it in Matthew's gospel does not go back to Jesus and indeed that some of its teaching is in some tension with Jesus' teaching. The other factor is the discomfort that many modern people feel over the stringent ethical demands of the Ser-

---

1. (Downers Grove, Ill.: InterVarsity Press, 2003), 11. Compare also David Buttrick in his *Speaking Jesus Homiletic Theology and the Sermon on the Mount* (Louisville: Westminster John Knox, 2002), 4: "Nowadays clergy teach courses on Parenting, Career Planning, Conflict Management, Grief Counselling, you-name-it, but we have neglected the Sermon on the Mount. We have turned away from the words of Jesus."

mon; the emphasis seems to be at odds with the joyful gospel of grace found elsewhere in the New Testament (notably in Paul's letters).[2]

1. The Question of the Origins of the Sermon

Doubts about the Sermon as Jesus' Teaching

The members of the Jesus Seminar in America speak for many scholars in concluding that rather little of the Sermon is clearly authentic teaching of Jesus.[3] They agree that *some* of the sayings in the Sermon probably go back to Jesus, but most do not, nor does the Sermon as a whole, which has been compiled out of different authentic and inauthentic sayings. Their view reflects that of those form critics who argue that the stories and sayings of Jesus were recalled in the earliest days of the church in a rather haphazard and unstructured way, not in coherent narratives or discourses.[4]

Two things about the Sermon on the Mount might be thought to confirm this view: first, some of the sayings found in Matthew's Sermon are found in entirely different contexts in Luke's gospel.[5] Second, others of the sayings have no parallel in Luke or anywhere else, but they have a strongly Matthean flavor; for example, Matthew 5:17 on Jesus coming to *fulfill* the law and the prophets (a very important idea for Matthew) and 5:20 on *righteousness* exceeding that of the scribes and Pharisees.[6] It looks to various scholars as though Matthew has composed the Sermon on the Mount partly out of sayings of Jesus, but considerably out of his own theological imagination and conviction.

This view has some superficial plausibility, but should not be taken for granted.[7]

---

2. It is also obviously in tension with postmodern pluralism.

3. See R. W. Funk and R. W. Hoover, *The Five Gospels: The Search for the Authentic Words of Jesus* (New York/Oxford: Macmillan, 1993), 138-59. Also, H. D. Betz and A. Y. Collins are quite agnostic about the dominical origin of the Sermon in their monumental *The Sermon on the Mount: A Commentary on the Sermon on the Mount, Including the Sermon on the Plain (Matthew 5:3–7:27 and Luke 6:20-49)* (Minneapolis: Fortress, 1995).

4. Gathering the individual traditions together came much later.

5. For example, the sayings about wealth and anxiety in Matt. 6:25-34 are found in Luke 12:22-32.

6. See, e.g., G. Stanton, *A Gospel for a New People: Studies in Matthew* (Edinburgh: T&T Clark, 1992), 305.

7. R. A. Guelich's *The Sermon on the Mount: A Foundation for Understanding* (Waco, Tex.: Word, 1982) is a particularly useful discussion of the Sermon. But see my review article: "Guelich on the Sermon on the Mount: A Critical Review," *TJ* 4 (1983): 92-108.

Jesus as a Teacher in Discourses

In the first place, the view that only individual sayings of Jesus and none of his "sermons" has been preserved for us seems to be tacitly accepted by much of the scholarly world, but deserves to be questioned. Jesus was without question a famous preacher whose teaching made a big impact. We may be confident that he did not just teach in one-liners or short sound bites; no teacher then or now teaches in that way. Of course, it could be that Jesus did teach or preach at some length, but that only individual and disconnected stories and sayings were remembered. But this seems entirely unlikely, given the power of his teaching and the memorization culture in which Jesus lived and taught.[8]

But is there any evidence that Jesus taught in discourses, and that they were remembered? The answer to this question is yes, since all the four gospels describe Jesus' teaching and record his discourses in their gospels.[9]

But it is not simply the evidence of the gospel texts as we have them that points in this direction. There is reason to believe that our gospels are drawing on earlier sources which also contained discourses of Jesus, and there is interesting corroborative evidence from Paul.

The Mission Discourse

To take two examples, there are four "mission discourses" attributed to Jesus in the synoptic gospels (in Matthew 10, Mark 6:7-13, Luke 9:1-6 and Luke 10:1-16, the last being addressed to the seventy). Scholars widely agree that there is a Markan and an independent non-Markan version of the discourse being utilized by the three synoptic evangelists. According to the two-source theory there was a Markan and a "Q" version.[10]

---

8. On the cultural context see R. Riesner, *Jesus als Lehrer* (Tübingen: Mohr, 1981).

9. It could be that all of the original discourses of Jesus were forgotten and that all of the discourses now attributed to Jesus in the gospels were actually composed or compiled by the evangelists, but this is an unnecessarily and improbably complicated hypothesis. (There is some parallel to the widely held scholarly view that the early church forgot who wrote the gospels and that the present attribution of the gospels to Matthew, Mark, Luke and John bears no relation to the historical facts. Martin Hengel rightly questions this view in his *The Four Gospels and the One Gospel of Jesus Christ: An Investigation of the Collection and Origin of the Canonical Gospels* [London: SCM, 2000]).

10. If we dispense with the Q hypothesis, there is still a strong case for believing Matthew to have access to a non-Markan version and for Luke knowing this version. For the complicated source criticism of the passage see D. L. Dungan, *The Sayings of Jesus in the Churches of Paul: The Use of the Synoptic Tradition in the Regulation of Early Church Life* (Oxford: Blackwell, 1971),

So far as Paul's evidence is concerned, this is found primarily in 1 Corinthians 9, where Paul speaks about his apostleship. He asks in v. 1, "Am I not an *apostle* . . . ? Are you not my *work* in the Lord?"; and then in what follows he asks, "Do we not have the *right* (Greek: ἐξουσία) *to eat and drink?*"; he goes on to talk further about the *rights* of the apostle, and then in v. 14 says, "In the same way the Lord commanded that those who proclaim the gospel should get their living by the gospel." Paul goes on to speak of what his *"reward"* as an apostle is.

Scholars generally have recognized v. 14 with its reference to the Lord's command as a reference to Jesus' teaching; it has widely been seen as a paraphrase of Matthew 10:10/Luke 10:7: "The worker is worthy of his hire/reward." What scholars have not noticed is how other things that Paul says about his apostleship in 1 Corinthians 9 (vv. 1, 4-6, 12, 17, 18) may also be echoes of Jesus' instructions to the apostles.

> Jesus sent (ἀποστέλλω) them out
> with *authority* (ἐξουσία),
> telling them to preach
> and to *eat and drink* what was set before them
> speaking of the evangelist's *work*
> and his *reward*

Paul is not quoting exactly from Jesus, let alone from one version of the discourse.[11] But it does seem probable that he is drawing in various ways on the discourse; he is not just picking up the one saying of Jesus that has been preserved in glorious isolation.

It is not necessarily the case that his Corinthian readers would have recognized the echoes. On the other hand, it is quite likely that they would have done so. Paul seems in 1 Corinthians 9 to be defending his apostleship, particularly in relation to his refusal to be financially maintained and his insistence on working with his hands. The probable, though not certain, inference must be that his critics knew the teaching of the Lord and were quoting it against him and his claim to be a true apostle.[12]

1-80; B. Fjärstedt, *Synoptic Tradition in 1 Corinthians: Themes and Clusters of Words in 1 Corinthians 1–4 and 9* (Uppsala: Uppsala University Press, 1974), 55-94; also my *Paul: Follower of Jesus or Founder of Christianity?* (Grand Rapids/Cambridge: Eerdmans, 1995), 190-200.

11. There are further possible links between Pauline teaching and Jesus' mission discourse: for example, when Paul speaks of wanting to make his gospel free of charge in 1 Corinthians 9:18, he may be echoing Matthew 10:8, "Freely you received, freely give." He may also show his knowledge of the Matthean instruction "Go . . . only to the lost sheep of the house of Israel" when he refers to Peter being commissioned to go to the circumcised in Galatians 2:7.

12. It is clear from various texts that Paul's apostleship was a controversial topic, and he

We know that Paul did pass on traditions of Jesus to the Corinthians from 1 Corinthians 11:23-25 and 15:3-5. The traditions referred to in those two texts are not just sound bites about the eucharist and resurrection, but seem to have included some narrative ("on the night that he was betrayed . . . ," 11:23). The traditions in those texts are passion-related narrative, not teaching of Jesus, and theoretically one might argue that Paul handed on only narrative about the passion and no teaching or discourses of Jesus. But there is no good reason to think that, and some reason to think the opposite.[13] So it is reasonable to conclude that in 1 Corinthians 9 he has Jesus' mission discourse in mind, and that his readers would have picked up the echoes.

The Eschatological Discourse

The same sort of conclusion is plausible with the eschatological discourse of Jesus. In 1 Thessalonians 4 and 5 Paul addresses the doubts of the Thessalonian Christians about Jesus' second coming. And in doing so he seems to echo Jesus' teaching repeatedly; thus, to take some examples, in 1 Thessalonians 4:16-17 Paul speaks of the Lord descending from heaven with the voice of an archangel, with the sound of a trumpet, and of Christians being caught up with the Lord in the clouds. This is unmistakably similar to Jesus' teaching in Matthew 24:30, 31: "they will see the Son of man coming on the clouds of heaven . . . and he will send his angels with a loud trumpet call, and they will gather his elect. . . ." Paul goes on in 1 Thessalonians 5:2 to talk about the day of the Lord coming like a thief in the night, and about the need to keep awake, which is very similar to the parable of the thief and the exhortation to keep awake in Matthew 24:43, 44// Luke 12:39, 40.[14] Of course, it could be argued that Matthew (and/or Luke) got his picture from Paul, not Paul from Jesus,[15] but it is unlikely that Paul or any other Christian would have compared the return of Jesus their Lord to the com-

---

goes out of his way to maintain the genuineness of his apostleship in relation to the "original" apostles in Galatians 1 and 2 and in 1 Corinthians 15:8-11. See also F. F. Bruce, *Paul, Apostle of the Free Spirit* (Carlisle, U.K.: Paternoster, 1980), 106-9.

13. Note Paul's use of the divorce traditions in 1 Corinthians 7:3, 4. Arguably he knows not just one saying of Jesus about divorce, but much of the teaching in Matthew 19:1-12 and parallels. See my *Paul: Follower or Founder?* for the whole Paul-and-Jesus question and pp. 242-46 on the marriage/divorce texts.

14. G. R. Beasley-Murray, *Jesus and the Last Days* (Peabody, Mass.: Hendrickson, 1993), 361, notes parallels between 1 and 2 Thessalonians and Jesus' teaching, commenting, "The reflections of the eschatological discourse in Paul's writings have been underestimated in recent years."

15. See M. D. Goulder, *Midrash and Lection in Matthew* (London: SPCK, 1974), 154.

ing of a thief. What is most likely is that Jesus himself used this striking image (as Matthew and Luke attest), and that Paul and others drew on Jesus' teaching (cf. 2 Pet. 3:10).

This conclusion is supported by 1 Thessalonians 4:15-17, where Paul responds to the Thessalonian Christians who are worried about the members of the church who have died before the Lord's return. Paul reassures them that they will not be lost in these words: "this we declare to you by a word from the Lord, that we who are alive, who are left until the coming of the Lord, will not precede those who have fallen asleep. . . ." No, "the dead in Christ will rise first. Then we who are alive . . . will be caught up to meet the Lord in the air, and so we will always be with the Lord." Scholars have been puzzled by Paul's reference to a word of the Lord: what is he referring to? The probable answer, though this is rarely recognized by scholars, is that Paul is referring to Jesus' parable of the wise and foolish virgins as in Matthew 25:1-13. The parable is about the delay of the master's return (which was the Thessalonians' problem): the wise virgins *fell asleep;* but when the bridegroom came, they *rose up* in order *to meet him* and (unlike their foolish colleagues who were unprepared) went into the banquet *with the* master. Paul interprets this parable of Jesus as a reassuring answer to the Thessalonians and their anxieties about their brothers and sisters who have fallen asleep.[16]

If this understanding of the text is correct, then we see that Paul specifically attributes his answer to the Lord's teaching (the "word of the Lord"), and we notice that Paul draws on various sayings of Jesus — all found in the eschatological discourse — in quick succession. It could be that he knew them as isolated sayings and that he, like Matthew and the other evangelists, gathered them together; but the simpler explanation is that he knew them already gathered in a discourse that came from the Lord.[17]

---

16. For this view and for fuller discussion of the eschatological teachings of Jesus and Paul see my *Paul: Follower or Founder?* 289-337, and my *Gospel Perspectives 4: The Rediscovery of Jesus' Eschatological Discourse* (Sheffield: JSOT, 1984). Also for some relevant observations on the parable and Paul see W. Schenk, "Auferweckung der Töten oder Gericht nach den Werken, Tradition und Redaktion in Matthäus xxv 1-13," *NovT* 8 (1966): 223-34; also K. P. Donfried, "The Allegory of the Ten Virgins (Matt 25:1-13) as a Summary of Matthean Theology," *JBL* 93 (1974): 415-28.

17. It is interesting, to say the least, that Paul seems particularly to be drawing on some traditions that are found only in Matthew's gospel (though the coming on the clouds is also in Mark and Luke, i.e., in the "Markan tradition" so-called, and the parable of the thief is also in Luke, i.e., in the "Q" tradition). This could be seen as problematic given the Two Source theory of synoptic origins; but that theory, despite its uses, should not be seen as a complete or fully adequate answer to source-critical questions, nor should it be used as a straitjacket that automatically excludes certain conclusions. James Dunn has recently reminded us of the priority of oral tradition and of the need to take that into account in reflecting on gospel origins; *Jesus Re-*

The Rock on Which to Build

I have necessarily oversimplified the argument and evidence considerably, but the conclusion is that Paul probably knew several of the discourses of Jesus, when writing to the Thessalonians in around AD 50 and to the Corinthians around AD 55.

This conclusion brings us back to the Sermon on the Mount. If the mission discourse and the eschatological discourse were known and taught in the churches in the 50s, then the probability is strong that the Sermon on the Mount comes into the same category. The specific evidence in this case is as follows:

Evidence for the Sermon on the Mount

(1) Matthew and Luke both know the Sermon independently of each other. Despite some scholars' doubts, it seems that the Sermon on the Mount in Matthew 5–7 is essentially the same as the Sermon on the Plain in Luke 6:20-49; they have much in common, both beginning with a beatitude on the poor and ending with the parable of building on the rock and the sand, and both Matthew and Luke presenting their respective versions as the first major sermon of Jesus. However, the wording of Matthew's and Luke's versions differs considerably, and this among other things makes it likely that their versions are independent.[18]

(2) Paul probably echoes the Sermon. This is most likely in Romans 12, where Paul says, "Bless those who persecute you; bless and do not curse.... Do not repay evil for evil.... Do not be overcome by evil, but overcome evil with good" (vv. 14-21). This is not a quote from Jesus as such, but both the thought and the language are strikingly like that found in the Sermons on the Mount and the Plain: "bless those who curse you, pray for those who abuse you" (Luke 6:27, 28).[19]

The same part of the Sermon seems to be quoted in the first letter of Peter: "not repaying evil for evil or abuse for abuse, but, on the contrary, blessing, because for this you were called, that you may inherit a blessing" (1 Pet. 3:9). There

---

membered (Grand Rapids/Cambridge: Eerdmans, 2003), 192-254. There are other examples of Paul showing knowledge of "M" traditions; e.g., in Galatians 1 and 2 Paul may well be alluding to the tradition about Peter the rock found in Matthew 16:16-20; see J. Chapman, "St Paul and the Revelation to St Peter, Matt. XVI,17," *Revue Bénédictine* 29 (1912): 133-47, and my *Paul: Follower or Founder?* 200-205.

18. So Dunn, *Jesus Remembered*, 231-34. They are frequently seen as different versions of Q.

19. On the use of the Sermon in Romans see the important discussion of Michael Thompson, *Clothed with Christ: The Example and Teaching of Jesus in Romans 12.1–15.13* (JSNTSup 59; Sheffield: JSOT, 1991).

are other possible echoes of the Sermon in 1 Peter (e.g. 2:12; 3:14; 4:13, 14),[20] and even more in the letter of James (e.g., 2:5; 5:1-2, 12).[21] This large number of parallels between the epistles and the Sermon is easy to explain if the Sermon on the Mount was (as the gospels might suggest) well-known teaching of Jesus.

Matthew's or Luke's Version?

But one further question needs to be addressed before we leave the issue of the origin of the Sermon. Matthew's and Luke's versions of the Sermon are significantly different, with Luke's version being much shorter. Many scholars conclude from this that Luke's is the more original version (approximating the Q version, if Q existed), and that Matthew has filled out the original version with sayings of Jesus from other contexts and with his own theological contributions.[22] So much of Matthew's version of the Sermon in his chapters 5–7 was not part of Jesus' original Sermon on the Mount.

This argument sounds plausible, but there are a number of considerations that may point in a different direction.[23]

First, there are things which indicate that Luke may in fact have known the Matthean form of the Sermon; for example, in 6:27, where Jesus says, "But I say to you who hear, Love your enemies." This "But I say to you" does not make especially good sense in the Lukan context, but it does make good sense in the context of Matthew's antitheses; thus in Matt. 5:43 Jesus says, "You have heard that it was said: 'Love your neighbor and hate your enemy.' But I say to you, 'Love your enemies.'"[24]

---

20. On the evidence of 1 Peter see the contrasting approaches of R. H. Gundry "'Verba Christi' in 1 Peter: Their Implications concerning the Authorship of 1 Peter and the Authenticity of the Gospel Tradition," *NTS* 17 (1966-67): 336-50, also idem, "Further *Verba* or *Verba Christi* in First Peter," *Bib* 55 (1974): 211-32, and E. Best, "1 Peter and the Gospel Tradition," *NTS* 18 (1967-68): 95-113. See also G. Maier, "Jesustradition im 1. Petrusbrief?" in D. Wenham, ed. *Gospel Perspectives 5: The Jesus Tradition outside the Gospels* (Sheffield: JSOT, 1984), 85-128.

21. On the evidence of James see P. H. Davids, "James and Jesus," in Wenham, ed., *Gospel Perspectives 5*, 63-84; P. J. Hartin, *James and the 'Q' Sayings of Jesus* (JSNTSup 47; Sheffield: JSOT, 1991); R. Bauckham, *James* (London: Routledge, 1999), 29-111.

22. So, e.g., U. Luz, *Matthew 1–7: A Commentary* (Minneapolis: Augsburg, 1989), 214: "Matthew has supplemented the Sermon on the Plain with other material."

23. It is worth commenting that a considerable number of scholars argue for Matthean priority, at least in relation to Luke, and assume that Luke has used and pruned Matthew. Those who think Luke used Matthew include, recently and lucidly, M. Goodacre, *The Synoptic Problem: A Way through the Maze* (London: Sheffield Academic Press, 2001).

24. Other possible indicators of Luke knowing Matthew's form of words include the inter-

It is easy to see how and why Luke, if he knew the Matthean antitheses, might have pruned the material radically. The antitheses reflect Matthew's interest, and that of his intended readers, in the interpretation of Old Testament law and in the comparison of Jesus and the scribes and Pharisees. Luke has no burning interest in these things in his gospel: he is not writing for Jewish-Christians, and after the beatitudes and the woes with their focus on poor and rich his version of the Sermon focuses almost entirely on Jesus' teaching about relationships — love of enemy, not judging, and the golden rule. He has no references to the ethics or the hypocritical piety of the scribes and Pharisees.

A second piece of evidence is from the letter of James. Patrick Hartin in his book *James and the Q Sayings of Jesus* speaks of "remarkable similarities between James and the Q sermon" and says that the vast majority of the sayings in the Q sermon can be paralleled in James.[25] However, the most remarkable parallel of all between James and the Sermon is in James 5:12, where James says, "Above all, my brothers, do not swear — not by heaven or by earth or by anything else. Let your 'Yes' be yes and your 'No', no, or you will be condemned," which quite strikingly parallels Matthew 5:34-37, one of the Matthean antitheses. This observation arguably undermines Hartin's view of James drawing on

---

jection in the middle of the Lukan sermon, "And he also told them this parable . . ." (6:39). This is exactly the point at which Luke has some sayings of Jesus that are not paralleled in Matthew, and may be Luke's way of introducing material, as if in brackets or a footnote.

Also, Luke 16:16, 17 and 18 may reflect knowledge of Matthew 5:17, 18 and 32. Note the sequence in Matthew and Luke: (1) a saying about the law and the prophets, (2) a comment on a jot or tittle not falling from the law, (3) a saying about divorce. Two things are worth mentioning about these sayings: (a) the Lukan saying about divorce has various formal similarities to the divorce saying in Matthew 5:32, which differentiate it from the divorce saying found in Mark 10:11, 12 and Matthew 19:8: there is the participial "everyone divorcing his wife," whereas in Mark it is "whoever divorces his wife," and the verb used is μοιχεύω (as in the commandment about not committing adultery), whereas in Mark 10:11 it is μοιχάομαι. (Matt. 5:32a starts like Luke, but then slips into the Markan form.) Scholars have identified Matthew 5:32 and Luke 16:18 as the Q form of the divorce saying. (b) It is not entirely easy to explain the Lukan sequence of sayings. We are first told that the law and the prophets were until John the Baptist, but that now we are in the era of the kingdom of God, then that not a jot or tittle will pass from the law, and finally that divorce and remarriage add up to adultery. Interestingly, all of this follows a statement strongly criticizing the Pharisees. It seems entirely possible that the critical reference to the Pharisees provoked a reflection on the passing of the old regime of the law and the prophets and the coming of the new era of the kingdom. Then that is clarified: it does not mean the abolition or (in Luke's language) the falling of the law (v. 17); indeed, Jesus' teaching on divorce illustrates his highly demanding ethic. Then the following parable of the rich man and Lazarus shows how the law and the prophets continue to be relevant and to speak to those who love money. If this is the Lukan train of thought, then it is not difficult to see how familiarity with the Sermon on the Mount in something like its Matthean form could have influenced Luke.

25. Hartin, *James and the 'Q' Sayings of Jesus*, 171.

Q in the Lukan form, and suggests that James may very well have known the Sermon in something like the Matthean form.[26]

My conclusion is that the Matthean form of the Sermon may well go back to Jesus.[27] But what then of the verses that express strongly Matthean ideas and themes, and which scholars have accordingly ascribed to Matthew as redactor rather than to Jesus? We noted how scholars have argued this for Matthew 5:17 on Jesus' fulfillment of the law and the prophets and for 5:20 where he speaks of "righteousness" exceeding that of the scribes and Pharisees. There is no question that both fulfillment and righteousness are top Matthew themes. But there is equally no question that both of the texts in question could well go back to Jesus: Jesus' interest in the fulfillment of the Old Testament is attested in all the gospels (e.g. Mark 1:14; Luke 4:21), and it is even possible that Matthew 5:17 is alluded to in Luke 24:44: "These are my words that I spoke to you while I was still with you, that everything written about me in the law of Moses and the prophets and the psalms must be fulfilled." As for righteousness, Jesus' interest in righteous living is also attested in all the gospels. It is true that the noun "righteousness" is not used on the lips of Jesus outside Matthew, but it would be most unwise to assume that he never used a word that is hugely important in the Old Testament.[28] We will say more on this as we turn to think further about the Sermon on the Mount and Paul in the second part of this article.

---

26. It is possible that Paul knows the oaths antithesis; see 2 Cor. 1:17, 18 and *Paul: Follower or Founder?* 271-74. For Paul's familiarity with Matthean tradition see our earlier argument about the parable of the wise and foolish virgins.

27. The Sermon in Matthew 5–7 fits with Jesus' Palestinian context (rather to the surprise of Betz in his commentary, since he postulates a largely Greek background to the Sermon). Individual terms like jot or tittle, the Aramaic word *Raca*, Mammon, and references to bringing your gift to the temple all sound Palestinian, and make sense in Jesus' context.

Although I see every reason for tracing the Sermon to Jesus, I do not rule out the possibility that Matthew and Luke have included in the Sermon some teaching of Jesus that was originally in other contexts. And I think it entirely likely that Luke has some wording that is more original that Matthew's.

28. One of the misuses of redaction criticism is when the critic identifies favorite ideas or expressions of a particular evangelist and then assumes that each appearance of that favorite idea or expression is redactional. This does not follow at all: Matthew found fulfillment in his traditions of Jesus, *and* it is a favorite theme of his. It may be that some of the uses of "righteousness" in Matthew are redactional, e.g., 5:6 and 5:33, and that Luke's form of words is more original (Luke 6:21; 12:31). This may also be the case in the first beatitude (cf. Matt. 5:3; Luke 6:20 and Jas. 2:5). But, even if this is the case, it does not mean that every use of "righteousness" in Matthew goes back to Matthew rather than Jesus.

2. The Stringent Demands of the Gospel

The Problematic Teaching

What are we to make of the stringent demands of the Sermon? Jesus tells his hearers to be perfect, not to have a lustful thought, and to love their enemies. A teacher making such demands must surely be on a different planet from most of us; the teaching can seem very depressing. The problem is made worse, arguably, by the way Jesus seems to insist on even the tiniest part of the Old Testament law continuing to be binding on his disciples. Not a jot or a tittle will pass from the law, he says in 5:18, and relaxing even the least of the laws will earn the lowest place in the kingdom (5:19). This sounds like the sort of legalistic Christianity that Paul for one rejected forthrightly, and that good Christians, including Protestants and evangelicals, have rejected ever since.

People have tried to get around this difficulty with the Sermon by arguing that Matthew understood Jesus to be speaking only for his own day (or until his resurrection), not for later generations. Others have claimed that Jesus never expected anyone to obey his teaching in the Sermon; it was intended to show us our sinfulness and our need of divine grace. Neither of these two ways out of the difficulty seems satisfactory. Jesus' words to his disciples, "You are the salt of the earth. . . . You are the light of the world. . . . Let your light shine . . . ," cannot reasonably be understood as only for his immediate disciples. Nor are they sensibly seen as intended simply to make us see our sin and our need of God's grace; Jesus wants his followers to live — as salt and light.

So what is to be done with the impossible demands of the Sermon? Three observations may help clarify this.

Gospel in Matthew

First, some things in Matthew's gospel may look legalistic and demanding; other things look very different. The gospel opens with the announcement of salvation through Jesus, for "he will save his people from their sins"; he will be "Immanuel, God with us" (1:21-23). Just before the Sermon on the Mount, Isaiah 9 is quoted: "the people dwelling in darkness have seen a great light, and for those dwelling in the land of the shadow of death, on them light has dawned" (4:16). Later in the gospel there is the famous invitation: "Come to me, all who labor and are heavy laden, and I will give you rest. . . . My yoke is easy, and my burden is light" (11:28-30); this sounds very different from Pharisaic legalism

(23:4).²⁹ In various places in Matthew's gospel it is clear that with Jesus the old age of the law and the prophets has ended and a new era has dawned, an era of freedom: Jesus uses that word in the curious story of the coin in the fish's mouth, when he discusses the temple tax with his disciples. He comments that "the sons" [i.e., his followers] are free; they are no longer bound by the obligations of the temple (17:24-27).³⁰ One greater than the temple has come — in Jesus (12:6; and greater than the Sabbath, 12:8); and when Jesus dies, the veil of the temple is torn in two, the way into God's presence has been opened up, and Jesus has brought forgiveness and life from the dead (27:51-54). This is the gospel of a new age of grace.

The Form and Content of the Beatitudes

My second observation about the demands of the Sermon has to do with the Sermon itself.

The Sermon begins with nine beatitudes, which may be helpfully set out as follows:

1. **Blessed are the poor in spirit,** *for theirs is the kingdom of heaven*.
2. **Blessed are those who mourn,** *for they will be comforted.*
3. **Blessed are the meek,** *for they will inherit the earth.*
4. **Blessed are those who hunger and thirst for <u>righteousness</u>,** *for they will be filled.*
5. **Blessed are the merciful,** *for they will be shown mercy.*
6. **Blessed are the pure in heart,** *for they will see God.*
7. **Blessed are the peacemakers,** *for they will be called sons of God.*
8. **Blessed are those who are persecuted because of <u>righteousness</u>, <u>for theirs is the kingdom of heaven</u>**.
9. *Blessed are you when people insult you, persecute you and falsely say all kinds of evil against you because of me. Rejoice and be glad, because great is your reward in heaven, for in the same way they persecuted the prophets who were before you.*

What is immediately clear from setting out the beatitudes in this way is that they are very carefully arranged. There are eight beatitudes in the third

---

29. But note the similarity to Sir. 24:19.

30. The proclamation of freedom with the call not to cause offense (σκανδαλίζω) is strongly reminiscent of Paul's teaching (e.g., 1 Cor. 8:9; Rom. 14:20).

person, "Blessed are so and so . . . ," and the ninth is in the second person, "Blessed are you." The ninth is the odd one out, and is arguably a sort of bridge from the general statements in beatitudes 1-8 into the rest of the Sermon, which is addressed directly to the disciples.

Beatitudes 1-8 may therefore be taken as a group. When they are, various things are notable: first, numbers 1 and 8 have the same promise, "for theirs is the kingdom of heaven." This probably suggests that all the beatitudes are about the kingdom of heaven, and about those who will receive it. In Matthew's gospel Jesus' message has just been summed up in 4:17: "Repent, for the kingdom of heaven has come near." And it is this kingdom that Jesus' ministry is about and that the Sermon on the Mount is about.

We notice, secondly, that the eight beatitudes fall into two blocks: the first four could all be described as rather passive — being poor in spirit, mourning, meek, hungry for righteousness; the second four are more active and ethical — showing mercy, being pure, making peace, being persecuted for righteousness in action. What is then interesting to observe is that the last of the first four and the last of the second four both speak of *righteousness* — hungering and thirsting for righteousness (no. 4) and being persecuted for righteousness (no. 8). This may not prove anything, but it is probably a further clue to the meaning of the Sermon. The Sermon is not just about the kingdom of heaven; it is specifically about the righteousness of the kingdom of heaven.[31]

But what does the arrangement of the beatitudes tell us about the righteousness of the kingdom? We noted that the first four beatitudes all speak in one way or another of people who know their need of God — the poor in spirit, the meek (not the pushy), the mourners, the hungry and thirsty for righteousness. The second four are ethical or practical — speaking of being merciful, pure in heart, peacemaking and being persecuted for righteousness' sake. This twofold structure arguably points to grace coming before works: turning to God hungry for righteousness comes before righteous living (and being persecuted for it!). The Sermon on the Mount is largely about the righteousness of the kingdom of God, ethical and practical righteousness, but the starting point for that sort of life is "Blessed are the poor in spirit. . . ." The kingdom of God is the grace of God breaking into history, and that grace generates the righteous-

---

31. It is intriguing to note that in the Greek the first four beatitudes (which all incidentally use words beginning with the letter π, πτωχός, πραεῖς, πενθοῦντες, πεινῶντες) are 36 words, and the second four are also 36 words; beatitude no. 1 is 12 words, and so is beatitude no. 8. This could be accidental, but is much more likely an indication of careful design. See helpfully on this as on other features of the Sermon C. H. Talbert, *Reading the Sermon on the Mount: Character Formation and Decision Making in Matthew 5–7* (Columbia: University of South Carolina, 2004), e.g., p. 49.

ness of the kingdom. The righteousness can come only when that grace of the kingdom of God is received.

This reading of the beatitudes is made the more likely if we recognize in the first four beatitudes echoes of Isaiah 61:1-3, where the Spirit-anointed one is sent to bring good news to the poor, to bind up the brokenhearted and to comfort all who mourn: Jesus is precisely that Spirit-anointed one, and his great Sermon starts with the grace of the kingdom of God before going on to the ethics of the kingdom.

The Context and Purpose of Matthew 5:17-20

But then what about 5:17-20, which demands obedience to the least of the Old Testament commands in a way that sounds legalistic? This brings us to a third observation. The key to this short passage lies, arguably, in the beginning and concluding verses: v. 17 says negatively that Jesus has not come to destroy the law and the prophets but to fulfill them, and v. 20 says positively that unless your righteousness exceeds that of the scribes and Pharisees you will not enter the kingdom of heaven. Why bother to say that Jesus has not come to destroy the law and the prophets and that he expects a higher righteousness than that of the scribes and Pharisees? Surely because some people argued that Jesus by his teaching or his way of life was undermining the law and the prophets and lowering the moral standards, contrast the Pharisees and scribes who set the highest of standards. We know that people did accuse Jesus exactly in those terms for his liberal attitude to the Sabbath and for his mixing with sinners; we know that later Christians, notably people like Paul, were similarly accused of abandoning the Jewish law and so encouraging sinful behavior. It is in response to that sort of accusation that Jesus in 5:17-20 replies very forcefully that he is not destroying the law and the prophets or lowering standards. No, he is "fulfilling" them, bringing in full the righteousness to which they are pointing and going even higher than the scribes and Pharisees.

This is then illustrated in the so-called antitheses that follow, where Jesus quotes the Old Testament–based teaching of the scribes and Pharisees and shows how much higher he goes, how much higher the righteousness of the kingdom of God is. The Old Testament and the Pharisees said "Don't kill" and "Don't commit adultery," while Jesus says "Don't even insult your brother or sister" and "Don't commit adultery in your heart." The righteousness of God's kingdom does not go skin deep: when God rules as king, there will not be outward respectability — e.g., not killing — and inward uncleanness (contrast the description of the Pharisees in 23:23-28); there will be integrity and righteousness that reaches the heart. When God rules as king, laws about divorce or oaths will not be needed; they were needed to deal with human sinfulness and weakness — whether in marriage or speaking (Matt. 19:8). God's kingdom will be different. God's kingdom will be marked by love of enemies, not just by an absence of revenge-taking. In God's kingdom the standard is, of course: "You therefore must be perfect as your heavenly Father is perfect" (5:48). So was Jesus undermining the Old Testament law and moral standards? Exactly the opposite: he was bringing the kingdom of God, in which the standard is perfection.

Seen in this context, the Sermon on the Mount is not depressingly difficult legalism.[32] Rather, it is a description of kingdom-of-heaven living, as well as a call to the disciples to live out their discipleship and their sonship of the heavenly Father. Jesus says, "Let your light so shine before people that they may see your beautiful deeds, and glorify your Father who is in heaven" (5:16). Such beautiful living does not come naturally, but is a manifestation of the kingdom of God and of the Holy Spirit.[33] The starting point is in the first four beatitudes — the acknowledgment of spiritual need and the seeking of God's righteousness. Those who start there will begin to live kingdom lives through the Holy Spirit.[34] Just as the kingdom of God brings physical healing to the sick who turn to Jesus in faith, so the kingdom of God brings practical transformation of disciples' lives. Not that Jesus in the Sermon on the Mount expects his disciples to achieve perfection in this life; no, he teaches them to pray, "Our Father, . . . forgive us our debts, as we forgive our debtors . . . ," and he expects them to need to receive and to give forgiveness (6:11-15). Nevertheless, God's intervention in Jesus — the coming of the kingdom of God — is to lead into righteousness that is higher than that of the Pharisees and toward the heavenly Father's perfection — whether in matters of relationships (5:21-48), or religion (6:1-18) or riches (6:19-34). This righteousness represents the fulfillment of the law and the prophets.[35] In Matthew's gospel Jesus has already spoken of his own calling "to fulfill all

---

32. Seen in this context, Matt 5:18, 19 are strong statements affirming the completeness of Jesus' fulfillment of the Old Testament laws; he does not leave any little law unfulfilled; he does not lower the standards at all. But the verses do not mean that Jesus expects his disciples to adhere to the Sabbath or temple laws, to take two examples, with the zeal of Pharisees (see 12:1-8) — because one greater than the temple and the Lord of the Sabbath has come, who fulfills those Old Testament institutions. See the discussion of these texts in R. Deines, *Die Gerechtigkeit der Torah im Reich des Messias: Mt 5,13-20 als Schlüsseltext der matthäischen Theologie* (Tübingen: Mohr, 2004).

33. Compare 19:26. R. Schnackenburg appropriately entitles his book on the Sermon *All Things Are Possible to Believers* (Louisville: John Knox, 1995). On the association of the kingdom and the Spirit see Matt. 12:28.

34. In this sense Jesus' yoke is an easy one (Matt. 11:28-30).

35. 5:17 and 7:12 seem to form an *inclusio* around the central teaching of the Sermon.

righteousness" (3:15); the disciples in the Sermon are challenged to follow Jesus in this calling.

Righteousness in Matthew and Paul[36]

If that is how Matthew understands the Sermon, then we are not far at all from some of Paul's teaching. Paul's interest in righteousness is well known and is most famously expressed in Romans 1:17, where he says that in the coming of Jesus "the righteousness of God is revealed," and in Romans 3:21, where he says, "But now the righteousness of God has been revealed, apart from the law, although witnessed to by the law and the prophets...." The exact meaning of the Greek phrase "δικαιοσύνη θεοῦ (righteousness of God)" has been discussed endlessly by scholars. Whatever the precise nuances, it is probable that Paul in speaking of righteousness coming in Jesus had in mind the numerous Old Testament passages which look forward to the day when God will intervene and establish righteousness in the world. One such passage is Isaiah 61, a famous chapter used by Jesus according to Luke 4:16-30 and echoed in other gospel passages, including the beatitudes. As we saw, in Isaiah 61 the prophet looks forward to God healing and saving his people, punishing wrong and establishing his covenant, and the chapter ends: "For as the soil makes the young plant come up and a garden causes seeds to grow, so the Sovereign Yahweh will make righteousness and praise spring up before all the nations" (v. 11). Other Old Testament passages speak of the coming of a Messiah who will bring righteousness, e.g., Isaiah 9:7; 11:4, and especially Jeremiah 23:5, 6: "Behold, the days are coming, declares Yahweh, when I will raise up for David a righteous branch, and he shall reign as king and deal wisely, and shall execute justice and righteousness in the land.... And this is the name by which he will be called: Yahweh is our righteousness."[37]

Paul surely had this promised righteousness in mind in Romans 1:17 and elsewhere. In 3:21 his "but now" points toward that eschatological direction, as does his reference to this revealed righteousness being "witnessed to by the law and the prophets." There is no question that Paul's theological thinking about

---

36. On righteousness in Matthew and Paul see R. Mohrlang, *Matthew and Paul: A Comparison of Ethical Perspectives* (SNTSMS 48; Cambridge: Cambridge University Press, 1984), and especially Deines, *Die Gerechtigkeit*. See also the discussions of A. J. M. Wedderburn, in the collection of essays *Paul and Jesus* (Sheffield: Sheffield Academic Press, 1989), 99-115, 117-43, and in his *The Reasons for Romans* (Edinburgh: T&T Clark, 1988), 108-22. On a closely related topic see M. W. Yeung, *Faith in Jesus and Paul* (WUNT 2.147; Tübingen: Mohr, 2002).

37. Compare the similar thought in Isa. 11:1, a text that has often been linked to Matt. 1:23.

Jesus and the Christian gospel has massively strong Old Testament roots, and that Paul sees Jesus as the fulfillment of the prophetic promises and vision.

The same is true of Matthew. And when Matthew associates Jesus and his kingdom teaching with righteousness, it is entirely probable that he is thinking of the Old Testament vision of eschatological righteousness. Thus, this must lie behind Jesus' programmatic words in Matthew 3:14 about his calling to "fulfill all righteousness." The righteousness that Jesus brings is not just ethical righteousness in general, but is specifically kingdom righteousness, as is explicit in 6:33 and implicit elsewhere.

Of course, it can be argued that righteousness in Paul and in Matthew are quite different. When Paul develops his argument about God's righteousness in a letter like Romans, he relates it particularly to the death of Jesus and to justification. The good news of Jesus is that there is now no condemnation, and that we who were under God's wrath have now been acquitted, by God's grace and through faith (see especially Romans 3). It is easy to conclude from this that for Paul "righteousness" is justification, whereas for Matthew it is ethical living.

But to make that contrast is to misinterpret Paul as well as Matthew. The eschatological righteousness which the Old Testament looked forward to included the forgiveness of sins and the restoration of relationships, but also the changing of people's lives. So it does for Matthew and for Paul. Thus in both Galatians and in Romans Paul focuses first on justification through faith, but then goes on to speak about Christian living. For Paul the Christian is one who is redeemed from sin and death through the death of Jesus, *so as to lead a new life.* In Romans 6 he emphasizes this, speaking of new life with Christ, and commenting, "Do not present your members (or body parts) to sin as instruments of unrighteousness, but present yourselves to God as those who have been brought from death to life, and your members to God as instruments of righteousness" (6:13). Paul here is speaking about righteousness in a strongly ethical sense. He goes on to comment that "just as you once presented your members (or body parts) as slaves to impurity and to lawlessness leading to more lawlessness, so now present your members as slaves to righteousness leading to sanctification" (v. 19). The contrast is between sin, impurity, lawlessness and desires/lusts on the one hand and righteousness on the other. We are very close to the Sermon on the Mount, where Jesus speaks of fulfilling the law (contrast lawlessness, 7:23), of purity of heart, of righteousness, and of cutting off the body parts that lead into sin (5:17, 8, 27-30).

Paul speaks in the same context of the Roman Christians having become "obedient from the heart to the standard of teaching to which you were committed" (6:17). What does he mean by that "standard" or "pattern" (Greek τύπος) of teaching? It seems probable that he is referring to the Christian instruction that converts would receive; it is tempting to wonder if such teaching included the Sermon on the Mount itself.[38]

In making such comparisons we need to beware of parallelomania,[39] i.e., of imagining significant connections between the Pauline teaching in Romans and Jesus' teaching in the Sermon on the Mount just because there are some similar words, phrases or ideas in two contexts. Finding similarities between Paul and the Sermon on the Mount does not mean that Paul was drawing on traditions of Jesus. However, there is further Pauline evidence. In 1 Corinthians 6:9 Paul says strikingly, "Don't you know that unrighteous people will not inherit the kingdom of God?" What is interesting about this is (a) that Paul rather rarely refers to "the kingdom of God?"[40] and (b) that he introduces the comment with the question "Don't you know?" What seems quite likely is that Paul uses the phrase and asks the question because he is here echoing teaching of Jesus which the Corinthian Christians have been taught. They have been taught sayings of Jesus such as Matthew 5:20: "Unless your righteousness exceeds that of the scribes and Pharisees, you will not enter the kingdom of heaven."[41] This view may be supported by the evidence of Romans 14:17, where Paul comments that, "The kingdom of God is not food and drink but righteousness and peace and joy in the Holy Spirit." Paul knows about the association of the kingdom of God with righteousness, probably as part of the teaching of Jesus; it is not just an idea of Matthew.[42]

Paul may also have known Matthew 5:17: Jesus speaks of having come not to abolish the law and the prophets but to fulfill them, and then goes on to explain his meaning in the antitheses that follow, which climax in the command to love your enemies (5:20-48). Paul in Romans 3:31 asks if his emphasis on faith nullifies the law; on the contrary, he says, we "uphold it." What does he mean? Various verses in Romans may help answer that question; thus in 3:21 Paul has spoken of the righteousness of God that has been manifested in Jesus being

---

38. This would fit in with our earlier observations about the frequent echoes of the Sermon in 1 Peter and James.

39. For the term see S. Sandmel, "Parallelomania," *JBL* 81 (1962): 1-13.

40. Paul's relatively infrequent use of the very Jewish concept of the kingdom of God in his letters probably reflects the Greek context of his mission and his letters; but his few references show that he was familiar with what was so central to Jesus' teaching.

41. Deines, *Die Gerechtigkeit*, 419-22, makes a very interesting comparison between Paul's teaching in 1 Thessalonians 4:1, 10 (where he urges the Thessalonians to continue in the teaching they had received and to abound [Greek περισσεύω] "all the more") and Matthew 5:20, where Jesus calls for righteousness that exceeds (περισσεύω).

42. Compare G. Johnston, "'Kingdom of God' Sayings in Paul's Letters," in P. Richardson and J. C. Hurd, eds., *From Jesus to Paul: Studies in Honour of Francis Wright Beare* (Waterloo, Ont.: Wilfrid Laurier, 1984), 143-56.

"witnessed to by the law and the prophets"; presumably in some sense that means that the law and the prophets were pointing forward to Jesus and so are being fulfilled by him. Rather differently, in Romans 8:3, 4 Paul comments on God through the death of Jesus doing what the law could not do, "so that the righteous requirement of the law might be fulfilled in us, who walk not according to the flesh, but according to the Spirit." Then in chapters 12 and 13 Paul explains how Christians should live, echoing Jesus' teaching about not returning evil for evil, but he also says this: "Do not owe anything to anyone except to love one another; for he who loves the other has fulfilled the law." He goes on to refer to the Old Testament commandments, and then comes back to saying, "Love works no evil to the neighbor; love, therefore, is the fulfillment of the law" (13:8-9). This idea of love fulfilling the law is not just in Romans, but is also attested in Galatians 5:14.[43]

Paul therefore uses language and ideas that are much closer to that of the Sermon on the Mount than is sometimes observed. Paul did indeed emphasize salvation through the grace of God and vigorously oppose attempts to impose Jewish law on Gentile converts. And yet he was also passionately concerned for righteous living. His desire and prayer for his converts was that "your love may abound more and more . . . so that you may approve what is excellent and so be pure and blameless for the day of Christ, filled with the fruit of righteousness that comes through Jesus Christ" (Phil. 1:9-11). Later in the same letter he speaks of his desire "that you may be blameless and innocent, children of God without blemish in the midst of a crooked and twisted generation, among whom you shine as lights in the world, holding fast to the word of life" (2:15, 16). The words of the Sermon on the Mount about letting "your light" shine are immediately brought to mind, as well as Jesus' words about living as children of the heavenly Father. Later Paul goes on to speak about striving for perfection (Phil. 3:12; cf. 1 Thess. 3:13; Col. 1:10).

There turns out to be no gulf fixed between Matthew and Paul; rather, the opposite. Both teach that Jesus saves the unrighteous from their sins through his death and by grace, both teach the importance of faith, and both teach that saying "Lord Lord," and even doing many mighty works in Jesus' name, are useless without living in love and thus fulfilling the law of Christ (Matt. 7:21-23; 1 Cor. 13:1-3). The Sermon on the Mount is addressing different questions from Paul's letter to the Romans, but its emphasis on beautiful, godly living does not

---

43. Scholars have commented with interest on the fact that Paul speaks of fulfilling the law, not doing it (e.g., S. Westerholm, *Perspectives Old and New on Paul: The "Lutheran" Paul and His Critics* (Grand Rapids/Cambridge: Eerdmans, 2004), 435. It seems entirely feasible that he has been influenced in the idea and the wording by Jesus himself.

contradict Paul's gospel of grace at all. On the contrary, Paul probably knew and taught and believed in the Sermon of his master.

Conclusion

We suggested at the start of this article that the Sermon on the Mount may have been neglected in the Christian church in recent years, partly because of critical doubts about its dominical origins, partly because of Protestant anxieties about a religion of works. My conclusion is that the doubts and anxieties are misplaced. The Sermon may and should be recognized as the pattern of Jesus' teaching to which Christian disciples have been committed and as the solid rock on which they should build their lives for eternity.

Balaam-Laban as the Key to the Old Testament Quotations in Matthew 2

David Instone-Brewer

Summary

Matthew 2 appears to pull proof-texts out of the Hebrew Scriptures in an almost random way. However, when it is read in the light of the ancient additions to the story of Balaam, the texts form the structure of a sermon based on Balaam's star. Early Jewish sources allude to a story about Balaam, who, in the identity of Laban, tried to kill Rachel's children, which included a messianic baby. They were protected in Egypt, but after the Exodus Balaam attacked again. Matthew's four quotations are each linked to this story, and a first-century Jewish reader would have recognized the story behind these links. The underlying message is that Jesus is the Messiah, and that Herod was like Balaam-Laban, the super-enemy of the Jews who tried to destroy the Messiah.

Matthew's Four Quotations

Matthew 2 leads the reader from the Magi who ask about the star, through the flight into Egypt, and finishes at the return to Nazareth. It includes four quotations from the "prophets": from Micah 5:2, 4 at v. 6; Hosea 11:1 at v. 15; Jeremiah 31:15 at v. 18; and an allusion from "the prophets" that "he will be called a Nazarene" at v. 23. The correspondence between the contents of this chapter and these texts appears to be flimsy and tendentious, and yet the author seems to think that these are convincing examples of fulfilled prophecy (vv. 5, 15, 17, 23).

Commentators have largely failed to find any common ground between these texts, and tend to treat them as isolated proof-texts, or texts from an early Christian list of testimonies, which have been applied without much regard to their original context. France, followed by Davies and Allison, has made a good attempt to find a common theme between them by pointing out that they each refer to a geographical location (Bethlehem, Egypt, Ramah and Nazareth), though they have difficulty finding the relevance of "Ramah."[1] This explanation does nothing to make these texts more convincing as "fulfillment" of prophecy because, as France suggests, the deeper meaning of these texts can only be appreciated by someone who has already accepted the conclusion that Jesus is Messiah.

This chapter is therefore either confused or confusing — either the author is writing in a sloppy and unconvincing manner, or we are missing something. In considering which possibility is more likely, we should dismiss two simplistic and condescending possibilities. First, we should not assume that the author is communicating only to those who are already convinced and therefore need only the merest hint to identify Jesus in these prophecies. His primary readership may well have been believers, but they were believers in a mission-oriented church, who mixed with unconvinced people every day. The whole tenor of the birth narratives is apologetic, so we would expect that these "fulfillment" prophecies were meant to be convincing to nonbelievers. Second, we should dismiss the assumption that ancient readers were gullible and easily convinced, while we, in contrast, are more intelligent and logical. Human intelligence has not increased measurably during the last few millennia, and the average Jewish reader was far better read in religious texts than most modern scholars, and they were just as skilled at following complex religious and exegetical reasoning.

We should assume instead that this chapter is confusing for us, partly perhaps because we are unpracticed at following their methods of reasoning, but mainly because we are ignorant of something with which first-century Jewish readers were very familiar. In other words, the author was assuming some knowledge which any Jewish reader of the time would possess, but which is unfortunately no longer readily available to a modern reader. The problem with this solution is that things which are very well known are often not recorded, but only alluded to, so the missing information may not now be available in an easily accessible form.

A modern example of something which is well known but poorly recorded is the stories regarding Father Christmas. Imagine scholars from a generation which had forgotten the Father Christmas stories, who were trying to piece together nineteenth-century allusions to this person from religious and historical

---

1. W. D. Davies and Dale C. Allison, *A Critical and Exegetical Commentary on the Gospel according to Saint Matthew* (3 vols.; ICC; Edinburgh: T&T Clark, 1988-97), 1:235, 268f. R. T. France, "The Formula-Quotations of Matthew 2 and the Problem of Communication," *NTS* 27 (1981): 233-51.

texts, and occasional letters and legal documents (which is roughly the extent of our records from the first century). They would find it very difficult to reconstruct the fable of Father Christmas from the sideways allusions which they might find in these documents. They might find references, for example, in a theology textbook ("Santa Claus is based on Saint Nicholas . . ."); or in a sermon ("a meal for the poor, unlike the traditional mince pie and cup of milk by the chimney, should be given without any hope of reward"); or in a church talk for children ("be good or you may get a piece of coal"); or in a letter ("John dressed in a Santa suit for the children's party"). But they would not find a straightforward retelling of this story, including the elves, reindeer, milk and mince pie, coal, presents, chimneys and white beard. This story was not passed on in books because it was told to the very young, so written texts contained only allusions to it. The scholars could of course cheat by referring to a children's book from the twentieth century (when parents needed extra help telling stories to their young), but a cautious and serious scholar would try to avoid using literature from a later time period.

We face a similar situation when we try to reconstruct a story which was familiar to all first-century Jews, such as the story of Balaam, which has many links with the details recorded in Matthew 2. In the intertestamental period, various additions to the biblical story transformed Balaam into a super-enemy who lived for hundreds of years and who tried to kill the baby ancestor of the Messiah.[2] First, when he was called Laban, he pursued the children of Rachel till they took refuge in Egypt. There Balaam's sons, Jannes and Jambres, advised Pharaoh to kill the children. Later, in the wilderness, Balaam attacked them again and he was finally killed, after prophesying about the star and scepter of the Messiah. The many examples of embellished rewritings of the Old Testament, such as Pseudo-Philo, the *Genesis Apocryphon,* and Josephus's *Jewish Antiquities,* suggest that such stories were very popular in the common Jewish mind-set of the first century. This particular series of stories is alluded to in various sources, but they are nowhere told in their entirety, so we have to reconstruct them from various ancient texts.

---

2. The sources about Balaam in the Targums, the LXX and the early rabbinic literature are conveniently summarized in G. Vermes, "The Story of Balaam," in *Scripture and Tradition in Judaism* (ed. G. Vermes; Leiden: Brill, 1961), 127-77, and by Louis Ginzberg, *The Legends of the Jews* (7 vols.; trans. H. Szold; Philadelphia: Jewish Publication Society, 1913-67), 1:369-76; 3:351-82. However, neither of them highlights the connection between Laban and Balaam.

Problems with "Early" Jewish Sources

There are very few sources which might reliably tell us about Jewish preaching and exegesis in Palestine-Syria of the first century. Most of the texts which have survived come from outside the area (such as Philo's works from Alexandria) or from outside mainstream Judaism (such as the documents from Qumran and apocalyptic sects) or from outside the time period (such as Targums and Midrashim). This leaves us with Josephus, who arguably represents mainstream synagogue interpretations, and the Septuagint, which sometimes preserves clues about the interpretations of the translators.

Some of the literature which was preserved at Qumran and nearby was probably also familiar in mainstream Judaism. In particular, we might assume that historical, ethical or sapiential works were of general interest, such as the Greek version of Ecclesiasticus, *Psalms of Solomon,* Third and Fourth Maccabees and Wisdom of Solomon. Some of the apparently sectarian works were probably also widely known outside Qumran and the various apocalyptic sects, because we find copies and translations of them in several locations. These include *Jubilees* and *Enoch* and perhaps works such as Pseudo-Philo, *Lives of the Prophets* and *Testaments of the Twelve Patriarchs.* Even though this literature was probably regarded somewhat like we regard the Arthurian legends — tales with stirring sentiments and moralizing conclusions which only the fanatics would read as historic — they are nevertheless a repository of well-known stories. These stories were probably not regarded as "true" by most Jews, but they would have been valued as quotable illustrations of universal truths and revelations, or simply as popular vehicles to which serious teaching could be attached.

Other sources which were recorded at a later date or outside Palestine-Syria can be useful when they display correlations with this literature. The Midrashim include a vast and varied collection of stories and interpretations which span from the first to the fifth centuries CE and sometimes later. These should be treated with caution because even when traditions appear to have an ancient origin, they are likely to have developed greatly in the meantime. Unlike halakhic rabbinic traditions, many of which can now be reliably dated, we do not yet have any way to date this haggadic material.[3]

The Targums are potentially useful because they are relatively conserva-

---

3. Dating methods for halakhic material are now well established, and the pre-70-CE traditions are now being dated systematically in David Instone-Brewer, *Traditions of the Rabbis from the Era of the New Testament (TRENT)* (1 vol., 5 vols. forthcoming; Grand Rapids: Eerdmans, 2004). When this project is complete, the results may provide clues by which haggadic material can be dated.

tive in their preservation of classical synagogue interpretations, though they too should be used with great care. These Aramaic translations adhere closely to the Hebrew text, but they also contain a varying number of interpolations and paraphrases to help the reader understand the text. For the non-Pentateuchal Old Testament we have only the *Targum Jonathan (Tg. Jon.)*, but for the Pentateuch we have three full versions and fragments of others. The three are:

- *Targum Onqelos (Tg. Onq.)* — the traditional rabbinic or Babylonian Targum which is usually very close to the Hebrew text.
- *Targum Pseudo-Jonathan (Tg. Ps.-J.)* — initially thought to be part of *Targum Jonathan*, which has the largest number of interpretive additions.
- *Targum Neofiti (Tg. Neof.)* — discovered in the Vatican last century, which is similar to *Tg. Onq.* but with some additions like those of *Tg. Ps.-J.* in the text and more of them added later in its margin.

There has been a welcome revival of interest in the Targums since the publication of the English translations edited by McNamara,[4] but the date of the traditions in these Targums is still completely uncertain. Written Targums existed from the second century BCE, as found at Qumran,[5] but the rabbinic Targums were written much later. Like other rabbinic literature, there was initially a reluctance to record Targums in a written form, lest it become confused with "Written Torah." A story about Gamaliel II (beginning of second century) suggests that he was willing to read a written Targum of Job, but he then destroyed it by burial to stop others from reading it, in contrast to his grandfather in the mid first century who buried it without reading it (*b. Shab.* 115a). Even if this story is not historically accurate, it presumably conveys the changing attitudes toward Targums which the Talmudic editors wished to record.

The Targum versions that we have were probable not written till after 70 CE, and they were also greatly reedited in the second century.[6] Nevertheless, they often preserve very early interpretations and allusions to stories which

---

4. Martin McNamara, ed., *The Aramaic Bible: The Targums* (Edinburgh: T&T Clark, 1992-).

5. A Targum of Job, 11QtgJob, has been found, which may be dated to the second century BCE, which is totally different from the rabbinic Targum. However, the small fragment of a Targum of Leviticus 16, 4QtgLev, probably from the first century BCE, is basically similar to *Targum Onqelos*.

6. See the useful discussion of dating the Targum of Isaiah by Bruce Chilton in *Aramaic Bible*, vol. 11, xx-xxxiii. McNamara summarizes the attempts to date Targums by comparisons with rabbinic halakhah, and warns against making firm conclusions from this data (*Aramaic Bible*, vol. IA, 41-42).

were well known in the first century but which are sometimes entirely missing from rabbinic collections.[7] This study will often refer to traditions in *Targum Pseudo-Jonathan* which are only partially confirmed by more dateable sources such as Josephus and the LXX. Although this is an uncertain way of discovering what was known and thought in the first century, I take comfort from the fact that I rely on the work of two great scholars of the past. This paper pulls together findings in two neglected studies by David Daube and Renée Bloch,[8] and draws implications from them.

When these findings are applied to Matthew 2, they provide a single theme which places its four OT citations into a sermonic structure which would have been easily recognized in the first century. I will suggest in this study that some concepts which are found primarily in the Targums should be regarded as intertestamental traditions, because they concur with briefer notices which we find in older sources and because they help to explain this difficult chapter in Matthew. Therefore, by a circular process, these targumic traditions will be shown to be ancient because they concur with older sources and because they cast light on a problematic passage in the NT.

Balaam-Laban, the Super-enemy of Israel

In targumic traditions, the story of Balaam starts with Laban. It is difficult to know if Laban and Balaam were really regarded as the same individual, or whether Laban was a kind of metaphorical forerunner. We do not know the subtleties of this identification because we merely have allusions to the fact.

> Num. 22:5: [Balak] sent messengers to **Laban the Aramaean, that is, Balaam** *(for he sought to swallow the people of the house of Israel),* the son of

---

7. McNamara gives the example of the gloss at Gen. 3:19 in *Tg. Ps.-J.* and *Tg. Neof.:* "But from the dust you are to arise again to give an account and a reckoning of all that you have done." Apart from *Gen. Rab.* 20:10 saying that Adam's "returning" to the dust hints at the resurrection, the nearest parallel to this gloss is found in the *Apocalypse of Moses*, a fourth-century Greek translation of a pre-Christian Hebrew document: "And the LORD said to him [Adam], 'I told you that you are dust and to dust you shall return. Now I promise to you the resurrection; I shall raise you on the last day in the resurrection with every man of your seed'" (*Apoc. Mos.* 41:2-3, in J. H. Charlesworth, *The Old Testament Pseudepigrapha* [2 vols.; London: Darton, Longman and Todd, 1983-85], 2:293).

8. David Daube, "The Earliest Structure of the Gospels," *New Testament Studies* 5 (1959): 174-87; Renée Bloch, "Ecriture et Tradition dans le Judaïsme, Aperçus sur l'origine du Midrash," *Cahiers Sioniens* 1 (1954): 9-34.

Beor, who *acted foolishly from the greatness of his wisdom. He did not spare Israel, the descendants of the sons of his daughters.* (Tg. Ps.-J.)⁹

Num. 31:8: *[Phineas said to Balaam]* "*Are you not* **Laban the Aramean, who sought to destroy Jacob our father, and went down to Egypt** . . . *you incited wicked Amalek against them, and now are you sent to curse them? But when you saw that your work did not take effect and the Memra of the Lord did not heed you, you persuaded the evil king Balak to put his daughters at the crossroads of the way to lead them astray, and because of this twenty-four thousand of them fell. Therefore there is no possibility again of sparing your life."* *And immediately he drew his sword from its sheath and slew him.* (Tg. Ps.-J.)

It may be argued that the identification of Laban with Balaam was a relatively late idea because *Targum Onqelos* and *Targum Neofiti* do not contain these two additions, and the other sources which preserve this idea are later rabbinic works.¹⁰ However, it is very common for *Targum Pseudo-Jonathan* to contain additions which are missing from the other two Targums, which are far less expanded, so this absence is not necessarily significant. Also, the earliest rabbinic tradition which refers to this idea is already questioning it and revising it, because the rabbis had some misgivings about the implication that Balaam was over 400 years old:

A Tanna taught: Beor, Cushan-rishathaim¹¹ and Laban the Syrian are identical; Beor denotes that he committed bestiality; Cushan-rishathaim that he perpetrated two evils upon Israel: one in the days of Jacob and the other in the days of the Judges. But what was his real name? Laban the Syrian.

Scripture writes, "the son of Beor"; [but also] his son [was] Beor.

R. Johanan said: His father [Beor] was as his son in the matter of prophecy. (*b. Sanh.* 105a, Soncino translation)

The first paragraph is attributed to an anonymous Tanna — i.e., a rabbinic authority who lived before 200 CE. This rabbi appears to be already familiar

---

9. All quotations from the Targums are taken from McNamara, *Aramaic Bible,* in which the deviations from the Hebrew text are indicated by italics. The words in bold are highlighted for the sake of this paper.

10. See Ginzberg, *Legends,* 6:123 n. 722.

11. See Judg. 3:8 — the king whom Israel served for eight years. The plural form of his name prompted the search for two identities, and the other is found in the days of Jacob, presumably because Israel served him for 2 × 7 years.

with the idea that Balaam (the "son of Beor") and Laban are the same individual. However, he has found a way to reduce the long life span which this implied by saying that actually Laban was identical with Beor, the father of Balaam. A later anonymous comment reduces the life span even further by suggesting that Laban was Balaam's grandfather, because Beor had a son called Beor. Finally R. Johanan bar Nappaha (c. 250-290 CE) completely removed the mystical element from this tradition by saying that Beor (i.e., Laban) was not his physical father, but only his father in prophecy. By the time of the next generation (c. 290-320 CE) R. Hanina is able to agree with an exegesis which said that Balaam lived only 33 years (*b. Sanh.* 106b).[12]

This discussion, which appears to have developed over a time period of two to four generations, shows at each step that the rabbis were moving away from the idea that Laban was identical with Balaam, not toward it. This implies that the straightforward identity of Laban and Balaam, as found in *Targum Pseudo-Jonathan,* was a very old idea, because each of these generations of rabbis are progressively distancing themselves from it.

In Genesis, Laban pursued Jacob because he left suddenly with a large flock which Laban considered to be his property, and because he suspected him of stealing a household god which Rachel, his daughter, had indeed stolen and successfully hid from him (Gen. 31:22-35). In the Hebrew Bible, it is Jacob who is angry at being treated wrongly while Laban is sad about losing his daughters, and they depart on amicable terms (see Gen. 31:36-54). However, in the Targums, Laban remains an enemy of Jacob and continues to pursue him. *Targum Pseudo-Jonathan* and *Targum Neofiti* both contain this tradition at Genesis 32:2-3 in slightly different language.

> Gen. 32:2-3: Jacob went on his way, and the angels of the Lord met him. (3) When Jacob saw them he said, *"These are not the camps of Esau that are coming to meet me, and neither are they* **the camps of Laban that are pursuing me again;** *but they are the camps of the Holy angels who have been sent from before the Lord."* (Tg. Ps.-J.)
>
> Gen. 32:2: And Jacob went on his journey, and angels from before the Lord overtook him. 3. And Jacob said when he saw them: *"Perhaps they are messengers from* **Laban, my mother's brother, who has returned to pursue after me;** *or the hosts of Esau, my brother, who comes to meet me, or hosts of*

---

12. This may be an anti-Christian comment — cf. R. T. Herford, *Christianity in Talmud and Midrash* (London: Williams & Norgate, 1903), 65f., but contra L. Ginzberg, "Some Observations of the Attitude of the Synagogue towards the Apocalyptic-Eschatological Writings," *JBL* 41-42 (1922-23): 115-36, esp. 121, n. 18.

angels from before the Lord come to deliver me from the hands of both of them." *(Tg. Neof.)*

This idea is also found in all three Targums for Deuteronomy 26 in words which are clearly related but are too dissimilar to have simple literary dependence on each other.

Deut. 26:5: And *you* shall answer and say before the Lord your God: "**Laban** the Aramaean *sought to destroy* our **father Jacob** from the beginning. *But you rescued him from his hand,* **and he went down to Egypt** and he sojourned there with a few people, *and he was blessed. (Tg. Neof.)*

Deut. 26:5: So you shall answer and say before the Lord your God: "Our father Jacob *descended to Aram Naharaim at the beginning, and (Laban) sought to destroy him,* but the Memra of the Lord saved him from his hands. Afterwards, **he went down to Egypt,** and he sojourned there with a small number of people. *(Tg. Ps.-J.)*

Deut. 26:5: In response, you should then recite before the Lord your God, "***Laban the Aramaean sought to destroy my ancestor,*** who went down to Egypt and lived there as a small nation." *(Tg. Onq.)*

This passage was part of the words recited in the Passover Haggadah, and the version in *Targum Onqelos* is very similar to some versions of the Haggadah which read: "An Aramean sought to destroy (אִיבַד) my father." This exegesis depends on a minor change of the Hebrew, "A wandering (*ober,* אֹבֵר) Aramean was my father," and was probably inspired by a wish to remove this rather disparaging description of Abraham.[13] This interpretation was already traditional and fixed by mishnaic times (i.e., by 200 CE — see *m. Pesiq.* 10.4), and probably much earlier.[14]

We are not told why Laban wants to pursue Jacob, but *Targum Pseudo-*

---

13. The LXX translation makes a similar attempt by translating, "My father forsook (יאבד) Aram."

14. L. Finkelstein argued that this exegesis originated in the second century BCE — see "The oldest Midrash: Pre-Rabbinic Ideals and Teachings in the Passover Haggadah," *HTR* 31 (1938): 291-317. Seeligmann thought that the tradition originated at the time of the Syrian Antiochus Epiphanes (early second century BCE), who caused many Jews to flee to Egypt, and he pointed to the LXX of Isa. 10:24, "that you may see the way to Egypt," as a reference to this — see I. L. Seeligmann, *The Septuagint Version of Isaiah: A Discussion of Its Problems, Mededelingen en verhandelingen van het Vooraziatisch-Egyptisch Genootschap. Ex Oriente Lux,* no. 9 (Leiden: E. J. Brill, 1948), 84-86.

Jonathan gives two indications that his target is a child who is the ancestor of the Messiah. First, the Targums link the sorrow of Rachel (who is the likely target of Laban's anger because she stole his household gods) with the coming of the Messiah:

> Gen. 35:18-21: As [Rachel's] soul departed — for *death came upon her* — she called his name "Son of my Agony"; but his father called him Benjamin. (19) And Rachel died and was buried **on the way to Ephrath, that is, Bethlehem**. . . . (21) *Jacob* journeyed on and pitched his tent beyond **the Tower of the Flock,** *the place from which the King Messiah will reveal himself at the end of days. (Tg. Ps.-J.)*

Another indication in *Targum Pseudo-Jonathan* that Laban's grand plan is to kill the child-ancestor of the Messiah, comes in the dream where God tells Jacob to flee to Egypt in order to escape Laban.

> Gen. 45:27–46:4: When [Jacob's sons] recounted to him all the words that Joseph had spoken with them, and when he saw the carriages that Joseph had sent to take him, the spirit *of prophecy, which had departed from him when they sold Joseph, returned and rested upon* their father Jacob. (28) And Israel said, "The Lord has done many *good things for me;* **he delivered me from** the hands of Esau and from **the hands of Laban,** *and from the hands of the Canaanites who pursued me; and I have seen and expected to see many consolations. But this I did not expect: that* my son Joseph was still alive. I will go then, and see him before I die" (46:1). Israel set out with all that was his, and came to Beer-sheba, and offered sacrifices to the God of his father Isaac. (2) *The Lord* spoke to Israel in a *prophecy* of the night and said, "Jacob! Jacob!" He said, "Here I am." (3) And he said, "I am God, the God of your father. **Do not be afraid to go down to Egypt** *because* of the slavery which I decreed with Abraham; for there I will make of you a great nation. (4) *It is* I who *in my Memra* will go down with you to Egypt. *I will look upon the misery of your sons, but my Memra will exalt you there;* **I will also bring your sons up from there.** *(Tg. Ps.-J.)*[15]

---

15. A variant reading of *Tg. Ps.-J.* Gen. 46.6-7 has "all his sons; he brought his seed and his grandsons," where the MT and orther targums have "sons" instead of "seed." The targumist is presumably attempting to remove the redundancy of repeating "sons" by pointing to the Messianic "seed" which Jacob also brought with him. For "seed" referring to a single Messiah, cf. 2 Sam. 7.12; 4QFlor = 4Q174.10f; Gal. 3.16. This highlighted the concept of a single Messianic "son" among the "sons."

These two texts point to the common thread which runs through the Balaam-Laban saga — which was the pursuit, not of Jacob, but of his children, and one messianic child in particular.

Balaam-Laban in Matthew 2

The first readers of Matthew's Gospel were presumably very familiar with the saga of Balaam-Laban and his pursuit of the child ancestor of the Messiah. The Aramaic targumic version was normally recited in the synagogue after a Hebrew Scripture reading, in order to help the non-scholars understand the day's reading of the Torah. There was probably no need to expand the targumic allusions to the Balaam story, though no doubt preachers would often expatiate upon this popular and lively tale.

Therefore, when Jews read the quotation of Micah 5 in Matthew, their minds would go directly to this saga, and find the other significant links which are highlighted in Matthew's narrative. Mary, like Rachel, was to give birth in Bethlehem of Ephrath (Matt. 2:5-6), and her child would be king of the Jews (Matt. 2:2) as Micah prophesied (Mic. 5:2), and he would be the Messiah (Matt. 2:4) as the Targum explained (*Tg. Ps.-J.* Gen. 35:21).

The theme of the Messiah in the Targum of Rachel's death appears to be prompted by the place names Bethlehem of Ephrath and the Tower of the Flock (or "of Ebal"), both of which are given messianic significance in Micah:

> Mic. 4:7-8: . . . and the LORD will reign over them in Mount Zion from now and for ever. (8) And you, **Tower of the Flock,** hill of the daughter of Zion, **to you he will come.** . . .

> Mic. 5:2-4: And you, **Bethlehem Ephratah,** who are least among the thousands of Judah, **out of you will come** to me one to become **a ruler in Israel,** and his coming is of old, from the days of eternity. (3) Therefore he will give them over till the time **the one giving birth** has given birth **and the rest of his brothers shall return** to the sons of Israel. (4) **And he shall pasture** in the strength of the LORD. . . . [MT Mic. 5:1-3]

Matthew conflates verses 2 and 4 of Micah 5 to juxtapose the twin concepts of a ruler being born in Bethlehem and his function as a shepherd. This emphasizes the origin of this prophecy in the narrative of Genesis 35:19-21, where Rachel is buried at Bethlehem but Jacob pitches his tent nearby at the Tower of the Flock, to which Micah sees the Messiah coming.

This prophecy in Micah probably prompted the concept that a special child was being born who would return together with his brothers. This inspired the idea in the Targum that Judah had a dream in which he was told to flee to Egypt to escape Laban where his special child ("your son") would be kept safe and that one day God would "bring your son out [of Egypt]."

Matthew records that Joseph, like Judah, had a dream in which God told him to flee to Egypt (Matt. 2:13; *Tg. Ps.-J.* Gen. 46:2-4), though the child-ancestor of the Messiah who was kept safe in Egypt is now the child-Messiah himself. The messianic reference in the targumic story of Jacob's dream is obvious to someone who expects to find it there ("I will bring your sons up from there . . . he brought his seed" — *Tg. Ps.-J.* Gen. 46:4, 6; cf. MT "bring you up"), but it is not convincing to the skeptic. Matthew therefore highlighted the inspiration behind this Targum, which lay in the strange wording of Hosea 11:1: "When Israel was a child, I loved him, and I called my son out of Egypt."

The wording of this prophecy suggests (to the keen eye of a Jewish interpreter) that there is a distinction between the child Israel whom God loves, and the son whom he calls out of Egypt, because if they were the same, Hosea would say: "I loved him and I called him out of Egypt." The Targumist replicates this strange ambiguity when he says that God told Jacob he would "look upon the misery of your son," and would "bring your son up from [Egypt]." Jacob had twelve sons, and if any individual could bear the title of the "son" whom God brought out of Egypt, it would be Jacob himself. And yet God tells Jacob that he would bring "your son" out of Egypt, which implied that this "son" was someone other than the nation which Jacob embodied. In Hosea, the identity of this infant is the young nation, but in the mind of the Targumist, there is another child — the Messiah or his ancestor.

The Child Messiah Predicted by the Sons of Balaam

The saga of Balaam-Laban continued while Jacob's family hid in Egypt because the sons of Balaam were magicians at the court of Pharaoh. According to widespread traditions in first-century extrabiblical literature, Pharaoh's magicians were called Jannes and Jambres,[16] whom some thought were the forefathers of

---

16. See Damascus Document 5:17-19 ("In days gone by, Moses and Aaron arose by the hand of the Prince of Lights [that is, the Good Spirit], but Belial [Satan] in his cunning raised up Yohana [Jannes] and his brother when Israel was saved for the first time") and the reference to them in 2 Tim. 3:8. The apocryphal book "Jannes and Jambres," which has survived in a very fragmentary form is difficult to date, but it may have existed in the first century CE.

the Magi.[17] But the secret of their "true" identity as the sons of Balaam was only alluded to in *Targum Pseudo-Jonathan:* Num 22:22: "And he [Balaam] was riding on his ass, and his two lads, Jannes and Jam(b)res."

This identity is not mentioned in any other Targum, but it is found in a different context in the later rabbinic work, *The Chronicles of Moses:* "And after they [Moses and Aaron] left, Pharaoh sent and called to Balaam the magician and Jannes and Jambaris [sic] his sons the sorcerers" (*Chronicles of Moses* cited in *Yalqut Shimoni* 173).

The Chronicles of Moses is of uncertain date, but it was known by rabbinic authorities in the late eleventh century, when it was cited in the ʿArukh dictionary which was completed in 1101.[18] Although it contains many traditions which are similar to *Targum Pseudo-Jonathan,* it is likely that these came from an entirely different source because this Targum was virtually unknown outside Palestine till after the eleventh century.[19]

Jannes and Jambres became part of the Balaam-Laban saga when they persuaded Pharaoh to kill the children of the Israelites, and they thereby continued the attempt by Laban to kill the special "son" of Jacob. In the Hebrew text, Pharaoh decided to kill the male Israelite children as a means of population control (Exod. 1:9f.) but *Targum Pseudo-Jonathan* added that this policy was inspired by a dream, which explains why he targeted only the male babies:

> Exod. 1:15: *And Pharaoh said (that while) he slept, he saw in his dream that all the land of Egypt was placed on one balance of a weighing-scales, and a lamb, the young (of an ewe), on the other balance of the weighing-scales; and the balance of the weighing-scales on which the lamb (was placed) weighed down. Immediately he sent and summoned all the magicians of Egypt and told them his dream. Immediately* **Jannes and Jambres,** *the chief magicians, opened their mouths and said to Pharaoh:* **"A son is to be born in the assembly of Israel, through whom all the land of Egypt is destined to be destroyed."** *Therefore Pharaoh,* the king of Egypt, *took counsel and said to the Jewish* midwives. . . ." *(Tg. Ps.-J.)*

---

17. Pliny, *Hist. Nat.* 30.11: "there is also another group of Magi who derive from Moses and Jannes and Jambres and the Jews." Philo calls Balaam a *magos* at *Life of Moses* 1.276, which is also his term for the magicians of Pharaoh (*Life of Moses* 1.92).

18. Bloch, "Ecriture et Tradition," n. 33. The ʿArukh is the great Talmudical dictionary composed by Nathan ben Jehiel of Rome.

19. R. Hai Gaon (c. 1038 CE) said: "We do not know who composed the Targum Yerushalmi; in fact we do not even know the Targum itself, and we have heard speak of it but little" — cited in McNamara, *Aramaic Bible,* 1A:1-2.

Jannes and Jambres warned Pharaoh about the special baby boy through whom Egypt would be destroyed. In Josephus's version, which is characteristically less miraculous, there is a clearer reference to Moses:

> One of those sacred scribes, who are very sagacious in foretelling future events truly, told the king, that about this time there would be a child born to the Israelites who, if he were reared, would bring the Egyptian domination low, and would raise the Israelites; that he would excel all men in virtue, and obtain a glory that would be remembered through all ages. Which thing was so feared by the king that, according to this man's opinion, he commanded that they should cast every male child which was born to the Israelites into the river, and destroy it. (Josephus, *Ant.* 2.9.2 §205)

Josephus's account appears to be a version of the Targumic story which is sanitized so that there is no offense to Egyptian fortune-tellers and a minimum of messianic fervor, but he is unable to completely remove the elements concerning a messianic triumph over the enemies of the Jews. Josephus's account suggests that these stories alluded to in *Targum Pseudo-Jonathan* already had a wide circulation and acceptance in mainstream first-century Judaism.

The story probably originated in order to explain the strange fact that Pharaoh killed all the male children supposedly in order to cut down the number of Israelites (Exod. 1:9-10). It would have been far more effective to kill all the female children and let the males grow up as slaves. This story delves behind the biblical text and finds the "real" reason why only the males were killed — because there was a secret prophecy from the Magi about a certain male leader.

The prophecy that through this child "all the land of Egypt is destined to be destroyed" (*Tg. Ps.-J.* — or, as in Josephus, that Egyptian domination would be brought low) clearly goes far beyond what Moses accomplished, who merely succeeded in helping his people escape. The origin of this idea about destruction was probably the prophecy of Isaiah 11, that the Messiah would "utterly destroy the tongue of the Egyptian sea" at the final Exodus, just as at the first (Isa. 11:15-16), because this chapter was often linked with the prophecy of Balaam (as we will see shortly).

When Israel did leave Egypt and cross the wilderness, they found Balaam waiting for them, ready to try again to destroy them. He attempted to curse them, but was thwarted, so he advised the king of Moab to cause them to sin with beautiful women, which resulted in the Lord killing 24,000 Israelites (Num. 25:1-9; 31:16). When Balaam tried to curse Israel, he was forced to deliver a prophecy which included the doom of the people who hired him: Num 24:17:

". . . A star shall come out of Jacob, and a scepter shall rise out of Israel, and shall dash the corners of Moab and destroy all the sons of Seth."

This mysterious prophecy of Balaam became the focus of much speculation, both within the Hebrew prophets and later. All three Targums give these words a messianic interpretation:

> Num. 24:17: A *king* will emanate *from* Jacob, and *the* **anointed one** *will be consecrated from* Israel. *(Tg. Onq.)*

> Num. 24:17: A *king is to arise* from *those of the house of* Jacob, *and a* **redeemer** *and ruler* from *those of the house of* Israel. *(Tg. Neof.)*

> Num. 24:17: *When the strong King from those of the house of Jacob shall rule, and the* **Messiah** *and the* **strong rod** *from Israel shall be* **anointed**. *(Tg. Ps.-J.)*

All three demonstrate an undoubted messianic interpretation, which is also found at Qumran (1QM 11:5-9; CD 7:18-21) and in the LXX,[20] though *Targum Pseudo-Jonathan* is, predictably, the most effusive and also gives us a clue as to where they gained their certainty about this interpretation — Isaiah 11:

> Isa. 11:1: A shoot will proceed from the stump of Jesse, and a branch from his roots will bear fruit. (2) And the Spirit of the Lord shall rest upon him, the Spirit of wisdom and understanding. . . . (4) He will judge the poor in righteousness. . . . He will strike the earth with the rod of his breath.

This apparently unrelated prophecy was regarded as intimately linked with the prophecy of Balaam, and the wording of them both is sometimes intertwined, e.g.:

> And after this there shall arise for you **a Star from Jacob** in peace: And a man shall arise from my posterity like the Sun of righteousness, walking with the sons of men in gentleness and righteousness, and in him will be found no sin. (2) And the heavens will be opened upon him to pour out the spirit as a blessing of the Holy Father. (3) And he will pour the spirit of grace on you. And you shall be sons in truth, and you will walk in his first and final decrees. (4) **This is the Shoot of God** most High; this is the fountain for the life of all humanity. (5) Then he will illumine **the scepter of my kingdom,** (6) and **from your root will arise the Shoot,** and through it will

---

20. The messianic interpretation is alluded to by translating "sceptre" as "a man."

arise **the rod of righteousness** for the nations, **to judge** and to save all that call on the Lord. (*T. Judah* 24:1-5)

Then the Lord will raise up a new priest, to whom all the words of the Lord will be revealed; and he will **execute a true judgment** upon the earth in the course of time. And **his star will arise** in heaven, as a king, lighting up the light of knowledge as by the sun of the day. . . . (7) And the glory of the Most High shall burst forth upon him. And **the spirit of understanding** and sanctification **shall rest upon him**.[21] (*T. Levi* 18:3)

The Child Messiah in Matthew 2

Raymond Brown concludes that the first half of Matthew 2 was deliberately written in such a way as to parallel the Balaam stories. Balaam and his two sons, Jannes and Jambres, who were called "magi" by Philo (*Life of Moses* 1.92), prophesied about the star which pointed to the Messiah, and the child from whom he would rise. As a result of this, Pharaoh ordered the death of all baby boys. The Balaam story ends when he "went off to his home" (Num. 24:25), just as the Magi "went away to their own country" (Matt. 2:12).[22] Matthew's details about Herod are told in very similar terms to Josephus's version of the story of Pharaoh — he consulted his magicians, expressed fear for his throne, and ordered the death of the baby boys.

But the child who comes out of Egypt in Matthew 2 is not a precursor of the Messiah like Moses (Deut. 18:15) or an ancestor of the Messiah, but the Messiah himself. Matthew makes sure that the reader's thoughts moved from Moses and the first exodus toward the Messiah and the second, eschatological exodus by referring to Rachel weeping for her children (Jer. 31:15). Jeremiah viewed the death scene of Rachel as a prophetic one — she was weeping not just because of the agony of her difficult labor, but because she could foresee the killing of her children.[23] Matthew's reference to Rachel keeps the readers thinking about the Balaam-Laban saga, but shifts this to the context of Jeremiah 31 — to the escha-

---

21. Translations from Charlesworth. Both are from *The Testament of the Twelve Patriarchs*, which is generally considered to be a pre-Christian Jewish work, though it has some Christian interpolations (e.g., *T. Levi* 4:1; 14:2; *T. Ash.* 7:3; *T. Benj.* 9:3) and this may also be one (as Davies and Allison believe — *Matthew*, 1:234).

22. R. Brown, *The Birth of the Messiah* (Garden City, N.Y.: Doubleday, 1977), 190-96.

23. Gen. 35:17-18 says that the midwife tried to comfort her, but she called her boy "Son of my Agony (אוֹנִי)." Jeremiah appears to create a midrash from this when he says that she "refused (מֵאֲנָה) to be comforted for her children, who are not (אֵינֶנּוּ)." In v. 16 the Lord says: "They will come again from the land of the enemy."

tological return of Israel from all corners of the earth (v. 8) and not just from Egypt as in the past (v. 32), and to a new covenant rather than the old broken one (vv. 31-34).

Matthew's account of their return from Egypt appears to be deliberately vague in some details. He says that Joseph decided to return after hearing that Herod the Great had died, but he had misgivings after hearing about the accession of Archelaus,[24] which were confirmed by a dream in which God told him to go to Galilee. But he is vague about the stage at which Joseph changed his mind. The most obvious way to write the account would be to say that he changed his mind before they set out, or that when they arrived in Judea they decided instead to continue moving north. However, Matthew's account appears to suggest that Joseph came to this decision during his journey, before he reached Judea, because "he was afraid to go there." This makes the reader envisage the family coming out of Egypt, thinking they were safe, and then finding out about the new danger while they were in the wilderness south of Israel. This would explain how they could set out for Judah, but not arrive, because they could skirt around the eastern edge of Judea and travel on toward Galilee. This heightens the parallels of the story with the Balaam-Laban saga: Israel left Egypt thinking they were safe because Laban had died, but when they got to Moab (southeast of Judea), they were met by Balaam who (in some mysterious way) was Laban, and who was still trying to kill them.

It is tempting to follow Daube's suggestion that Matthew was also making a hidden criticism of the whole Herodian family (including Herod the Great, Archelaus, Herod Antipas who ruled during Jesus' lifetime, and Herod Agrippa I who succeeded him). The hidden criticism is that they were all Idumeans (Edomites), and not real Jews. The country of Idumea became Jewish in the second century BCE,[25] though they were often regarded as second-class Jews (cf. m. Soṭ. 7.8). Matthew deliberately highlighted parallels between Balaam-Laban and Herod, who both killed many children of Israel in an attempt to kill the child-messiah. Daube suggests that an unspoken link is found in the well-known words of the Passover Haggadah when it cites Deuteronomy 6:5: "An Aramean sought to destroy my father" (see above). He points out that "Aramean" (ארמי) and "Idumea" (אדמי) differ only by the tiniest difference between the letters *dalet* and *resh*. This hidden reference would have been noticed by Jewish readers, but not by any Gentiles who happened to read the work.

---

24. Archaelaus was Herod's named heir, but Herod Antipas pursued his rival claim, which resulted in a few very turbulent years in Judea.

25. Josephus says that they were converted by force (*Ant.* 13.9.1), but their support of the Jewish nation makes this questionable. The debate and literature are summarized in Lester L. Grabbe, *Judaism from Cyrus to Hadrian* (Minneapolis: Fortress, 1992), 2:329-31.

The Nazarene and His "Scepter"

The final "fulfillment prophecy" in Matthew 2 is the most obscure mainly because the source of the text is difficult to identify and partly because the significance seems minor. The only prophecy which speaks about anyone being called anything like a "Nazarene" is in Judges (13:5, 7; 16:17, LXX Ναζιραῖος), where the angel says that Samson will be a "Nazirite." It is difficult to relate this text to Jesus, whose lifestyle was neither like that of Samson nor of an alcohol-abstaining Nazirite (cf. the description of himself at Luke 7:34, which he reports and does not dispute: "a gluttonous man and a drunkard").

This solution became even more difficult after the discovery in 1962 of a synagogue inscription in Caesarea which included the name of Nazareth in Hebrew, spelling it "Natzereth" (using a *tzade*, not a *zayin*). This is the earliest record of the Hebrew spelling of this village, and it confirms the reading found in later rabbinic literature.[26] This spelling means that Matthew was calling Jesus a "Natziri" and not a "Naziri," so this is very unlikely to be a reference to "Nazirite" (which is spelled with a *zayin*).

The term "Natziri" is well known in rabbinic writings as a name for Jesus and for Christians — Jesus is called "Yeshu Natzeri" (or "Notzeri," depending on how it is vocalized), and his disciples are called "Notzerim." This designation is found mainly in portions of the Talmud which were considered to be derogatory to Christians and were therefore censored out of the printed editions.[27] We do not know why it was considered derogatory, but probably it combined the accusation that he had no legitimate father (so that he was named after a place instead of "ben Joseph") with the fact that he came from a very low-class village. Some ancient versions of the daily prayer, the Eighteen Benedictions, contain a curse against the Notzerim,[28] and early Christians regarded

---

26. See Ray Pritz, "He Shall Be Called a Nazarene" (*Jerusalem Perspective,* online at http://www.jerusalemperspective.com/Default.aspx?tabid=27&ArticleID=1638).

27. Jesus is called "Notzri" at *b. Sanh.* 43a, 103a, 107b; *b. Sot.* 47a; *b. 'Abod. Zar.* 16b, 17a, and his followers are called "Notzrim" in *b. 'Abod. Zar.* 6a; *b. Ta'an.* 27b. Most of these been preserved only in older manuscripts. These censored passages are collected in Hebrew/Aramaic with English translations by R. T. Herford in *Christianity in Talmud and Midrash* (London: Williams & Norgate, 1903).

28. The twelfth of the Eighteen Benedictions reads, in the Geniza version (which probably represents the earliest form which has been preserved): "For the apostates let there be no hope, and may the kingdom of the arrogant be quickly uprooted in our days; and may *notzerim* and *minim* instantly perish; may they be blotted from the book of the living, and not be written with the righteous. Blessed are you, Lord, humbler of the arrogant." See William Horbury, "The Benediction of the *Minim* and Early Jewish-Christian Controversy," *JTS* N.S. 33 (1982): 19-61; David Instone-Brewer, "The Eighteen Benedictions and the *Minim* before 70 CE," *JTS* N.S. 54 (2003): 25-44.

this as a reference to themselves — Justin Martyr said repeatedly that Jews curse Christians in the synagogue and speak disparagingly about them after their prayers (*Dial.* 16, 93, 95, 96, 123, 133), and Tertullian said that "the Jews call us 'Nazareni'" because of Jesus (*Adv. Marc.* 4.8.1).

Matthew's readers would presumably be familiar with the name "Yeshu Natzeri," and perhaps they were already themselves being called "Natzerim" in some early versions of the curse in the Jewish daily prayer. Matthew wished to relate this name both to the town of Natzereth and to a prophecy "in the prophets" — but which "prophets"?

The spelling of "Natzeri" with a *tzade* makes it likely that the prophecy he was referring to is Isaiah 11:1: "A shoot will come forth from the stem of Jesse, and a branch *(netzer)* from his roots will bear fruit." Although the word "branch" *(netzer)* occurs in this context only once, there are similar prophecies which use slightly different vocabulary: Isaiah 53.2, "tender shoot *(yonek)*"; Jeremiah 23:5 and 33:15, "a righteous plant *(tsemach)* for David"; Zechariah 3:8 and 6:12, "my servant, the Branch *(tsemach)*." These other prophecies might explain why Matthew generalized the source as "the prophets" rather than just Isaiah,[29] and his readers would have little difficulty identifying the Isaiah prophecy because it was an important messianic focus in early Jewish traditions (e.g., 4Q161 pIsa. 3:11-25; Rom. 15:12).

This final "prophecy" about Jesus' title as "Natzeri" brings the readers back to the Balaam's prophecy of the star in Numbers 24:17, because this became closely linked with the Isaiah 11 prophecy in the intertestamental period (see *T. Judah* 24:1-5 and *T. Levi* 18:3 above). Both passages bring the readers back to the beginning of Matthew 2 — Balaam's prophecy brings them back to the "star" and Isaiah's equivalent of Balaam's scepter ("rod of his mouth," Isa. 11:4) reminds a knowledgeable reader about "striking the judge of Israel with a rod on his cheek" (just before Matthew's quotation in Mic. 5:1).[30] As soon as a star was mentioned, Matthew's readers would have started thinking about Balaam's prophecy of the "star which will rise out of Jacob" portending that a deliverer would dash their enemies with his scepter (Num. 24:17), especially as

---

29. This explanation was already recognized by various Church Fathers, though they also thought that it referred to Jesus' holy lifestyle as typified in the Nazirite vow — both interpretations are found side-by-side in Chromaticus, *Tractate on Matthew* 7.2; Jerome, *Commentary on Matthew* 1.2.23; Cyril of Alexandria, *Fragment* 16. They are conveniently cited in M. Simonetti, *Matthew 1–13*, in T. C. Oden, ed., *Ancient Christian Commentary on Scripture*, 1a (Downers Grove, Ill.: InterVarsity Press, 2001), 37f.

30. This link makes it likely that Matthew is consciously alluding to this passage in 26:26 and 27:30, where both the Jews and the Romans strike him, both in the context of a scene of judgment.

the wording of the LXX is so similar to the Magi's word's "We saw the star when it rose."[31]

The parallels with the stories of Balaam-Laban are not so close as to make us conclude that Matthew is constructing his infancy narratives in order to fit in these stories. Matthew appears to have a set of stories from which he draws parallels, and the fact that these sometimes appear to be forced suggests that his narrative is determined by the traditions about Jesus rather than the stories about Balaam-Laban.

Conclusion: Matthew 2 is a Proem Sermon

Balaam's prophecy therefore marks both the beginning and the end of the series of quotations in chapter 2, and Matthew could be sure that Numbers 24:17 was in the mind of any Jewish reader, even though he never alluded to it. As soon as Balaam was introduced in this way, Matthew steered his readers through a series of scriptural citations which remind them of the various stages in the saga of Balaam-Laban. The prophecy about Bethlehem Ephratah, the site of Rachel's grave, takes them to Rachel, the origin of Laban's anger, and then "call my son out of Egypt" reminds them of the dream when God told Jacob to escape there, even though their baby sons were killed there by the sons of Balaam. The weeping of Rachel when she foresaw the suffering before the final eschatological exodus reminded them that the first exodus and that the special child whom Balaam-Laban was trying to kill was not merely Moses, but the coming Messiah. The final prompt that the Jews themselves call Jesus "the Natzeri" left the readers with the conclusion that Jesus is that Messiah, the "branch" of Isaiah 11, who was linked with the "star" of Numbers 24:17.

Therefore this chapter would have been read as an exposition of a Torah text (Num. 24:17) by means of a series of texts from the prophets. The Torah text has not been cited, but the chapter opens with a concept from that text (the star) and ends by leading back to that same text via the linked concepts in Isaiah 11. This structure was very familiar to anyone attending synagogue in the first century and beyond, because it follows the most common sermonic structure of the time — the Proem sermon.

Hundreds of examples of Proem sermons have survived in *Midrash*

---

31. Matt. 2:2: τὸν ἀστέρα ἐν τῇ ἀνατολῇ; cf. LXX Num. 24:17: ἀνατελεῖ ἄστρον. The form of the phrase in Matthew can be translated "in the East," though it is similar to the technical phrase "in its rising" (with an additional αὐτοῦ — see Davies and Allison ad loc.) and the LXX parallel supports this translation.

Rabbah and other rabbinic literature.[32] The first readers of Matthew would have felt as comfortable and familiar with this structure as any Baptist who hears the preacher say "The first of my three points is . . . ," or any Catholic who hears "The Saint we remember on this day is. . . ." The fact that the underlying text is never mentioned is entirely normal for this type of sermon. First-century Jewish listeners would be able to identify the opening text, and be able to recognize the links to that text, and they would be waiting for the final link to bring them satisfyingly back home to the original text.

Not all of Matthew's readers would have appreciated his use of these stories. The fact that the Targum writers can assume their readers would know this story suggests that Matthew can do the same, but not everyone had a high regard for them. In particular, we see the rabbis were trying to discredit the idea of the Balaam-Laban identity and probably had a very low view of this popular mythology.[33] More sophisticated readers would think about the contexts of each citation and consider the way in which Matthew found a messianic interpretation in each case, while ignoring the structure based on a popular story as irrelevant. They might have wanted to make a different structure based on Moses, or David, but Matthew chose something different. Gentile readers would not know the Balaam-Laban stories and would probably not realize that there was any need to justify the use of these various texts, except as prophecies of a Jewish Messiah. All readers, at all levels, could understand that Matthew regarded the Old Testament as a signpost to the messianic credentials of Jesus. As France has pointed out, Matthew can be read on many levels.

Therefore the Jewish original readers of Matthew 2 would not have regarded the four citations of Scripture as "isolated and disparate proof-texts" (which is how many modern readers regard them) but as the formal structural markers of a careful exposition of Balaam's prophecy, leading to the conclusion that the baby Jesus is the Messiah, as foretold in the Hebrew Scriptures.

---

32. See the introduction by Isaiah Sonne in Jacob Mann, *The Bible as Read and Preached in the Old Synagogue* (vol. 1, New York: KTAV, 1971; vol. 2, Cincinnati: Hebrew Union College, 1966). Unfortunately, the rabbinic collections which contain these sermons were compiled relatively late, and the individual sermons are almost impossible to date. However, it is possible to identify this sermon form in the NT — see John Westerdale Bowker, "Speeches in Acts: A Study in Proem and *Yelammedenu* Form," *NTS* 14 (1967): 96-111, esp. p. 100.

33. This is perhaps similar to the approbation directed against me when I used quotations from the "Terminator" films to illustrate a Gospel sermon ("Trust me," "I'll be back," and "Judgment Day is inevitable"). Older Christians were uncertain about using illustrations from such a popular and disreputable source, though younger uncommitted listeners thought that the comparison was amusing and memorable.

"The Virgin Will Conceive":
Typological Fulfillment in Matthew 1:18-23

James M. Hamilton Jr.

Introduction

What does Isaiah 7:14 mean in its own context? Does Matthew[1] show awareness of this context? Does he respect it, and, for that matter, how does he use the word "fulfilled"?[2] Is the validity of the way that Matthew quotes Isaiah 7:14 affected by whether or not the Hebrew term *'almah* (עַלְמָה) refers strictly to a "virgin"?[3] In this essay, I will address each of these issues as I seek to demonstrate the thesis that Matthew was not claiming that the OT prophet was making a future prediction about Israel's Messiah when he wrote, "Now the whole of this has happened in order that what was spoken by the Lord through the

---

1. Authorship of the first gospel is disputed (see, e.g., Martin Hengel, *The Four Gospels and the One Gospel of Jesus Christ* [Harrisburg, Pa.: Trinity Press International, 2000], 65-78). I follow E. Earle Ellis, *The Making of the New Testament Documents* (Boston: Brill, 2002), 36: "The second-century sources probably identify the four Evangelists correctly. The arguments against these identifications are not decisive and often rest on questionable assumptions. . . ."

2. See especially the aorist passive forms of πληρόω in Matt. 1:22; 2:15, 17, 23. Cf. also the use of the verb elsewhere in Matthew at 3:15; 4:14; 5:17; 8:17; 12:17; 13:35, 48; 21:4; 23:32; 26:54, 56; 27:9. For the formula ἵνα πληρωθῇ, which is used only in Matthew and John, see Matt. 1:22; 2:15; 4:14; 12:17; 21:4. For the formula ὅπως πληρωθῇ, see Matt. 2:23; 8:17; 13:35. Ellis writes of ἵνα πληρωθῇ, "Along with other 'fulfilment' formulas, it is favoured by the Hebraist missioners to underscore their perception of salvation history as it is consummated in Jesus" (E. Earle Ellis, "Biblical Interpretation in the New Testament Church," in *Mikra: Text, Translation, Reading and Interpretation of the Hebrew Bible in Ancient Judaism and Early Christianity* [CRINT 2.1; Philadelphia: Fortress, 1988; reprint Peabody, Mass.: Hendrickson, 2004], 693). For extensive bibliography, see Warren Carter, "Evoking Isaiah: Matthean Soteriology and an Intertextual Reading of Isaiah 7–9 and Matthew 1:23 and 4:15-16," *JBL* 119 (2000): 503 n. 1.

3. Ulrich Luz (*Matthew 1–7* [Minneapolis: Augsburg Fortress, 1989], 123-24) writes, "Luther declared his willingness to pay the 'stubborn, condemned Jews' a hundred guilders if Isa. 7:14 really means 'young woman' and not 'virgin.' He owes them."

prophet might be fulfilled, saying, 'Behold, the virgin will have in the womb, and she will bear a son, and they will call his name Immanuel, which is, having been translated, God with us" (Matt. 1:22-23).[4] The thesis of this essay offers one way to understand how it can be that Matthew *both* respects the OT contexts of the texts he cites *and* sees them being fulfilled in Jesus.

Not a few authors have held the position that Isaiah 7:14 predicted the coming of the Messiah in the distant future.[5] On the other hand, some are extremely confident that this position is untenable, and Jensen goes so far as to say, "No critical scholar today holds that Isaiah directly foretold the birth of Jesus of a virgin."[6] But it seems that this does not have to be an issue of being a "critical scholar" (with its overtones of the rejection of the supernatural), though it is an issue of interpreting Isaiah 7:14 in its own historical and literary context. One does get the impression that the sacrosanctity of this passage has kept some from allowing Isaiah 7:14 to mean what it appears to say,[7] while, on the other side, an iconoclastic attitude, or at least the perception of such,[8] has prevented

---

4. Unless otherwise noted, all translations are my own. I deliberately seek to be as direct as possible in these translations. For the text form Matthew employed here, see Richard Beaton, *Isaiah's Christ in Matthew's Gospel* (SNTSMS 123; Cambridge: Cambridge University Press, 2002), 88-90.

5. See, e.g., Justin Martyr, *First Apology*, chap. 33 (*ANF* 1:174); idem, *Dialogue with Trypho*, chs. 43 (*ANF* 1:216) and 66 (*ANF* 1:231); Irenaeus, *Against Heresies* 21.4 (*ANF* 1:452); Origen, *Against Celsus* 1.34-35 (*ANF* 4:410-11); Patrick Fairbairn *The Typology of Scripture* (Grand Rapids: Eerdmans, 1963 [1845-47]), 1:380; Leonhard Goppelt, *Typos: The Typological Interpretation of the Old Testament in the New* (Grand Rapids: Eerdmans, 1982; reprint Wipf and Stock, 2002 [1939]), 84 n. 103; Robert Horton Gundry, *The Use of the Old Testament in St. Matthew's Gospel: With Special Reference to the Messianic Hope* (NovTSup 18; Leiden: Brill, 1967), 226-27; Edward J. Young, *The Book of Isaiah* (3 vols.; Grand Rapids: Eerdmans, 1965), 1:283-94; C. F. D. Moule, "Fulfilment-Words in the New Testament: Use and Abuse," *NTS* 14 (1968): 297; George M. Soares Prabhu, *The Formula Quotations in the Infancy Narrative of Matthew: An Enquiry into the Tradition History of Mt 1-2* (AnBib 63; Rome: Biblical Institute Press, 1976), 251; Daniel Schibler, "Messianism and Messianic Prophecy in Isaiah 1-12 and 28-33," in *The Lord's Anointed* (ed. Philip E. Satterthwaite, Richard S. Hess, and Gordon J. Wenham; Grand Rapids: Baker, 1995), 100 n. 55.

6. Joseph Jensen, "Immanuel," in *ABD* 3:393.

7. Thus Rikki E. Watts, "Immanuel: Virgin Birth Proof Text or Programmatic Warning of Things to Come (Isa. 7:14 in Matt. 1:23)?" in *From Prophecy to Testament* (ed. C. A. Evans; Peabody, Mass.: Hendrickson, 2004), 92: "Although it is widely recognized that Isa. 7:14 does not appear to predict a viriginal conception, that as far as we can tell the oracle was not understood messianically in contemporary Judaism, and that Jesus' miraculous origin is hardly of major concern in the NT, the general opinion is that this has not prevented Matthew from ingeniously reading the Immanuel oracle as a prophecy of Jesus' virgin birth."

8. Luz (*Matthew 1-7*, 124) writes, "The traditional church interpretation . . . turns out to be evidence of Christian sin."

some who believe in the virgin birth (as I do) from accepting arguments regarding the context of Isaiah 7:14.[9] My objective in this essay is to argue for an understanding of Matthew's use of Isaiah 7:14 which allows the text to mean what it says in its OT context. That is to say, I am not arguing against the virgin birth by saying that Isaiah was not predicting it. Matthew's testimony to the virgin birth of Jesus is sufficient for it to be established. The question for this study is how Matthew understands and claims fulfillment for the OT.

Affirming that when read in the broad context of Isaiah's messianic expectation the text does contribute to Isaianic Messianism, I will nevertheless argue here that in the immediate context of Isaiah 7 the statement in verse 14 refers to something that will take place during the life of King Ahaz.[10] While it may be true that the prophecy has a dual application,[11] the interpretation I will present incorporates Matthew's understanding of the Isaianic context.[12] The crucial premise for my argument is that Matthew does not mean by *fulfillment* what many assume that he means (the realization of a future prediction). For example, Gundry writes that Matthew pursues a course of "transforming historical statements in the OT — those concerning the Exodus and the Babylonian Exile — into messianic prophecies."[13] If it were shown that Matthew does refer to things long ago predicted now coming to pass when he uses fulfillment language, my thesis would be falsified.[14]

I am positing a clarification of one aspect of the range of meaning of the word "fulfill" (πληρόω). Delling describes the places where the word is used for

---

9. Raymond E. Brown notes, "The RSV was burned by fundamentalists in some parts of the United States because it used 'young woman' rather than 'virgin' in Isa. 7:14 — a sign to the book burners that the translators were denying the virginal conception of Jesus! The reading 'virgin' was imposed by a decision of the American bishops on the reluctant Catholic translators of the NAB" (*The Birth of the Messiah* [ABRL; New York: Doubleday, 1993 {1977}], 146 n. 37).

10. So also Geoffrey W. Grogan, "Isaiah," in *The Expositor's Bible Commentary* (ed. F. E. Gaebelein; vol. 6; Grand Rapids: Zondervan, 1986), 63-64; John N. Oswalt, *The Book of Isaiah Chapters 1–39* (NICNT; Grand Rapids: Eerdmans, 1986), 209-13; John H. Walton, "Isa 7:14: What's in a Name?" *JETS* 30 (1987): 289, 297; John D. W. Watts, *Isaiah 1–33* (WBC; Waco, Tex.: Word, 1985), 97-101; Brown, *Birth of the Messiah*, 147; Donald A. Hagner, *Matthew 1–13* (WBC; Dallas: Word, 1993), 20.

11. As argued by J. A. Motyer, "Context and Content in the Interpretation of Isaiah 7:14," *TynBul* 21 (1970), 124, and R. H. Gundry, *Matthew* (2nd ed.; Grand Rapids: Eerdmans, 1994), 25.

12. Contra John D. W. Watts, *Isaiah 1–33*, 103: "A second factor facilitated the use of Isa. 7:14 in Matthew. A hermeneutical method was in general use which allowed verses to be separated from their contexts."

13. Gundry, *Matthew*, 37. Similarly Michael Knowles, *Jeremiah in Matthew's Gospel: The Rejected-Prophet Motif in Matthean Redaction* (JSNTSup 68; Sheffield: Sheffield Academic Press, 1993), 226.

14. Cf. Grogan, *Isaiah*, 64.

the fulfillment of prophecy as follows: "'To complete,' 'to fulfill' prophetic sayings which were spoken with divine authority and which can thus be called directly the words of God."[15] It is not clear, however, what sort of fulfillment he has in mind, and this complaint can be made against the relevant section of BDAG as well, where we read that the word is used of "the fulfillment of divine predictions or promises."[16] The assessment of Davies and Allison is similarly vague: "Matthew's formula is a development of the early Christian use of πληρόω to indicate OT texts fulfilled in the story of Jesus."[17] So these authors agree that "fulfill" (πληρόω) can be used to point to the fulfillment of OT texts, but is this a *predictive* fulfillment or a *typological* fulfillment? Delling makes reference to typological fulfillment in his discussion, but he cites only Luke 22:16 as a possible instance. This essay will propose that Matthew has typological fulfillment in view when he states that something has been fulfilled in 1:22; 2:15, 17, and 23. I know of no other treatment that has argued for the typological understanding I seek to set forth, not even studies of typology.[18]

When we examine the five texts cited in the first two chapters of Matthew's Gospel,[19] we find that in their original contexts only Micah 5:2 might be construed as a prophecy about the distant future. And when Matthew cites this text he does not use a form of the word "fulfill" (πληρόω) but introduces the citation with the words, "for so it has been written through the prophet" (Matt. 2:5). In the other four cases, the verb "fulfill" is used, and each time, in Hagner's words, "the quoted texts themselves are . . . not even predictive of future events."[20] To draw the conclusion from this that Matthew has no regard for historical or literary context when he cites the OT[21] would be to rush to a conclusion that assumes a meaning of the word "fulfilled" that Matthew might not, in fact, intend.

---

15. Gerhard Delling, "πληρόω," in *TDNT*, 6:295.

16. BDAG, s.v., 829.

17. W. D. Davies and Dale C. Allison, *A Critical and Exegetical Commentary on the Gospel according to Saint Matthew* (3 vols.; ICC; Edinburgh: T&T Clark, 1988-97), 3:574.

18. Cf. Fairbairn, *Typology of Scripture*, 1:380; Goppelt, *Typos*, 84 n. 103. My interpretation differs from J. Daniélou's *From Shadows to Reality: Studies in the Biblical Typology of the Fathers* (London: Burns & Oates, 1960), 15.

19. (1) Isaiah 7:14 in Matthew 1:22-23; (2) Micah 5:2 in Matthew 2:5-6; (3) Hosea 11:1 in Matthew 2:15; (4) Jeremiah 31:15 (with Genesis 37:30) in Matthew 2:17-18; and (5) no identifiable text in Matthew 2:23.

20. Hagner, *Matthew 1–13*, lv.

21. As, for example, Rudolf Bultmann and S. V. McCasland do. See Bultmann, "Prophecy and Fulfillment," trans. James C. G. Greig, in *Essays on Old Testament Hermeneutics* (ed. Claus Westermann; Richmond, Va.: John Knox, 1963), 51-52; and S. V. McCasland, "Matthew Twists the Scriptures," *JBL* 80 (1961): 143-48; reprinted in *The Right Doctrine from the Wrong Texts* (ed. G. K. Beale; Grand Rapids: Baker, 1994), 146-52 (reprint cited herein), see esp. 147, 149.

Predictive or Typological Fulfillment?

Concentrating mainly on the first text cited, Isaiah 7:14, I will argue that when Matthew speaks of the OT being "fulfilled" he refers to *typological* rather than *predictive* fulfillment.[22] At the risk of oversimplification I offer these brief explanations of predictive and typological fulfillment.[23]

Predictive fulfillment would require that when Matthew states that something has been fulfilled, he means that the prophet was speaking specifically of the coming of the Messiah in the distant future. As Young put it in his commentary on Isaiah with reference to 7:14, "This is prediction, and in the birth of Jesus Christ it found its fulfillment."[24] Matthew does appear to cite some OT texts this way (e.g., Micah 5:2 in Matthew 2:5-6), but, as noted above, in this instance he does not use the verb "fulfill" in the citation formula. If we maintain that Matthew has predictive fulfillment in view when he refers to the OT being *fulfilled* in Jesus, the OT contexts create problems for our proposed interpretations. If Matthew has predictive fulfillment in view, Bultmann's allegation might be on the mark: "the writers in the New Testament do not gain new

---

22. For excellent surveys of the issues generated by the technique called typology, see David Baker, "Typology and the Christian Use of the Old Testament," *SJT* 29 (1976): 137-57; reprinted in *The Right Doctrine from the Wrong Texts* (ed. G. K. Beale; Grand Rapids: Baker, 1994), 313-30 (reprint cited herein), and R. T. France, *Jesus and the Old Testament* (Vancouver: Regent College Press, 1998 [1971]), 38-43. For a study of the use of typology in the Old Testament, see Francis Foulkes, *The Acts of God: A Study of the Basis of Typology in the Old Testament* (London: Tyndale, 1955; reprinted in *The Right Doctrine from the Wrong Texts,* 342-71, reprint cited herein). For typology in extrabiblical Jewish literature, see Goppelt, *Typos,* 23-58. Ellis ("Biblical Interpretation," 173) writes, "Typological interpretation had been employed earlier in Judaism [citing the exodus as the model or 'type' by which the OT prophets understood God's subsequent acts of redemption of Israel and the Gentiles; cf. Isa. 40–66] and became, in early Christianity, a basic key by which the scriptures were understood." So also William Horbury, "Old Testament Interpretation in the Writings of the Church Fathers," in *Mikra,* 766: "Typology . . . is already found within the OT (as in passages on a new exodus). . . ." For the typological use of the OT in the OT prophets, see also Gerhard von Rad, *Old Testament Theology* (2 vols.; OTL; trans. D. M. G. Stalker; Louisville: Westminster John Knox, 1962, 1965), 2:323: "They looked for a new David, a new Exodus, a new covenant, a new city of God: the old had thus become a type of the new and important as pointing forward to it" (cf. 272, 365); Walther Eichrodt, "Is Typological Exegesis an Appropriate Method?" trans. James Barr, in *Essays on Old Testament Hermeneutics,* 234: "even in Old Testament prophecy itself typology is already playing a part" (citing numerous examples, 234-35).

23. For other brief descriptions of the relationship between typology and prediction-fulfillment, see Eichrodt, "Typological Exegesis," 229; Knowles, *Jeremiah in Matthew's Gospel,* 226.

24. Young, *Isaiah,* 1:294.

knowledge from the Old Testament texts, but read from or into them what they already know."[25]

As we consider typological fulfillment, we begin by noting with Alsup that "Much of what was later used to discredit typology was based on the misperceptions of typology as allegory stemming from developments within [the] patristic period."[26] Typological fulfillment is neither allegory nor *sensus plenior*,[27] and in contrast to predictive fulfillment, it does not necessarily maintain that the prophet is looking into the distant future and prophesying about something outside his own historical context.[28] Rather, typological fulfillment in the life of Jesus refers to the *fullest expression of a significant pattern of events*.[29] Thus, typological interpretation sees in biblical narratives a divinely intended pattern of events. Events that take place at later points in salvation history correspond to these and intensify their significance.[30] As Ellis writes,

---

25. Bultmann, "Prophecy and Fulfillment," 54. See also Richard T. Mead, "A Dissenting Opinion about Respect for Context in Old Testament Quotations," *NTS* 10 (1964): 279-89, reprinted in Beale, ed., *The Right Doctrine from the Wrong Texts*, 153-63, see esp. 154-55, where Mead alleges that in Matt. 2:18 "the historical Old Testament situation is thoroughly disregarded." Contrast Goppelt (*Typos*, 204), arguing that in their use of typology the NT authors respect the meaning of OT texts: "When Christian salvation is read into the OT, both the OT and the reality of Christ are distorted."

26. John E. Alsup, "Typology," in *ABD* 6:684. See Goppelt, *Typos*, 203-5, where he argues that "the *Epistle of Barnabas* . . . has abandoned the most important aspect of NT typology."

27. Hagner seems to conflate *sensus plenior* with typology. He describes *sensus plenior* as "a fuller or deeper sense within the quoted material not understood by the original author but now detectable in the light of the new revelatory fulfillment" (*Matthew 1–13*, lvi). Thus far what he is describing can be called *sensus plenior*, but in his next sentence he brings in what seems to be better described as typology, drawing no distinction between the two: "This is not an arbitrary, frivolous misuse of the texts, as is sometimes claimed, but *a reasoned practice that assumes a divinely intended correspondence between God's saving activity at different times in the history of redemption*" (emphasis added). The italicized words are similar to the definition of typology adopted here, emphasizing historical correspondence and escalation. See the helpful discussion in Douglas J. Moo, "The Problem of *Sensus Plenior*," in *Hermeneutics, Authority, and Canon* (ed. D. A. Carson and John D. Woodbridge; Grand Rapids: Zondervan, 1986), 179-211, esp. 202: "The *sensus plenior* is to be distinguished from typology; the former has to do with the deeper meaning of *words*, the latter with the extended meaning of *things*."

28. See France, *Jesus and the Old Testament*, 39-42. Some of the typology in the OT, for instance in Isaiah 40–66, is looking beyond its own historical context into the eschatological future.

29. Delling ("πληρόω," in *TDNT*, 6:296) writes, "Fulfilment means that in the today of the NT God's saving will achieves its full measure in the Christ event. The NT concept of fulfilment is summed up in the person of Jesus."

30. E. Earle Ellis, "Foreword" to Leonhard Goppelt, *Typos* (trans. Donald H. Madvig; Grand Rapids: Eerdmans, 1982; reprint Wipf and Stock, 2002 [1939]), x. Baker rejects "increase" or "progression" from type to antitype as a characteristic of typology ("Typology and the Chris-

"typology views the relationship of OT events to those in the new dispensation not as a 'one-to-one' equation or correspondence, in which the old is repeated or continued, but rather in terms of two principles, historical correspondence and escalation."[31]

In order to argue that *typological* rather than *predictive* fulfillment is in view in the early chapters of Matthew, this study will focus primarily on Matthew's first use of the "fulfillment" formula. Other texts will be brought in as corroborating evidence after both Isaiah 7 and Matthew 1 have been examined.

The Context of Isaiah 7:14

Isaiah 7:1 identifies the historical time frame in which the sign of Immanuel was given: "And it came about in the days of Ahaz, son of Jotham, son of Uzziah, king of Judah."[32] Isaiah 7:1-6 gives insight into the political context that the sign of

---

tian Use of the Old Testament," 326). But since the Christians conceive of themselves as those upon whom the "ends of the ages have come" (1 Cor. 10:11), all things — including the fulfillment of types — take on greater significance (see also Matt. 11:11, where the least in the Kingdom of Heaven is greater than John the Baptist, the greatest OT prophet). Even in the OT the "new Exodus" will make the "former things" to be forgotten (Isa. 43:18-19). Eichrodt ("Typological Exegesis," 233-34) writes, "typology is concerned with the depiction in advance of an eschatological, and therefore an unsurpassable, reality, which stands toward the type in the relation of something much greater or of something antithetically opposed." Similarly Foulkes, *The Acts of God*, 343, 356. Darrell L. Bock (*Proclamation from Prophecy and Pattern: Lucan Old Testament Christology* [JSNTSup; Sheffield: Sheffield Academic, 1987], 49-50) identifies the presence or absence of escalation as the feature that distinguishes typology from analogy.

31. Ellis, "Foreword," x; Goppelt, *Typos*, 202. Horbury ("Old Testament Interpretation in the Writings of the Church Fathers," 766) writes, "Typology can be said to differ from allegorical interpretation in that it takes seriously the historical setting of an OT law or event; type and antitype identify some correspondence between different stages in a sacred history, whereas allegory elicits timeless truth from beneath the veil of the biblical 'letter', which may be regarded as having no reference to history." The entry on "types" in the *Oxford Dictionary of the Christian Church* (3rd ed.; ed. E. A. Livingstone; Oxford: Oxford University Press, 1997), is similar: "In theology, the foreshadowings of the Christian dispensation in the events and persons of the OT.... A Christian type differs from allegory in that the historical reference is not lost sight of. Types are looked upon, however, as having a greater significance now than was apparent in their pre-Christian OT context" (1649); so also Goppelt discussing Philo (*Typos*, 52). Eichrodt ("Typological Exegesis," 225) writes: "The so-called *tupoi* . . . are persons, institutions, and events of the Old Testament which are regarded as divinely established models or prerepresentations of corresponding realities in the New Testament salvation history. These latter realities, on the basis of 1 Peter 3:21, are designated 'antitypes'" (cf. 227, where Eichrodt distinguishes between allegory and typology).

32. In this discussion I am concerned only with the text of Isaiah as it stands. For a discus-

Immanuel addresses. The king of Syria, Rezin, has aligned himself with Pekah, the son of King Remaliah of Israel — the northern kingdom in the divided realm of Israel and Judah (7:1).[33] Their plans to attack the southern kingdom of Judah (7:1-2, 5-6) in order to set up a puppet king there (7:6) were made known to Ahaz, the king of Judah, and these plans quailed him and his people (7:2).

Yahweh responds to Ahaz's fright by sending Isaiah to meet Ahaz (7:3). Isaiah is to reassure Ahaz that what Syria and Israel are planning will neither stand nor come to pass (7:7). Rather, the enemies of Judah will have their heads broken (7:8-9).[34] Ahaz is urged to ask for a confirming sign from Yahweh that he might trust that the danger from the north will not materialize (7:10-11).[35] Ahaz refuses to "test Yahweh" (7:12), but Isaiah sees the refusal to ask for a sign as an indication of faithlessness. He responds to Ahaz's refusal with a denunciation (7:13) and the sign of Immanuel (7:14).

The sign of Immanuel is not limited to the statement in 7:14; it continues through chapter 8. The statement in 7:16 roots the sign of Immanuel firmly in the historical context with which the chapter is dealing, "For before the boy knows to reject the evil and choose the good, the land before whose two kings you are terrified will be deserted."[36] This appears to mean that a child will be born in the near future, and that before this child is old enough to discern good and evil the threat from Syria and Israel will be resolved by the devastation of Ephraim, the northern kingdom of Israel, and Syria. This devastation seems to be the subject of 7:17–8:10, as the prophet describes the coming of Assyria against Syria, Israel, and then Judah. The devastation of the land appears to result in underpopulation because of the many slain (7:21-25), and it is apparently this scarcity of people that results in the abundance of food Immanuel will en-

---

sion of the redactional history of the text, see H. G. M. Williamson, "The Messianic Texts in Isaiah 1–39," in *King and Messiah in Israel and the Ancient Near East* (ed. John Day; JSOTSup 270; Sheffield: Sheffield Academic, 1998), 244-50.

33. Israel is referred to as Ephraim in 7:2, 5, 8, 9, 17, etc. Cf. Siegfried Hermann, "Ephraim (Person)," in *ABD* 2:551.

34. The head-shattering language may echo Genesis 3:15, calling Ahaz to trust in Yahweh's promise.

35. Whether Isa. 7:10-25 is continuing the encounter with Ahaz on the highway to the fuller's field (7:3) or represents a later proclamation does not affect the thesis of this study. From a literary perspective, the juxtaposition of the two oracles to Ahaz with no indication of a change in time or place would seem to indicate that the two are to be read together.

36. "The sign cannot refer to Jesus, argued Ibn Ezra, since it calls for verification in the near future" (Joseph Blenkinsopp, *Isaiah 1–39* [AB; Garden City, N.Y.: Doubleday, 2000], 233). "Some authors emphasize the difficulty of relating Immanuel to Isaiah's historical context in order to favor a more strictly messianic interpretation" (Joseph Jensen, "Immanuel," in *ABD* 3:393).

joy when he has matured enough to know the difference between good and evil (cf. 7:15 with 7:22).[37]

Significantly, there is no direct evidence that the child to be born will be from the line of David, and it appears from the near context that the child might be Isaiah's (8:3),[38] though this is disputed.[39] The reference in Isaiah 8:18 to Isaiah and the children given to him being signs and portents in Israel fits with the three children named (Shear-jashub, Immanuel, and Maher-shalal-hash-baz) being his.[40] The relevance of the birth of the child to the threat from Syria and Israel is seen again in 8:3-4, where Isaiah fathers a child (8:3), and the word comes that "before the child knows how to call, 'my father,' or, 'my mother,' the wealth of Damascus [Syria, 7:8] will be carried away along with the spoil of Samaria [Israel/Ephraim, 7:9] before the king of Assyria." This statement appears to elaborate upon 7:16, and if that is the case, it is tempting to identify Maher-shalal-hash-baz (8:1, 3) with Immanuel (7:14; 8:8, 10).[41]

The identification of Maher-shalal-hash-baz with Immanuel appears to be corroborated by 8:5-7, where Rezin and Pekah are still in view (8:6), and the promise that they will be swept away by the king of Assyria is restated in 8:7. The overflowing flood of the Assyrian army will not stop in the north, however, but will continue down into the land of Judah, the land of Immanuel (8:8).

The promise to Ahaz from 7:7 that the plan of Syria and Israel "will not stand (לֹא תָקוּם)" was verified by the promised sign of Immanuel (7:14), and this appears to be restated in 8:10. Following the breaking (רֹעוּ) and shattering (חַתּוּ) of the peoples (8:9; cf. the breaking of Ephraim [חַתּ] in 7:9), the promise comes again: "but it will not stand because of Immanuel (וְלֹא יָקוּם כִּי עִמָּנוּ אֵל)" (8:10).[42] This restates the assurance to Judah that they will not be over-

---

37. So Joseph Jensen, "Immanuel," in *ABD* 3:394. For other options, and the dialogue is extensive, see the discussion and bibliography cited in Rikki E. Watts, "Immanuel," 98-99.

38. "Ibn Ezra, followed by Rashi, identified the young woman as Isaiah's wife and Immanuel as his son" (Blenkinsopp, *Isaiah 1-39*, 233). Cf. Von Rad, *Old Testament Theology*, 2:173-74. This was Jerome's view as well, and H. G. M. Williamson in 1998 called it "increasingly popular" ("The Messianic Texts in Isaiah 1-39," 245; see too the bibliography he cites in note 15).

39. For an argument against this view, see Walton, "Isa 7:14: What's in a Name?" 295-97. Cf. Blenkinsopp, *Isaiah 1-39*, 233: "by now the scholarly debate on the designation of the woman and the name of the child practically defies documentation." Rikki E. Watts concludes, "the text as it stands offers nothing specific. . . . It is also worth noting that if Shear-jashub is not himself the remnant, nor Maher-shalal-Hash-Baz the spoiler, then it is unlikely that this second child is himself somehow 'God with us'" ("Immanuel," 96).

40. Cf. H. G. M. Williamson, *Variations on a Theme: King, Messiah and Servant in the Book of Isaiah* (Carlisle, U.K.: Paternoster, 1998), 102-3.

41. Cf. Motyer, "The Interpretation of Isaiah 7:14," 124.

42. Most English translations follow the Greek translation of the OT at 8:10, rendering

come by Syria and Israel: the plan will not stand because God has given a sign to his people — Immanuel, God is with us — and this sign guarantees his promise for them. The words of Isaiah 8:12, "Do not call conspiracy all that this people calls conspiracy, and neither fear nor tremble (plural verbs) at what he (singular pronominal suffix, referring to Ahaz in 7:2?) fears," could be referring to the conspiracy between Syria and Israel to unseat Ahaz. Since Ahaz has apparently rejected Isaiah's message (7:12-13), Isaiah commits his words to his disciples (8:16) and resolves to wait for Yahweh (8:17), noting that he and his children are "signs and portents in Israel from Yahweh of hosts who dwells on Mount Zion" (8:18).

Thus, it seems that in the context of Isaiah 7–8, the promise of the birth of a child who will be named Immanuel is a sign that guarantees God's promise that the plan concocted by Syria and Israel to dethrone Ahaz and replace him with one they can control will not stand. God's people were threatened and uncertain. God promised through Isaiah that they would be delivered from these circumstances, and the promise of deliverance was guaranteed by the birth of a child. This child would be born to a mother who could have been a virgin when the promise was made, or perhaps she was simply a young woman of marriageable age — depending upon the meaning of the Hebrew word ʿalmah (עַלְמָה). But there is no indication in the text that this woman would not conceive through intercourse with a man.[43] If, as I have suggested, the birth of Maher-

---

עִמָּנוּאֵל not as I have it here, "Immanuel," but along the lines of, "It will not stand, for God is with us" (ESV, HCSB, NAB, NASU, NIV, NRSV, NLT, TANAK, etc.). These translations do not follow the Greek translation at 8:8, however, where most transliterate "Immanuel," but the TANAK renders, with the Greek, "with us is God." BHS indicates no distinction in the spacing of עִמָּנוּאֵל — it is spaced the same way in 7:14, 8:8, and 8:10. The Vulgate, like most ETs and LXX, has "Emmanuhel" at 7:14 and 8:8 and "nobiscum Deus" at 8:10. The Targum interprets "your land, O Immanuel" in 8:8 with "your land, O Israel," and "because of Immanuel (or, for God is with us)" in 8:10 as "for God is our help (or, because in our help is God, our God)."

43. Joseph Jensen, "Immanuel," in *ABD* 3:395. Gundry suggests that "we should have expected ʾishah if marriage were contemplated before conceiving and giving birth. The adjective [חָרָה] emphasizes the state of the ʿalmah's pregnancy, as if it had already begun; so that we must understand she conceives and bears in her status as ʿalmah.... Second, if marriage is not contemplated, ʿalmah is used in the sense of a young married woman. To this writer's knowledge, such a meaning for ʿalmah has never been demonstrated" (*The Old Testament in St. Matthew's Gospel*, 226-27). Gundry's suggestion that pregnancy is viewed as if it has already begun is countered by Jensen ("Immanuel," in *ABD* 3:393): "'the young woman . . .' will conceive (or: has conceived — the Hebrew does not clearly specify). . . ." Similarly, Grogan (*Isaiah*, 63). The usage of ʿalmah is, of course, endlessly disputed. It seems to me that neither of Gundry's objections derive from an exegetical analysis of Isaiah 7, but from the prior conviction that Isaiah is predicting what would take place 700 years later when Jesus was born of the virgin Mary. Rikki E. Watts writes, "Did Isaiah envisage this as a miraculous virgin birth? It is now widely agreed that

shalal-hash-baz is the realization of the promise, then the child appears to have been conceived when Isaiah "drew near to the prophetess" (8:3). This is my reading of the passage, but my argument is not falsified if the child is Ahaz's, or if one of the other proposed interpretations is adopted. The child's name, Immanuel, is apparently a reflection of the confidence of those who believed that God would keep his promise and protect them by his presence. In the wider context, there are pointers toward a child to be born who will be Mighty God (9:6),[44] but the child immediately in view in Isaiah 7:14 is a child whose birth will be relevant during the life of Ahaz. As Oswalt puts it, "To suppose that the sign did not occur in any sense until 725 years after the fact flies in the face of the plain sense of the text."[45]

Taken as a whole, Isaiah is a book fraught with Messianism, and this can be poignantly felt in chapters 7–11. It might be that Matthew read Isaiah 7:14 more in light of the many messianic statements in Isaiah and the OT than in the light of its immediate context in chapter 7, and if so, then perhaps Matthew read Isaiah 7:14 as a predictive prophecy of *the* Messiah.[46] But this interpretation does not appear to fit either Matthew or Isaiah. Matthew's fulfillment formulas in chapters 1 and 2 do not support this suggestion, as will be seen below, and in contrast to many passages in Isaiah that bear no explicit historical connections, there are many historical notices in chapters 7 and 8 which serve to anchor Isaiah 7:14 to a particular point in Israel's history. Taken in the context of Isaiah 7, it

---

he did not and, had it not been for Matthew's use of this text, it is extremely doubtful if anyone would ever have read it so" ("Immanuel," 100).

44. Oswalt (*Isaiah 1–39*, 246) insists that "such extravagant titling was not normal for Israelite kings," but Blenkinsopp suggests the translation "Hero Warrior" (*Isaiah 1–39*, 246, cf. 250). It is curious that Isaiah 9:6 is not cited in the NT as a proof-text for the deity of the Messiah (Appendix IV of NA[27], "Loci Citati Vel Allegait," lists only Luke 1:32 next to Isa. 9:6, but the correspondences in wording do not constitute a citation), nor does it seem that those who heralded Jesus as the Messiah were necessarily expecting that he be God incarnate. The "Son of God" language has these overtones, but it can be explained as referring to a human ruler who rules the way God would growing out of 2 Sam. 7:14 (cf. the peacemakers who are called "sons of God" in Matt. 5:9). It may be that in the case of Isa. 9:6 we have *sensus plenior*, Isaiah speaking better than he knows (for biblical recognition of *sensus plenior*, see John 11:51-52).

45. Oswalt, *Isaiah 1–39*, 208; similarly Luz, *Matthew 1–7*, 124.

46. So J. Gresham Machen, *The Virgin Birth of Christ* (San Francisco: Harper & Row, 1930), 291-92. Rikki E. Watts ("Immanuel," 104) insists that there is no "evidence that Isa 7:14 was ever understood in terms of a future messianic hope," but Hagner suggests, "Two things in particular were responsible for the later perception of this secondary level of meaning: the name given to the child . . . and the surrounding passages. . . . The promised son of Isa 7:14 thus became readily identifiable as that son of David who would bring the expected kingdom. . . . Accordingly, probably sometime in the third century B.C., the Greek translators of Isa 7:14 apparently regarded the passage as having a deeper meaning, as yet unrealized" (*Matthew 1–13*, 20).

is hard to deny that verse 14 directly predicts a child who would be born *during* rather than *after* Ahaz's life, and perhaps this accounts for the fact that Isaiah 7:14 "does not appear to have been widely cited in early Jewish literature and never in connection with a messianic figure."[47] Williamson rightly states, "in the immediate context the prediction of [Immanuel's] birth is securely tied to the prevailing historical circumstances of the reign of Ahaz, so that a long-range messianic prediction is ruled out, at least at the primary level."[48] If it is the case that the sign applies to Ahaz's day, and if Matthew respected the Isaianic context, what did he mean that the birth of Jesus "fulfilled" what was spoken in Isaiah 7:14?

The Context of Matthew 1:22-23

By opening with the statement that Jesus the Messiah is the son of David, son of Abraham, the Gospel of Matthew presents Jesus as the fulfillment of the promises to David and Abraham (1:1). A genealogy containing three sets of fourteen is then presented (Matt. 1:2-17).[49] This genealogy is geared to engender an expectation that the last days have come. "The new, Messianic age has dawned."[50]

In the last days, all that was spoken by the prophets would be fulfilled. As Davies and Allison note, "The early church found in the Scriptures the declared will of divine providence and believed that the life of Jesus in its every detail completely fulfilled that will. Thus arose the NT's distinctive sense of fulfillment and its distinctive πληρόω-formulas."[51] All of history was to culminate in the coming of the Kingdom of God. Yahweh would judge the nations from Jerusalem, the capital of the globe to which the nations would stream to learn his Torah (Isa. 2:1-4). Gloom would be banished, dawn would bring great joy, and the oppressor would be "broken as [in the past when God had delivered his people through Gideon] on the day of Midian" (Isa. 8:23–9:3 [ET 9:1-4]).[52] The

---

47. Beaton, *Isaiah's Christ in Matthew's Gospel*, 91.
48. Williamson, *Variations on a Theme*, 109.
49. The letters of the name David according to *gematria* add up to fourteen (ד 4 + ו 6 + ד 4), and, perhaps also of significance, in the three sets of fourteen there are six sets of seven, Messiah Jesus being the "head of the seventh seven, the seventh day of history, the dawn of the eternal sabbath" (Davies and Allison, *Matthew*, 1:162). Davies and Allison cite parallels (*1 Enoch* 93.1-10; 91.12-17), but note that "Matthew expressly writes of three fourteens, not six sevens." See too the comments on *gematria*, ibid., 163-65, where they conclude, "The name, David, is the key to the pattern of Matthew's genealogy."
50. France, *Jesus and the Old Testament*, 79.
51. Davies and Allison, *Matthew*, 1:211.
52. Foulkes ("The Acts of God," 343) writes that the prophets and historians of Israel "could assume . . . that as he had acted in the past, he could and would act in the future."

wilderness would become as the Garden of Eden (Isa. 51:3). With all these blessings would come a "branch from the stem of Jesse" (Isa. 11:1). His reign would be marked by the Spirit of Yahweh (11:2), resulting in just judgment (11:3-5) and the end of the age-old enmity between the seed of the woman and the seed of the serpent (11:8). There is little indication that these promises would not all be realized together, so the already/not yet dimension of the Kingdom Jesus brings is a surprise for all who are looking for the consolation of Israel.

After the genealogy, the opening chapters of Matthew show the recapitulation of the history of Israel in the life of Jesus. Following Matthew 1:18-25, which will receive more attention shortly, Jesus is presented as in danger from an evil ruler, much as Moses was. Just as the nation found itself in Egypt, and just as Moses was to command Pharaoh to release God's son Israel, so now God's son Jesus is summoned from Egypt. Just as there was weeping when the nation went into exile, so there was weeping after Herod slaughtered the infants of Bethlehem. Just as a voice in the wilderness heralded the return from exile, so John the Baptist prepared the way for Jesus. Just as the nation was tested in the wilderness before passing through the Jordan to possess the land, Jesus was baptized in the Jordan before being tested in the wilderness (see Matt. 1–4). At the head of these correspondences (and several others) between the life of Jesus and the history of Israel stands the account of Jesus' birth in Matthew 1:18-25.

In Isaiah's day, Judah was under threat from Syria and Ephraim. In the days Matthew narrates in his opening chapters, the nation is under threat from Rome, whose constant presence testified to the nation's ongoing subjugation.[53] In Isaiah's day the king, though a descendant of David, was faithless. In the days described in the first chapters of Matthew, the king over Jerusalem is also faithless, but now he is not even Jewish, to say nothing of the fact that he is not a descendant of David.[54] On the name of the child Carter observes a possible connection, "As with Isaiah's Immanuel, the child Jesus is a sign of resistance to imperial power. The name Immanuel contests imperial claims that Domitian is a *deus praesens* (Statius, *Silv.* 5.2.170) or θεὸς ἐπιφανής."[55] It seems that in Isaiah's day a believing remnant hoped to experience the fulfillment of the promises of God. Isaiah encouraged this remnant to believe that the birth of a child of promise was God's way of guaranteeing that he would deliver those faithful

---

53. Carter ("Evoking Isaiah," 507-8) writes, "The Isaiah texts evoke a situation of imperial threat, thereby establishing an analogy with the situation of the Gospel's authorial audience also living under imperial power, that of Rome, and also promised God's salvation (1:21)."

54. Carter ("Evoking Isaiah," 508) notes that response to the prophetic word colors the context: "The Isaiah texts . . . also raise the questions of how people will respond."

55. Carter, "Evoking Isaiah," 513. I am not necessarily convinced that Matthew is as late as Domitian.

to him (Isa. 8:20). A believing remnant within Israel persisted in the first century,[56] and for them too, the birth of a child of promise is a sign that God is going to keep his promises. Indeed, the early Christians saw all the promises confirmed in Jesus (cf. 2 Cor. 1:20).[57]

In addition to the historical correspondences between the details of Isaiah 7 and the time of the birth of Jesus, there is also an aspect of *escalation,* whereby the meaning of these events is intensified by the coming of the Messiah and the period in salvation history that begins with his arrival. Just as the significance of the time is increased, so also are the details from Isaiah 7 to Matthew 1. When we compare Isaiah 7 with Matthew 1, we see that whereas a woman who, perhaps, was a virgin conceived a child when Isaiah drew near (Isa. 7:14; 8:3), Joseph "was not knowing her until she bore a son; and he called his name Jesus" (Matt. 1:25). So while the woman in Isaiah 7:14 may or may not have been a virgin, Matthew testifies that Mary was and makes it explicit that she remained so until after Jesus' birth. Whereas the deliverance guaranteed by the birth of a child in Isaiah has to do with the threat from Syria and Ephraim, the deliverance guaranteed by the birth of the child in Matthew goes deeper: "he will save his people from their sins" (Matt. 1:21).[58] The child of which Isaiah speaks will be named "Immanuel" because his birth testifies to God's faithfulness to his promise not to abandon his people Israel (e.g., Deut. 31:6).[59] The child whose birth Matthew narrates, by contrast, will represent in his own person God's presence with his people (cf. Matt. 28:20).[60]

On this understanding, the sense in which Matthew's narrative *fulfills* Isaiah 7:14 has everything to do with *historical correspondence* and *escalation,*

---

56. See esp. Luke 2:25-35, 36-38, where Simeon and Anna are representatives of this remnant who welcome the birth of Jesus.

57. Carter ("Evoking Isaiah," 510-11) points out that these correspondences "are part of a larger pattern of God's ways of working." He cites themes of "resistance and the refusal to trust God's saving work, of imperial power as a means of divine punishment, and of God's saving the people from imperial power," and notes that "similar themes . . . could be elaborated in relation to the exodus, to prophetic views of Babylon's roles . . . , to the Deuteronomic view of exile . . . , to 2 Maccabees' perception of Antiochus Epiphanes as punisher of the people and as the one from whom God will liberate the people . . . , and to Pompey's violation of Jerusalem and the temple."

58. Similarly Rikki E. Watts, "Immanuel," 113: "In this case, at least 'fulfillment' seems better understood in paradigmatic terms: as Yahweh had acted in the past, so he would act again. Matthew sees Isa. 7:14 not as a proof-text for some long foretold virgin birth . . . but instead as a scriptural elucidation of the significance of Jesus, which elucidation works only if Jesus is already believed to be the climax of Israel's history."

59. For more on this theme in the Pentateuch, see James M. Hamilton Jr., "God with Men in the Torah," *WTJ* 65 (2003): 113-33.

60. Cf. also Carter, "Evoking Isaiah," 511.

whereas it has to do with *predictive fulfillment* only when Isaiah 7:14 is read as a contribution to Isaianic Messianism rather than as a contribution to Isaiah 7. Thus, Matthew can be seen to be respecting the context of Isaiah 7–8 and claiming that Isaiah 7:14 is indeed *fulfilled* (typologically) in the birth of Jesus. Davies and Allison write, "Later Judaism apparently did not understand Isa. 7.14 messianically; at least we have no positive evidence that it did. What Jewish traditions we do have connect the verse with Hezekiah (Justin, *Dial.* 43; *Exod. Rab.* on 12.29; *Num. Rab.* on 7.48). Thus the application of Isa. 7.14 to the Messiah is evidently peculiarly Christian."[61] This peculiarly Christian reading of Isaiah 7:14 is informed by the peculiar events of the birth of Jesus.

If this proposal is on the mark, the nuance of the Hebrew word *'almah,* so much discussed, is *irrelevant.* Taking Matthew's citation of Isaiah 7:14 as an instance of typological fulfillment, we see that there is historical correspondence and escalation, regardless of whether the Hebrew word refers strictly or primarily to a virgin. Thus the charge made by Bultmann and many others that "the Old Testament text only becomes of use when it is understood in a sense contrary to the original wording, according to the LXX text"[62] is eviscerated. The whole discussion of what *'almah* means, particularly in Proverbs 30:19 and Song of Songs 6:8, turns out to have been a red herring. Isaiah 7:14 does not predict that one day 700 years in the future the virgin Mary will give birth to the Messiah, nor does Matthew claim that it did. Matthew saw a particular pattern of events in Isaiah 7–8, and he claimed that this pattern of events was *fulfilled* in the corresponding, intensified pattern of events surrounding the birth of Jesus at the dawn of the new age. In the life of Jesus the pattern came to its fullest expression.

Typological Fulfillment in Matthew

If we reject typological fulfillment as a hermeneutical key with which to unlock the fulfillment language in Matthew, we are forced either to ignore the OT context or to conclude that "Matthew shows little awareness that the prophets might actually have been delivering oracles of crucial relevance to their original audiences."[63] With this perspective, it would indeed be difficult to "remove the interpreter's frustration with Matthew's use of the OT,"[64] and this would support the conclusion that Matthew's exegetical methods are illegitimate and

---

61. Davies and Allison, *Matthew,* 1:213.

62. Bultmann, "Prophecy and Fulfillment," 53.

63. David D. Kupp, *Matthew's Emmanuel: Divine Presence and God's People in the First Gospel* (SNTSMS 90; Cambridge: Cambridge University Press, 1996), 167.

64. Kupp, *Matthew's Emmanuel,* 169.

should not be practiced by modern interpreters of the Bible. If, on the other hand, typological fulfillment is practiced in the NT, might the NT's interpretations of the OT serve as an example of how modern interpreters should read the text?

The following brief explanations are offered in an attempt to embrace the perspective that might have driven Matthew's "fulfillment" formulas. Hosea 11:1 is famously cited in Matthew 2:15. In its OT context, this verse is manifestly not a prediction that one day the Messiah will be summoned from Egypt. Rather, the reference in Hosea 11:1 to God's son is a reference to the nation, as the statements preceding and following the words Matthew cites show. Before the words "and out of Egypt I called my son" (Hos. 11:1b) are the words, "When Israel was a youth I loved him" (11:1a). Then 11:2a reads, "They called to them, thus they went from before them" (so BHS), or, as most English translations have it (taking into account the Greek and Syriac translations), "Just as I called them, so they departed from my presence." This seems to be a reference to the nation of Israel being brought out of Egypt and sustained in the wilderness only to rebel against Yahweh, who had redeemed them. Matthew neither introduces this quotation because he is unable to find a better "proof-text" nor because he has failed to understand what Hosea was saying. Rather, Matthew cites these words because just as the nation, the collective son of God, was led out of Egypt by the pillar of fire and cloud to failure in the desert, so Jesus, the singular Son of God, was summoned out of Egypt and then led out to the desert by the Spirit to succeed against temptation (Matt. 4:1-11).[65] The historical circumstances correspond to one another, but the stakes are higher and Jesus is found faithful where the nation grumbled and rebelled.[66] The fulfillment of Hosea 11:1 in Matthew 2:15 is typological, as the elements of historical correspondence and escalation show.

France describes Jeremiah 31:15 as a "note of gloom in a chapter of joy."[67]

---

65. Similarly R. T. France, "The Formula-Quotations of Matthew 2 and the Problem of Communication," *NTS* 27 (1981): 233-51, reprinted in *The Right Doctrine from the Wrong Texts*, 114-34, see 125-26.

66. For a similar assessment, see Daniélou, *From Shadows to Reality*, 156-60. Against what I have articulated, John H. Sailhamer writes, "When Matthew quoted Hos 11:1 as fulfilled in the life of Christ, he was not resorting to typological interpretation. Rather, he was drawing on the *sensus literalis* from the book of Hosea and it, in turn, was drawn from Hosea's exegesis of the *sensus literalis* of the Pentateuch" ("Hosea 11:1 and Matthew 2:15," *WTJ* 63 [2001]: 91). I am sympathetic with Sailhamer's presentation, particularly with his argument that the OT is thoroughly messianic. He appears to have reservations about the legitimacy of typology (he refers to Matthew "resorting to" it again in his conclusion [96]). For somewhat more harsh objections to his argument, see Dan McCartney and Peter Enns, "Matthew and Hosea: A Response to John Sailhamer," *WTJ* 63 (2001): 97-105.

67. France, "Formula-Quotations," 128.

The chapter is replete with announcements that Yahweh will bring his people back from exile, but that good news necessarily entails the bad news — exile is coming. So, for example, there are references to those who survive the sword (31:2), to rebuilding and return to joy (31:4-5), to a return to the land (31:8), to the fact that the one who scattered Israel will shepherd them (31:10). But all of these promises of restoration assume that destruction is coming. Thus, it is not precisely correct to say, "In citing Jer. 31.15, Matthew has chosen the one verse in Jeremiah 31 that is negative in outlook."[68] The promises of restoration in the future are simultaneously promises of destruction in the present, as the broader context of Jeremiah shows. The reality of these coming woes accentuates the relief guaranteed by Yahweh's everlasting love for his people (31:3). Verse 15 is in this same vein: a matriarch of Israel, Rachel, is depicted as a figurative mother weeping for those slain in the devastating judgment that will come, but this is immediately followed by the call not to weep (31:16) because the future is hopeful (31:17).

The historical correspondences here are not hard to recognize.[69] The historical situation is anything but "thoroughly disregarded."[70] In Jeremiah's day, the devastation wrought by the enemies of the people of God is going to be swallowed up in the merciful salvation Yahweh will work for Israel. At the birth of Jesus, the wicked king Herod calls for the cruel murder of the babies of Bethlehem, but the lamentation deepens the joy felt that the Messiah escapes to bring salvation. And the salvation he brings is enriched because the pain has made it more precious.

Jeremiah's promises of the return from exile included God raising up David their King to lead them (30:9). The people returned to the land and waited for the Messiah, and Matthew proclaims that now, at long last, Jeremiah's oracles of the return from exile are fulfilled in the coming of Jesus. Jeremiah is pointing to the future restoration of God's people in these chapters, but the words cited in Matthew 2:18 are not predictive words.[71] Rather, it seems that Matthew is pointing to the correspondence between the weeping of the nation as it was sent into

---

68. Knowles, *Jeremiah in Matthew's Gospel*, 38.

69. *Pace* Knowles, *Jeremiah in Matthew's Gospel*, 41: "references to the context of Jeremiah 31 prove altogether elusive"; and Soares Prabhu, *Formula Quotations*, 261: "scarcely anything in the narrative links up with the quoted text."

70. Contra Mead, "Dissenting Opinion," 154-55.

71. For the text form of the citation of Jer. 31(LXX 38):15 in Matt. 2:18, see Knowles, *Jeremiah in Matthew's Gospel*, 36-38, and for more detail, Maarten J. J. Menken, "The Quotation from Jeremiah 31(38).15 in Matthew 2.18: A Study of Matthew's Scriptural Text," in Steve Moyise, ed., *The Old Testament in the New Testament* (JSNTSup 189; Sheffield: Sheffield Academic, 2000), 106-25.

exile and the weeping of the women of Bethlehem when their babes were slain. Just as the nation was exiled, Jesus was exiled to Egypt, from which, like the nation, he would be summoned to conquer the land. From these historical correspondences — and from the increased significance of the Messiah's conquest of the land — the fulfillment in view in Matthew 2:17-18 appears to be of a typological rather than a predictive stripe. If we reject typological fulfillment in these Matthean "fulfillment formulas," we must conclude with Knowles, "Matthew's use of Jer. 31.15 does not take account either of its biblical context or of its predominant interpretation in the Jewish schools and synagogues."[72] Since Matthew is seeking to persuade his contemporaries, and since there is evidence of typological interpretation in both the OT and in early Jewish literature,[73] this way of viewing the material seems more plausible.[74]

There is no OT text that states that the Messiah will be called a Nazarene, prompting many explanations of the words, "that what was spoken through the prophets might be fulfilled, that he shall be called a Nazarene" (Matt. 2:23). Eusebius connects the villages of Nazareth and Cochaba to those who were able to trace their Davidic descent (*Hist. eccl.* 1.7.14), which might indicate that families of the line of David had used words like "branch" (נֵצֶר) (Isa. 11:1) and "star"

---

72. Knowles, *Jeremiah in Matthew's Gospel*, 43, cf. also 39: "the verse evidently appeared to Matthew so applicable to the fate of Herod's victims that he ignored its original intent." As I understand typology, it draws attention to the divinely intended pattern of events which are seen to correspond to what takes place in the life of Jesus and later the church, and whose significance is heightened by the new stage in salvation history. Therefore, I cannot agree with Knowles's assertion that "Matthew's use of Jer. 31.15 . . . represents the essence of typology," though it suffers from "Ignoring altogether the original context of the passage" (*Jeremiah in Matthew's Gospel*, 51-52, see a similar typological explanation of Hos. 11:1, maintaining that it too is cited "entirely out of context" on pp. 225-26). Knowles acknowledges that typology is marked by historical correspondence and escalation (229 and n. 1). Though contemporary critical OT scholars do not always do this, Matthew would have based his understanding of Israel's history on the text of the OT, which is to say that he would have based it upon the OT context. I do not see how we can say that Matthew is pointing to historical correspondences between the life of Jesus and the history of Israel *and* disregarding the context of the OT passages he cites.

73. See especially Pseudo-Philo 12:3, which is quoted below in the conclusion of this study. Comparisons with earlier events in the history of Israel appear in Pseudo-Philo at 17:3; 32:1, 16; 40:2; 45:2; 54:2. These comparisons appear to reflect perceived historical correspondences between events at different points in Israel's history, and thus Baker would call them *typology*. Bock, on the other hand, might classify them as *analogy* since escalation is not explicit (see note 30 above).

74. Knowles (*Jeremiah in Matthew's Gospel*, 44) agrees with Bultmann: "Matthew's exegesis does not focus in the first instance on the text at hand, but rather, beginning with the revelatory event of Jesus' life, seeks a scriptural text that will reaffirm what is, in effect, already known" (see nn. 21 and 25 above).

(Aramaic, כּוֹכְבָא) (Num. 24:17) to name their villages because of the messianic significance of these terms. The fulfillment formula in Matthew 2:23 might thus refer to the way that the hope for a shoot from the root of Jesse is realized. Most explanations of this fulfillment formula appeal in some way to the word "branch (נֵצֶר)" in Isaiah 11:1. The lack of a text predicting what Matthew claims here makes it difficult to see this instance of the fulfillment formula in Matthew as the fulfillment of a prediction about the future from the standpoint of the OT prophet. The "fulfillment" is, again, pointing to the broader hope for the Davidic "branch," and the move to Nazareth corresponds to this hope reflected in the naming of the village. When Jesus moves to Nazareth, the hope for the Davidic branch reflected in the naming of the village comes home.[75] If this is correct, Matthew is claiming that Jesus is the fulfillment of the prophecies of a "branch man." A typological understanding — emphasizing historical correspondence and escalation — would then be able to incorporate a text like Zechariah 6:11-12, where the high priest Joshua is heralded as "the Branch."

Conclusion

I have argued that Isaiah 7:14 points to a child who will be born during the lifetime of King Ahaz, and that Matthew respects the historical context of this prophecy in Isaiah 7, claiming in Jesus a *typological* rather than a *predictive* fulfillment of Isaiah 7:14. The chief characteristics of typological interpretation are historical correspondence and escalation, and I have argued that this approach can help us understand the "fulfillment" language in Matthew 2:15, 17-18, and 23. This seems to have been a common method of interpretation, as we can see from the words of Matthew's contemporaries. For instance, it seems that Matthew was not the only early Christian to use "fulfillment" language to point to typological fulfillment. Bock argues that the citation of Isaiah 61 in Luke 4:17-19 as being "fulfilled" in Jesus (4:21) is an instance of "typological-prophetic" fulfillment.[76]

---

75. This explanation of Matt. 2:23 would appear to be strengthened by Carter's observation ("Evoking Isaiah," 506): "An audience elaborates the gaps or indeterminacies of a text to build a consistent understanding not by supplying whatever it likes but by utilizing the tradition it shares with the author. The common traditions provide the audience with a frame of reference, the 'perceptual grid,' for its interpretive work. Precisely this phenomenon is evident through the Gospel's opening genealogy (Matt. 1:1-17). The list of names (Abraham, Isaac, Jacob, etc.) requires the audience's elaborative work by evoking its knowledge of much more extensive and common traditions."

76. Bock, *Proclamation from Prophecy and Pattern*, 108-11, 276. See also the fulfillment language in Luke 22:16, where Jesus says that he will not again eat the Passover until it is "fulfilled"

The same is true of Pseudo-Philo, who describes in his *Biblical Antiquities* at 12:3 the people's response to Moses when he comes down from the mountain with the law and a shining face as follows: "And while he was speaking, they did not heed him, *so that the word spoken* in the time when the people sinned by building the tower *might be fulfilled,* when God said, 'And now unless I stop them, everything that they will propose to do they will dare, and even worse.'"[77] As in Matthew, so here — the words that are fulfilled are not predictive words; rather, the author is pointing to both historical correspondence and escalation. This technique might also inform what Matthew intends when he describes Jesus fulfilling all righteousness in 3:15 and the law in 5:17, but these texts are beyond the scope of this project. My objective here was to present a plausible case that Matthew understood and respected the context of Isaiah 7:14.

---

in the Kingdom of God. Delling writes, "The passover is a reminder of deliverance from Egypt; along these lines the OT and the eschatological events are perhaps contrasted as type and antitype" ("πληρόω," in *TDNT,* 6:296).

77. *LAB* 12:3, as translated by Donald J. Harrington in *OTP* 2:320 (original italics removed and emphasis added). I gladly thank Preston Sprinkle for alerting me to this reference. The nearest parallel to this in Pseudo-Philo seems to be 56:1, "And in that time the sons of Israel desired and sought for a king, and they gathered to Samuel and said, 'Behold now you are old, and your sons do not walk in your ways. And now appoint over us a king to govern us, because the word has been fulfilled that Moses said to our fathers in the wilderness, saying, "Appoint from your brothers a ruler over you."'" The text alluded to, Deut. 17:15, is a command rather than a prediction. See the other comparisons with earlier events in Israel's history in Pseudo-Philo cited in n. 73 above.

The Rhetoric of Hearing: The Use of the Isaianic Hearing Motif in Matthew 11:2–16:20

Jeannine K. Brown

Matthew 11:2–16:20 follows on the heels of the initial stages of Jesus' ministry to Israel (4:17–11:1) and narrates the increasingly polarized responses of various Matthean characters and character groups to Jesus' preaching and healing ministry.[1] It focuses on questions about Jesus' identity as he teaches, heals, feeds crowds, and engages in and withdraws from conflict with his antagonists. The various responses to Jesus' identity in this section of Matthew range from attribution of his power to Beelzebub (12:24) to the notion that he is John the Baptist *redivivus* (14:1-2) to faith that he is the Messiah, the Son of David (15:21-28; 16:13-20). Interwoven among these responses is the motif of hearing, which derives from Matthew's reliance upon the hearing motif from Isaiah. Matthew's hearing motif is properly considered a subtheme of his motif of understanding. While the theme of understanding has received significant focus in Matthean studies, there has been less attention to the secondary motif of hearing.[2] Nevertheless, the hearing motif is integrally connected to Matthew's theme of understanding. An exploration of its backdrop in Isaiah illuminates the impact of the hearing motif on Matthew's plot and his implied reader.[3]

---

1. Carter understands Matt. 11:2–16:20 to be the gospel's third narrative block, focusing on responses to Jesus. Warren Carter, *Matthew at the Margins: A Sociopolitical and Religious Reading* (Maryknoll, N.Y.: Orbis, 2000), 249.

2. Gerhard Barth provided the foundation work on the theme of understanding in "Matthew's Understanding of the Law," in G. Bornkamm, G. Barth, and H. J. Held, *Tradition and Interpretation in Matthew* (Philadelphia: Westminster, 1963), 58-164. For a review of the literature on understanding as it relates to the Matthean disciples, see Jeannine K. Brown, *The Disciples in Narrative Perspective: The Portrayal and Function of the Matthean Disciples* (SBLAB 9; Atlanta: Society of Biblical Literature, 2002), 6-12, 18-24.

3. For a discussion of the concept of the implied reader using narrative-critical methods, cf. Brown, *Disciples*, 123-28. In the rest of the essay, "reader" will be used as a shorthand to indicate this construct of the "implied reader."

The Relationship of Hearing and Understanding in Matthew 11:2–16:20

The plot of Matt. 11:2–16:20 begins with John the Baptist's question focused on the identity of Jesus: "Are you the one who is to come, or are we to wait for another?" (11:3).[4] Matthew takes up this question in subsequent pericopae from different angles.[5] First, Jesus himself answers John's question by referencing the language of Isaiah 35 and 61, which points to Israel's restoration. Then Matthew takes up a comparison of John and Jesus in which he implies that Jesus is the one who ushers in the kingdom (11:11-15) and who himself embodies wisdom and Torah (11:19, 25-30). After the narration of various controversies between Jesus and his adversaries followed by Jesus withdrawing from them (12:15; 14:13; cf. also 15:21; 16:4), the question of Jesus' identity is once again explicitly raised by Herod (14:1-2), who wrongly supposes that Jesus is John the Baptist raised from the dead. In the rest of Matthew 14–16, the plot centers on Jesus' feeding of the crowds and his healing ministry before moving to the climactic confession of Jesus as the Messiah by his disciples at 16:13-20, a pericope that clearly culminates the emphasis on Jesus' emerging identity in 11:2–16:20.

Related to the plotting of Jesus' identity in this section of Matthew are the varied responses to Jesus by the characters who interact with him. As who Jesus is becomes more clear, the responses to him grow more polarized. "Revelation and disclosure of the identity of Jesus are the context for the rejection . . . [and] acceptance motif[s]."[6] Between John's questioning of Jesus' Messianic identity (11:2) and Peter's dramatic confession of Jesus as Messiah (16:16), we witness a range of responses. These include lack of repentance and rejection (11:16-24; 13:53-58); challenge (12:1-14, 38-45; 15:1-11; 16:1-4); attribution of Jesus' Messianic deeds to Satan (12:22-28); understanding (11:25-30; 16:13-20); misunderstanding (14:1-2; 15:15-20; 16:5-12); little faith (14:22-33);[7] and great faith (15:21-28). It is in the subplot of responses to Jesus that the reader encounters the motifs of hearing and understanding, since it is primarily other characters *in relation to Jesus* who are described by the terms for hearing and understanding.

---

4. The NRSV will be used for biblical quotations unless otherwise specified.

5. Cecilia Deutsch identifies the theme of Jesus' identity in 11:2–13:58. Cecilia Deutsch, *Hidden Wisdom and Easy Yoke: Wisdom, Torah and Discipleship in Matthew 11.25-30* (JSNTSup 18; Sheffield: JSOT, 1987), 24.

6. Deutsch, *Hidden Wisdom*, 24.

7. Cf. also the disciples' little faith fleshed out in the feeding miracles at 14:13-21; 15:32-39. As Verseput notes, "The deliberate parallels between [the second feeding miracle] and the first feeding account render the disciples' continued lack of insight into the mighty power of Jesus all the more incomprehensible for the reader . . . , impressing upon him the utter foolishness of their 'little faith'" (19). Donald J. Verseput, "The Faith of the Reader and the Narrative of Matthew 13:53–16:20," *JSNT* 46 (1992): 14-19.

An interesting pattern emerges as the reader follows the concepts of hearing and understanding through this section of Matt. 11:2–16:20. We could liken the pattern to that of a tag-team relay. In Matt. 11:2–13:52, hearing rather than understanding is the preferred way of talking about responses to Jesus and his teaching. In Matt. 13:1–16:20, understanding becomes a crucial rubric for these responses. The overlapping of terms for these two concepts in the parables discourse of Matthew 13 (13:1-52) provides the most detail on the relationship between the two concepts. Language of hearing, which is prominent in Matthew 11–12, shifts to language of understanding in the parables discourse, with understanding serving as an important concept of reception in Matthew 14–16.

Analysis of the specific occurrences of terms for hearing and understanding illuminates the following contours: Language for hearing and understanding (in relation to reception of Jesus and his message) is used by both Jesus and the narrator.[8] Jesus refers to the importance of *hearing* in Matthew 11–12 four times[9] and only once in Matt. 13:53–16:20 (in explicit connection with understanding; 15:10). In addition, Matthew indicates that hearing is thematic in chapters 11–13 through the inclusio at 11:2 and 14:1 (using ἀκούω) as well as the reference to hearing in the fulfillment quotation of 12:18-21 (12:19).[10] Once the reader arrives at the parables discourse in Matthew 13, references to hearing abound, with the term ἀκούω occurring sixteen times in Jesus' speech.

Alternately, the key terms for understanding do not occur in Matthew until the parables discourse of chapter 13. In that chapter, συνίημι occurs six times (13:13, 14, 15, 19, 23, 51). Following the parables discourse (Matt. 13:53–16:20), terms for understanding, specifically συνίημι and νοέω, occur six times.[11] Across Matt. 13:1–16:20, these two terms for understanding come from the

---

8. In Matthew's plot, it is not at all surprising to encounter regularly the verb for hearing (ἀκούω), since reporting what various characters hear from other characters is prevalent in narration. Therefore, greater attention will be given to ἀκούω in Jesus' speech as well as occurrences that are shown to be prominent via strategic placement (e.g., Matt. 11:2; 14:1, where ἀκούω forms part of an inclusio around Matthew 11–13).

9. Possibly seven, given the text-critical issue at 11:15; 13:9 and 43. In each case, the issue is the presence of ἀκούειν following ὦτα: ὁ ἔχων ὦτα [ἀκούειν] ἀκουέτω. It is most probable that the inclusion of the infinitive in each case is secondary, since (1) the longer phrase occurs elsewhere in the Gospels (e.g., Mark 4:9, 23); and (2) there is little reason for scribes to drop the infinitive if original. Cf. Bruce M. Metzger, *A Textual Commentary on the Greek New Testament* (3d ed.; Stuttgart: United Bible Societies, 1971), 29.

10. Eco notes the importance of placement as an indicator of a theme, referring to the "strategic placement" of theme words or ideas (as distinct from reiterative placement). Umberto Eco, *The Role of the Reader: Explorations in the Semiotics of Texts* (Bloomington: Indiana University Press, 1979), 26. For more on the inclusio of 11:2 and 14:1, cf. the discussion below.

11. Συνίημι at 15:10 and 16:12 (with the adjectival ἀσύνετος at 15:16); νοέω at 15:17; 16:9, 11.

mouth of Jesus, except at 16:12, where it is the narrator who uses the term to describe the disciples. So there is a general movement regarding the placement of the Greek words for hearing and understanding, from hearing in Matthew 11–13 to understanding in Matthew 13–16.[12] The effects of this movement for the reader of Matthew will be explored in the final section of this paper. First, however, we will explore the motif of hearing in Matt. 11:2–16:20, especially as it intersects with the same theme drawn from Isaiah.

The Motif of Hearing in Matthew 11:2–16:20

In Matthew 11–12, the importance of hearing Jesus rightly is introduced in relation to his emerging identity.[13] The introduction of the hearing concept then blossoms in the parables discourse where hearing takes on primary significance and where it is interwoven with the theme of understanding. As the theme of understanding takes over and the motif of hearing recedes, there is one more significant occurrence of the hearing motif in 11:2–16:20, where it is paired with understanding (15:10). An important connection that emerges at each of these key "hearing junctures" is Matthew's placement of Isaianic quotations (cf. 11:5; 12:18-21; 13:14-15; and 15:8-9) alongside the motif of hearing. This connection suggests that to grasp the import of Matthew's hearing motif it will be important to examine the Isaiah texts he cites and reflect upon how they are used in relation to hearing. We will examine in turn the four junctures of Isaiah quotations and Matthew's hearing references: 11:2-19; 12:1-32; 13:1-23; and 15:1-20.

Matthew 11:2-19

Matthew uses ἀκούω three times in the passage that introduces 11:2–16:20, emphasizing the prominence of the hearing motif by its initial placement. In re-

---

12. Exploration of the hearing motif in Matthew focuses on the lexical level, since the motif is signaled primarily through the word ἀκούω. Yet a narrative analysis of this motif will necessarily look beyond lexical occurrence to ways in which (lack of) hearing is portrayed in Matthew's story. As Neyrey observes regarding Matthew 12, "The Scribes and the Pharisees... are clearly *not* listening to 'greater than Jonah' or 'greater than Solomon'. Some people, then, are willfully refusing to listen to the voice of God's messengers"; Jerome H. Neyrey, "The Thematic Use of Isaiah 42,1-4 in Matthew 12," *Bib* 63 (1982): 461. In this way, comprehending hearing as a narrative-conceptual motif in Matthew is the broader aim of this study.

13. Characterization in ancient narration is much less about character development (which is primarily a psychological category and so a modern one) than about character revelation. That is, it is typical for ancient biographers to gradually reveal what they understand to already be a part of a person's nature (φύσις). See my discussion of this issue in Brown, *Disciples*, 49-53.

sponse to John the Baptist's question of whether Jesus is the one they are expecting, Jesus responds, "Go and tell John what you hear (ἀκούω) and see: the blind receive their sight, the lame walk, the lepers are cleansed, the deaf hear (ἀκούω), the dead are raised, and the poor have good news brought to them" (11:4b-5a; cf. Isa. 35:5). According to Matthew's Jesus, anyone hearing his message and seeing his works (τὰ ἔργα τοῦ Χριστοῦ; 11:2) should be able to recognize that the restoration of Israel heralded in Isaiah has begun. That hearing is an important part of right response to Jesus is further emphasized at 11:15: "The one who has ears ought to hear" (ἀκούω; my translation).[14] The same phrase will recur twice in the parables discourse of chapter 13, tying Matthew 11–13 together by means of the hearing motif.

Another indication that hearing is significant in this section of Matthew is its usage at 11:2 and 14:1 in similar ways in two passages that are structurally connected. At 11:2, John hears while in prison of the deeds of the Messiah (ἀκούσας . . . τὰ ἔργα τοῦ Χριστοῦ), which prompts his question to Jesus through John's disciples. At 14:1-2, Herod hears reports (ἤκουσεν . . . τὴν ἀκοήν) about Jesus' miraculous powers and comes to the mistaken conclusion that he is John the Baptist risen from the dead.[15] The ties between these sections include the subplot related to John the Baptist and references to both John and Herod hearing about Jesus' activity and wondering about his identity. In particular, Jesus' activity is described in a similar way in both stories. In Matt. 11:2-5, the deeds of the Messiah are described by miraculous activity: the blind receiving sight, the lame walking, the leprous cured, the deaf hearing, the dead raised. At 14:1, Herod has heard reports of Jesus' miraculous powers.[16]

In addition, the placement of these two stories is significant. Matt. 11:2-19 introduces increasingly diverse responses to Jesus' identity by asking in John's voice, "Are you the one who is to come?" After narrating the various ways characters answer this question and react to Jesus, Matthew introduces the parables discourse to illustrate in parabolic form the range of responses to Jesus. Almost immediately after the parables discourse,[17] Herod's confused identification of

---

14. Or "the one who has ears to hear ought to hear." Cf. discussion of this text-critical issue above.

15. Matthew then narrates in proleptic form the death of John at the behest of Herod (14:3-12).

16. At 14:2, Matthew uses δυνάμεις. Note the use of the same term at 11:20 to sum up Jesus' activity as it has been described in 11:2-19.

17. Luz signals the presence of an inclusio around Matthew 13 at 12:46-50 and 13:53-58 by pointing to the theme of Jesus' family with associated catchwords. Ulrich Luz, *Matthew 8–20* (trans. James E. Crouch; Hermeneia; Minneapolis: Fortress, 2001), 301. This, in turn, points to 11:2-6 and 14:1-12 as lead stories for their respective sections (11:2–13:58; 14:1–16:20) in 11:2–16:20,

Jesus with John the Baptist emphasizes the importance of recognizing rightly who Jesus is. This lead story is followed by narration focused primarily on more positive responses of the disciples, the crowds, and the Canaanite woman.[18] Finally, the whole section culminates in Peter's confession on behalf of the disciples of Jesus' true identity as Messiah (16:16).

Matthew's use of Isaiah in 11:2-19 confirms the importance of the hearing motif for the evangelist at this juncture. First, his introduction to the citation makes it clear that what people are hearing and seeing in the ministry of Jesus should confirm his true identity (11:4). Second, the citation, which is actually a conflation of borrowed language and phraseology from Isaiah (Isa. 35:5-6; 61:1; cf. also 29:18),[19] further elaborates on the motif of hearing in Matthew's narrative. One of the specific activities appropriated from Isa. 35:5-6 is the restoration of hearing to the deaf. As we will see in more detail below, the theme of hearing/not hearing is an important one in Isaiah. According to Isaiah, part of what God will do when Israel's restoration is enacted is to unstop the ears of God's wayward people, who are metaphorically pictured as deaf. Isa. 35:5 provides a vision of restoration, when "the eyes of the blind shall be opened, and the ears of the deaf unstopped."[20] In this way, the Isaianic connection made at Matt. 11:5 affirms both who Jesus is as the enactor of restoration and one proper way of responding to his identity, namely, hearing rightly who he is and what he is bringing. As Matthew affirms at the end of this pericope in relation to John's precursory ministry to Jesus: "The one who has ears ought to hear" (11:15: ὁ ἔχων ὦτα ἀκουέτω).[21]

---

both of which are pointedly focused on Jesus' identity and misunderstanding about it. Deutsch delineates 11:2–13:58 as a discreet section of narrative (*Hidden Wisdom*, 21-22).

18. The portrayal of disciples in Matthew is not uniformly positive, however. At times, they provide an example to emulate, as when they leave their work to follow Jesus (4:18-22). At other points in the narrative, the disciples exhibit less than ideal discipleship (Brown, *Disciples*, 91-93, 119-20). For example, they are routinely defined by "little faith" (8:26; 14:31; 16:8; 17:20; cf. 6:30). Matthew also portrays the crowds in mixed fashion in the narrative (e.g., 12:23; 13:11-13).

19. W. D. Davies and Dale C. Allison, *Matthew* (ICC; Edinburgh: T&T Clark, 1991), 2:242.

20. There seems to be a dual level to the hearing motif in Isaiah: both physical restoration of hearing (35:5) and restoration of insight (metaphorical hearing) are in view (e.g., Isa 42:18-19; 48:6-8; 50:4-5; 52:13-15; cf. 6:9-10). In fact, Isa. 35:5 may well involve the return of both physical and metaphorical hearing, given the abundance of metaphor throughout the chapter.

21. Another proper response is to avoid stumbling over Jesus (11:6). The stumbling motif is often related to misunderstanding Jesus' identity in Matthew; see, e.g., 11:6. For a helpful discussion of the connection of these themes, cf. Andrew H. Trotter, "Understanding and Stumbling: A Study of the Disciples' Understanding of Jesus and His Teaching in the Gospel of Matthew" (Ph.D. diss., University of Cambridge, 1986), 229-30.

Matthew 12:1-32

In Matt. 12:1-32 the motif of hearing is again paired with an Isaianic quotation. The pericope begins with the withdrawal of Jesus following a confrontation with the Pharisees (12:15). This is the first of three such withdrawals (ἀναχωρέω) which follow confrontations with Jesus (cf. also 14:13; 15:21).[22] Yet as he withdraws from controversy, Jesus is once again approached by the crowds, who bring their sick to him. Jesus heals the sick and warns them not to reveal his identity (12:16). It is at this point in the narrative that Matthew includes a fulfillment quotation from Isa. 42:1-4.

This particular Matthean Old Testament citation has generated much discussion and debate, not only because it is one of the lengthier Matthean fulfillment quotations but also because of questions regarding its connection to its Matthean context.[23] Early offerings on the topic of the contextual connections of 12:18-21 (Isa. 42:1-4) focused on the way in which the quotation, particularly 12:19, illustrates the Messianic secret motif immediately preceding the quotation: "[Jesus] ordered them not to make him known" (12:16). More recent suggestions have worked to take seriously why a full four verses from Isaiah make their way into Matthew's narrative. Beaton, for example, emphasizes that the Isaiah text as well as its appropriation by Matthew focus on the theme of justice coming through God's chosen servant.

> The inclusion of Isa. 42.1-4 . . . offers a scriptural basis for the countercultural perspective of Jesus' messiahship and kingship (11.6). In addition to depicting a compassionate servant who identifies with and aids broken humanity, it links these deeds with justice. . . . Matthew's Jesus, in a nonconfrontational manner, offers justice to the poor, sick and lame and to the harassed crowds burdened with the weight and oppression of the legal interpretations of the Jewish establishment (cf. 9.36; 15.1-20; 23.4, 24).[24]

In his thesis, Beaton suggests that Matthew's fulfillment quotations are bi-referential. To use the terminology of narrative criticism, the quotations function both at the story and at the discourse levels of the narrative. For Beaton,

---

22. Note also 16:4, where καταλείπω is used.

23. For a thorough treatment, cf. Richard Beaton, *Isaiah's Christ in Matthew's Gospel* (SNTSMS 123; Cambridge: Cambridge University Press, 2002). Since discussion of the text forms used in the Matthean Old Testament citations falls outside the parameters of this paper, cf. Beaton as well as Gundry and Stendahl on this topic. Robert H. Gundry, *The Use of the Old Testament in Matthew's Gospel with Special Reference to the Messianic Hope* (Leiden: E. J. Brill, 1967); Krister Stendahl, *The School of St. Matthew* (2d ed.; Philadelphia: Fortress, 1968).

24. Beaton, *Isaiah's Christ*, 165.

The Rhetoric of Hearing

the quotation's function in the story of Jesus highlights three ideas: the secrecy motif, the Pharisaic threat of Matthew 12, and the healings performed by Jesus as an expression of his compassionate ministry (12:19-20a). On the discourse level, Matthew is showing the reader that Jesus fulfills the Messianic expectation to establish justice (12:18, 20b-21).[25]

Beaton's work helpfully argues for and attends to the multiple connections between the Isa. 42:1-4 citation and its context in Matthew. I would point out an additional connection, this one focused on the hearing motif in Matthew drawn from Isaiah. In the center of the Isaiah quotation, this affirmation is made about the servant of the Lord: "He will not wrangle or cry aloud, nor will anyone hear his voice in the streets" (12:19; Isa. 42:2). As Neyrey has noted, if we compare Matthew's rendering of the latter half of this verse with both the MT and the LXX, we see that Matthew has heightened the emphasis on hearing as a human response.[26]

MT: וְלֹא־יַשְׁמִיעַ . . . קוֹלוֹ

LXX: οὐδὲ ἀκουσθήσεται . . . ἡ φωνὴ αὐτοῦ

Matt: οὐδὲ ἀκούσει τις . . . τὴν φωνὴν αὐτοῦ

The active voice of ἀκούω in Matthew's form of the citation focuses attention on the responsibility of the hearer for what is heard. As Neyrey comments, "Matt's version is . . . rendered in a direction which points less to the speaker's plan *not* to be heard and more to rejection by the hearers themselves."[27]

This instance of the hearing motif from Isaiah is shaped by Matthew toward his subplot of the varied responses to Jesus' identity, which is then illustrated and elaborated in the context of Matthew 11–12. For example, Matthew 12 highlights the negative response of the Pharisees toward Jesus. They accuse Jesus' disciples of breaking the Sabbath (12:1-14). They attribute Jesus' authority not to God but to the prince of demons (12:22-32). In fact, in the latter pericope, it is when the Pharisees *hear* that the people wonder if Jesus is the Son of David that they claim he drives out demons by Beelzebub (12:24). They do not hear in a right fashion, even as the people suggest the proper perspective toward Jesus' identity. Neyrey comments, "Belief vs. unbelief — clearly some are *not* listening to [Jesus'] voice."[28]

---

25. Beaton, *Isaiah's Christ*, 149-51.
26. Jerome H. Neyrey, "Isaiah in Matthew," 461.
27. Neyrey, "Isaiah in Matthew," 461 (author's emphasis).
28. Neyrey, "Isaiah in Matthew," 461. Much of the rest of Matthew 12 (12:33-45) continues to illustrate varied responses by contrasting good and bad fruit and in the inappropriate request for a sign from Jesus to prove his identity.

Matthew 13:1-23

After illustrating positive and negative responses in narrative form in Matthew 11–12 (with more emphasis on the negative than the positive), the evangelist crafts a discourse centered on a number of Jesus' parables to represent the right and wrong kinds of responses to Jesus. Wrapped around the parables discourse are two stories that touch on Jesus' familial connections (12:46-50; 13:53-58). That these two accounts function as an *inclusio* is signaled by their common catchwords, μήτηρ, ἀδελφός, and ἀδελφή.[29] The parallel stories highlight two contrasting responses to Jesus. On the one hand, familial connection to Jesus is extended to all who do the Father's will (12:50). Alternately, rejection of and stumbling over Jesus is illustrated by Jesus' hometown, who question the source of Jesus' authority and power (13:54-57) and in the end are typified by unbelief (13:58).

Between these two points, the right and wrong kinds of responses are played out in a series of parables told by Jesus (13:1-52). We hear of these responses in parabolic visions of good soil and "bad" soil (13:13-18), wheat and weeds (13:24-30), and good and bad fish (13:47-50). The focus on response is specifically tied to God's reign;[30] it is the possible responses to the message of the kingdom preached by Jesus that are the focus of Matthew 13.[31] Proper responses to the kingdom message include reception and fruitfulness (13:23), and prizing the kingdom above all else (13:44-46).

The motif of hearing plays out in the tension between these right and wrong responses. The prominence of the motif is evident both in its clustered focus in 13:13-19 and in its strategic placement at 13:9 and 13:43 in the repeated invitation, "The one who has ears ought to hear," which was introduced at 11:15. We will look at these two thematic moments in turn, beginning with the latter.

The expression, ὁ ἔχων ὦτα ἀκουέτω, is repeated three times in Matthew 11–13, and its placement seems to be significant. The expression first occurs at 11:15 in the introductory passage revolving around John the Baptist. After John sends followers to question Jesus about his identity, Jesus identifies John for his hearers: John is "Elijah who is to come" (11:14). Then Jesus issues the call to hear. In

---

29. Luz, *Matthew 8–20*, 301.

30. I am sympathetic to those who choose to translate βασιλεία in Matthew as "the reign (of God)" in order to indicate the more dynamic nature of the Greek term in its Gospels' usage, though I will use both "kingdom" and "God's reign" in the following discussion. Cf. Carter, *Matthew at the Margins*, 571-72, n. 8.

31. The terminology "message of the kingdom" is explicit at 13:19. The standard introductory formula to the parables of this chapter is "The kingdom of heaven is like . . ." (13:24, 31, 33, 44, 45, 47).

this context, "The one who has ears ought to hear" is a *call to understand and accept* John the Baptist as the Elijah-type Messianic forerunner. Hearing is more than auditory perception; it is about understanding and acceptance. Similarly, the use of the expression at 13:9 and 13:43 in the parables chapter emphasizes hearing (ἀκούω) as understanding. The very first parable of Matthew 13 is the parable of the sower; and the admonition at the end of this parable ("the one who has ears ought to hear") refers to the various responses to God's reign illustrated in the parable. The phrase functions as a call to understand and respond rightly to God's reign. Ultimately, this right response involves bearing fruit as the good soil of the parable does. Finally, the same expression at 13:43 caps Jesus' explanation of the parable of the weeds requested by the disciples.[32] In this instance, it again functions as a call to understand and ultimately to respond to God's reign as the righteous ones described in 13:43.[33]

In addition to the reiteration of the expression ὁ ἔχων ὦτα ἀκουέτω, the clustering of ἀκούω in the early part of Matthew 13 is pronounced. In fact, we could describe 13:9-19 as a cacophony of references to ears and hearing, given the many occurrences of οὖς and ἀκούω![34] To understand the significance of the hearing motif in this section of Matthew 13, we will need to determine the ways in which it is used. A close reading of 13:9-23 suggests that "hearing" is used in at least two senses. In some occurrences, ἀκούω is used to indicate mere apprehension of sound — hearing as physical act alone. For example, the first use of ἀκούω in 13:13 (from Isa. 6:9) fits this sense: "Though seeing, they do not see; though *hearing,* they do not hear or understand." At other points, ἀκούω indicates right reception of what is heard. In its second usage at 13:13, ἀκούω approaches the concept of understanding.[35] In fact, the two senses are interwoven throughout 13:13-23. Hearing as mere sound apprehension occurs at 13:14, 19-23, while hearing as movement toward or including understanding is implied at 13:15-16.[36]

---

32. This expression occurs at the conclusion of both the first parable spoken to the crowds (13:3-9) and the first parable spoken to the disciples alone (13:37-43).

33. As I note elsewhere, "this phrase occurs at key junctures in the [parables] chapter, capping off the first pericope in each major section. As such, it invites the reader to be one of those who listen carefully to . . . these parables, drawing the reader into Jesus' teaching in a more direct fashion." Jeannine K. Brown, "Direct Engagement of the Reader in Matthew's Discourses: Rhetorical Techniques and Scholarly Consensus," *NTS* 51 (2005): 29.

34. Ears that either hear or do not hear; cf. 13:9, 15, 16.

35. As Luz notes, "seeing and hearing are not simply identical to understanding, but they are associated with it. 'Seeing eyes' and 'hearing ears' are the basis on which understanding can grow" (Luz, *Matthew 8-20*, 247).

36. Wesley G. Olmstead, *Matthew's Trilogy of Parables: The Nation, the Nations, and the Reader in Matthew 21.28–22.14* (SNTSMS 127; Cambridge: Cambridge University Press, 2003), 157.

Yet the intermingling of the two senses of hearing does not occur for the first time in Matthew 13. Rather, it begins in Matthew 11–12 in the sections we have already examined. In Matthew's narrative, the reader has already encountered those who hear Jesus but do not rightly understand or interpret what they are hearing. John the Baptist is unsure that what he has heard indicates Jesus' Messianic status (11:2-3). Herod, who hears of the miracles of Jesus, is characterized by an even greater misunderstanding of Jesus' identity (14:1-2). The Pharisees also hear but do not understand who Jesus is (12:23-24). Hearing as mere auditory perception does not guarantee understanding. In contrast to mere auditory perception, however, Jesus calls all who have ears to hear, that is, to understand the import of his words (11:15): "The one who has ears ought to hear." In Jesus' call to the crowds (cf. 11:7) to hear rightly, we also notice Matthew speaking to the implied reader to use her ears according to their true purpose — for comprehension.

The reader, therefore, comes to Matthew 13 with these two possible senses for ἀκούω.[37] While some occurrences fit clearly into either one or the other of the two senses, there are some usages of ἀκούω that seem ambiguous. Specifically, the four usages at 13:16-17 do not seem to fit entirely either of the two senses already described. Matt. 13:16-17 functions both as the culmination of the Isaiah quotation of 13:14-15 and as a transition to Jesus' interpretation of the parable of the soils which begins at 13:18. The further complexity of the hearing motif in 13:16-17 revolves around its eschatological nuance. The four uses of ἀκούω at 13:16-17 focus less upon sensory hearing or even hearing as understanding than upon *when* the hearing occurs. The disciples are considered blessed because they hear what many of the righteous and the prophets of former days longed to hear. It is unlikely that the contrast is between those who merely hear (the prophets of old) and those who hear and understand (the disciples).[38] The contrast of 13:16-17 is almost entirely a *temporal* one. What the faithful believers prior to the coming of the kingdom longed for the disciples now experience. They have experienced the arrival of Jesus, who heralds the kingdom, and beyond this, who inaugurates the kingdom in his preaching and

---

37. These are two of the possible senses of ἀκούω according to BDAG: "to have or exercise the faculty of hearing" (37) and "to hear and understand a message" (38).

38. While Jesus indicates that the disciples are given knowledge of the secrets of the kingdom (13:11), Matthew does not seem to be *emphasizing* the disciples' understanding in this section (Trotter, "Understanding and Stumbling," 77). Rather, their knowledge consists of their being privy to Jesus' interpretations of parables (cf. 13:18-23, 37-43). The disciples' own affirmation that they do understand (13:51) should be read with attention to the narrator's point of view and to the narrative picture of what the disciples do and do not understand about Jesus' teaching (e.g., 15:16; 16:8-12). Cf. Brown, *Disciples*, 109-11.

miraculous activity.[39] The blessing bestowed on the disciples at 13:16 is precisely the eschatological blessing already proclaimed in the kingdom beatitudes (5:3-12). The time of the reversal of Israel's fortune envisioned in Isaiah's new exodus has arrived.[40]

Our discussion of Matthew 13 thus far invites explanation of Matthew's usage of Isaiah 6 in the parables chapter. Isa. 6:9-11 in Matt. 13:14-15 is probably the most examined Isaiah text in Matthew, given the general tenor of the evangelist's usage, which seems to indicate that Jesus speaks in parables to encourage misunderstanding! It is significant that the text which Matthew cites here is the culmination of Isaiah's call narrative. When Isaiah sees a vision of God exalted and holy (6:1-4), he is immediately struck by his own uncleanness (6:5-7). After being purified, Isaiah responds to the call of Yahweh to go to the people of Israel (6:8): "Here am I; send me!" The nature of Isaiah's mission is then spelled out in Isa. 6:9-13: Isaiah's audience is a stubborn, unseeing, and unhearing people.

> And [the Lord] said, "Go and say to this people: 'Keep listening, but do not comprehend; keep looking, but do not understand.' Make the mind of this people dull, and stop their ears, and shut their eyes, so that they may not look with their eyes, and listen with their ears, and comprehend with their minds, and turn and be healed." Then I said, "How long, O Lord?" And he said: "Until cities lie waste without inhabitant, and houses without people, and the land is utterly desolate; until the LORD sends everyone far away, and vast is the emptiness in the midst of the land. Even if a tenth part remain in it, it will be burned again, like a terebinth or an oak whose stump remains standing when it is felled." The holy seed is its stump.

In an intgriguing study of Isa. 6:9-13, Beale marshals evidence for his thesis that these verses express God's judgment upon Israel for its idolatry.[41] The form of judgment is that of coming to resemble the objects of their worship, idols that can neither see nor hear. Beale finds support for this thesis first in the closely parallel language of Ps. 135:15-17a: "The idols of the nations are silver and gold, the work of human hands. They have mouths, but they do not speak; they have eyes, but they do not see; they have ears but they do not hear." The psalmist's contention is that those who trust in idols will become like

---

39. Davies and Allison refer to the prophets and the righteous of old longing to see "the eschatological revelation of God" (*A Critical and Exegetical Commentary on the Gospel according to Saint Matthew* [3 vols.; IC; Edinburgh: T&T Clark, 1988-97], 2:394).

40. For the theme of the new exodus in Mark, cf. Rikki E. Watts, *Isaiah's New Exodus in Mark* (WUNT 2; Tübingen: Mohr, 1997).

41. G. K. Beale, "Isaiah VI 9-13: A Retributive Taunt against Idolatry," *VT* 41 (1991): 257-78.

those very idols: "Those who make them and all who trust them shall become like them" (Ps. 135:18).[42]

Beale finds significant support for his thesis from within Isaiah as well, particularly in the use of idol terminology at 6:13. The reference to burning the terebinth tree has parallels with Isa. 1:29-31, where this language is tied to idolatrous practices. Beale concludes that both in Isa. 6:13 and in 1:29-31 "rebellious Israel is metaphorically portrayed as becoming 'like' the idols ('cultic trees') which they worshipped. Israel will become like these trees, resembling their destructive destiny, as expression of the ironic principle abstractly stated in [Ps 135:18]."[43]

If Beale is correct, then Isaiah's call is to proclaim a message to a people who will be unable to see, hear, or understand it, given their increasing resemblance to the unresponsive idols they have chosen to worship. If this is the fundamental nature of Isaiah's ministry, then it is not difficult to understand why hearing is an important motif in Isaiah. Any kind of reversal of this judgment will in all likelihood involve a call to see and hear truly (i.e., understand). In fact, this is what we see in Isaiah; as the eschatological vision of a new exodus is set forth, the call to hear is regularly reiterated.[44]

As we turn to Matthew's use of Isaiah 6, we hear Jesus intentionally framing his ministry to Israel by evoking Isaiah's ministry to Israel: they are both called to preach a message in large measure to unresponsive and unhearing people. In Matthew's context, the evangelist offers this as an explanation for the variety of responses, many of them negative, which arise from Jesus' presence with and ministry to Israel. Matthew shapes the hearing motif, especially in the parables discourse, to suggest that adequate hearing is hearing that moves toward understanding. In addition, reception, acceptance, and fruitfulness in relation to what one hears are the ultimate goals of hearing. This seems to be the focus of the kind of hearing referred to in the interpretation of the parable of the soils: "But as for what was sown on good soil, this is the one who hears the word and understands it, who indeed bears fruit and yields, in one case a hundredfold, in another sixty, and in another thirty" (13:23).

This emphasis is important, given the tendency to dwell on the division between those who understand and those who do not in Matthew 13. A sharp distinction between the uncomprehending crowds and the discerning disciples has typically been seen at 13:10-17. As we will see below, the disciples do not earn this uniformly positive portrayal. In the end, beyond the crowds and the

---

42. Beale, "Idolatry," 258.
43. Beale, "Idolatry," 260.
44. Cf. discussion of Isaiah's hearing motif below.

disciples, *the implied reader* is issued a call to hear rightly in Matthew 13. It is crucial to attend to the way in which Matthew's audience is invited to use their ears to hear and understand through the explanation of the parable of the soils and particularly in the dual refrain: "The one who has ears ought to hear" (13:9, 43). Whatever is secret and hidden from various character groups in Matthew is fully disclosed to the reader of Matthew.[45]

The connections between Isaiah 6 and Matthew 13 indicate that, even at the turning point between this age and the age to come, the prophetic message is not fully heard and grasped. One reason given in the parables chapter is the unexpected nature of the kingdom. The parables of the mustard seed (13:31-32) and yeast (13:33) at a minimum communicate the kingdom as seemingly inconspicuous and hidden in its early manifestation.[46] This helps to explain the varied responses, not all positive, to God's reign as revealed in Jesus' ministry. "Both parables teach that the coming of the kingdom begins not with a grand, public spectacle but with a hidden presence."[47] The result of these varied responses is eschatological judgment portrayed in the parables of the weeds (13:24-30; with interpretation at 13:36-42) and the fish (13:47-50). At the end of the age, though not until then, all allegiances will be seen clearly.[48] While evildoers will be punished, "the righteous will shine like the sun in the kingdom of their Father" (13:43).

Matthew 15:1-20

The final combination of Matthew's hearing motif with an Isaianic text citation in Matt. 11:2–16:20 is found at Matt. 15:1-20, where Jesus cites Isa. 29:13. During a dispute over why his disciples do not follow hand-washing traditions of the elders, Jesus turns the tables on the Pharisees and scribes by accusing them of disobeying the Torah itself in their focus on keeping such traditions. Then Jesus invokes Isaiah's condemnation of the hypocrisy of his day to combat the hypocrisy Jesus perceives in his opponents: "This people honors me with their lips, but their hearts are far from me; in vain do they worship me, teaching human precepts as doctrines" (Matt. 15:8-9; Isa. 29:13).

Even though the Isaiah quotation itself does not focus on hearing, the context from which this quotation is taken highlights the Isaianic theme of hearing

---

45. Cf. the final section below.

46. Though supremely valuable, as communicated by the twin parables of the hidden treasure (13:44) and the costly pearl (13:45-46).

47. Davies and Allison, *Matthew*, 2:421.

48. There is emphasis in the parable of the weeds on *delayed* judgment, since it is not so very easy for Jesus' followers to determine "weeds" from "wheat" (13:28-30).

and understanding. First, immediately following the citation verses, the reader of Isaiah hears the result of the people's hypocrisy: "So I will again do amazing things with this people, shocking and amazing. The wisdom of their wise shall perish, and the discernment of the discerning shall be hidden" (Isa. 29:14; LXX: τὴν σύνεσιν τῶν συνετῶν κρύψω for the latter clause). Second, in subsequent verses, the reversal of Israel's fortune is envisioned (29:17-24). In this reversal context, the language of hearing is invoked: "On that day the deaf shall hear the words of a scroll, and out of their gloom and darkness the eyes of the blind shall see" (29:18; LXX begins: καὶ ἀκούσονται ἐν τῇ ἡμέρᾳ ἐκείνῃ).

It is not surprising, then, that Jesus follows the citation from Isaiah with these words to the crowds (15:10): "Listen and understand" (ἀκούω and συνίημι, respectively).[49] In Isaiah, what had been hidden from God's people because of hypocrisy and superficial worship will be made clear ("the deaf will hear . . .") in the final day. Matthew seems to evoke this wider Isaianic context in his shaping of 15:1-20. In Jesus, the potential for restored hearing (and so understanding) has arrived. As people observe the ministry of Jesus and his interactions, the invitation to hear and understand emerges. Yet there is no guarantee that all will respond with proper hearing and understanding. The motif of hearing/not hearing derived from Isaiah finds its way into Matthew's telling of the story of Jesus.

Hearing and Not Hearing in Isaiah

As we have looked at the intersection of Matthew's hearing motif and his use of Isaiah citations in 11:2–16:20, it has become clearer that Matthew had a significant store of material in Isaiah from which to draw this motif. With each of the Isaiah citations explored above, we have begun to discern the contours of the theme of the hearing motif from Isaiah. Although this study focuses primarily on Matthew, an overview of significant ways in which *hearing* and *not hearing* emerge in the final form of Isaiah will assist our exploration of this borrowed theme in Matt. 11:2–16:20.[50]

From the beginning of Isaiah, the importance of hearing is hallmarked, as the heavens and earth are called *to listen* to God's complaint against his people

---

49. The fact that Matthew's Jesus speaks these words to the crowds, who have been described as lacking knowledge of the kingdom secrets at 13:11, should make us cautious of asserting that the crowds are unable to hear or understand in the end.

50. My exploration of Matthew's use of Isaiah does not depend on any particular view of Isaianic unity or authorship. For a discussion of the hearing motif with attention to issues of authorship, cf. R. E. Clements, "Beyond Tradition-History: Deutero-Isaianic Development of First Isaiah's Themes," *JSOT* 31 (1985): 101-6.

(שָׁמַע; 1:2), and the people are called *to hear* God's complaint themselves (שָׁמַע; 1:10). In addition, the theme of Israel's incomprehension, which is often tied to their ability to hear (e.g., 6:10; 29:18-24; 32:3-4), is introduced at the very beginning of the book (1:3): "The ox knows its owner, and the donkey its master's crib; but Israel does not know, my people do not understand (בִּין)." In fact, in the Septuagint of Isaiah 1, Israel's choice or ability to hear becomes the deciding factor in their destiny (καὶ ἐὰν θέλητε καὶ εἰσακούσητέ μου . . . ἐὰν δὲ μὴ θέλητε μηδὲ εἰσακούσητέ μου; 1:19-20).[51]

The theme of hearing is centrally focused by way of Isaiah's call narrative in 6:1-13. Isaiah's mission focuses on an audience who is unable to hear and understand his message.[52]

> And he said, "Go and say to this people:
> '**Keep listening** (שָׁמַע), *but do not comprehend;*
> keep looking, but do not understand.'
> Make the mind of this people dull,
> and stop their ears,
> and shut their eyes,
> so that they may not look with their eyes,
> and **listen** (שָׁמַע) **with their ears,**
> and comprehend with their minds,
> and turn and be healed" (6:9-10).[53]

This aspect of Isaiah's mission receives continued emphasis beyond Isaiah 6. Israel's obduracy expressed in their inability to hear, raised in a programmatic way in the Isaianic call narrative, is reiterated across Isaiah.[54] In Isaiah 30,

---

51. These verses conclude the first oracle of Isaiah (1:2-20).

52. If Beale is correct, they are unable to do so because of their idolatry, which renders them more and more like the deaf and blind idols they worship ("Idolatry").

53. Aitken notices that hearing (and seeing) are central to Isaiah's experiences just prior to 6:8-13 and concludes that "the experience of Isaiah stands in part as a model of what is to be denied to the people through his preaching: Isaiah has 'seen' and 'heard' — and, by implication, he 'understands'; the people will also see and hear, but they will not understand." K. T. Aitken, "Hearing and Seeing: Metamorphoses of a Motif in Isaiah 1–39," in *Among the Prophets: Language, Image, and Structure in the Prophetic Writings* (ed. Philip R. Davies and David J. A. Clines; JSOTSup 144; Sheffield: JSOT, 1993), 19.

54. A combination of hearing and sight is present in most of the passages discussed here. Cf. Beale's discussion of lack of sight (which along with lack of hearing fits the wider theme of Israel's incomprehension) and its frequent connection to idolatry; e.g., Isa 29:9-10; 42:16-20; and 44:8-20 ("Idolatry," 272-74). As Clements observes, "the theme of Israel's blindness and deafness, understood in a metaphorical and spiritual sense, is clearly of central importance to Isa. 40–55" (Clements, "Isaiah's Themes," 102).

for instance, not only is Israel described as rebellious "children who will not hear (שָׁמַע) the instruction of the LORD," but they actively oppose hearing from God by telling the prophets, "let us hear (שָׁמַע) no more about the Holy One of Israel" (30:9, 11). In addition, language of a people with ears but unable to hear is repeated at 42:18-20 and 43:8, even as these deaf ones are called to listen (42:18).[55] Finally, it is clear in Isaiah that the threat of judgment hangs over Israel's obduracy. "I will destine you to the sword, and all of you shall bow down to the slaughter; because, when I called, you did not answer, when I spoke, you did not listen" (שָׁמַע) (65:12).

Yet it is not only the theological problem of hearing that is thematic in Isaiah. The solution to their lack of hearing and obduracy is also supplied. Isaiah anticipates a time when the hearing of the people will be restored. As Evans has noted, "after the judgment, there is restoration, in which perception returns (attended by righteousness, justice, and trust in God)."[56] So in Isaiah 29 we read, "On that day the deaf shall hear (שָׁמַע) the words of a scroll, and out of their gloom and darkness the eyes of the blind shall see" (29:17-18). The refrain of restoration of hearing (and sight) recurs in Isaiah 32: "Then the eyes of those who have sight will not be closed, and the ears of those who have hearing (שָׁמַע) will listen" (32:3).[57] These texts are set in the context of future redemption and envision a renewed hearing resulting in understanding as characteristic of God's people. An eschatological reversal of the receptivity of Israel is set forth in contrast to their current obdurate state.

There is, however, a final way in which the motif of hearing weaves its way through Isaiah which complicates a simple temporal distinction between Israel's current lack of hearing and their future ability to hear. The numerous injunctions to *hear* that occur across Isaiah imply that hearing which results in understanding is always a possibility. Isaiah's audience (its hearers!) is presumed to have the capacity to respond to these many injunctions. For example, Isaiah addresses rulers of the people whom he defines as "scoffers" to "hear the word of the LORD" (28:14; שִׁמְעוּ דְבַר־יְהוָה). In fact, as the oracle continues, the prophet calls them to stop scoffing (28:22) and instead to "Listen, and hear my

---

55. Evans indicates that Isa. 42:18f., although negatively cast with language of obduracy, hints of coming promise. "Second Isaiah declares that it is time for Israel to wake up and recognize what God has accomplished in recent times." Craig A. Evans, *To See and Not Perceive: Isaiah 6.9-10 in Early Jewish and Christian Interpretation* (JSOTSup 64; Sheffield: JSOT, 1989), 44. This holds true for Isa 43:1-13 as well, where judgment and restoration are announced.

56. Evans, *Isaiah 6.9-10*, 46. In addition to Isa. 29:17-18; 32:3 (discussed above), cf. also Isa. 30:19-22.

57. Cf. also Isaiah 43, where the reversal of deafness is again echoed: "Bring for the people . . . who are deaf . . . and let them hear . . ." (43:8-9).

voice; / Pay attention, and hear my speech" (28:23). Clearly, even those with great propensity to *not* hear (scoffers) may respond to the call to listen. This idea is most potently communicated in the injunction to the deaf to hear and the blind to see (42:18; cf. also 42:23). Yet it is not only the most stubborn or deaf who are called to hear. At 44:1, *all the people of Israel* are called to listen to Yahweh (cf. also 48:1, 12). If these are real invitations to hear, then the possibility of reversal of obduracy for Isaiah's audience is real as well.[58]

This brief review of hearing in Isaiah should demonstrate that it is a significant Isaianic motif, especially as it belongs to the broader theme of Israel's obduracy and lack of understanding. The hearing motif also finds some literary resolution in the eschatological reversal of hearing — the time will come when the people will hear and respond rightly to Yahweh. We have already noted in our discussion above that this same eschatological emphasis is discernible in the use of the hearing motif in Matthew 13. We will explore this and other connections between Isaiah and Matthew in the final section of this paper.

Hearing and Not Hearing: Polyvalence and Rhetoric in Matthew's Use of Isaiah

At this point, a number of similarities between Isaiah's and Matthew's hearing themes become apparent.[59] First, the connection between hearing and understanding in Isaiah finds expression in Matthew as well. While the themes are often interconnected in individual passages in Isaiah (cf. explicit connection at 6:9-10; 43:9-10), the movement in Matthew is one in which hearing (Matthew 11–13) transitions to understanding (Matthew 13–16). Some instances of hearing in Isaiah (mere auditory perception) are contrasted with understanding, while in other cases hearing virtually includes understanding. Matthew picks up this patent connection to emphasize that hearing alone is not an adequate response to Jesus' ministry. Hearing that moves to understanding and then to obedience is right hearing (e.g., 13:23). It seems significant that the evangelist moves from language of hearing in Matthew 11–13 to that of understanding in Matthew 13–16. The effect of this connection and movement motivates the implied audience to strive to understand Jesus' message as they hear it.

---

58. Cf. injunctions to hear across Isaiah: 1:2, 10; 18:3; 32:9; 33:13; 34:1; 47:8; 49:1; 51:1, 4, 21; 66:5. "The rhetorical call for attention [using "hear/give heed"] is one of the most characteristic stylistic features of prophetic diatribe and protreptic." Joseph Blenkinsopp, *Isaiah 1–39* (AB; New York: Doubleday, 2000), 182. Blenkinsopp provides examples from Isaiah as well as from across the Hebrew Bible.

59. In this study, the focus from Matthew has been on Matt. 11:2–16:20.

Second, a significant part of the contrast between not hearing and hearing in Isaiah as well as Matthew seems to be of an eschatological nature. The restoration of Israel's hearing in Isaiah will come "on that day" (29:18; בַּיּוֹם הַהוּא), when God will act graciously toward Israel and hearing again will bring about understanding. As we have seen in our discussion of the Isaiah quotations in Matt. 11:2–16:20, the hearing motif also emerges in those moments when the eschatological nature of Jesus' work is emphasized. This seems to be, in part, because Matthew highlights Isaiah precisely at those junctures in which the evangelist is emphasizing the eschatological activity of God in Jesus the Messiah. For example, we saw in Matt. 11:2-19 that Matthew cites Isaiah's vision of the deaf hearing (11:5) as one indication that the Messianic age has arrived.

Matthew most directly emphasizes the eschatological restoration of hearing at 13:16-17, where the contrast is given between the disciples who are blessed because their ears hear the message of God's reign in Jesus and the prophets and righteous people of old who did not have the opportunity to hear Jesus' message. Clearly, in this case, the contrast is not between a rebellious, obdurate people and the disciples, since the prophets and righteous ones are said to have longed to hear what the disciples now hear (Matt. 13:17). Instead, the contrast is primarily a temporal one. The disciples are blessed to be recipients of Jesus' ministry and preaching. This observation helps us make sense of the contrast in the parables chapter between the crowds and the disciples as well. Since the crowds are those to whom the Isaiah 6 citation is directed, it is clear that they do not hear in a way that brings understanding. Yet, because the disciples are not only contrasted with the crowds (as ones who have been "given to know the secrets of the kingdom of heaven"; 13:11), but also with the prophets and righteous ones, whose only disadvantage seems to have been an eschatological one, we must be careful not to presume full understanding by the disciples. That they are privy to eschatological preaching (here, the parables and their interpretation) does not guarantee that they understand fully; it only shows their blessed stance in relation to those who do not sit at the same pivotal moment in God's salvation history and to the crowds who lack receptivity and are not privy to the full disclosure that the disciples receive (i.e., the parables' interpretations). "In the first contrast, the crowd's lack of receptivity and understanding is played against the disciples' possession of both . . . In the second contrast, the lack of historical fortune of the prophets and righteous men is contrasted with the disciples' good fortune."[60]

A third similarity between the hearing motif in Isaiah and Matthew focuses on the calls to hear that resound across both writings. In Isaiah, the call is often to hear *the word of Yahweh* (e.g., 1:10; 28:14; 66:5; cf. also 28:23). In addition, the in-

---

60. Trotter, "Understanding and Stumbling," 75.

junction to hear is a broad one; it goes out, for example, to Israel (44:1; 48:1, 12; 51:4), to all peoples or nations (18:3; 34:1), and to the faithful or righteous ones (51:1, 7). In Matthew, the thrice-repeated refrain, "The one who has ears ought to hear" (11:15; 13:9, 43), comes on the lips of Jesus and is spoken in reference to John the Baptist's role in bringing God's reign into history and in reference to Jesus' parables. The call in each case is to understand; and the call is issued to characters at the gospel's story level as well as to the reader on Matthew's discourse level.[61]

In fact, given the invitations to hear, especially in Matthew 13, it is unlikely that hearing would be viewed as an activity only a select group could fulfill. Anyone with ears can do it (11:15; 13:9, 43). And since in Jesus the eschatological moment for deaf ears to open has come (11:5), Matthew's reader will be encouraged to understand the calls to hear as true invitations to hearing and acceptance. In Matthew's view, his reader sits at the right time of salvation history: "Blessed are your eyes, for they see, and your ears, for they hear" (13:16).[62]

Having explored the connections between hearing in Isaiah and in Matthew, we can now bring them together to address how the hearing motif functions in Matthew. Since ἀκούω is used in more than one way by the evangelist, even within the same passage, its polyvalence functions to encourage the reader toward proper hearing. By providing contrasting ways of hearing, from mere auditory perception to understanding to acceptance, the audience is invited to consider their own way of hearing.[63] The implicit question raised is, *What kind of hearer will I be?* When hearing without understanding happens, as when Herod hears reports about Jesus' activity but wrongly identifies Jesus as John the Baptist raised from the dead (14:1-2), the reader is challenged to hear in a superior way.[64] Those in the story that hear but do not understand provide a foil for the reader that encourages proper hearing.[65] As Combrink observes, "The commands to listen (and understand) (11:5; 13:9, 43; 15:10; *cf.* also 17:5) would thus be relevant to the implied reader too as a challenge not to react in the same manner as Jesus' opponents."[66]

---

61. These are Chatman's terms for the two levels of narrative. Cf. Seymour Chatman, *Story and Discourse: Narrative Structure in Fiction and Film* (Ithaca: Cornell University Press, 1978); and Brown, *Disciples*, 35.

62. For the argument that Matthew more directly addresses his reader in the gospel's five discourses, cf. Brown, "Direct Engagement," 24-33.

63. According to Phillips, successful seeing and hearing results in action. Gary A. Phillips, "History and Text: The Reader in Context in Matthew's Parables Discourse," *Semeia* 31 (1985): 125.

64. Cf. also 13:13 for hearing without understanding.

65. For this reading effect in relation to the Matthean disciples, cf. Brown, *Disciples*, 128-33.

66. H. J. Bernard Combrink, "The Structure of the Gospel of Matthew as Narrative," *TynBul* 34 (1983): 89.

In addition, when hearing that leads to understanding, acceptance, and fruit bearing is described in the narrative, Matthew's implied reader is drawn to emulate this kind of hearing: "But as for what was sown on good soil, this is the one who *hears* the word and *understands* it, who indeed *bears fruit* and yields, in one case a hundredfold, in another sixty, and in another thirty" (13:23; italics mine). As Olmstead says, "In this narrative, hearing in its fullest sense can never be separated from obeying. The one who does not bear fruit does not hear and understand."[67] This kind of full hearing is what is intended in the three calls to hear at 11:15; 13:9 and 13:43 (cf. also 15:10): "The one who has ears ought to hear." The call is not simply to perceive sound physically. Matthew's Jesus is calling his audience to hearing that involves understanding and leads to acceptance. At the same time, Matthew is with rhetorical emphasis inviting his reader to this kind of right hearing.

Conclusion

In this essay, I have argued that Matthew picks up on Isaiah's motif of hearing/not hearing (especially in 11:2–16:20) and that his reliance on it can be seen more clearly by examining the Isaiah quotations in this part of Matthew. In addition, I contend that Matthew uses this motif in similar ways to its use in Isaiah, namely (1) to explain the rejection of God's message (through Jesus); (2) to point to the eschatological restoration of hearing (now begun in Jesus); and (3) to call the reader to true or full hearing, which evidences itself in understanding and acceptance. Matthew accomplishes this final task by weaving the Isaianic motif of hearing emphasized by means of Isaiah quotations into his subplot of varying responses to Jesus' ministry.

In this subplot, those who *hear* Jesus encompass the full spectrum of characters and character groups. In Matthew's story, Jesus' antagonists hear, John the Baptist hears, the disciples hear, and so do the crowds. Yet hearing does not guarantee right hearing, which expands to include understanding and even acceptance of Jesus and his message. While hearing can simply indicate auditory perception, at other points, hearing approximates understanding (11:15; 13:9; and 13:43) and paves the way for acceptance and fruit bearing.

Given the flexibility of ἀκούω in Matthew,[68] hearing functions as a rhetorical device that invites the reader into an active stance toward her own hearing.

---

67. Olmstead, *Matthew's Trilogy of Parables*, 109.
68. To refer to auditory perception or to include understanding; cf. discussion of Matt. 13:1-23 above.

As hearing is used to identify various responses to Jesus' message and ministry, more than one way of hearing is proposed for the reader. This polyvalence in relation to hearing is a rhetorical strategy that draws the reader toward understanding and accepting Jesus and his teachings.

Reflections on the Writing of a Commentary on the Gospel of Matthew

R. T. France and John Nolland

Three of the contributors to the present volume, and to the conference that lay behind it, have written commentaries on the Gospel of Matthew; indeed, one published two commentaries (three books) on Matthew. So there seemed to be value in including in the present work some reflection on the process of producing a commentary on this Gospel.[1] The initial reflections are those of John Nolland, followed by those of Dick (R. T.) France keyed to the sections of Nolland's remarks (not all Nolland's sections are used, and where France is commenting on a narrower front this is indicated in the heading). For Donald Hagner's reflections on the writing of a commentary on Matthew an earlier essay can be consulted.[2]

Reflections 1: Nolland

The Commentary Genre

What is one doing in writing a commentary? A survey of commentaries soon makes it clear that there is no uniform answer to this question. Of course there are certain kinds of background information that will be found in most, if not

---

1. D. A. Hagner, *Matthew* (WBC 33A-B; Dallas: Word, 1993-95); J. Nolland, *The Gospel of Matthew* (NIGTC; Grand Rapids: Eerdmans, 2005); R. T. France, *The Gospel according to Matthew: An Introduction and Commentary* (Leicester, U.K./Grand Rapids: Inter-Varsity Press/Eerdmans, 1985); idem, *The Gospel of Matthew* (NICNT; Grand Rapids: Eerdmans, 2007); and cf. *Matthew: Evangelist and Teacher* (Exeter/Downers Grove, IL: Paternoster/InterVarsity, 1989).

2. See D. A. Hagner, "Writing a Commentary on Matthew: Self-conscious Ruminations of an Evangelical," *Semeia* 72 (1995): 51-72.

Material from this essay has drawn upon "The Purpose and Value of Commentaries," *JSNT* 29 (2007): 305-11 and is reproduced here with permission.

all commentaries: almost all commentaries offer discussion of matters such as authorship and dating; and almost all commentaries devote a large part of their scope to commenting on blocks of text dealt with sequentially. But these common features do little more than identify the genre at the most general of levels, and leave the question of the specific investments of the commentator almost entirely open. In general, one is likely to try to write a commentary which is something like the commentaries one has found most helpful, or a commentary that has the qualities one wished one could have found in commentaries one has consulted and been disappointed with; and the commentary thus produced is likely to be at some level a reflection of how the commentator is personally constituted. Of course commentators will always work hard at trying to see things from the point of view of their intended readers, but in the case of the more detailed commentaries, which inevitably assume a better-informed reader who is prepared to invest effort, the more personal factors tend to leave the most obvious stamp on the product.

The Meeting Point of the Author's Viewpoint and Reader Viewpoints

I write as an Evangelical scholar, but I do not intend my work to be in any sense an in-house product. (In-house products have a place, even an important place, but most of the time I do not think that it is my role to work in that way.) Most of my conversation partners for the commentary do not share my specific faith perspectives; some do not have a faith perspective at all. I am grateful for their work and have learned from the whole range, and I would like to feel that I could communicate with the whole range. I have, therefore, given a good deal of thought to the question of how presuppositions should be allowed to function. Whatever one's presuppositions, it is a real turnoff to those who do not share some or all of them to find that the results being offered in a work are to a large degree a reworked restatement of the starting assumptions. I have tried hard to avoid this possibility. I have sought to write in such a way that readers with various sets of presuppositions can engage with and benefit from my work, without feeling that everything depends on coming from exactly the same starting point. I will have my blind spots, no doubt, but I have tried to generate an open texture of communication.[3] I have of course worked with assumptions of various kinds,

---

3. There has been development in my own approach since the production of my commentary on Luke (J. Nolland, *Luke* [WBC 35A-C; 3 vols.; Dallas: Word, 1989-93]), but the basic impulses of my scholarship have not changed. When the reviews appeared I was disappointed by various reviews in which I found that I was learning much more about the reviewer than I was about an evaluation of my work from which I might be able to benefit. I was finding out that the

but even then I have tried to work with my assumptions in such a way that the materials under investigation are allowed the power to nuance or even at times dislodge and entirely refashion starting assumptions. I have wanted to have a lightness of touch in relation to presuppositions.

Commentaries and Their Own Time Period

That commentaries are of their own period is evident from looking at commentaries from different periods. One could think of this negatively, and accuse the commentators of imposing their own perspectives on the biblical text; and no doubt plenty of that does happen. But one can also look at this positively and recognize that a commentary does and should involve a coming-to-terms-with and not simply the offering of a compendium of information about. Commenting inevitably involves, whether consciously or not, the bringing together of the horizons that belong to the text and the horizons that belong to the interpreter. Good commenting demands, I think, an openness in this conversation between horizons. If the horizons of the interpreter are dominant, then the text is unlikely to have been heard in more than a superficial manner: it will have been stretched upon a procrustean bed. If the horizons of the text are given exclusive dominance, then the danger is of a product that is technical and sterile, and distances readers from the text. But while commentaries are of their own period, it is also true that the best of commentaries tend to transcend their age. Calvin's commentaries continue to be worth reading in a way that Luther's are not to the same degree. Most of the nineteenth- and early-twentieth-century commentaries now look very stuck in their time period, but among others Adolf Schlatter and Godet — for somewhat different reasons — still repay at least selective attention. There is a cultural and historical specificity about any reading of a New Testament Gospel, but if these are texts that engage with God and with profound dimensions of what it is to be human, then those readings which have been most sensitive to the timeless within the timely will still have a capacity to address people at other times and in other places. Commentators cannot be their own best judges as to how well they have scored in this area. But as a commentator I have sought to listen to, indeed to prayerfully listen to, and not simply

---

reviewer and I had different assumptions and priorities, and little more. There was nothing wrong with pointing that out, but perhaps it was hardly fair to evaluate the work primarily on the basis of whether it shared the reviewer's particular presuppositions! Happily, other reviewers, whether they shared some of my specific starting points or not, were able to engage creatively with the work, see its strengths and offer useful critique.

master the text of the Gospel of Matthew. My eclectic approach to methods has been in part guided by a wish to avoid the kind of up-to-dateness that is in danger of soon becoming an out-of-dateness, as scholarly fashions move on.

Methodological Investments

My central concern in the commentary is with how Matthew tells his story and with the story he has to tell. The work is oriented to the nexus of communication between author and reader through the mediation of a rhetorically and structurally sophisticated text. Though it will be evident to any reader that some scholarly methods have influenced me more than others, my work is committedly eclectic. I am indebted to quite a range of methods for their capacity to illuminate, but I have been struck by the narrowness introduced into many works by the studious implementation of a method of inquiry, and also by the technical verbiage that especially the more recent methods often generate. I take sources seriously and with some regularity try to see how Matthew has edited his sources to serve the purposes of his narrative. My Matthew commentary is, however, not as oriented to source matters and tradition history as was my work on Luke — in part out of concern not to cover the same ground again. Nonetheless, there continues to be a major investment in historical background. The whole commentary is, broadly speaking, redaction-critical, inasmuch as I see Matthew as a careful editor of sources — a fairly conservative editor, but one who carefully integrates his material to present a well-considered whole message. There is narrative-critical investment in the commentary. Something of my interest here is caught in the words of T. L. Donaldson[4] when he speaks of "narrative worlds that readers can enter and experience through the act of reading." I am quite interested in how rhetoric works and consider Matthew to be a highly rhetorical work. I am persuaded that most people will have initially encountered the Gospel of Matthew as something to be heard rather than as something to be read; but at the same time it seems to me that the encoding used by Matthew is much too subtle to allow oral possibilities to limit interpretation. I have been modestly touched by Structuralist approaches, but in the end I generally find structure more illuminating. I find sociologically oriented studies very interesting, but am suspicious of the degree to which the results are predetermined by the chosen Sociological model. I am quite interested in Reader Response issues, but mostly in terms of the Gospel author's orchestration of the reading process (I have not

---

4. T. L. Donaldson, "The Mockers and the Son of God (Matthew 27.37-44): Two Characters in Matthew's Story of Jesus," *JSNT* 41 (1991): 4.

considered it necessary to distinguish the many hypothetical kinds of readers identified in Reader Response Theory) — but see further below. I have less time for ideological readings or for the hermeneutics of suspicion. I care about many of the things that Feminists care about, but do not have Feminist priorities. I have a particular interest in close reading of the inner logic of the unfolding text. I welcome Postmodern critique of the objectivity of Enlightenment rationalism and the flexibility that Postmodernism has brought to scholarship, but not its deconstructionist priorities or its radical hostility to all metanarratives.

I want to say a little more about how, in the writing of the commentary, I have thought about the process of reading. I have tried to write with a recognition of the intrinsic limitations involved in all attempts at communication. One way this shows up in the commentary is by the attempt made to indicate levels of confidence. I have wanted to mark different levels of confidence about judgments offered in the commentary. And I have wanted to distinguish between matters which are treated as foundational and matters where I have a judgment (and reasons for it), but which is not something that I have been prepared to construct an edifice on the basis of.

Issues of intrinsic limitations of communication, however, also run deeper. Inevitably, but also appropriately, I will understand what the other is seeking to communicate somewhat in connection with the horizons of my own life and experience — that is what I have to connect it to, if it is to have any significance for me. There is an "I" involved here, or better there is a series of "I-s": there is the "I" of my individuality; there is the "I" in my Christian identity with its individual and corporate dimensions; there is the "I" in my scholarly identity as part of the conversation of the scholarly fraternity; and surely there are others. I have been conscious that all of these "I-s" have a stake in my attempts to read appropriately and to appropriate what I read.

But there are yet other issues here. What writers produce will never be a perfect encoding of what they have in mind. They will say both more and less than they intend. More because the writing is informed not only by their conscious intentions, but also by aspects of what makes them up of which they are not at all or only partially conscious. More because they are making use of larger thought constructions and cultural artifices of which they may be only inchoately aware, or only partially aware, and which once evoked have resonances of their own that inevitably escape the control of the writer. More because it is a reader who must finally integrate into some significant whole what is being offered by the text; and readers in their attempts at integration inevitably make conscious or unconscious appeal to things that never entered the mind of the author. But also less because all attempts at communication are only partially successful. This might be because the producer of the text assumes, often quite unconsciously, a framing context within which what is being said makes its proper sense, but is only able imperfectly to provide that context directly within a text of any reasonable compass. (One reason for stressing the importance of original readers is that they may be assumed to share a good deal more than subsequent readers of the framing context assumed by the author.) This may be because no real reader is ever quite an ideal reader. Coding will be missed; coding will be disputed between readers; necessary background information will be imperfectly known, or not known at all. Conscious of these matters, I have wanted to recognize a certain fluidity of understanding as appropriate for a text like the Gospel of Matthew.

While real authors, however, hope for ideal readers, they are unlikely, if they have reflected on the matter, to assume ideal readers. Real authors are content with something less than an ideal reception of the text. They will be looking for successful and effective communication, not ideal communication; and they will expect to communicate to different readers to different degrees and at different levels. It is very likely that a Gospel writer like Matthew worked instinctively or consciously with an awareness that he would communicate to different degrees to different readers. He produces a text in which the large movements of the story could hardly be lost on even the most minimally attentive hearer of an oral performance of the Gospel. But he also produces a text with extremely complex cross-references and allusions to materials from the OT and wider Jewish tradition. He can hardly have assumed that all his intended readers would be able to decipher the complex coding he makes use of. He produces a text in which the large structural blocks and elements of the more detailed structuring are very obvious indeed, but in which, despite the very evident intense investment in structuring, the details of the intended structure evade even the most attentive of readers (sometimes the structure markers can be identified more readily than their function).

Despite all the appropriate qualifications and limitations, I have written with a confidence that with a document like the Gospel of Matthew a real writer successfully communicates with real readers in a transaction that can be ultimately satisfying for both parties. But I have also been content to see that there is to some degree — but only to some degree — a place for a plurality of interpretations of this Gospel.

Do Commentaries Write Themselves?

Novelists sometimes say that once their projects got under way the novels to some degree wrote themselves, with the starting point established and the interplay of characters once created dictating the direction of development, and resisting fiercely the author's attempts to control the development. I have found writing a commentary to be a bit like that. When I wrote on Luke I had a natural beginning point in a passage — Luke 4:16-30 — that I had worked extensively on in my doctoral research. I was fortunate to have already carefully attended to a piece that was programmatic for the Gospel of Luke, and I was able to work backward and forward from that pivot point. Nothing comparable offered itself for making a start on Matthew. However, I had spent ten years engaged with the Gospel of Luke before turning my attention to Matthew. So my first assumption was that I had commented already on a good deal of the material in Matthew and would be able to adapt this quickly to the Matthean frame. But such was not at all the case. I spent the best part of two years reading widely in the Matthean scholarship and exploring the text of the Gospel before I wrote a word. The Matthean world proved to be such a different world from the Lukan — so different that I was initially quite disoriented by the contrast. In the end I simply started from the beginning. By the time I had finished exploring the opening genealogy I had already begun to glimpse the central importance of the Jewish heritage for this Gospel writer. In many ways it has been a recognition of the immense Jewishness of this Gospel that has centrally shaped the commentary that has been produced — this is one respect in which the commentary, once begun, wrote itself.

The Commentator's Range of Answerability

There is inevitably a certain comprehensiveness of answerability involved in writing a commentary. People will look in it for everything they ever wanted to know about Matthew; and people will inevitably be disappointed in one respect or another. Inevitably a priority of importance must be established; otherwise what are already large books would become ridiculous and quite unusable. Some priorities are consciously set (e.g., see discussion below of *Heilsgeschichte*), and some are set in relation to expectations about readership (is one addressing people for whom the world of biblical scholarship or even the world of the Bible is quite unknown, or can one assume a broad general acquaintance with the world of the scholarly study of the Bible? — can one assume that readers will view the Gospel of Matthew as a privileged text, or are they as likely to come from outside the world of Christian faith? — will Christian readers expect explicit connections to be made between the biblical text and their own context of Christian discipleship, or will they be content to see the commentary's contribution as providing them with the raw material for such exploration?). But most priorities emerge indirectly from the sustained three-way conversation that goes on between the author of the commentary, the body of existing Matthean scholarship, and the text of the Gospel itself: the evident preoccupations of the Gospel itself must be respected; what lots of scholars have identified as important can hardly be ignored; light on matters that one has personally found puzzling surely must be included.

One of the decisions necessary for establishing priorities was that of what to do with *Wirkungsgeschichte* — the history of the effects of a text over time. Attention to *Wirkungsgeschichte* has clearly functioned to allow fresh access to the substance of the Bible message, after the erosive effect of Enlightenment-inspired research which had increasingly bracketed out the central concerns of the text. As I have made use of various commentaries which have made a significant investment in reporting the *Wirkungsgeschichte*, I have concluded that it is a very blunt instrument that most of the time illuminates the vicissitudes of the history of the church more than it illuminates the biblical text itself. But a life of personal Christian discipleship and engagement with the life of the church have their own ways of providing relevant horizons in relation to which to attempt to elucidate biblical texts in ways that attend to the fundamental investments of the texts themselves. And the truth is that to the degree that one is inevitably a product of the *Wirkungsgeschichte*, it has its impact on one as an interpreter whether one likes it or not, and to some extent whether one knows all the specifics of the *Wirkungsgeschichte*. For good or ill, attention to the *Wirkungsgeschichte* has not been part of the agenda for this commentary.

Compromises about Readership

I have wanted to write a work that would be serviceable for as wide an audience as possible. I have tried hard to limit as much as possible the use of jargon. But I soon discovered that there were compromises to be made if the scope of the work was to be kept within any reasonable bounds. Explaining everything for the sake of the novice takes a lot of words, and may in the end compromise the seriousness with which others who have no need of such introduction will take the work. I hope I have found a middle ground.

Engaging the Scholarship

I have thought of myself as serving a kind of apprenticeship by engaging with the existing scholarly literature in as comprehensive a manner as possible. But I have not wanted to produce a commentary on the scholarship or even a digest of the scholarship. I have wanted the commentary to focus squarely on the text of Matthew, and not on the scholarship on Matthew. I have been very happy to gather up insights scattered through the specialist literature; and I have wanted to evaluate within a larger framework the many suggestions that have been made about particular features of the Gospel text. But while I have tried to acknowledge every specific debt, I have minimized the citation of fellow scholars.

The Whole and the Parts

One of the challenges in writing a commentary is that of insuring that the questions one seeks to answer relate to all the appropriate levels for interpretation. Questions at the level of detail are easy to identify, but they constantly threaten to overwhelm the enterprise, so that a reader becomes lost in an endless rehearsal of detail. Standing back from the detail is as important as becoming immersed in the detail. As a natural "bottom up" thinker I tend to get to the bigger picture by building it up from the level of detail and am less at home with spelling out the detail in relation to an overview that is first put into place. To some degree the big picture for me is something that is always in the process of emerging, and my temptation is to defer adequate attention to questions of the big picture. I have found that a close attention to structure and flow of thought have been invaluable in lifting me beyond detail to reflect on the role of material in relation to the larger shape of the story. Matthew creates a complex set of hierarchies in his Gospel that help to control the detail of his material in relation to the whole that he is creating. Attention to thematic development, literary linkages and structural markers have all helped to insure that I have traveled up through the levels of questions from those that relate to detail to those that relate to the big picture.

Matters of Introduction

Matters of introduction turn up at the beginning of commentaries, and mine is no exception. But there is a question as to the status to be given to what is said there. Are these the working assumptions (appropriately articulated and defended) on which the rest of the commentary work rests? In my own case this is only minimally so. Though these matters are, logically, preliminary to engagement with the Gospel, the facts about them generally cannot be determined without attention to the Gospel. And in many cases the facts about them continue to be a matter of debate. In the various areas I have provided a discussion and indicated my own judgments and my reasons for them. But I have been reluctant to make these judgments working assumptions for the commentary.

Procedurally, I paid detailed attention to the questions of introduction only after I had completed in draft the whole commentary. I have tried to make my attention to questions of introduction answerable to an exploration of the whole text of the Gospel rather than bringing to the study of the text of the Gospel a set of pre-existing conclusions about introductory matters. Sometimes in the scholarship it becomes glaringly obvious that the material of the Gospel is being made to conform to conclusions already reached about matters of introduction. Admittedly these conclusions have arisen in part out of a consideration of features of the Gospel, but they then seem to me to have become a procrustean bed in relation to all the other features of the Gospel. As I have explored my way through Matthew and pondered the scholarly views, judgments about matters of introduction have not served as a guiding star helping me to find my way from text to text through the various possible construals. I claim no pristine purity here. I am aware that I will have been influenced by background assumptions of which I am not fully conscious. I am also aware that the more of the Gospel text I had explored in detail, the more the exploration of a new piece was inevitably, and to a point I believe properly, conditioned by the earlier work. I only want to say that I have done all within my power to avoid placing a straightjacket over the reading of the Gospel based upon conclusions about matters of introduction. And I have said to my readers that there should be a provisionality about how they bring to the reading of the Gospel and of my commentary on the Gospel the conclusions of this introduction.[5]

Dating Matthew

I did my work on the commentary with a broad assumption that the Gospel of Matthew was, as virtually everybody agrees, a first-century document, but I had assumed nothing more precise. Only as I worked on the materials of chapter 24 did the conviction come that the materials of this chapter can be made to

---

5. The one clear exception to my pattern of leaving detailed consideration of matters of introduction to the end has to do with my working assumption that Matthew had available to him the Gospel of Mark, or something much like it. More tentatively, I have also assumed that the writer of the Gospel of John did not have access to any of the Synoptic Gospels. I think that Matthew wrote in a source-rich environment, with materials often coming to him in more forms than we can any longer identify. This view is explained and defended in the Introduction, but it does not function as a foundational assumption for the commentary proper.

make good sense only if they are understood to make assumptions about the destruction of Jerusalem and its temple in the first century that in the event proved not to be true in every respect. This conviction in turn offered me the alternatives of a post-70 document that had faithfully incorporated a pre-70 perspective, despite its evident errors from a post-70 perspective — but Matthew seemed to be not at all adverse to editing his materials to enable them to serve most helpfully his own specific purposes — or the possibility that we were dealing with a pre-70 document. This in turn led me to review all the Gospel materials where there was any possibility that a post-70 environment was in some way being reflected. None of the scholarly claims along these lines seemed to me to have a very solid basis to them; a general first-century Jewish setting, whether pre- or post-70, seemed quite adequate in every case, and especially so when the limitations of the knowledge base from which we reconstruct first-century Judaism is properly admitted to. And it was clear that there were various features of the Gospel which, while they did not require that the temple still be standing and in use, had their most natural sense against the background of such an assumption. Did the source situation have any bearing on the likelihood of a pre-70 date for the Gospel? My work on Luke had led me to the conclusion that the best dating option for that Gospel was either in the period of resurgent nationalism leading up to the Jewish war or in the period soon after the war, when that period was still freshly in focus. Since I had been convinced that Luke used Mark, a yet earlier date for Mark became a necessary part of the picture. But the possibility of a pre-70 date for Mark, while not universally favored, is well represented in the scholarship, and I considered my work on Luke to be a fresh argument in favor of a pre-70 date for Mark. Perhaps all three Synoptic Gospels were composed in a fairly narrow time band, the later two inspired by the first, and by other now lost attempts to provide an account of Christian origins with the fundamental shape of an account of the "career" of Jesus.

Matthew as Theologian?

From my work on Matthew I have become convinced that it articulates a clear enough set of theological beliefs, but a couple of qualifications to this are of some importance. First, Matthew writes as a pastoral theologian and not as a systematic thinker. His concern is to address and challenge, and despite the highly structured nature of his Gospel he should not be looked to for systematic instruction about the Christian faith. This sometimes means that it is not really possible to clarify from within the Gospel what the relationship is between aspects of Matthew's theological vision. Second, Matthew has a story to tell, not simply a set of beliefs to articulate, and the story mode gives an event-shape to Matthew's beliefs: this is what has happened; this is what is to happen; this is what Matthew's readers are being encouraged to relate themselves to in an appropriate manner. It is the drama of the story and how it works as a story which have priority over the set of beliefs which comes to expression. At the end of the day, except in a secondary and derivative sense, "What does Matthew believe about . . . ?" is not quite the right sort of question to be asking Matthew.

A central area in which it has proved difficult to integrate aspects of Matthean theology is in connection with soteriology. On the one hand, Matthew's Gospel insists that the living out of Jesus' vision of an abundant righteousness is a fundamental necessity for entry into the kingdom. Near enough is not good enough for disciples of Jesus. They are to discover the full depth and range of what is involved in how God calls upon us to live. They are to live a life of uncompromising love toward even their enemies, and their lives are to be sharply focused on the service of God. However, although the Matthean Jesus makes no concessions to laxity, he does not seem to be making sinless perfection a condition for entry into the kingdom. A heart for the new ways must be there, but human frailty is well recognized in the strong Matthean emphasis on the importance of forgiveness: extended to others and received ever afresh from God.

This, perhaps, prepares us for what is, on the other hand, Matthew's clear investment in the idea that Jesus' death to be viewed as a saving event, as *the* saving event. At the Last Supper the kingdom language which has been prominent throughout the Gospel is displaced by covenant language, and the pouring out of Jesus' blood in death is identified as the means of forgiveness and that by which the (renewed) covenant is to be sealed. Just how we are to understand this is not entirely clear. But imagery of ransom and of sacrifice is made use of. Jesus is certainly not seen as absorbing the wrath of God in such a way as to leave no room for other manifestations of his wrath. The judgment to come upon the people of Jerusalem makes that clear. Jesus does, however, seem to function as a kind of lightning rod for the coming wrath of God, which is to be spent on him so that others may be spared the wrath that is justly their due. But to which others does this apply? The answer will finally be: only those who are prepared to align themselves with Jesus and all that he stands for. God's ways are marked by generosity to the repentant but severity to the rebellious. Even in his salvific death Jesus calls to a new way of life. And Matthew holds out the hope that Jesus' death and vindication through resurrection will open the ears of many to his message who were deaf to it during his lifetime.

That Matthew does not think that the cross as salvific is some sort of alternative to the stringent demands of discipleship is clear in 20:25-28, where, precisely as salvific, the cross becomes the supreme example of the servant role to which the disciples are summoned. To understand the relationship between grace and demand has always been a challenge for Christians, as it has been for Jews. In our primary documents they tend to stand side by side, as both of ultimate significance, but the interrelationship between the two is not immediately transparent. The Gospel of Matthew is no exception. The proclamation of the kingdom is the proclamation of God's saving intervention (5:3-10), but it also makes repentance urgent (4:17). Jesus healed and fed, but he also taught, inspired, challenged and threatened with judgment. He taught a practice of unceasing forgiveness, but paradoxically he announced that there would be no forgiveness from God for those who were not prepared to be forgiving (18:22, 35).

Conclusion

I have commented briefly on a range of matters that have come into focus for me in the process of writing a detailed commentary on the Gospel of Matthew. No doubt there are others that I have left unaddressed. I might have commented more extensively on what I see as the pervasive Jewishness of this Gospel; there will be those who fear that I do not allow sufficiently for its Christian distinctiveness. For me the writing of a commentary has taken me through the whole gamut of emotional responses from exhilaration, excitement and a sense of privilege to frustration, boredom and perplexity. Problem solving is an important ingredient to my personality (perhaps it has something to do with the fact that I came into Biblical Studies from a background of Mathematics and Physics), and this Gospel has given me plenty of problems to look for solutions to. There is a quiet satisfaction in having seen the project through to completion.

Reflections 2: France

John Nolland has done a fine job of setting out, in a typically thoughtful and measured way, the sort of issues that confront any commentator, and some of the specifics of commenting on Matthew. I am grateful for his open acknowledgment of some of the personal and professional dilemmas involved. I am in basic agreement with a majority of what he has written, and so shall not repeat it in these briefer comments. I shall confine myself to underlining and expanding on a few of his points which have also been important to me, and to setting out some of the methodological peculiarities which arose for me because I had already written both a shorter ("popular") commentary (the Tyndale Commentary, 1985) and a sort of extended introduction (*Matthew: Evangelist and Teacher*, 1989) to this gospel.

The Commentary Genre

I began my 2002 commentary on Mark with the declaration: "I have tried to write the sort of commentary I like to use. Whether this is what other readers are looking for will depend on what they think a biblical commentary should be. But I hope there are enough other people who share my expectations to make the enterprise worthwhile."[6] I have found, like John (n. 3), that reviews often reveal more about the reviewer than about the book. There were those reviewers who obviously fell into the category of those who like the same type of commentary, and others who did not, but the latter can be divided into those whose reviews did little more than state this fact, and those who tried to assess the commentary on its own terms. To the latter I am very grateful: they are the most valuable reviews. Incidentally, another thing I noticed about reviewers is that most rely on the introduction to give them a taste of the approach of the commentary, and some showed little sign of having read further; so I took a big gamble in dispensing with the traditional introduction in my new commentary (see below); I wonder what this will do to the review process!

So what is "the sort of commentary I like to use"? It is, I think, very traditional. I turn to a commentary for help with exegesis. In practice I fear that most often this is in relation to specific texts, often problem texts, but I am aware that in so doing I am not being fair to the commentator, since the detail must be read in the light of the interpretation of the passage (and indeed the book) as a whole. It is commonplace these days to speak about the importance of reading a gospel as a single, continuous story rather than as a collection of independent units; the difference from the days when form criticism dominated study of the gospels is breathtaking. So a central concern of the commentator must be to trace, and to help readers to follow, the flow of the narrative and the development of themes through the gospel as a whole. I have therefore attempted to locate each new section, large or small, within the narrative development, and the introductory comments on individual pericopes may in some cases take as much space as comment on individual verses. To quote my Mark commentary again: "The verse-by-verse comment on details of the text which occurs within each section is intended as supplementary to the introductory

---

6. R. T. France, *The Gospel of Mark* (NIGTC; Grand Rapids: Eerdmans, 2002), 1.

comments on the section itself and to be read only in that light. In other words, reference only to what I have to say under a given verse number may not represent all or even the most important part of what I have to say about the significance of that verse in its setting."[7] This approach requires of the reader a more sophisticated approach than the traditional verse-by-verse commentary, but it is one which the narrative integrity of the text demands. A gospel is not just a collection of verses.

My overriding concern with exegesis means that I devote less space than many commentators to issues of source and tradition criticism. I am more interested in what the text says than in how it came to exist in its present form. Synoptic comparisons often throw helpful light on Matthew's distinctive "take" on a given saying or incident, but I have not felt obliged to comment on them where there is no obvious exegetical payoff. Nor have I always felt it necessary to account for Matthew's "omissions." Like John (n. 5), I have my doubts about the adequacy of a simple two-document hypothesis, and believe that the process of gospel-writing among the first-century churches was more complex and probably involved more varied contacts than a simple "Who-copied-whom?" approach allows for.[8] So I have not always assumed that Mark represents the earliest accessible form of a given tradition, nor that Matthew is always consciously relating to or deviating from Mark's version, even though it seems clear to me that Matthew has been strongly influenced by Mark both in the overall structure of his gospel and in much of its content. But the first gospel is not a "revised Mark," but something new and with a life of its own, and it is that life that I want to discover and convey.

There are of course other ways of writing a commentary, some dramatically different from mine. I remember the experience of being asked to review Fernando Belo's *Materialist Reading of the Gospel of Mark*[9] and struggling to find any point of contact between what he was looking for in the text and the approach I had inherited from my Western historico-grammatical tradition; and there was the same lack of connection between the means by which he sought meaning and those that came naturally to me. It was seldom that I found sufficient common ground to make any meaningful reference to Belo in my own commentary. Matthew too has been well represented among "alternative"

---

7. France, *Gospel of Mark*, 2.

8. I still stand by the assessment of the Synoptic Problem which I set out in *Matthew: Evangelist and Teacher*, 24-49.

9. F. Belo, *A Materialist Reading of the Gospel of Mark* (translated from the French; Maryknoll, NY: Orbis, 1981). The author is a Portuguese Catholic of Marxist convictions. The flavor of the book may perhaps be gauged by the heading of the introduction: "K/X or the Problematic" [K/X refers to MarK and MarX].

approaches to commentary writing, though I am not aware of any quite as "alternative" as Belo. One notices, for instance, Warren Carter's tendency to discover political nuances in the text which have escaped earlier "bourgeois" exegetes (reminiscent of Ched Myers' earlier interpretation of Mark). I think the commentator must be content to "let a thousand flowers bloom," recognizing that one's own is but one of the available approaches, and one that will not resonate with everyone. Sometimes welcome new insights will come from these different perspectives. But that is no reason to abandon one's own tradition of exegesis where it still seems to offer what at least some readers from one's own cultural background (and possibly from others) continue to find illuminating. The commentator remains an interpreter, and that interpretation will result from the commentator's own interaction, within the bounds of his or her cultural framework, with the text.

Methodological Investments: A Variety of Readers

I resonate strongly with John's comments on Matthew's "awareness that he would communicate to different degrees to different readers." Many years ago I proposed such an approach especially to Matthew's formula-quotations.[10] I argued that Matthew, like the authors of some of the best "children's" fiction and television shows, catered to readers at all levels. At one extreme were those who simply noted superficial links between the story line and details of the quoted text; at the other were the more sophisticated readers who, with their wider scriptural knowledge and more creative interpretative method, were able to discern several further "bonus" levels of meaning which Matthew had encoded in his text. As with parables, the more you bring to the text, the more you get out of it. No doubt there were shared interpretative patterns and in-group conventions between Matthew and at least some of his projected readers, some of which may be difficult or impossible for us now to reconstruct with any confidence. Hence the happy hunting-ground for scholarly ingenuity which especially the formula-quotations have become. The commentator can but draw attention to some of these possibilities, recognizing that among his or her own readers there is likely to be a similar range both of expertise and of willingness to think new thoughts. But it is my impression that Matthew's "surprising" uses of scripture, for which evangelicals in the past used to feel the need to apologize, are now more healthily accepted as the mark of a creative explora-

---

10. "The Formula-Quotations of Matthew 2 and the Problem of Communication," *NTS* 27 (1980-81): 233-51.

tion of the scriptural heritage in the light of the coming of the Messiah which must surely have been one of the most exciting elements in first-century Christian life and thought.

Do Commentaries Write Themselves?

I wish they did! Especially with a book of the length and density of Matthew it is a long, hard slog, one which I undertook with considerable reluctance having just spent ten years doing the same for the much less tightly packed and shorter Gospel of Mark. But now that I am retired it has been easier to find the time, and the work ground remorselessly on, not as quickly as I had hoped, but at least within not much more than four years this time.

But my situation was different from John's. He came "fresh" to Matthew from Luke. I came immediately from Mark, but having been focused on (and published on) Matthew for many years before that. So I suppose that on many issues I could already see where I was going, both in terms of having been exposed to the scholarly literature for some time and in the fact that I had already had to formulate, and publish, my views on many (most) of the key issues. But, on the other hand, a decade is a long time in scholarship, and the shape of academic discussion had changed in significant ways. And of course I was older, if not wiser; I could not take it for granted that I would still agree with what I had said earlier. In fact, in the event, I quite often did not (and the new commentary draws attention to this from time to time).

My Tyndale commentary was designed for readers who could not be assumed to be familiar with academic discussion, and was in any case so constrained by space limits that it was not possible, even if desirable, to enter into debate in any depth. On the other hand, my *Matthew: Evangelist and Teacher* was intended as a guide through scholarly debate for the beginning specialist student, and its scope allowed a fuller consideration of such issues than most commentary introductions can afford. Now I had the opportunity to produce a commentary at that sort of level. But I did not want to simply repeat in an expanded form what I had already said. So a new start was needed, but not a standing start; my mind was already well stocked, but the approach must be different.

My method has been the same that I followed in my Mark commentary, to write a first draft of what I wanted to say on each section before turning to the other commentaries, relevant articles, and the like, so as to insure that I was making a distinctive contribution rather than simply responding to other people's commentaries. The difference this time was that my own earlier commentary and book on Matthew (and, where appropriate, my commentary on Mark) came into the same category: they too were kept on one side until I had written my first draft. As a result, the approach to many sections is significantly different, based on the way I now approach the text twenty years later. At times, as mentioned above, I was surprised to find what I had previously written and now wished to take a different line.

The more generous scale of the NICNT series has allowed me to take much fuller account of other people's contributions. I have done this largely in the footnotes, which are therefore quite extensive. It is there that most of the interaction with other views and interpretations is found. Sometimes further reading led me to modify my first draft, but generally the main text reflects my own interaction with the text, the footnotes more my interaction with scholarship.

The Commentator's Range of Answerability: Wirkungsgeschichte

When Childs's great Exodus commentary came out in 1974, I was among those who hailed its "canonical" approach as a breath of fresh air. I still believe that it was, and is, a model of how scripture can and should be understood as part of an ongoing process, so that the subsequent reception of the text is taken into account along with its synchronic relations. And while this is preeminently true of Old Testament scripture in relation to its development in the New Testament, it seems to me also that the responses of readers to New Testament texts, both within and beyond the New Testament period, are an interesting and potentially significant part of our engagement with the text as scripture.

But, as John has illustrated in several ways, the commentator is always confronted by the need to make choices over what should and should not be included in the space available, and these choices must be made in the light of what are expected to be the primary interests of one's readers. It quickly became clear that in a primarily exegetical commentary any significant survey of the history of interpretation of the text, even if I had been equipped to provide it, would have been an unjustifiable luxury. Fortunately, however, in the case of Matthew the commentator is spared any anxiety on this point by the great commentary of Luz, which devotes a good deal of space and vast erudition to tracing the fate of each pericope particularly in patristic (and often Reformation) interpretation. It is perhaps the nearest thing we have to a "Childs-type" commentary on Matthew (though I suspect Luz would not be entirely comfortable with that designation!). It is a pleasure to be able to refer the interested reader gratefully to a job already admirably done, and thus with a clear conscience to refrain from my own account of the *Wirkungsgeschichte* of the gospel.

Matters of Introduction

Like John, I always write the introduction last. But this time it is rather different. I find myself in the same situation as Howard Marshall when he wrote his NIGTC commentary on Luke. He had recently published his introductory book on Luke,[11] the foundation volume of the series in which my *Matthew: Evangelist and Teacher* is found. As a result the "Introduction" section of his commentary consists of only eight pages, on which he comments: "Instead of an introduction to the Gospel of Luke, . . . what is offered here is a brief introduction to the commentary."[12] This seemed to me a good example to follow, both because it would be tedious to go over the same ground again and also because the result was a welcome reduction in the size of an already swelling volume. True, in Howard's case the interval between introduction and commentary was a mere eight years, in my case seventeen, but I still find myself able to echo Howard's claim: "The further study involved in the completion of the commentary . . . has not led me to alter my basic understanding of Luke in any vital points." Perhaps I am too old and set in my ways to think new thoughts — or perhaps I got it right then! At any rate, I too have dispensed with the customary introductory coverage of all the general issues relating to the study of the gospel which I had already covered in my earlier book, and hope that the reader who is interested to know what I think on these matters will be willing to resort to that fuller treatment. Instead, I have used the introduction to highlight a number of issues to which the commentary repeatedly refers but which are better dealt with first in a more general way. It contains brief summaries on the structure of the gospel, the significance of Galilee and Judea in Matthew's narrative outline, the nature and aims of the five discourses, and the formula-quotations. There is only the briefest summary of my views on the date, authorship, literary relations and social setting of the gospel — enough, I hope, to placate the outraged reviewer who does not have access to *Matthew: Evangelist and Teacher*, but no attempt to cover all the ground again or to justify again the stance I had already taken on these issues. There is no attempt at a systematic "theology of Matthew."

This unconventional approach is the result of my own specific situation. It is not the way I would write the introduction to a commentary on a book on which I had not previously published; see my Mark commentary for a more conventional approach.

---

11. I. H. Marshall, *Luke: Historian and Theologian* (Exeter, U.K.: Paternoster, 1970).
12. I. H. Marshall, *The Gospel of Luke: A Commentary on the Greek Text* (NIGTC; Exeter, U.K.: Paternoster, 1978), 29.

Dating Matthew

As a longtime advocate of a pre-70 date for Matthew (and a slightly earlier date for Mark) I am pleased to see John's cautiously open conclusion on this issue. But I fear the discussion is often skewed by a quite unnecessary assumption of an ideological commitment (hence perhaps John's guarded conclusion?). It is taken for granted that "evangelicals" will favor an early date and "liberals" (i.e., mainstream scholarship) a later one. I suppose there is some truth in this in that evangelicals tend to defend Jesus' temple sayings as real prediction whereas others prefer to regard them as *ex eventu*. But that is not the only issue involved in dating a gospel. After all, it was Harnack, hardly an arch-conservative, who gave one of the strongest boosts to dating the gospels in the sixties; and J. A. T. Robinson was hardly a defender of evangelical theology. The arguments put forward by Gundry for dating Matthew in the sixties still remain to be adequately answered. The problem is that the whole dating scheme for the gospels (and indeed other NT documents) is interconnected, and once you admit the possibility that the traditional scheme is insecurely based many hitherto unquestioned assumptions become vulnerable. It is more comfortable to stay with the "received wisdom" of the twentieth century.

Conclusion

More could be commented on, but this must suffice. Writing this commentary was a stimulating, if demanding, process. But I will not be in a hurry to write another commentary — and fortunately no one is asking me to!

Bibliography

Ådna, Jostein. *Jesu Stellung zum Tempel*. Wissenschaftliche Untersuchungen zum Neuen Testament 2.119. Tübingen: Mohr Siebeck, 2000.

Aitken, K. T. "Hearing and Seeing: Metamorphoses of a Motif in Isaiah 1–39." Pages 12-41 in *Among the Prophets: Language, Image, and Structure in the Prophetic Writings*. Edited by P. R. Davies and D. J. A. Clines. Journal for the Study of the Old Testament: Supplement Series 144. Sheffield: JSOT Press, 1993.

Albright, W. F., and C. S. Mann. *Matthew: A New Translation with Introduction and Commentary*. Garden City, N.Y.: Doubleday, 1971.

Allen, E. "Greek Syntactical Analysis: An Investigation into the Relationship between Conjunctions and Contextual Variables in the Gospel of Matthew." M.Sc. thesis, University College London, September 1999.

———, and V. Farewell. "Statistical Analysis of the Choice of Conjunction in the Gospel of Matthew." Appendix to *Sentence Conjunctions in the Gospel of Matthew: καί, δέ, τότε, γάρ, οὖν and Asyndeton in Narrative Discourse*, by S. L. Black. Journal for the Study of the New Testament: Supplement Series 216. Studies in New Testament Greek 9. London: Sheffield Academic Press, 2002.

Allen, W. C. *A Critical and Exegetical Commentary on the Gospel According to S. Matthew*. 3d ed. International Critical Commentary. Edinburgh: T&T Clark, 1912.

Allison, D. C., Jr. "Matt. 23:39 = Luke 13:35b as a Conditional Prophecy." *Journal for the Study of the New Testament* 18 (1983): 75-84.

———. *The New Moses: A Matthean Typology*. Minneapolis: Fortress, 1993.

Alsup, J. E. "Typology." Pages 682-85 in *Anchor Bible Dictionary* 6. Edited by David Noel Freedman et al. New York: Doubleday, 1992.

Anderson, J. C. *Matthew's Narrative Web: Over, and Over, and Over Again*. Journal for the Study of the New Testament: Supplement Series 91. Sheffield: JSOT Press, 1994.

Andreoli, D. "Il velo squarciato nel Vangelo di Matteo." *Biblical Studies on the Web* 1 (1998): 35-40.

Arvedson, T. *Das Mysterium Christi: Eine Studie zu Mt. 11.25-30*. Leipzig: Alfred Lorentz, 1937.

Aune, D. E. *Prophecy in Early Christianity and the Ancient Mediterranean World.* Grand Rapids: Eerdmans, 1983.
Bacon, B. W. *Studies in Matthew.* London: Constable, 1930.
Baker, D. "Typology and the Christian Use of the Old Testament." *Scottish Journal of Theology* 29 (1976): 137-57. Repr. pages 313-30 in *The Right Doctrine from the Wrong Texts.* Edited by G. K. Beale. Grand Rapids: Baker, 1994.
Barnett, F. W. "Characterization and Christology in Matthew: Jesus in the Gospel of Matthew." *Society of Biblical Literature Seminar Papers* 28 (1989): 588-603.
Barton, S. C. "Dislocating and Relocating Holiness: A New Testament Study." Pages 198-200 in *Holiness: Past and Present.* Edited by Stephen C. Barton. London: T&T Clark, 2003.
———. *The Spirituality of the Gospels.* London: SPCK, 1992.
Battistella, E. L. *Markedness: The Evaluative Superstructure of Language.* Albany: State University of New York Press, 1990.
Bauckham, R. J. "The Coin in the Fish's Mouth." Pages 219-52 in *Gospel Perspectives 6: The Miracles of Jesus.* Edited by D. Wenham and C. Blomberg. Sheffield: JSOT Press, 1986.
———. *James.* London: Routledge, 1999.
———. "Jesus' Demonstration in the Temple." Pages 72-89 in *Law and Religion: Essays on the Place of the Law in Israel and Early Christianity.* Edited by B. Lindars. Cambridge: James Clarke, 1988.
———. "The Parable of the Royal Wedding Feast (Matthew 22:1-14) and the Parable of the Lame Man and the Blind Man *(Apocryphon of Ezekiel)*." *Journal of Biblical Literature* 115 (1996): 447-64.
———. "The Parting of the Ways: What Happened and Why." *Studia Theologica* 47 (1993): 135-51.
———. "Synoptic Parousia Parables Again." *New Testament Studies* 29 (1983): 129-34.
Bauer, D. R. *The Structure of Matthew's Gospel: A Study in Literary Design.* Journal for the Study of the New Testament: Supplement Series 31. Sheffield: JSOT Press, 1988.
Baum, A. D. "Bildhaftigkeit als Gedächtnishilfe in der synoptischen Tradition." *Theologische Beiträge* 35 (2004): 4-16.
———. "Experimentalpsychologische Erwägungen zur synoptischen Frage." *Biblische Zeitschrift* 42 (2000): 37-55.
———. "Die lukanische und chronistische Quellenbenutzung im Vergleich: Eine Teilanalogie zum synoptischen Problem." *Ephemerides theologicae lovanienses* 78 (2002): 340-57.
———. "Der mündliche Faktor. Teilanalogien zu den Minor Agreements aus der Oral Poetry-Forschung und der experimentellen Gedächtnispsychologie." *Biblica* 85 (2004): 264-72.
———. "Oral Poetry und synoptische Frage. Analogien zu Umfang, Variation und Art der synoptischen Wortlautidentität." *Theologische Zeitschrift* 59 (2003): 17-34.
Beale, G. K. *The Bible and the Church's Mission: A Biblical Theology of the Temple.* New Studies in Biblical Theology. Downers Grove, Ill.: InterVarsity Press, 2004.
———. "Isaiah VI 9-13: A Retributive Taunt against Idolatry." *Vetus Testamentum* 41 (1991): 257-78.
Beasley-Murray, G. R. *Jesus and the Kingdom of God.* Grand Rapids: Eerdmans, 1986.

———. *Jesus and the Last Days.* Peabody, Mass.: Hendrickson, 1993.
Beaton, R. *Isaiah's Christ in Matthew's Gospel.* Society for New Testament Studies Monograph Series 123. Cambridge: Cambridge University Press, 2002.
Becker, Hans-Jürgen. *Auf der Kathedra des Mose. Rabbinisch-theologisches Denken und antirabbinische Polemik in Matthäus 23, 1-12.* Arbeiten zur neutestamentlichen Theologie und Zeitgeschichte 4. Berlin: Institut Kirche und Judentum, 1990.
———. "Die Zerstörung Jerusalems bei Matthäus und den Rabbinen." *New Testament Studies* 44 (1998): 59-73.
Beckwith, R. *The Old Testament Canon of the New Testament and Its Background in Early Judaism.* Grand Rapids: Eerdmans, 1985.
Belo, F. *A Materialist Reading of the Gospel of Mark.* Translated from the French. Maryknoll, N.Y.: Orbis, 1981.
Benoit, P. "La mort de Judas." Pages 341-59 in Vol. 4 of *Exégèse et théologie.* 4 vols. Edited by P. Benoit. Paris: Cerf, 1961-82.
Berger, David *The Jewish-Christian Debate in the High Middle Ages: A Critical Edition of the Nizzahon Vetus, with an Introduction, Translation and Commentary.* Philadelphia: Jewish Publication Society of America, 1979.
Best, E. "1 Peter and the Gospel Tradition." *New Testament Studies* 18 (1967-68): 95-113.
Bestgen, Y. "Segmentation Markers as Trace and Signal of Discourse Structure." *Journal of Pragmatics* 29 (1998): 775.
Betz, H. D. "The Logion of the Easy Yoke and of Rest (Mt. 11:28-30)." *Journal of Biblical Literature* 86 (1967): 10-24.
———, and A. Y. Collins, *The Sermon on the Mount: A Commentary on the Sermon on the Mount, Including the Sermon on the Plain (Matthew 5:3–7:27 and Luke 6:20-49),* Hermeneia: A Critical and Historical Commentary on the Bible. Minneapolis: Fortress, 1995.
Black, M. "The Christological Use of the Old Testament in the New Testament." *New Testament Studies* 18 (1971): 1-14.
Black, S. L. *Sentence Conjunctions in the Gospel of Matthew: καί, δέ, τότε, γάρ, οὖν and Asyndeton in Narrative Discourse.* Journal for the Study of the New Testament: Supplement Series 216. Studies in New Testament Greek 9. London: Sheffield Academic Press, 2002.
Blank, S. H. "Death of Zechariah in Rabbinic Literature." *Hebrew Union College Annual* 13 (1938): 327-46.
Blenkinsopp, Joseph. *Isaiah 1–39.* Anchor Bible Commentary. Garden City, N.Y.: Doubleday, 2000.
Bloch, R. "Ecriture et Tradition dans le Judaïsme le Judaïsme, Aperçus sur l'origine du Midrash." *Cahiers Sioniens* 1 (1954): 9-34.
Bock, D. L. *Proclamation from Prophecy and Pattern: Lucan Old Testament Christology.* Journal for the Study of the New Testament: Supplement Series 12. Sheffield: Sheffield Academic, 1987.
Bockmuehl, Markus. *Jewish Law in Gentile Churches: Halakhah and the Beginning of Christian Public Ethics.* Grand Rapids: Baker, 2000.
———. "'Let the Dead Bury Their Dead': Jesus and the Law Revisited." Pages 23-48 in

Markus Bockmuehl, *Jewish Law in Gentile Churches*. Repr. from *Journal of Theological Studies* N.S. 49 (1998): 553-81.

Bons, E., ed. *"Car c'est l'amour qui me plait, non le sacrifice . . .": Recherches sur Oseé 6:6 et son interprétation juive et chrétienne*. Journal for the Study of Judaism: Supplement Series 88. Leiden, Boston: Brill, 2004.

Bornkamm, G., G. Barth, and H. J. Held. *Tradition and Interpretation in Matthew*. Translated by P. Scott. London: SCM, 1963.

Bower, G. H., and L. S. Bolton. "Why Are Rhymes Easy to Learn?" *Journal of Experimental Psychology* 82 (1969): 453-61.

Brawley, Robert L. "Reverberations of Abrahamic Covenant Traditions in the Ethics of Matthew." Pages 26-46 in *Realia Dei: Essays in Archaeology and Biblical Interpretation*. Edited by Prescott H. Williams, Jr. and Theodore Hiebert. Scholars Press Homage Series 23. Atlanta: Scholars Press, 1999.

Brooke, G. J. "4Q500 1 and the Use of Scripture in the Parable of the Vineyard." *Dead Sea Discoveries* 2 (1995): 279-85.

Brower, K. *Holiness in the Gospels*. Kansas City: Beacon Hill, 2005.

———. "Jesus and the Lustful Eye: Matthew 5:28." *Evangelical Quarterly* 76 (2004): 291-309.

———, and A. Johnson, eds. *Holiness and Ecclesiology in the New Testament*. Grand Rapids: Eerdmans, 2007.

Brown, J. K. "Direct Engagement of the Reader in Matthew's Discourses: Rhetorical Techniques and Scholarly Consensus." *New Testament Studies* 51 (2005): 19-35.

———. *The Disciples in Narrative Perspective: The Portrayal and Function of the Matthean Disciples*. Society for Biblical Literature Academia Biblica 9. Atlanta: Society of Biblical Literature, 2002.

Brown, R. E. *The Birth of the Messiah*. Anchor Bible Reference Library. New York: Doubleday, 1993 [1977].

———. *The Death of the Messiah: A Commentary on the Passion Narratives in the Four Gospels*. 2 vols. New York: Doubleday, 1994.

Bruce, F. F. *Paul: Apostle of the Free Spirit*. Carlisle, U.K.: Paternoster, 1980.

Bruner, F. D. *The Christbook, Matthew 1–12*. Vol. 1 of *Matthew: A Commentary*. Revised and Expanded Edition. Grand Rapids: Eerdmans, 2004.

Bryan, C. *A Preface to Mark: Notes on the Gospel in Its Literary and Cultural Settings*. Oxford: Oxford University Press, 1993.

Bultmann, R. "Prophecy and Fulfillment." Pages 50-75 in *Essays on Old Testament Hermeneutics*. Edited by Claus Westermann. Translated by J. C. G. Greig. Richmond: John Knox, 1963.

Burger, C. "Jesu Taten nach Matthäus 8 und 9." *Zeitschrift für Theologie und Kirche* 70 (1973): 272-87.

Burnett, F. *The Testament of Jesus-Sophia: A Redaction-Critical Study of the Eschatological Discourse in Matthew*. Washington, D.C.: University Press of America, 1979.

Buth, R. "Perspective in Gospel Discourse Studies, with Notes on *Euthus, Tote* and the Temptation Pericopes." *Selected Technical Articles Related to Translation* 6 (1982): 8.

Buttrick, D. *Speaking Jesus: Homiletic Theology and the Sermon on the Mount*. Louisville: Westminster John Knox, 2002.

Byrskog, Samuel. *Jesus the Only Teacher: Didactic Authority and Transmission in Ancient Israel, Ancient Judaism and the Matthean Community.* Coniectanea biblica: New Testament Series 24. Stockholm: Almqvist & Wiksell International, 1994.

Cargal, T. B. "'His Blood Be upon Us and upon Our Children': A Matthean Double Entendre?" *New Testament Studies* 37 (1991): 101-12.

Carroll, J. T., and J. B. Green. *The Death of Jesus in Early Christianity.* Peabody, Mass.: Hendrickson, 1995.

Carson, D. A. "Do the Prophets and the Law Quit Prophesying before John? A Note on Matthew 11:13." Pages 179-94 in *The Gospels and the Scriptures of Israel.* Journal for the Study of the New Testament: Supplement Series 104. Edited by C. A. Evans and R. W. Stegner. Sheffield: Sheffield Academic Press, 1994.

———. "Matthew." Pages 3-599 in Vol. 8 of *The Expositor's Bible Commentary.* Edited by Frank E. Gaebelein. Grand Rapids: Zondervan, 1984.

Carter, W. "Evoking Isaiah: Matthean Soteriology and an Intertextual Reading of Isaiah 7-9 and Matthew 1:23 and 4:15-16." *Journal of Biblical Literature* 119 (2000): 503-20.

———. *Matthew at the Margins: A Sociopolitical and Religious Reading.* Maryknoll, N.Y.: Orbis, 2000.

———. *Matthew: Storyteller, Interpreter, Evangelist.* Peabody, Mass.: Hendrickson, 1996.

Chapman, J. "St Paul and the Revelation to St Peter, Matt. XVI, 17." *Revue Benedictine* 29 (1912): 133-47.

Charlesworth, J. H. *The Old Testament Pseudepigrapha.* 2 vols. London: Darton, Longman and Todd, 1983-85.

Chatman, S. *Story and Discourse: Narrative Structure in Fiction and Film.* London: Cornell University Press, 1978.

Chester, Andrew. "Messianism, Torah and Early Christian Tradition." Pages 318-41 in *Tolerance and Intolerance in Early Judaism and Christianity.* Edited by G. N. Stanton and G. G. Stroumsa. Cambridge: Cambridge University Press 1998.

Chilton, B. D. *A Galilean Rabbi and His Bible: Jesus' Own Interpretation of Isaiah.* London: SPCK, 1984.

———. "God's Vineyard and Its Caretakers." Pages 381-406 in *Jesus and His Contemporaries: Comparative Studies.* Edited by Craig A. Evans. Arbeiten zur Geschichte des antiken Judentums und des Urchristentums 25. Leiden: Brill, 1995.

———. *Profiles of a Rabbi: Synoptic Opportunities in Reading about Jesus.* Brown Judaic Studies 177. Atlanta: Scholars Press, 1989.

Chronis, H. L. "The Torn Veil: Cultus and Christology in Mark 15:37-39." *Journal of Biblical Literature* 101 (1982): 97-114.

Clements, R. E. "Beyond Tradition-History: Deutero-Isaianic Development of First Isaiah's Themes." *Journal for the Study of the Old Testament* 31 (1985): 95-113.

Cohen, S. J. D. "The Destruction: From Scripture to Midrash." *Prooftexts* 2 (1982): 18-39.

Collins, R. F. "Matthew's *ENTOLAI:* Towards an Understanding of the Commandments in the First Gospel." Pages 1325-48 in Vol. 2 of *The Four Gospels 1992.* FS F. Neirynck. 3 vols. Edited by F. van Segbroeck et al. Bibliotheca ephemeridum theologicarum lovaniensium 100. Leuven: Leuven University Press, 1992.

Combrink, H. J. B. "The Structure of the Gospel of Matthew as Narrative." *Tyndale Bulletin* 34 (1983): 61-90.

Comrie, B. *Aspect: An Introduction to the Study of Verbal Aspect and Related Problems.* Cambridge Textbooks in Linguistics. Cambridge: Cambridge University Press, 1976.

Cope, O. L. *Matthew: A Scribe Trained for the Kingdom of Heaven.* Catholic Biblical Quarterly Monograph Series 5. Washington: Catholic Biblical Association of America, 1976.

Cousland, J. R. C. *The Crowds in the Gospel of Matthew.* Novum Testamentum: Supplement Series 102. Leiden: Brill, 2002.

Croft, W., and D. A. Cruse. *Cognitive Linguistics.* Cambridge: Cambridge University Press, 2004.

Cullmann, O. *Christ and Time.* Translated by F. Filson. London: SCM, 1962.

Cummings, J. T. "The Tassel of His Cloak: Mark, Luke, Matthew — and Zechariah." Pages 47-61 in *Studia Biblica 1978*: II. *Papers on the Gospels 2.* Edited by Elizabeth Anne Livingstone. Journal for the Study of the New Testament: Supplement Series 2. Sheffield: JSOT Press, 1980.

Cunningham, Philip A. "Actualizing Matthean Christology in a Post-Supersessionist Church." Pages 563-75 in Vol. 2 of *When Judaism and Christianity Began: Essays in Memory of Anthony J. Saldarini.* Edited by A. J. Avery-Peck, D. Harrington and J. Neusner. Journal for Jewish Studies: Supplement Series 85. Leiden: Brill, 2004.

Dalman, G. *Orte und Wege Jesu.* 3d ed. Gütersloh: C. Bertelsmann, 1924.

Daniélou, J. *From Shadows to Reality: Studies in the Biblical Typology of the Fathers.* London: Burns & Oates, 1960.

Daube, D. "The Earliest Structure of the Gospels." *New Testament Studies* 5 (1959): 147-87. Repr. pages 329-41 in Vol. 1 of *New Testament Judaism: Collected Works of David Daube.* Edited by Calum Varmichael. Berkeley: University of California Press, 2000.

———. *The New Testament and Rabbinic Judaism.* London: Athlone Press, 1956.

Davids, P. H. "James and Jesus." Pages 63-84 in *Gospel Perspectives 5: The Jesus Tradition outside the Gospels.* Edited by D. Wenham. Sheffield: JSOT Press, 1885.

Davies, G. I. "The Presence of God in the Second Temple and Rabbinic Doctrine." Pages 32-36 in *Templum Amicitiae: Essays on the Second Temple Presented to Ernst Bammel.* Edited by W. Horbury. Journal for the Study of the New Testament: Supplement Series. Sheffield: JSOT Press, 1991.

Davies, W. D. *The Gospel and the Land.* Berkeley: University of California Press, 1974.

———. *The Setting of the Sermon on the Mount.* Atlanta: Scholars Press, 1989.

———, and D. C. Allison. *A Critical and Exegetical Commentary on the Gospel according to Saint Matthew.* 3 vols. ICC. Edinburgh: T&T Clark, 1988-97.

Deines, Roland, *Die Gerechtigkeit der Tora im Reich des Messias: Mt 5,13-20 als Schlüsseltext der matthäischen Theologie.* Wissenschaftliche Untersuchungen zum Neuen Testament 177. Tübingen: Mohr Siebeck, 2005.

deSilva, D. *Honor, Patronage, Kinship, and Purity: Unlocking New Testament Culture.* Downers Grove, Ill.: InterVarsity Press, 2000.

Deutsch, C. *Hidden Wisdom and Easy Yoke: Wisdom, Torah and Discipleship in Matthew 11.25-30.* Journal for the Study of the New Testament: Supplement Series 18. Sheffield: JSOT Press, 1987.

———. "Wisdom in Matthew: Transformation of a Symbol." *Novum Testamentum* 32 (1990): 13-47.

Dodd, C. H. *The Parables of the Kingdom*. London: Nisbet, 1935.

Doering, Lutz. *Schabbat. Sabbathalacha und -praxis im antiken Judentum und Urchristentum*. Texte und Studien zum antiken Judentum 78. Tübingen: Mohr Siebeck, 1999.

Donaldson, T. L. "The Law That Hangs (Matthew 22:40): Rabbinic Formulation and Matthean Social World." *Catholic Biblical Quarterly* 57 (1995): 689-709.

———. "The Mockers and the Son of God (Matthew 27.37-44): Two Characters in Matthew's Story of Jesus." *Journal for the Study of the New Testament* 41 (1991): 3-18.

Donfried, K. P. "The Allegory of the Ten Virgins (Matt 25:1-13) as a Summary of Matthean Theology." *Journal of Biblical Literature* 93 (1974): 415-28.

Doohan, L. *Matthew: Spirituality for the 80's and 90's*. Santa Fe: Bear, 1985.

Dungan, D. L. *The Sayings of Jesus in the Churches of Paul: The Use of the Synoptic Tradition in the Regulation of Early Church Life*. Oxford: Blackwell, 1971.

Dunn, J. D. G. "Altering the Default Setting: Re-envisaging the Early Transmission of the Jesus Tradition." *New Testament Studies* 49 (2003): 139-75.

———. "Jesus and Oral Memory: The Initial Stages of the Jesus Tradition." *Society of Biblical Literature Seminar Papers* 136 (2000): 287-326. Repr. pages 84-145 in *Jesus: A Colloquium in the Holy Land*. Edited by D. Donnelly. New York: Continuum, 2001.

———. *Jesus Remembered*. Christianity in the Making 1. Grand Rapids: Eerdmans, 2003.

Eckstein, Hans-Joachim. "Die 'bessere Gerechtigkeit.' Zur Ethik Jesu nach dem Matthäusevangelium." *Theologische Beiträge* 32 (2001): 299-316.

Eco, U. *The Role of the Reader: Explorations in the Semiotics of Texts*. Bloomington: Indiana University Press, 1979.

Eichrodt, W. "Is Typological Exegesis an Appropriate Method?" Pages 224-45 in *Essays on Old Testament Hermeneutics*. Edited by C. Westermann. Translated by J. Barr. Richmond: John Knox, 1963.

Ellis, E. E. "Biblical Interpretation in the New Testament Church." Pages 691-725 in *Mikra: Text, Translation, Reading and Interpretation of the Hebrew Bible in Ancient Judaism and Early Christianity*. Compendia rerum iudaicarum ad Novum Testamentum 2.1. Philadelphia: Fortress, 1988. Repr. Peabody, Mass.: Hendrickson, 2004.

———. "Foreword" to Leonhard Goppelt, *Typos*. Translated by Donald H. Madvig. Repr. Grand Rapids: Eerdmans, 1982. Repr. Wipf and Stock, 2002.

———. *The Making of the New Testament Documents*. Boston: Brill, 2002.

Elman, Y. "Orality and the Redaction of the Babylonian Talmud." *Oral Tradition* 14 (1999): 52-99.

Eloff, M. "Exile, Restoration and Matthew's Genealogy of Jesus ὁ Χριστός." *Neotestamentica* 38 (2004): 75-87.

———. "From the Exile to the Christ: Exile, Restoration and the Interpretation of Matthew's Gospel." D.Th. diss., The University of Stellenbosch, 2002.

Evans, Craig A. "Aspects of Exile and Restoration in the Proclamation of Jesus and the Gospels." Pages 299-328 in *Exile: Old Testament, Jewish and Christian Conceptions*. Edited by J. M. Scott. Leiden: Brill, 1997.

———. "God's Vineyard Parables of Isaiah 5 and Mark 12." *Biblische Zeitschrift* 28 (1984): 82-85.

———. "Jesus' Action in the Temple: Cleansing or Portrait of Destruction?" *Catholic Biblical Quarterly* 51 (1989): 237-70.

———. "Jesus and Zechariah's Messianic Hope." Pages 373-88 in *Authenticating the Activities of Jesus*. Edited by B. Chilton and C. A. Evans. New Testament Tools and Studies 28.2. Leiden: Brill, 1999.

———. "Predictions of the Destruction of the Herodian Temple in the Pseudepigrapha, Qumran Scrolls, and Related Texts." *Journal for the Study of the Pseudepigrapha* 10 (1992): 89-147.

———. *To See and Not Perceive: Isaiah 6.9-10 in Early Jewish and Christian Interpretation.* Journal for the Study of the Old Testament: Supplement Series 64. Sheffield: JSOT Press, 1989.

Fairbairn, P. *The Typology of Scripture*. Repr. Grand Rapids: Eerdmans, 1963.

Finkelstein, L. "Introductory Study to *Pirke Abot*." *Journal of Biblical Literature* 57 (1938): 13-50.

———. "The Oldest Midrash: Pre-Rabbinic Ideals and Teachings in the Passover Haggadah." *Harvard Theological Review* 31 (1938): 291-317.

Fitzmyer, J. A. "Anti-Semitism and the Cry of 'All the People.'" *Theological Studies* 26 (1965): 667-71.

Fjärstedt, B. *Synoptic Tradition in 1 Corinthians: Themes and Clusters of Words in 1 Corinthians 1-4 and 9*. Uppsala: Uppsala University Press, 1974.

Foster, Paul, *Community, Law and Mission in Matthew's Gospel*. Wissenschaftliche Untersuchungen zum Neuen Testament 2.177. Tübingen: Mohr Siebeck, 2004.

Foulkes, F. *The Acts of God: A Study of the Basis of Typology in the Old Testament*. London: Tyndale, 1955. Repr. pages 342-71 in *The Right Doctrine from the Wrong Texts*. Edited by G. K. Beale. Grand Rapids: Baker, 1994.

France, R. T. "Chronological Aspects of 'Gospel Harmony.'" *Vox Evangelica* 16 (1986): 33-59.

———. "The Formula-Quotations of Matthew 2 and the Problem of Communication." *New Testament Studies* 27 (1980-81): 233-51. Repr. pages 114-34 in *The Right Doctrine from the Wrong Texts*. Edited by G. K. Beale. Grand Rapids: Baker, 1994.

———. *The Gospel according to Matthew: An Introduction and Commentary*. Tyndale New Testament Commentaries 1. Leicester, U.K./Grand Rapids: Inter-Varsity Press/Eerdmans, 1985.

———. *The Gospel of Mark*. New International Greek Testament Commentary. Grand Rapids: Eerdmans, 2002.

———. *The Gospel of Matthew*. New International Commentary on the New Testament. Grand Rapids: Eerdmans, 2007.

———. *Jesus and the Old Testament*. Repr. Vancouver: Regent College, 1998.

———. *Matthew: Evangelist and Teacher*. Grand Rapids: Zondervan, 1989.

Frankemölle, H. "Antijudaismus im Matthäusevangelium? Reflexionen zu einer angemessenen Auslegung." Pages 168-98 in *Studien zum jüdischen Kontext neutestamentlicher Theologien*, FS J. Gnilka. Edited by H. Frankemölle. Stuttgarter Biblische Aufzatzbände Neues Testament 37. Stuttgart: Katholisches Bibelwerk, 2005.

———. *Jahwebund und Kirche Christi: Studien zur Form- und Traditionsgeschichte des Evangeliums nach Matthäus*. Neutestamentliche Abhandlungen 10. Münster: Aschendorff, 1974.

Franzmann, M. H. *Follow Me: Discipleship according to Saint Matthew.* St. Louis: Concordia, 1961.
Freyne, S. *Galilee from Alexander the Great to Hadrian, 323 B.C.E. to 135 C.E.: A Study of Second Temple Judaism.* Wilmington, Del.: Glazier, 1980.
———. *Galilee, Jesus and the Gospels: Literary Approaches and Historical Investigations.* Dublin: Gill & Macmillan, 1988.
Funk, R. W., and R. W. Hoover. *The Five Gospels: The Search for the Authentic Words of Jesus.* New York/Oxford: Macmillan, 1993.
Garbe, Gernot. *Der Hirte Israels. Eine Untersuchung zur Israeltheologie des Matthäusevangeliums.* Wissenschaftliche Monographien zum Alten und Neuen Testament 106. Neukirchen-Vluyn: Neukirchener, 2005.
Garland, David E. *The Intention of Matthew 23.* Novum Testamentum: Supplement Series 52. Leiden: Brill, 1979.
———. "The Temple Tax in Matthew 17:24-25 and the Principle of Not Causing Offense." Pages 69-98 in *Treasures New and Old: Recent Contributions to Matthean Studies.* Edited by D. R. Bauer and M. A. Powell. Society of Biblical Literature Symposium Series 1. Atlanta: Scholars Press, 1996.
Gärtner, B. *The Temple and the Community in Qumran and the New Testament: A Comparative Study in the Temple Symbolism of Qumran Texts and the New Testament.* Cambridge: Cambridge: University Press, 1965.
Gatzwieler, K. "Les récits de miracles dans L'Évangile selon Saint Matthieu." Pages 209-20 in *L'Évangile selon Matthieu: Rédaction et Théologie.* Edited by M. Didier. Bibliotheca ephemeridum theologicarum lovaniensium 29. Gembloux: Duculot, 1972.
Gerhardsson, B. *The Ethos of the Bible.* Translated by Stephen Westerholm. Philadelphia: Fortress, 1981.
———. "The Hermeneutic Program in Matthew 22:37-40." Pages 129-50 in *Jews, Greeks and Christians: Religious Cultures in Late Antiquity, Essays in Honor of William David Davies.* Edited by R. Hamerton-Kelly and R. Scroggs. Leiden: Brill, 1976.
———. *The Mighty Acts of Jesus according to Matthew.* Lund: Gleerup, 1979.
Gielen, Marlis. *Der Konflikt Jesu mit den religiösen und politischen Autoritäten seines Volkes im Spiegel der matthäischen Jesusgeschichte.* Bonner biblische Beiträge 115. Bodenheim: Philo, 1998.
Ginzberg, L. *The Legends of the Jews.* Translated from the German manuscript by Henrietta Szold. 7 vols. Philadelphia: Jewish Publication Society of America, 1913-67.
———. "Some Observations of the Attitude of the Synagogue towards the Apocalyptic-Eschatological Writings." *Journal of Biblical Literature* 41-42 (1922-23): 115-36.
Givón, T. *Functionalism and Grammar.* Amsterdam: John Benjamins, 1995.
———. *Syntax: An Introduction.* 2 vols. Amsterdam: John Benjamins, 2001.
Goldenberg, R. "Early Rabbinic Explanations to the Destruction of Jerusalem." *Society of Biblical Literature Seminar Papers* 21 (1982): 517-25.
Goldin, J. "The Two Versions of *Abot de Rabbi Nathan*." *Hebrew Union College Annual* 19 (1945/46): 97-120.
Gomulicki, B. R. "Recall as an Abstractive Process." *Acta Psychologica* 12 (1956): 77-94.
Goodacre, M. *The Synoptic Problem: A Way through the Maze.* London: Sheffield Academic Press, 2001.

Goppelt, L. *Typos: The Typological Interpretation of the Old Testament in the New*. Translated by D. H. Madvig. Repr. Grand Rapids: Eerdmans, 1982. Repr. Wipf and Stock, 2002.

Goulder, M. D. *Midrash and Lection in Matthew*. London: SPCK, 1974.

Grabbe, Lester L. *Judaism from Cyrus to Hadrian*. Minneapolis: Fortress, 1992.

Green, J. B. *The Gospel of Luke*. New International Commentary on the New Testament. Grand Rapids: Eerdmans, 1997.

Greenberg, J. H. *Language Universals: With Special Reference to Feature Hierarchies*. The Hague: Mouton, 1966.

Grice, H. P. "Logic and Conversation." Pages 41-58 in *Speech Acts*. Vol. 3 of *Syntax and Semantics*. Edited by P. Cole and J. L. Morgan. New York: Academic Press, 1975.

———. *Studies in the Way of Words*. Cambridge, Mass.: Harvard University Press, 1989.

Grogan, G. W. "Isaiah." Pages 3-354 in Vol. 6 of *The Expositor's Bible Commentary*. Edited by Frank E. Gaebelein. Grand Rapids: Zondervan, 1986.

Guelich, R. A. *The Sermon on the Mount: A Foundation for Understanding*. Waco, Tex.: Word, 1982.

Gundry, R. H. "Further *Verba* or *Verba Christi* in First Peter." *Biblica* 55 (1974): 211-32.

———. *Matthew: A Commentary on His Handbook for a Mixed Church under Persecution*. 2nd ed. Grand Rapids: Eerdmans, 1994.

———. *Matthew: A Commentary on His Literary and Theological Art*. Grand Rapids: Eerdmans, 1982.

———. *The Use of the Old Testament in St. Matthew's Gospel with Special Reference to the Messianic Hope*. Novum Testamentum: Supplement Series 18. Leiden: Brill, 1967.

———. "'Verba Christi' in 1 Peter: Their Implications concerning the Authorship of 1 Peter and the Authenticity of the Gospel Tradition." *New Testament Studies* 17 (1966-67): 336-50.

Gurtner, D. M. *The Torn Veil: Matthew's Exposition of the Death of Jesus*. Society for New Testament Studies Monograph Series 139. Cambridge: Cambridge University Press, 2007.

Haenchen, E. "Matthäus 23." *Zeitschrift für Theologie und Kirche* 48 (1951): 38-63.

Hagner, Donald A. "Balancing the Old and the New: The Law of Moses in Matthew and Paul." *Interpretation* 51 (1997): 20-30.

———. "Ethics and the Sermon on the Mount." *Studia Theologica* 51 (1997): 44-59.

———. *Matthew*. 2 vols. WBC 33A-B. Dallas: Word, 1993, 1995.

———. "Matthew: Apostate, Reformer, Revolutionary?" *New Testament Studies* 49 (2003): 193-209.

———. "New Things from The Scribe's Treasure Box (Mt 13:52)." *Expository Times* 109 (1998): 329-34.

———. "Righteousness in Matthew's Theology." Pages 101-20 in *Worship, Theology and Ministry in the Early Church: Essays in Honor of Ralph P. Martin*. Edited by M. J. Wilkins and T. Paige. Sheffield: JSOT Press, 1992.

———. "The *Sitz im Leben* of the Gospel of Matthew." Pages 27-68 in *Treasures New and Old: Recent Contributions to Matthean Studies*. Edited by D. R. Bauer and M. A. Powell. Society of Biblical Literature Symposium Series 1. Atlanta: Scholars Press, 1996.

———. "Writing a Commentary on Matthew: Self-conscious Ruminations of an Evangelical." *Semeia* 72 (1995): 51-72.
Halliday, M. A. K. *Explorations in the Functions of Language*. London: Edward Arnold, 1973.
———. *An Introduction to Functional Grammar*. 3d ed. Revised by Christian M. I. M. Matthiessen. London: Arnold, 2004.
Hamilton, J. M., Jr. "God with Men in the Torah." *Westminster Theological Journal* 65 (2003): 113-33.
Hare, D. R. A. "How Jewish Is the Gospel of Matthew?" *Catholic Biblical Quarterly* 62 (2000): 264-77.
Hartin, P. J. *James and the 'Q' Sayings of Jesus*. Journal for the Study of the New Testament: Supplement Series 47. Sheffield: JSOT Press, 1991.
Hawkins, J. C. *Horae Synopticae: Contributions to the Study of the Synoptic Problem*. Repr. 2nd ed. Oxford: Clarendon, 1968.
Hawthorne, G. F., and O. Betz, eds. *Tradition and Interpretation in the New Testament*. Grand Rapids: Eerdmans, 1987.
Heil, J. P. *The Death and Resurrection of Jesus: A Narrative-Critical Reading of Matthew 26–28*. Minneapolis: Fortress, 1991.
Held, H. J. "Matthew as Interpreter of the Miracle Stories." Pages 165-299 in *Tradition and Interpretation in Matthew*. Edited by G. Bornkamm, G. Barth, and H. J. Held. Translated by P. Scott. London: SCM, 1963.
Hengel, Martin. *The Charismatic Leader and His Followers*. Translated by J. C. G. Greig. Edited by J. Riches. 2nd ed. Edinburgh: T&T Clark, 1996.
———. *The Four Gospels and the One Gospel of Jesus Christ: An Investigation of the Collection and Origin of the Canonical Gospels*. London: SCM, 2000.
Herford, R. T. *Christianity in Talmud and Midrash*. London: Williams & Norgate, 1903.
Hermann, S. "Ephraim (Person)." *Anchor Bible Dictionary* 2:551-53.
Holladay, W. L. *A Concise Hebrew and Aramaic Lexicon of the Old Testament: Based upon the Lexical Work of Ludwig Koehler and Walter Baumgartner*. Leiden: Brill, 1988.
Honoré, A. M. "A Statistical Study of the Synoptic Problem." *Novum Testamentum* 10 (1968): 59-147. Repr. pages 70-122 in *The Synoptic Problem and Q: Selected Studies from Novum Testamentum*. Edited by D. E. Orton. Leiden: Brill, 1999.
Hood, R. T. "The Genealogies of Jesus." Pages 1-15 in *Early Christian Origins: FS H. R. Willoughby*. Edited by Allen P. Wikgren. Chicago: Quadrangle, 1961.
Horbury, W. "The Benediction of the *Minim* and Early Jewish-Christian Controversy." *Journal of Theological Studies* N.S. 33 (1982): 19-61.
———. "Old Testament Interpretation in the Writings of the Church Fathers." In *Mikra: Text, Translation, Reading and Interpretation of the Hebrew Bible in Ancient Judaism and Early Christianity*. Compendia rerum iudaicarum ad Novum Testamentum 2.1. Philadelphia: Fortress, 1988. Repr. Peabody, Mass.: Hendrickson, 2004.
Horsley, R. A. *Hearing the Whole Story: The Politics of Plot in Mark's Gospel*. Louisville: Westminster John Knox, 2001.
Howell, D. B. *Matthew's Inclusive Story: A Study in the Narrative Rhetoric of the First Gospel*. Journal for the Study of the New Testament: Supplement Series 42. Sheffield: JSOT Press, 1990.

Hummel, Reinhart. *Die Auseinandersetzung zwischen Kirche und Judentum im Matthäusevangelium*. Beiträge zur evangelischen Theologie 33. München: Chr. Kaiser 1963. 2nd ed. 1966.
Hunter, A. M. *A Pattern for Life: An Exposition of the Sermon on the Mount, Its Making, Its Exegesis and Its Meaning*. Rev. ed. Philadelphia: Westminster, 1965.
Instone-Brewer, D. "The Eighteen Benedictions and the Minim Before 70 CE." *Journal of Theological Studies* N.S. 54 (2003): 25-44.
———. *Traditions of the Rabbis from the Era of the New Testament (TRENT)*. Grand Rapids: Eerdmans, 2004-.
Jensen, J. "Immanuel." *Anchor Bible Dictionary* 3:392-95.
Johnson, L. T. "The New Testament's Anti-Jewish Slander and Conventions of Ancient Rhetoric." *Journal of Biblical Literature* 108 (1989): 419-41.
Johnson, M. D. *The Purpose of the Biblical Genealogies: With Special Reference to the Setting of the Genealogies of Jesus*. 2nd ed. Society for New Testament Studies Monograph Series 8. London: Cambridge University Press, 1988.
Johnson-Laird, P. N. *Mental Models: Toward a Cognitive Science of Language, Inference, and Consciousness*. Cambridge: Cambridge University Press, 1983.
Johnston, G. "'Kingdom of God' Sayings in Paul's Letters." Pages 143-56 in *From Jesus to Paul*. Edited by P. Richardson and J. C. Hurd. Waterloo, Ont.: Wilfrid Laurier, 1984.
Juel, D. *Messiah and Temple: The Trial of Jesus in the Gospel of Mark*. Society of Biblical Literature Dissertation Series 31. Missoula, Mont.: Scholars Press, 1977.
Kähler, M. *The So-Called Historical Jesus and the Historic Biblical Christ*. Translated by C. E. Braaten. Philadelphia: Fortress, 1964.
Kammler, Hans-Christian. "Sohn Gottes und Kreuz. Die Versuchungsgeschichte Mt 4,1-11 im Kontext des Matthäusevangeliums." *Zeitschrift für Theologie und Kirche* 100 (2003): 163-86.
Kampling, R. *Das Blut Christi und die Juden. Mt 27,25 bei den lateinischsprachigen christliche Autoren bis zu Leo dem Grossen*. Neutestamentliche Abhandlungen 16. Münster: Aschendorff, 1984.
Keener, C. S. *A Commentary on the Gospel of Matthew*. Grand Rapids: Eerdmans, 1999.
Kempson, R., Wilfried Meyer-Viol, and Dov Gabby. *Dynamic Syntax: The Flow of Language Understanding*. Oxford: Blackwell, 2001.
Kessler, H. L. "Through the Veil: The Holy Image in Judaism and Christianity." *Kairos* 32 (1990): 53-77.
Kingsbury, J. D. *Matthew as Story*. 2nd ed. Philadelphia: Fortress, 1988.
———. *Matthew: Structure, Christology, Kingdom*. Philadelphia: Fortress, 1975.
———. "Observations on the 'Miracle Chapters' of Matthew 8–9." *Catholic Biblical Quarterly* 40 (1978): 559-73.
Kloppenborg, J. S. *Excavating Q: The History and Setting of the Saying Gospel*. Minneapolis: Fortress, 2000.
Knibb, M. A. "The Exile in the Literature of the Intertestamental Period." *Heythrop Journal* 17 (1976): 253-72.
Knowles, M. *Jeremiah in Matthew's Gospel: The Rejected-Prophet Motif in Matthean Redaction*. Journal for the Study of the New Testament: Supplement Series 68. Sheffield: Sheffield Academic Press, 1993.

Kosmala, H. "'His Blood on Us and on Our Children' (The Background of Mat 27,24-25)." *Annual of the Swedish Theological Institute* 7 (1968/9): 94-126.
Krentz, E. "The Extent of Matthew's Prologue: Toward a Structure of the First Gospel." *Journal of Biblical Literature* 83 (1964): 409-14.
Kroeger, Paul R. *Analyzing Syntax: A Lexical-Functional Approach*. Cambridge: Cambridge University Press, 2004.
Kupp, D. D. *Matthew's Emmanuel: Divine Presence and God's People in the First Gospel*. Society for New Testament Studies Monograph Series 90. Cambridge: Cambridge University Press, 1996.
Landmesser, Christoph. *Jüngerberufung und Zuwendung zu Gott. Ein exegetischer Beitrag zum Konzept der matthäischen Soteriologie im Anschluß an Mt 9,9-13*. Wissenschaftliche Untersuchungen zum Neuen Testament 133. Tübingen: Mohr Siebeck, 2001.
Langacker, R. W. *Concept, Image, and Symbol: The Cognitive Basis of Grammar*. Cognitive Linguistics Research 1. Berlin: Mouton de Gruyter, 2002.
Lasker, Daniel J. *The Refutation of Christian Principles by Hasdai Crescas*. SUNY Series in Jewish Philosophy. Albany, N.Y.: State University of New York Press, 1992.
———. *R. Ùasdai Crescas, Sefer Bittul Iqqarei Ha-Nozrim: Translation of Joseph Ben Shem Tov*. Ramat Gan: Bar-Ilan University Press/Beer-Sheva: Ben-Gurion University of the Negev Press, 1990.
———, and Sarah Stroumsa, eds. *The Polemic of Nestor the Priest*. Qiṣṣat Mujādalat al-Usquf *and* Sefer Nestor ha-Komer. Introduction, Critical Editions, Annotated Translations and Commentary. 2 vols. Jerusalem: Ben-Zvi Institute for the Study of Jewish Communities in the East, 1996.
Légasse, S. "L''anti-judaisme' dans l'Évangile selon Matthieu." Pages 417-28 in *L'Évangile selon Matthieu: Rédaction et théologie*. Edited by M. Didier. Bibliotheca ephemeridum theologicarum lovaniensium 29. Gembloux: Duculot, 1972.
Lerner, M. B. "The External Tractates." Pages 367-409 in *The Literature of the Sages*, vol. 1: *Oral Tora, Halakha, Mishna, Tosefta, Talmud, External Tractates*. Compendia rerum iudaicarum ad Novum Testamentum 2.3.1. Philadelphia: Fortress, 1987.
Levine, Amy-Jill. *The Social and Ethnic Dimensions of Matthean Salvation History*. Studies in the Bible and Early Christianity 14. Lewiston-Queenstown: Mellen, 1988.
Lightfoot, R. H. *Locality and Doctrine in the Gospels*. London: Hodder & Stoughton, 1938.
Lincoln, A. T. "Matthew — A Story for Teachers?" Pages 103-26 in *The Bible in Three Dimensions*. Edited by D. J. A. Clines et al. Sheffield: JSOT, 1990.
Livingstone, E. A., ed. *Oxford Dictionary of the Christian Church*. 3d ed. Oxford: Oxford University Press, 1997.
Lohmeyer, E. *Das Evangelium des Matthäus*. 4th ed. Göttingen: Vandenhoeck & Ruprecht, 1967.
———. *Galiläa und Jerusalem*. Göttingen: Vandenhoeck & Ruprecht, 1936.
———. "Das Gleichnis von de bösen Weingärtnern." *Zeitschrift für systematische Theologie* 18 (1941): 242-59.
Lona, Horacio E. *Die "wahre Lehre" des Kelsos*. Kommentar zu frühchristlichen Apologeten. Ergänzungsband 1. Freiburg: Herder, 2005.
Longenecker, B. W. "Rome's Victory and God's Honour: The Jerusalem Temple and the Spirit of God in Lukan Theodicy." Pages 90-102 in *The Spirit and Christian Origins*.

Edited by G. N. Stanton, B. W. Longenecker, and S. C. Barton. Grand Rapids: Eerdmans, 2004.
Lord, A. B. "The Gospels as Oral Traditional Literature." Pages 33-91 in *The Relationship among the Gospels: An Interdisciplinary Dialogue.* Edited by W. O. Walker. San Antonio: Trinity University Press, 1978.
Louw, J. P. "The Structure of Mt 8:1–9:35." *Neotestamentica* 11 (1977): 91-97.
———, and E. A. Nida, eds. *Greek-English Lexicon of the New Testament Based on Semantic Domains.* 2d ed. New York: United Bible Societies, 1989.
Lowe, M. "Who Were the *Ioudaioi?*" *Novum Testamentum* 18 (1976): 101-30.
Luomanen, Petri. *Entering the Kingdom of Heaven: A Study on the Structure of Matthew's View of Salvation.* Wissenschaftliche Untersuchungen zum Neuen Testament 2.101. Tübingen: Mohr Siebeck, 1998.
Lust, J., E. Eynikel, and K. Hauspie. *A Greek-English Lexicon of the Septuagint.* 2 vols. Stuttgart: Deutsche Bibelgesellschaft, 1996.
Luz, U. "The Disciples in the Gospel according to Matthew." Pages 98-128 in *The Interpretation of Matthew.* Edited by Graham Stanton. Philadelphia/London: Fortress/SPCK, 1983.
———. *Das Evangelium nach Matthäus.* EKKNT. 4 vols. Zürich: Benziger, 1985-2002.
———. *Matthew 1–7: A Commentary.* Translated by Wilhelm C. Linss. Hermeneia. Edinburgh: T&T Clark, 1989.
———. *Matthew 8–20.* Translated by J. E. Crouch. Hermeneia. Minneapolis: Fortress, 2001.
———. *The Theology of the Gospel of Matthew.* Translated by J. B. Robinson. Cambridge: Cambridge University Press, 1995.
———. "Die Wundergeschichten von Mt 8–9." Pages 149-65 in *Tradition and Interpretation in the New Testament.* Edited by G. F. Hawthorne and O. Betz. Grand Rapids: Eerdmans, 1987.
Lyons, J. *Introduction to Theoretical Linguistics.* Cambridge: Cambridge University Press, 1968.
Machen, J. G. *The Virgin Birth of Christ.* San Francisco: Harper & Row, 1930.
Maier, G. "Jesustradition im 1. Petrusbrief?" Pages 85-128 in *Gospel Perspectives 5: The Jesus Tradition outside the Gospels.* Edited by D. Wenham. Sheffield: JSOT Press, 1984.
Mann, J. *The Bible as Read and Preached in the Old Synagogue.* Vol. 1. New York: KTAV, 1971. Vol. 2. Cincinnati: Hebrew Union College, 1966.
Marshall, I. H. *The Gospel of Luke: A Commentary on the Greek Text.* New International Greek Testament Commentary Series. Exeter, U.K.: Paternoster, 1978.
———. *Luke: Historian and Theologian.* Exeter, U.K.: Paternoster, 1970.
———, S. Travis, and I. Paul. *A Guide to the Letters and Revelation.* Vol. 2 of *Exploring the New Testament.* Downers Grove, Ill.: InterVarsity Press, 2002.
Martling, C. H., and S. E. Staxäng, eds. *Kommentar till evangelieboken, Högmässotexterna.* Part 3. Stockholm: Uppsala, 1964.
Mason, S. "Pharisaic Dominance before 70 CE and the Gospels' Hypocrisy Charge (Matt 23:2-3)." *Harvard Theological Review* 83 (1990): 363-81.
Matera, F. J. "John the Baptist in Matthew's Gospel." *Journal of Biblical Literature* 99 (1980): 383-405.

———. *Law and History in Matthew's Gospel*. Analecta biblica 71. Rome: Pontifical Biblical Institute, 1976.

———. "The Plot of Matthew's Gospel." *Catholic Biblical Quarterly* 49 (1987): 233-53.

———. "Salvation History in Matthew: In Search of a Starting Point." *Catholic Biblical Quarterly* 37 (1975): 203-15.

———. *The Vision of Matthew: Christ, Church and Morality in the First Gospel*. New York: Paulist Press, 197.

McCartney, D., and P. Enns. "Matthew and Hosea: A Response to John Sailhamer." *Westminster Theological Journal* 63 (2001): 97-105.

McCasland, S. V. "Matthew Twists the Scriptures." *Journal of Biblical Literature* 80 (1961): 143-48. Repr. pages 146-52 in *The Right Doctrine from the Wrong Texts*. Edited by G. K. Beale. Grand Rapids: Baker, 1994.

McConnell, R. A. "Law and Prophecy in Matthew's Gospel." Ph.D. diss., University of Basel, 1964.

McIver, R. "Implications of New Data Pertaining to the Problem of Synoptic Relationships." *Australian Biblical Review* 45 (1997): 20-39.

———, and M. Carroll, "Experiments to Develop Criteria for Determining the Existence of Written Sources, and Their Potential Implications for the Synoptic Problem." *Journal of Biblical Literature* 121 (2002): 667-87.

McKelvey, R. J. *The New Temple: The Church in the New Testament*. Oxford: Oxford University Press, 1969.

McKnight, Scot. "A Loyal Critic: Matthew's Polemic with Judaism in Theological Perspective." Pages 55-79 in *Anti-Semitism and Early Christianity: Issues of Polemic and Faith*. Edited by C. A. Evans and D. A. Hagner. Minneapolis: Fortress, 1993.

McNamara, M., ed., *The Aramaic Bible: The Targums*. Edinburgh: T&T Clark, 1992-.

Mead, R. T. "A Dissenting Opinion about Respect for Context in Old Testament Quotations." *New Testament Studies* 10 (1964): 279-89. Repr. pages 153-63 in *The Right Doctrine from the Wrong Texts*. Edited by G. K. Beale. Grand Rapids: Baker, 1994.

Meier, John P. "The Historical Jesus and the Historical Law: Some Problems within the Problem." *Catholic Biblical Quarterly* 65 (2003): 52-79.

———. *Matthew*. New Testament Message 3. Wilmington, Del.: Michael Glazier, 1981.

Menken, M. J. J. "The Quotation from Jeremiah 31(38).15 in Matthew 2.18: A Study of Matthew's Scriptural Text." Pages 106-25 in *The Old Testament in the New Testament*. Edited by Steve Moyise. Journal for the Study of the New Testament: Supplement Series 189. Sheffield: Sheffield Academic Press, 2000.

Merkel, H. "Die Überlieferung der Alten Kirche über das Verhältnis der Evangelien." Pages 566-90 in *The Interrelation of the Gospels*. A Symposium led by M.-É. Boismard, W. R. Farmer, and F. Neirynck. Jerusalem, 1984. Edited by D. L. Dungan. Bibliotheca ephemeridum theologicarum lovaniensium XCV. Leuven: Leuven University Press, 1990.

Metzger, B. M. *A Textual Commentary on the Greek New Testament*. 3d ed. Stuttgart: United Bible Societies, 1971.

Michel, O. "Ναός." *TDNT* 4:880-90.

Miller, R. J. "The Rejection of the Prophets in Q." *Journal of Biblical Literature* 107 (1988): 225-40.

Minear, P. S. *Matthew: The Teacher's Gospel*. New York: Pilgrim, 1982.

Minsky, M. "A Framework for Representing Knowledge." Pages 211-77 in *The Psychology of Computer Vision*. Edited by P. H. Winston. New York: McGraw-Hill, 1975.

Moffitt, D. M. "Righteous Bloodshed, Matthew's Passion Narrative and the Temple's Destruction: Lamentations as a Matthean Intertext." *Journal of Biblical Literature* 125 (2006): 299-320.

Mohrlang, Roger. *Matthew and Paul: A Comparison of Ethical Perspectives*. Society for New Testament Studies Monograph Series 48. Cambridge: Cambridge University Press, 1984; repr. as paperback edition, 2004.

Moiser, J. "The Structure of Matthew 8–9: A Suggestion." *Zeitschrift für die neutestamentliche Wissenschaft und die Kunde der älteren Kirche* 76 (1985): 117-18.

Moo, D. J. "Jesus and the Mosaic Law." *Journal for the Study of the New Testament* 20 (1984): 3-49.

———. "The Problem of *Sensus Plenior*." Pages 179-211 in *Hermeneutics, Authority, and Canon*. Edited by D. A. Carson and J. D. Woodbridge. Grand Rapids: Zondervan, 1986.

Morgan, Robert. "Towards a Critical Appropriation of the Sermon on the Mount: Christology and Discipleship." Pages 157-91 in *Christology, Controversy and Community*. Festschrift D. R. Catchpole. Edited by D. G. Horrell and Chr. M. Tuckett. Novum Testamentum: Supplement Series 99. Leiden: Brill, 2000.

Morgenthaler, R. *Statistische Synopse*. Zürich: Gotthelf, 1971.

Morris, L. *The Gospel according to Matthew*. Pillar New Testament Commentary. Grand Rapids: Eerdmans, 1992.

Motyer, J. A. "Context and Content in the Interpretation of Isaiah 7:14." *Tyndale Bulletin* 21 (1970): 118-25.

Moule, C. F. D. "Fulfilment-Words in the New Testament: Use and Abuse." *New Testament Studies* 14 (1968): 293-320. Repr. in C. F. D. Moule, ed. *Essays in New Testament Interpretation*. Cambridge: Cambridge University Press, 1982. Repr. from *New Testament Studies* 3 (1956): 3-36.

Moulton, J. H., and G. Milligan. *Vocabulary of the Greek Testament*. Peabody, Mass.: Hendrickson, 1997. Repr. of *Vocabulary of the Greek Testament*. London: Hodder & Stoughton, 1930.

Mournet, T. C. *Oral Tradition and Literary Dependency: Variability and Stability in the Synoptic Tradition and Q*. Wissenschaftliche Untersuchungen zum Neuen Testament 2.195. Tübingen: Mohr, 2005.

Murphy, Frederick J. "The Jewishness of Matthew: Another Look." Pages 377-403 in Vol. 2 of *When Judaism and Christianity Began: Essays in Memory of Anthony J. Saldarini*. 2 vols. Edited by A. J. Avery-Peck, D. Harrington and J. Neusner. Journal for the Study of Judaism: Supplement Series 85. Leiden: Brill, 2004.

Murray, J. D. "Connectives and Narrative Text: The Role of Continuity." *Memory and Cognition* 25 (1997): 228.

Nesbitt, C., and G. Plum. "Probabilities in a Systemic-Functional Grammar: The Clause Complex in English." Pages 6-38 in *Theory and Application*. Vol. 2 of *New Developments in Systemic Linguistics*. Edited by R. P. Fawcett and D. Young. Open Linguistics Series. London: Pinter, 1988.

Neugebauer, Fritz. "Die dargebotene Wange und Jesu Gebot der Feindesliebe. Erwägungen zu Lk 6,27-36/Matt. 5,38-48." *Theologische Literaturzeitung* 110 (1985): 865-76.
Neusner, J. *The Fathers according to Rabbi Nathan: An Analytical Translation and Explanation*. Brown Judaic Studies 114. Atlanta: Scholars Press, 1986.
———. "Judaism in a Time of Crisis: Four Responses to the Destruction of the Second Temple." *Judaism* 21 (1972): 313-27.
Neyrey, J. H. "The Thematic Use of Isaiah 42:1-4 in Matthew 12." *Biblica* 63 (1982): 457-73.
Nickelsburg, G. W. E. *Jewish Literature between the Bible and the Mishnah: A Historical and Literary Introduction*. London: SCM, 1981.
Nineham, D. E. "The Genealogy in St Matthew's Gospel and Its Significance for the Study of the Gospel." *Bulletin of the John Rylands University Library of Manchester* 58 (1975-76): 421-44.
Nolan, B. M. *The Royal Son of God: The Christology of Matthew 1–2*. Orbis biblicus et orientalis 23. Göttingen: Vandenhoeck & Ruprecht, 1979.
Nolland, J. *The Gospel of Matthew*. New International Greek Testament Commentary. Grand Rapids: Eerdmans, 2005.
———. *Luke*. Word Biblical Commentary 35A-C. 3 vols. Dallas: Word, 1989-93.
———. "The Mandate: Love of Enemies: Matt. 5:43-48." *Anvil* 21 (2004): 23-33.
Novakovic, Lidija. *Messiah, the Healer of the Sick: A Study of Jesus as the Son of David in the Gospel of Matthew*. Wissenschaftliche Untersuchungen zum Neuen Testament 2.170. Tübingen: Mohr Siebeck, 2003.
Olmstead, W. G. *Matthew's Trilogy of Parables: The Nation, the Nations, and the Reader in Matthew 21.28–22.14*. Society for New Testament Studies Monograph Series 127. Cambridge: Cambridge University Press, 2003.
Oswalt, J. N. *The Book of Isaiah, Chapters 1-39*. New International Commentary on the New Testament. Grand Rapids: Eerdmans, 1986.
Overman, J. A. *Church and Community in Crisis: The Gospel according to Matthew*, the New Testament in Context. Valley Forge, Pa.: Trinity Press International, 1996.
———. *Matthew's Gospel and Formative Judaism: The Social World of the Matthean Community*. Minneapolis: Fortress, 1990.
Park, E. C. *The Mission Discourse in Matthew's Interpretation*. Wissenschaftliche Untersuchungen zum Neuen Testament 2.121. Tübingen: Mohr Siebeck, 2000.
Phillips, G. A. "History and Text: The Reader in Context in Matthew's Parables Discourse." *Semeia* 31 (1985): 111-38.
Powell, M. A. "Do and Keep What Moses Says (Matthew 23:2-7)." *Journal of Biblical Literature* 114 (1995): 419-35.
———. "The Plot and Subplots of Matthew's Gospel." *New Testament Studies* 38 (1992): 187-204.
Pritz, R. "He Shall Be Called a Nazarene." *Jerusalem Perspective,* online at http://www.jerusalemperspective.com/Default.aspx?tabid=27&ArticleID=1638.
Przybylski, B. *Righteousness in Matthew and His World of Thought*. Society for New Testament Studies Monograph Series 41. Cambridge: Cambridge University Press, 1982.
Reicke, B. "Die Entstehungsverhältnisse der synoptischen Evangelien." *Aufstieg und Niedergang der römischen Welt* 2.25.2 (1984): 1758-91.
———. *The Roots of the Synoptic Gospels*. Philadelphia: Fortress, 1986.

Repschinski, Boris. *The Controversy Stories in the Gospel of Matthew: Their Redaction, Form and Relevance for the Relationship between the Matthean Community and Formative Judaism*. Forschungen zur Religion und Literatur des Alten und Neuen Testaments 189. Göttingen: Vandenhoeck & Ruprecht, 2000.

Reumann, J. *"Righteousness" in the New Testament: "Justification" in the United States Lutheran-Roman Catholic Dialogue*. Philadelphia/New York: Fortress/Paulist, 1982.

Ridderbos, H. N. *Matthew*. Translated by R. Togtman. Grand Rapids: Zondervan, 1987.

Riesner, R. *Jesus als Lehrer*. Tübingen: Mohr, 1981.

Rist, J. M. *On the Independence of Matthew and Mark*. Society for New Testament Studies Monograph Series 32. Cambridge: Cambridge University Press, 1978.

Robertson, A. T. *A Grammar of the Greek New Testament in the Light of Historical Research*. 4th ed. Nashville: Broadman, 1934.

Robinson, J. A. T. "Elijah, John and Jesus." *New Testament Studies* 4 (1958): 263-81. Repr. pages 28-52 in *Twelve New Testament Studies*. Edited by J. A. T. Robinson. Studies in Biblical Theology 34. London: SCM, 1962.

Robinson, J. M., et al. *The Critical Edition of Q*. Hermeneia. Minneapolis: Fortress, 2000.

Rubin, D. C., S. E. Wetzler, and R. D. Nebes. "Autobiographical Memory across the Lifespan." Pages 202-21 in *Autobiographical Memory*. Edited by D. C. Rubin. Cambridge: Cambridge University Press, 1986.

Sailhamer, J. H. "Hosea 11:1 and Matthew 2:15." *Westminster Theological Journal* 63 (2001): 87-96.

Saldarini, Anthony J. "Boundaries and Polemics in the Gospel of Matthew." *Biblical Interpretation* 3 (1995): 239-65.

———. "Delegitimation of Leaders in Matthew 23." *Catholic Biblical Quarterly* 54 (1992): 659-80.

———. *The Fathers according to Rabbi Nathan (Abot de Rabbi Nathan Version B). A Translation and Commentary*. Studies in Judaism in Late Antiquity 11. Leiden: Brill, 1975.

———. "The Gospel of Matthew and Jewish-Christian Conflict." Pages 37-61 in *Social History of the Matthean Community: Cross-Disciplinary Approaches*. Edited by David L. Balch. Minneapolis: Fortress, 1991.

———. *Matthew's Christian-Jewish Community*. Chicago/London: University of Chicago Press, 1994.

———. "Reading Matthew without Anti-Semitism." Pages 166-84 in *The Gospel of Matthew in Current Study*. Edited by D. E. Aune. Grand Rapids: Eerdmans, 2001.

———. "Varieties of Rabbinic Response to the Destruction of the Temple." *Society of Biblical Literature Seminar Papers* 2 (1982): 437-58.

Sanders, E. P. *Jesus and Judaism*. London: SCM, 1985.

Sandmel, S. "Parallelomania." *Journal of Biblical Literature* 81 (1962): 1-13.

Schank, R. C., and R. P. Abelson. *Scripts, Plans, Goals and Understanding*. Hillsdale, N.J.: Lawrence Erlbaum, 1977.

Schank, R., and M. Burstein. "Artificial Intelligence: Modeling Memory for Language Understanding." Pages 145-66 in *Disciplines of Discourse*. Vol. 1 in *Handbook of Discourse Analysis*. Edited by T. A. van Dijk. London: Academic Press, 1985.

Schechter, S. *Aboth de Rabbi Nathan*. Hildesheim: Olms, 1979.

Schenk, G. "τὸ ἱερόν." *TDNT* 3:235.

Schenk, W. "Auferweckung der Töten oder Gericht nach den Werken, Tradition und Redaktion in Matthäus xxv 1-13." *Novum Testamentum* 8 (1966): 223-34.

Schibler, D. "Messianism and Messianic Prophecy in Isaiah 1–12 and 28–33." Pages 87-104 in *The Lord's Anointed*. Edited by P. E. Satterthwaite, R. S. Hess, and G. J. Wenham. Grand Rapids: Baker, 1995.

Schillebeeckx, E. *Christ: The Christian Experience in the Modern World.* ET. London: SCM, 1980.

Schnackenburg, R. *All Things Are Possible to Believers.* Louisville: John Knox, 1995.

Schweizer, Eduard. *Das Evangelium nach Matthäus.* Das Neue Testament Deutsch, vol. 2. Göttingen: Vandenhoeck & Ruprecht, 1973.

———. *The Good News according to Matthew.* Translated by D. E. Green. London: SPCK, 1976.

———. *Matthäus und seine Gemeinde.* Stuttgart: K. B. W. Verlag, 1974.

Seccombe, David P. "The Forceful Who Seize the Kingdom." Cape Town, 2001.

Seeligmann, I. L. *The Septuagint Version of Isaiah: A Discussion of Its Problems*, Mededelingen en verhandelingen van het Vooraziatisch-Egyptisch Genootschap. Ex Oriente Lux, no. 9. Leiden: Brill, 1948.

Segal, E. M., J. F. Duchan, and P. J. Scott. "The Role of Interclausal Connectives in Narrative Structuring: Evidence from Adults' Interpretations of Simple Stories." *Discourse Processes* 14 (1991): 27-55.

Senior, Donald. "Between Two Worlds: Gentiles and Jewish Christians in Matthew's Gospel." *Catholic Biblical Quarterly* 61 (1999): 1-23.

———. "Directions in Matthean Studies." Pages 5-21 in *The Gospel of Matthew in Current Study.* Edited by D. E. Aune. Grand Rapids: Eerdmans, 2001.

———. *The Passion Narrative according to Matthew.* Bibliotheca ephemeridum theologicarum lovaniensium 39. Leuven: Leuven University Press, 1975.

———. *What Are They Saying about Matthew?* Revised and updated edition. New York: Paulist Press, 1996.

Sim, David C. *Apocalyptic Eschatology in the Gospel of Matthew.* Society for New Testament Studies Monograph Series 88. Cambridge: Cambridge University Press, 1996.

———. "Christianity and Ethnicity in the Gospel of Matthew." Pages 171-95 in *Ethnicity and the Bible.* Biblical Interpretation Series 19. Edited by M. G. Brett. Leiden: Brill, 1996.

———. *The Gospel of Matthew and Christian Judaism: The History and Social Setting of the Matthean Community.* Edinburgh: T&T Clark, 1999.

———. "The Gospel of Matthew and the Gentiles." *Journal for the Study of the New Testament* 57 (1995): 19-48.

Simonetti, M., and T. C. Oden, eds. *Ancient Christian Commentary on Scripture,* vol. 1a: *Matthew 1–13.* Downers Grove, Ill.: InterVarsity, 2001.

Smith, J. Z. "The Temple and the Magician." Pages 233-47 in *God's Christ and His People: Studies in Honour of Nils Alstrup Dahl.* Edited by J. Jervell and W. A. Meeks. Oslo: Universitetsforlaget, 1977.

Snodgrass, Klyne. "Matthew and the Law." Pages 99-127 in *Treasures New and Old: Recent Contributions to Matthean Studies.* Edited by D. R. Bauer and M. A. Powell. Society of Biblical Literature Symposium Series 1. Atlanta: Scholars Press, 1996.

———. *The Parable of the Wicked Tenants: An Inquiry into Parable Interpretation.* Tübingen: Mohr Siebeck, 1983.
Soares Prabhu, G. M. *The Formula Quotations in the Infancy Narrative of Matthew: An Enquiry into the Tradition History of Mt 1–2.* Analecta Biblica 63. Rome: Biblical Institute Press, 1976.
Sperber, D., and D. Wilson. *Relevance: Communication and Cognition.* 2d ed. Oxford: Basil Blackwell, 1995.
Stanton, Graham N. "The Communities of Matthew." *Interpretation* 46 (1992): 379-91.
———. *A Gospel for a New People: Studies in Matthew.* Edinburgh: T&T Clark, 1992.
Stassen, G., and D. Gushee. *Kingdom Ethics.* Downers Grove, Ill.: InterVarsity, 2003.
Steck, O. H. *Israel und das gewaltsame Geschick der Propheten: Untersuchungen zur Überlieferung des deuteronomistischen Geschichtsbildes im Alten Testament, Spätjudentum, und Urchristentum.* Wissenschaftliche Monographien zum Alten und Neuen Testament 23. Neukirchen-Vluyn: Neukirchener, 1967.
Stemberger, G. *Einleitung in Talmud und Midrasch.* 8th ed. München: Beck, 1992.
Stendahl, K. "Quis et Unde? An Analysis of Matthew 1–2." Pages 94-105 in *Judentum, Urchristentum, Kirche: Festschrift für J. Jeremias.* Edited by W. Eltester. Berlin: Töpelmann, 1960. Repr. pages 69-80 in *The Interpretation of Matthew.* Edited by G. N. Stanton. Edinburgh: T&T Clark, 1995.
———. *The School of St. Matthew,* 2d ed. Philadelphia: Fortress, 1968.
Stratton, G. M. "The Mnemonic Feat of the 'Shass Pollak.'" *Psychological Review* 24 (1917): 244-47. Repr. pages 311-14 in *Memory Observed: Remembering in Natural Contexts.* Edited by U. Neisser. San Francisco: Freeman, 1982.
Strecker, G. "The Concept of History in Matthew." *Evangelische Theologie* 26 (1966): 57-74. Repr. pages 67-84 in *The Interpretation of Matthew.* Edited by G. N. Stanton. London: SPCK, 1983.
———. *Der Weg der Gerechtigkeit: Untersuchung zur Theologie des Matthäus.* Dritte, durchgesehene und erweiterte Aufl. Göttingen: Vandenhoeck & Ruprecht, 1971.
Suggs, M. J. *Wisdom, Christology, and Law in Matthew's Gospel.* Cambridge, Mass.: Harvard University Press, 1970.
Sullivan, D. "New Insights into Matthew 27:24-25." *New Blackfriars* 73 (1992): 453-57.
Syreeni, Kari. "Matthew, Luke, and the Law: A Study in Hermeneutical Exegesis." Pages 126-55 in *The Law in the Bible and in Its Environment.* Edited by T. Veijola. SESJ 51 = Publications of the Finnish Exegetical Society 51. Göttingen: Vandenhoeck & Ruprecht, 1990.
Talbert, C. H. *Reading the Sermon on the Mount: Character Formation and Decision Making in Matthew 5–7.* Columbia: University of South Carolina Press, 2004.
Tan, K. H. *The Zion Traditions and the Aims of Jesus.* Society for New Testament Studies Monograph Series 91. Cambridge: Cambridge University Press, 1997.
Tatum, W. B. "The Origin of Jesus Messiah (Matt 1, 18a): Matthew's Use of Infancy Traditions." *Journal of Biblical Literature* 96 (1977): 528-29.
Telford, W. R. *The Barren Temple and the Withered Tree: A Redaction-Critical Analysis of the Cursing of the Fig-Tree Pericope in Mark's Gospel and Its Relation to the Cleansing of the Temple Tradition.* Journal for the Study of the New Testament: Supplement Series 1. Sheffield: JSOT Press, 1980.

Theissen, G. *The Miracle Stories of the Early Christian Tradition.* Philadelphia: Fortress, 1983.

———. *The Shadow of the Galilean.* ET. London: SCM, 1987.

Thompson, M. *Clothed with Christ: The Example and Teaching of Jesus in Romans 12.1–15.13.* Journal for the Study of the New Testament: Supplement Series 59. Sheffield: JSOT Press, 1991.

Thompson, W. G. "Reflections on the Composition of Mt 8.1–9.34." *Catholic Biblical Quarterly* 33 (1971): 365-88.

Thysman, R. *Communauté et directives éthiques: La catéchèse de Matthieu.* Gembloux: J. Duculot, 1974.

Torrey, C. C. "The Foundry of the Second Temple at Jerusalem." *Journal of Biblical Literature* 55 (1936): 247-60.

Trotter, A. H. "Understanding and Stumbling: A Study of the Disciples' Understanding of Jesus and His Teaching in the Gospel of Matthew." Ph.D. diss., Cambridge University, 1986.

Twelftree, G. H. *Jesus the Miracle Worker.* Downers Grove, Ill.: InterVarsity Press, 1999.

Upton, J. A. "The Potter's Field and the Death of Judas." *Concordia Journal* 8 (1982): 213-19.

Vahrenhorst, Martin. *"Ihr sollt überhaupt nicht schwören." Matthäus im halachischen Diskurs.* Wissenschaftliche Monographien zum Alten und Neuen Testament 95. Neukirchen-Vluyn: Neukirchener, 2002.

van der Kwaak, H. "Die Klage über Jerusalem (Matth. xxiii 37-39)." *Novum Testamentum* 8 (1966): 156-70.

Vermes, G. *Jesus the Jew: A Historian's Reading of the Gospels.* London: Collins, 1973.

———. "The Story of Balaam." Pages 127-77 in *Scripture and Tradition in Judaism: Haggadic Studies.* Studia post-Biblica. Edited by G. Vermes. Leiden: Brill, 1961.

Verseput, D. J. "The Faith of the Reader and the Narrative of Matthew 13:53–16:20." *Journal for the Study of the New Testament* 46 (1992): 3-24.

Viviano, Benedict. Review of R. Deines, *Die Gerechtigkeit der Tora im Reich des Messias: Mt 5,13-20 als Schlüsseltext der matthäischen Theologie.* Wissenschaftliche Untersuchungen zum Neuen Testament 177. Tübingen: Mohr Siebeck, 2005. *Freiburger Zeitschrift für Philosophie und Theologie* 52 (2005): 790-94.

Vledder, E.-J. *Conflict in the Miracle Stories: A Socio-Exegetical Study of Matthew 8 and 9.* Journal for the Study of the New Testament: Supplement Series 152. Sheffield: Sheffield Academic Press, 1997.

von Dobbeler, Axel. "Die Restitution Israels und die Bekehrung der Heiden. Das Verhältnis von Mt 10,5b.6 und Mt 28,18-20. Erwägungen zum Standort des Matthäusevangeliums." *Zeitschrift für die neutestamentliche Wissenschaft und die Kunde der älteren Kirche* 91 (2000): 18-44.

von Dobbeler, Stephanie. "Auf der Grenze. Ethos und Identität der matthäischen Gemeinde nach Mt 15,1-20." *Biblische Zeitschrift* Neue Folge 45 (2001): 55-79.

Von Rad, Gerhard. *Old Testament Theology.* 2 vols. Old Testament Library. Translated by D. M. G. Stalker. Louisville: Westminster John Knox, 1962, 1965.

Walker, P. W. L. *Jesus and the Holy City: New Testament Perspectives on Jerusalem.* Grand Rapids: Eerdmans, 1996.

Walker, R. *Die Heilsgeschichte im ersten Evangelium*. Göttingen: Vandenhoeck & Ruprecht, 1967.
Walton, J. H. "Isa 7:14: What's in a Name?" *Journal of the Evangelical Theological Society* 30 (1987): 289-306.
Watts, J. D. W. *Isaiah 1–33*. Word Biblical Commentary. Waco, Tex.: Word, 1985.
Watts, R. E. "Immanuel: Virgin Birth Proof Text or Programmatic Warning of Things to Come (Isa 7:14 in Matt 1:23)?" Pages 92-113 in *From Prophecy to Testament*. Edited by C. A. Evans. Peabody, Mass.: Hendrickson, 2004.
———. *Isaiah's New Exodus and Mark*. Wissenschaftliche Untersuchungen zum Neuen Testament 2. Tübingen: Mohr, 1997.
Wedderburn, A. J. M. *Paul and Jesus*. Sheffield: Sheffield Academic Press, 1989.
———. *The Reasons for Romans*. Edinburgh: T&T Clark, 1988.
Weinfeld, M. "The Charge of Hypocrisy in Matthew 23 and in Jewish Sources." *Immanuel* 24/25 (1990): 52-58.
Wenham, D. "Guelich on the Sermon on the Mount: A Critical Review." *Trinity Journal* 4 (1983): 92-108.
———. *Paul: Follower of Jesus or Founder of Christianity?* Grand Rapids/Cambridge: Eerdmans, 1995.
———. *Gospel Perspectives 4: The Rediscovery of Jesus' Eschatological Discourse*. Sheffield: JSOT, 1984.
Weren, W. J. C. "The Use of Isaiah 5, 1-7 in the Parable of the Tenants [Mark 12, 1-12; Matthew 21, 33-46]." *Biblica* 79 (1998): 1-26.
Westerdale Bowker, J. "Speeches in Acts: A Study in Proem and *Yelammedenu* Form." *New Testament Studies* 14 (1967-68): 96-111.
Westerholm, S. *Perspectives Old and New on Paul: The "Lutheran" Paul and His Critics*. Grand Rapids/Cambridge: Eerdmans, 2004.
Wick, Peter. "Die Antithesen der Bergpredigt als paränetische Rhetorik. Durch scheinbaren Widerspruch zu einem neuen Verständnis." *Judaica* 52 (1996): 156-78.
Wilckens, U. *Weisheit und Torheit: Eine exegetisch-religionsgeschichtliche Untersuchung zu 1. Kor. 1 und 2*. Tübingen: Mohr Siebeck, 1959.
Wilk, Florian. *Jesus und die Völker in der Sicht der Synoptiker*. Beihefte zur Zeitschrift für die neutestamentliche Wissenschaft 109. Berlin: de Gruyter, 2002.
Wilkins, M. J. *Discipleship in the Ancient World and Matthew's Gospel*. 2nd ed. Grand Rapids: Baker, 1995.
———. *Following the Master: Discipleship in the Steps of Jesus*. Grand Rapids: Zondervan, 1992.
Williamson, H. G. M. "The Messianic Texts in Isaiah 1–39." Pages 238-70 in *King and Messiah in Israel and the Ancient Near East*. Edited by John Day. Journal for the Study of the Old Testament: Supplement Series 270. Sheffield: Sheffield Academic Press, 1998.
———. *Variations on a Theme: King, Messiah and Servant in the Book of Isaiah*. Carlisle: Paternoster, 1998.
Wink, W. *John the Baptist in the Gospel Tradition*. Society for New Testament Studies Monograph Series 7. Cambridge: Cambridge University Press, 1968.
Wright, N. T. *The New Testament and the People of God: Christian Origins and the Question of God*. Vol 1. Minneapolis: Fortress, 1992.

Yang, Y.-E. *Jesus and the Sabbath in Matthew's Gospel*. Journal for the Study of the New Testament: Supplement Series 139. Sheffield: Sheffield University Press, 1997.
Yeung, M. W. *Faith in Jesus and Paul*. Wissenschaftliche Untersuchungen zum Neuen Testament 2.147. Tübingen: Mohr Siebeck, 2002.
Young, E. J. *The Book of Isaiah*. 3 vols. Grand Rapids: Eerdmans, 1965.
Zahn, Theodor. *Das Evangelium nach Matthäus*. 4th ed. Kommentar zum Neuen Testament 1. Leipzig: Deichertsche, 1922. Repr. Wuppertal: R. Brockhaus, 1984.

Index of Modern Authors

Aitken, K. T., 263
Allen, E., 42
Allison, D. C., Jr., 40, 41, 46, 59n.18, 87, 92, 103, 104, 105, 136, 137, 141-43, 148, 150, 152, 207, 222, 226, 231, 239, 242, 259
Alsup, J. E., 233
Andreoli, D., 128, 152

Bacon, D. W., 112
Baker, D., 233, 245
Barton, S. C., 179
Battistella, E. L., 36
Bauckham, R. J., 128, 129, 137, 138, 153
Baum, A. D., vii
Beale, G. K., 259, 260, 263
Beasley-Murray, G. R., 191
Beaton, R., 140, 254, 255
Becker, H. J., 61, 63, 67
Beckwith, R., 144
Belo, F., 284
Berger, D., 59
Betz, H. D., 47, 58, 176, 188, 196
Blenkinsopp, J., 235, 236, 238, 265
Bloch, R., 212, 235
Bock, D. L., 234, 245, 246
Bockmuehl, M., 55, 66
Brawley, R. L., 75, 79
Brower, K., 179, 186
Brown, J. K., vii, 248, 251, 253, 257, 258, 267
Brown, R. E., 121, 150, 222, 230

Bruner, F. D., 46
Bultmann, R., 232, 233, 242, 245
Burger, C., 39-41, 43, 46
Buth, R., 49
Buttrick, D., 187

Cargal, T. B., 168
Carson, D. A., 95, 96
Carter, W., 138, 228, 240, 241, 246, 248, 285
Charlesworth, J. H., 212
Chatman, S., 267
Chester, A., 55
Chilton, B. D., 211
Clements, R. E., 262, 263
Collins, A. Y., 188
Collins, R. F., 79
Combrink, H. J. B., 267
Cullmann, O., 85

Dalman, G., 132
Daube, D., 212, 223
Davids, P. H., 194
Davies, W. D., 40, 41, 46, 87, 92, 95, 103-5, 136, 137, 141-43, 148, 150, 152, 207, 222, 226, 231, 239, 242, 259
Deines, R., vii, 65, 71, 72, 201, 202, 204
Deutsch, C., 132, 138, 249, 253
Donaldson, T. L., 273
Dungan, D. L., 189
Dunn, J. D. G., 192, 193

313

INDEX OF MODERN AUTHORS

Eckstein, H. J., 70
Eco, U., 250
Eichrodt, W., 232, 234
Ellis, E. E., 228, 232-34
Eloff, M., vii, 88
Evans, C. A., 60, 141, 264

Finkelstein, L., 8, 215
Foster, P., 53, 57, 62
Foulkes, F., 234, 239
France, R. T., vii, 108, 140, 143, 145, 207, 208, 227, 243, 270, 282
Frankemölle, H., 154
Franzmann, M. H., 185

Garbe, G., 57
Garland, D. E., 102, 103
Gerhardsson, B., 39, 139
Givón, T., 28-31
Golden, J., 8
Goodacre, M., 194
Goppelt, L., 233, 234
Greenberg, J. H., 29
Grice, H. P., 27
Guelich, R. A., 188
Gundry, R. H., 138, 142, 194, 230, 237, 254, 289
Gurtner, D. M., vii, 151
Gushee, D., 187

Hagner, D. A., vii, 49, 57, 67, 80, 100, 139, 141, 143, 145, 231, 233, 238, 270
Halliday, M. A. K., 32, 33
Hamilton, J. M., vii
Hare, D. R. A., 57
Hartin, P. J., 195
Held, H. J., 39-41, 43, 46
Hengel, M., 189
Horbury, W., 232, 234
Horsley, R. A., 114
Howell, D. A., 86, 87, 93

Instone-Brewer, D., vii, 210, 224

Jensen, J., 229, 235, 237
Johnson, L. T., 157
Johnson-Laird, P. N., 26, 27

Kähler, M., 138
Kingsbury, J. D., 40, 41, 43, 46, 86, 106, 111, 129
Knowles, M., 144-46, 245
Kroger, P. R., 31

Langacker, R. W., 29
Livingstone, E. A., 234
Lohmeyer, E., 128, 152
Longenecker, B. W., 130
Louw, J. P., 40, 41, 46
Luz, U., 39, 46-48, 50, 51, 55, 57, 74-76, 134, 137, 149, 189, 228, 229, 252, 257, 283

Marshall, I. H., 27, 288
Mason, S., 159
McKnight, S., 78, 80
McNamara, M., 211-13, 216, 219
Mead, R. T., 233
Meier, J. P., 85, 86, 104
Morgenthaler, R., 2
Moule, C. F. D., 74
Murray, J. D., 30, 31

Nesbitt, C., 32
Neyrey, J. H., 251, 255
Nineham, D. E., 91, 92
Nolland, J. H., vii, 54, 73, 76, 78, 82, 270, 271, 282

Olmstead, W. G., 146, 147
Oswalt, J. N., 238
Overman, J. A., 53, 66, 73

Phillips, G. A., 267
Przybylski, B., 174

Reicke, B., 14, 23
Robertson, A. T., 24
Robinson, J. A. T., 96, 289
Robinson, J. M., 144

Sailhamer, J. H., 243
Saldarini, A. J., 53, 56, 60, 61, 66
Sanders, E. P., 123
Schechter, S., 8
Schnackenburg, R., 201

Index of Modern Authors

Seeligmann, I. L., 215
Segal, E. M., 30, 31
Senior, D., 63, 87
Sim, D. C., 53, 55, 63
Snodgrass, K., 78
Soares Prabhu, G. M., 244
Sperber, D., 45
Stanton, G. N., 57, 89
Stassen, G., 187
Stendahl, K., 254
Strecker, G., 86, 101
Sullivan, D., 168
Syreeni, K., 56, 83

Telford, W. R., 140, 151
Thompson, W. G., 39-41, 43, 46

Vahrenhorst, M., 53, 66
Verseput, D. J., 249

Viviano, B., 56, 70, 74
Vledder, E.-J., 47
von Dobbeler, A., 53
von Dobbeler, S., 63
von Rad, G., 115

Walker, P. W. L., 86, 108, 110, 127
Watts, J. D. E., 230
Watts, R. E., 236-38, 241
Weinfeld, M., 158
Wenham, D., vii
Wick, P., 65
Williamson, H. G. M., 239
Wright, N. T., 91, 92, 102

Yang, Y.-E., 78
Young, E. J., 232

Zahn, T., 56

Index of Subjects

Abram, Abraham, 72, 88-94, 239
Anti-Semitism, 56, 63, 108, 122, 128, 130, 154-69

Balaam-Laban: background, 207, 212-13; in Matthew, 217, 222
Beatitudes, 58, 73, 80, 171, 175, 180, 198-201

Dating of Matthew, 279-80, 289
David, 71, 88-94, 106-7, 171, 239
Disciples, 266

Eschatological Future, 60, 180
Exile, 91-92, 94, 107

"Fulfill," 230-31, 239-47; predictive, 232; typological, 233

Gentile, 161; mission, 55, 183
Grammar: 28, 32; conjunctions: use of, 34-36

Healing, 39-41, 139-41

Idolatry, 259-60

Jesus: Christology, 57, 67, 142; discipleship, 44-46, 49-50, 81-83, 177-78, 183-86; hearing, 251-62; passion of, 121; saving work, 281-82

Jerusalem, 108-9, 113, 116, 125-27
John the Baptist, 99-100, 248-49
Judaism, 56; Jewishness of Matthew's gospel, 128-29, 153, 173-74

Law, 58-63, 64, 76, 79, 82, 176-78, 197
Linguistics: redundancy, 25-26, 50-52; markedness, 29-33, 50-52; mental representations, 26-29, 50-52

Markan Priority, 24, 111, 284
Messiah, 71, 83, 89
Miracles, 140
Moses, 176-77

"Natziri," 224-25

Parables, 118-19, 172, 261
Pharisees, 157
Pilate, culpability in the death of Jesus, 166-69

Righteousness, 174-76, 179-82, 202-4

Sabbath, 61, 67-68, 115, 128, 134-35
Sermon on the Mount, 79, 81, 170, 178, 187-206; origin of, 188-96
Sermon on the Plain, 194-96
Shekinah, 103, 145
Son of Man, 122, 124, 126, 162

Temple, 123, 128, 134-53; destruction of, 145-46; οἰκία, 130-31; ἱερόν, 131; ναός, 131-32, 143, 148, 149
Torah. *See* Law
Typology, 229

Veil, 151
Virgin Birth, 106, 208, 228-29

Zion. *See* Jerusalem

Index of Ancient Sources

OLD TESTAMENT

Genesis
1–11	93
1:28	90
2:1-4	94
2:2-3	90
3:15	235n.34
3:19	212n.7
4:12-14	94
4:13-14	94
12:1-3	89, 90, 93
31:22-35	214
31:36-54	214
32:2-3	214
32:22-30	99
35:17-18	222n.23
35:18-21	216
35:19-21	217
37:30	231n.19
45:27–46:4	216

Exodus
1:9f	219
1:9-10	220
12:2	90n.22
20:12	66n.43
21:15	66n.43
21:17	66n.43
29:46	90n.22

Leviticus
11:44-45	185
13–14	59n.18
19:17	64n.39
19:18	64n.39
20:9	121
21:18-19	139n.58
26:13	67n.46

Numbers
12:13-15	59n.18
15:38-39	59
15:40	59
24:17 (LXX)	220, 225, 226n.31, 246
24:25	222
25:1-9	220
31:16	220

Deuteronomy
6:5	223
6:7	12n.20
17:15	247n.77
18:15	222
19:10	121
21:1-9	166
22:12	59
23:1-2 (LXX)	173
27–28	102
28:48	67n.46
31:6	241

Joshua
2:19	121

Judges
3:8	213n.11
13:5, 7	224
16:17	224

1 Samuel
1:9 (LXX)	132n.14
3:3 (LXX)	132n.14
21:7 (LXX)	130n.8, 150

2 Samuel
1:16	121
5:8	139n.58
7	89, 136n.36
7:5-16	89
7:12	216
7:13	90
7:14	238n.44
7:28-29	90
14:4-11	167n.27
22:7	132n.14

1 Kings
1–10	90n.22
6:3	132n.14
6:5	132n.14
6:17	132n.14
6:33	132n.14

Index of Ancient Sources

6:36	132n.14	5:28	145n.91	1:2-20	263n.51
7–10	18	6:5	132n.14	1:10	265n.58
7:21	132n.14			1:19-20	263
7:50	132n.14	**Nehemiah**		1:29-31	260
8:10-20	90n.22	9:26	153	2:1-4	239
9:6-9	145	13:1 (LXX)	173	5:1-7	118, 142
12:4-14	67n.46			5:2 (LXX)	141
18:1-16	132n.16	**Psalms**		5:24-25	142
		5:7	132n.14	6:9	257
2 Kings		10:5	132n.14	6:9-10	102
18:16	132n.14	17:6	132n.14	6:9-11	259
21:10-15	152n.124	24:4	167n.25	6:9-13	259
23:4	132n.14	26:4	132n.14	6:13	260
24:13	132n.14	26:6 (25 LXX)	167n.25	7:10-25	235n.35
		27:2	132n.14	7:14	102, 241, 228n.3,
1 Chronicles		28:9	132n.14		229n.7, 230n.9,
17	136	44:15	132n.14		230n.12, 231n.19,
21:27	160n.13	48:2	110		238n.46, 241n.58,
28:8 (LXX)	173	64:4	132n.14		242
28:11	132n.13	67:29	132n.14	8:3	241
29:4 (LXX)	131	73:13 (72 LXX)	167n.25	8:20	241
		78:1	132n.14	8:23–9:3	239
2 Chronicles		96 (95 LXX)	161n.15	9	97
1–10	90n.22	107:23-32	50	9:1-2	102, 113
3:17	132n.14	118	104, 105	9:2	197
4–9	18	118:22	118, 142	9:4	67
4:7	132n.14	118:26	125, 130n.8, 146,	9:6	238n.44
4:8	132n.14		150, 162	10:24 (LXX)	215n.14
4:22	132n.14	129:21	64n.39	10:27	67
5:11–6:11	90n.22	135:8	260	11:1	202n.37, 240, 245
6	91n.25	135:15-17a	259	11:1-4	221
6:13 (LXX)	131	135:18	260	11:4	225
8:12	132n.13	137:2	132n.14	11:15-16	220
15:8	132n.13	143:12	132n.14	14:25	67
24:17-23	132n.16			18:3	265n.58
24:20-22	143n.85, 144	**Proverbs**		28:11f	76
24:21-22	144	1:20-33	153n.129	28:16	142
26:16	132n.14	30:12 (LXX)	166n.24	29:9-10	263n.54
27:2	132n.14	30:19	242	29:13	102, 261
29:3-7	140n.62	30:20 (LXX)	166n.24	29:14 (LXX)	262
29:7	132n.13			29:17-18	264
29:17	132n.13	**Song of Songs**		29:18 (LXX)	253
36:7	132n.14	6:8	242	30:19-20	264n.56
				32:3	264
Ezra		**Isaiah**		32:9	265n.58
3:30	145n.91	1–39	102	33:13	265n.58
5:14	132n.14	1:2	265n.58	34:1	265n.58

319

35:5	252, 253n.20	24:1	132n.14	**Hosea**		
35:5-6	253	26:6	146n.101	6:6 (LXX)	59, 69, 134	
40–66	232n.22, 233n.28	26:18	146n.101	11:1	207, 218, 231n.19,	
40–55	263n.54	27:11	67n.46		243, 245n.72	
40	107	29	123	11:4	67n.46	
40:3	102	29:7	90n.23			
42:1-4	102, 254, 255	31:15 (LXX)	222, 231n.19,	**Joel**		
42:2 (LXX)	255		244, 245	2:27	146n. 95	
42:16-20	263n.54	32:6-9	150n.120	3:5	132n.14	
42:18	264n.55	35:14	67n.46	3:16-17	146n.95	
42:18-19	253n.20	47:6	160n.13			
43:1-13	264n.55			**Amos**		
43:8-9	264n.57	**Lamentations**		8:3	132n.14	
43:18-19	234n.30	1:10 (LXX)	173			
44:8-20	263n.54	1:14	67n.46	**Jonah**		
47:7	67	5:5	67n.46	1:5 (LXX)	50	
47:8	265n.58			2:5	132n.14	
48:6-8	253n.20	**Ezekiel**		2:8	132n.14	
49:1	265n.58	8:6	145			
50:4-5	253n.20	8:12	145	**Micah**		
51:1	265n.58	8:16	132n.14	2:5 (LXX)	173	
51:3	240	9:3	145	3:12	146n.101	
51:4	265n.58	9:9	145	4:7-8	217	
51:21	265n.58	10:1-22	103	5:1	225	
52:1	109	10:18-19	124	5:2	207, 217, 231n.19,	
52:13-15	253n.20	11:22-23	124, 145		232	
53:4	102	34:27	67n.46	5:2-4	217	
56:7 (LXX)	102, 130, 138,	41:1	132n.14			
	144n.88, 150	41:4	132n.14	**Zechariah**		
60:7 (LXX)	130, 138, 150	41:15	132n.14	3:8	225	
61:1	253	41:21	132n.14	6:11-12	246	
62:11	109	41:23	132n.14	6:12	225	
64:10-11 (64:9-10		41:25	132n.14	7:3	66	
LXX)	103, 145	45:9 (LXX)	131	8:9	132n.14	
65:2	103			8:19	66	
66:5	265n.58	**Daniel**		8:23 (LXX)	59, 60	
66:6	132n.14	4:26	132n.14	9:9	109, 117, 171	
66:24	107	5:2	132n.14	11:12 (LXX)	150n.120	
		5:3	132n.14	11:13 (LXX)	149	
Jeremiah		7:14	104	14:4	145, 14	
2:30	153	9:24	109			
5:5	67n.46	9:24-27	92	**Malachi**		
7:4	132n.14	9:27	147	3	107	
7:8-15	146n.101	11:31	147	3:1	132n.14	
7:11	144n.88	12:11	147			
9:10-11	146n.101					
19:1-13	150n.120					

Index of Ancient Sources

NEW TESTAMENT

Matthew

Ref	Pages
1–11	133
1–4	240
1	241
1:1	71, 88, 89, 90, 94, 239
1:1-17	71, 87, 246n.75
1:2	94
1:2-17	92, 239
1:12	91
1:13-15	92n.27
1:16	71
1:17	87, 88, 90, 93, 94, 107
1:18	182
1:18-23	228
1:18-25	87, 240
1:20	71, 182
1:21	71, 77, 82n.85, 87, 93, 104, 241
1:21-23	197
1:22	75, 102n.55, 228n.2, 231
1:22-23	229, 231n.19, 239
1:23	60, 71, 90n.22, 94, 103, 202n.37
1:25	241
2	75, 207, 209, 212, 217, 222, 226, 227
2:1	113
2:1-12	71
2:2	113, 217, 226
2:2-6	71
2:3	114, 120, 165n.21
2:4	217
2:5	113, 231
2:5-6	217, 231n.19, 232
2:6	113
2:11	130, 133
2:12	114, 222
2:13	218
2:14	114
2:15	75, 228n.2, 231, 243, 246
2:17	75, 228n.2, 231
2:17-18	231n.19, 245, 246
2:18	233n.25, 244
2:22	114
2:23	75, 115, 228n.2, 231, 245, 246
3:1	114
3:2	72, 96
3:3	96, 102n.55
3:4	68n.48, 96n.37
3:5	114, 115
3:6	71
3:7-10	114
3:8	58
3:9	88n.18
3:11	182
3:11-14	96
3:12	99
3:14	203
3:15	58n.16, 61, 72, 74, 75, 80, 82, 174, 202, 228n.2, 247
3:16	182
4:1-11	131, 133, 243
4:3	149
4:5	108, 109, 115, 133
4:6	149
4:8	72
4:9	133
4:12	114
4:12-16	113
4:14	75, 228n.2
4:14-16	102n.55
4:15	161n.15
4:17	72, 96, 100, 111, 113, 199, 282
4:17–11:1	248
4:18-22	15, 253
4:19	79, 82n.85
4:19-22	178
4:23	72, 170
4:24-25	115
4:25	116
5–7	79, 170, 177, 193, 194, 196n.27
5:1	177, 198
5:1–7:29	106
5:2	198
5:3	100, 171, 180, 196n.28, 198
5:3-10	58, 102, 282
5:3-12	259
5:3–7:27	58
5:4	174, 198
5:5	174, 198
5:6	70n.51, 73, 80, 82, 174, 196n.28, 198
5:7	174, 198
5:8	174, 198, 203
5:9	174, 198, 238n.44
5:10	73, 74, 171, 175, 180
5:11	65n.41, 79, 175
5:11-16	73
5:12	79
5:13	179
5:13-16	69, 74, 76, 82n.85, 185
5:16	74, 81, 82, 185, 201
5:17	59, 60, 67n.44, 73, 74, 75, 76, 77, 80, 128, 139, 142, 150, 152, 177, 178, 188, 195n.24, 196, 200, 201n.35, 203, 204, 228n.2, 247
5:17-19	56, 173
5:17-20	57, 64, 65n.41, 70, 72, 73, 74, 77, 78, 200
5:18	61, 62, 70n.52, 76, 77, 176, 195n.24, 197, 201n.32
5:18-19	134
5:19	67, 72, 77, 79, 197, 201n.32
5:20	72, 80, 81, 82, 135, 161, 175, 188, 196, 200, 204
5:20-48	204
5:21	62, 78, 82
5:21-48	64, 82, 201
5:22	176
5:22-25	64
5:23	59, 143

INDEX OF ANCIENT SOURCES

5:23-24	115, 130, 133, 134, 148, 150n.119, 152	7:23	58, 62n.29, 203	8:24	50
5:24	133	7:24	187	8:25	48
5:27-30	203	7:24-27	131, 173, 178	8:25-26	48, 49, 50, 51
5:28	64, 176	7:28	100, 111, 120	8:26	48, 49, 50, 51, 253n.18
5:29	72	7:28-29	97	8:27	50, 51
5:31	64, 69	8	136	8:28	42n.48
5:32	176, 195n.24	8:1	42n.48	8:28-34	40
5:33	64, 196n.28	8:1-4	40, 133	9:1-8	40
5:34	176	8:1-15	40	9:2-6	71
5:34-37	195	8:1-17	39, 40	9:4	66
5:35	108, 110, 115	8:1-22	38	9:6	130
5:38-39	160	8:1–9:34	39, 40, 41, 46, 47, 48, 51, 133	9:7	130
5:38-42	64	8:2	59n.18	9:9	178
5:39	64, 176	8:3	65	9:10	66, 71, 131
5:43	64n.39, 194	8:4	58, 59, 60, 130, 133, 140, 148	9:11	134
5:44	176	8:5	42n.48	9:13	59, 71, 134
5:45	65, 81, 82	8:5-13	40	9:15	66
5:48	65, 72n.58, 81, 184, 201	8:6	131	9:17	65n.41
6:1	81, 82, 175	8:9	38, 39, 40, 41, 46, 51	9:18	42n.48, 45
6:1-18	161, 175, 201	8:10	44, 50	9:18-31	39
6:2	175	8:11	88n.18, 105, 107, 122	9:20	59, 65
6:5	175, 188n.5	8:12	105, 107	9:23	131
6:9	174	8:14	131	9:25	65
6:9-10	106	8:14-17	40	9:27	71
6:11-15	201	8:16-17	43	9:28	131
6:12	185	8:16-22	40, 41	9:32	42n.48
6:14	15	8:17	40, 102n.55, 228n.2	9:32-34	39
6:16	175	8:18	40, 43	9:33	42n.48
6:16-18	66	8:18-22	37, 39, 40, 41, 43, 46, 51	9:33-34	47
6:17	66	8:18-27	37, 40, 41, 51, 52	9:35	72, 170
6:19-34	201	8:18–9:17	39	9:36	68, 254
6:25	135	8:19	43, 46	10	97, 165n.21, 170, 189
6:27	194	8:19-20	43	10:1-15	183
6:30	253n.18	8:20	43	10:5	62, 161
6:32	82, 161n.15	8:21	44, 45, 46	10:5-6	97, 183
6:33	80, 81, 82n.85, 175, 184, 203	8:21-22	43, 45	10:5-8	97
7:5	68n.50	8:22	40, 44, 45, 46, 50, 66, 178	10:6	93, 97, 101, 130
7:6	174	8:23	39, 40, 41, 45, 46, 51	10:7	72
7:12	62, 65, 67n.44, 179, 201n.35	8:23-27	37, 39, 40, 46, 48, 50, 51, 52	10:8	190n.11
7:13	72	8:23-34	39	10:8-14	184
7:19	68			10:9	82n.85
7:21	58, 72, 177, 186			10:10	190
7:21-23	106n.67, 205			10:12	131
				10:13	131
				10:14	131
				10:16	98

10:16-22	65n.41	11:13	67n.44, 75, 83, 96, 102, 171	12:18-21	250, 251, 254
10:18	97, 161n.15			12:19	250, 255, 258
10:19-20	182	11:14	96n.37, 171, 256	12:19-20	255
10:23	162	11:15	95, 250n.9, 252, 256, 258, 267, 268	12:20-21	255
10:24-25	177			12:21	161n.15
10:32-33	173, 181	11:16	98n.47, 102	12:22-28	249
10:34-39	65n.41	11:16-19	95, 98, 153n.129, 165n.21	12:22-32	255
10:37	66n.43			12:23	71, 253n.18
10:37-38	177	11:16-24	249	12:23-24	258
10:37-39	173, 181	11:19	66, 71, 97, 249	12:24	248, 255
10:38	178	11:20-24	153n.129, 165n.21	12:25	131
10:42	97	11:24	106n.67	12:28	171
11–13	251, 252, 265	11:25	95, 97, 99, 101	12:29	131
11–12	250, 251, 255, 256, 258	11:25-26	95	12:31	71, 77
		11:25-28	94	12:33-45	255n.28
11	102	11:25-30	138, 249	12:35	181, 228n.2
11:1	95, 97, 100, 111, 177	11:27	94	12:38-45	249
11:1-18	94, 101	11:28	94, 95	12:39	95, 98n.47
11:1-24	94	11:28-30	67, 107, 181, 197, 201n.34	12:41	115, 135
11:1–12:50	94			12:42	90n.22, 115, 135
11:2	71, 249, 250, 252	11:30	175	12:44	130
11:2-3	258	12	251n.12, 255	12:45	98n.47, 102
11:2-5	252	12:1	67	12:46-50	252n.17, 256
11:2-6	252n.17	12:1-8	67, 201n.32	12:48	228n.2
11:2-19	251, 252, 253, 266	12:1-14	134, 249, 255	12:49-50	182
11:2–13:52	250	12:1-32	251, 254	12:50	177, 256
11:2–16:20	248, 249, 250, 251, 261, 262, 265n.59, 266, 268	12:1-50	94	13	95, 170, 250, 252, 256, 257, 258, 259, 260, 261, 265, 267
		12:3	67n.47, 71		
		12:4	150		
11:3	95, 97, 249	12:5	68n.48, 131, 135	13–16	251, 265
11:4	253	12:5-6	115, 134	13:1	131
11:4-5	171, 252	12:6	108, 115, 122, 130, 131, 134, 135, 149, 198	13:1-23	251, 256
11:4-6	100			13:1–16:20	250
11:5	100, 251, 253, 266, 267			13:3-9	257n.32
		12:7	59, 134	13:9	250n.9, 257, 261, 267, 268
11:6	253n.21	12:8	161n.15, 198		
11:7	258	12:9-13	67	13:9-19	257
11:7-11	114	12:9-14	67	13:9-23	257
11:8	130	12:10	68	13:10-17	260
11:9	96	12:12	68	13:11	99, 165n.21, 171, 262n.49, 266
11:9-14	95	12:14	65n.41, 68, 98, 131, 168		
11:10	96			13:11-13	253n.18
11:11	100, 116, 234n.30	12:15	68, 114, 249, 254	13:12	80
11:11-15	66, 95, 249	12:16	254	13:13	250, 257
11:12	88n.16, 96, 97, 99, 100, 101, 139	12:17	228n.2	13:13-18	256
		12:17-21	102n.55	13:13-19	256
11:12-13	95, 99, 102	12:18	182, 255	13:13-23	257

323

13:14	250, 257	14:1	250	16:12	65n.41, 68n.50, 250n.11, 251
13:14-15	102n.55, 251, 258, 259	14:1-2	248, 249, 252, 258, 267	16:13-20	136, 248, 249
13:15	250, 257n.34	14:1-12	252n.17	16:14	114, 123
13:15-16	257	14:4-12	15	16:16	171, 249, 253
13:16	257n.34, 259, 267	14:13	114, 249, 254	16:16-20	71, 193n.17
13:16-17	171, 258, 266	14:20	80	16:18	63n.37, 136, 172, 173
13:17	266	14:22-33	15, 249	16:19	69
13:18	258	14:31	253n.18	16:21	100, 111, 116, 172, 177
13:18-23	258n.38	14:34-36	15	16:21–20:34	116
13:19	250, 256	14:36	59	16:22-23	15
13:19-23	257	14:58	148	16:24	77, 177
13:23	250, 256, 260, 265, 268	15:1	115	16:24-26	184
		15:1-11	15, 68, 249	16:24-27	172
13:24	256n.31	15:1-20	251, 254, 261, 262	16:24-28	178
13:24-30	256, 261	15:2	60, 65n.41, 68n.50	16:27	161, 162, 178
13:28-30	261n.48	15:6-9	60	16:27-28	162
13:31	256n.31	15:8-9	102n.55, 251, 261	17:5	267
13:31-32	261	15:10	250, 251, 262, 267, 268	17:10-13	15
13:31-33	172			17:12	171
13:32	135	15:11	68	17:17	165n.21
13:33	156n.31, 261	15:12	65n.41	17:20	253n.18
13:34	15	15:14	115	17:24	61, 69, 79, 131
13:35	93	15:15-20	15, 249	17:24-25	61
13:36	131	15:16	250n.11, 258n.38	17:24-27	198
13:36-42	261	15:17	68, 250n.11	17:24-29	137
13:37-43	257n.32, 258n.38	15:20	60, 68	17:25	131
13:41	62n.29	15:21	15, 114, 249, 254	17:26	131
13:43	250n.9, 256, 257, 261, 267, 268	15:21-28	248, 249	17:27	69, 131, 137
		15:22	71	18	170
13:44	256n.31	15:24	62, 101, 130	18:1-4	97
13:44-46	172, 184, 256	15:25-28	15	18:3	69, 72
13:45	256n.31	15:29	15	18:3-4	186
13:47	256n.31	15:29-31	69	18:3-6	77
13:47-50	256, 261	15:32	80	18:6	69
13:51	250, 258n.38	15:32-38	69	18:6-7	182
13:51-52	177	15:32-39	15, 69	18:8	72
13:52	180	15:37	80	18:8-9	15
13:53	97, 100, 111	16:1-4	249	18:12-14	68
13:53-58	15, 249, 252n.17, 256	16:4	249, 254n.22	18:15-17	182
		16:5-12	249	18:17	172
13:53–16:20	250	16:6	60	18:18	69
13:54	120	16:7-11	15	18:20	106, 145, 173, 181
13:54-57	256	16:8	112, 253n.18	18:22	282
13:54-58	165n.21	16:8-12	258n.38	18:35	282
13:58	256	16:9	250n.11	19:1	97, 100, 111
14–16	249, 250	16:11	60, 250n.11		

Index of Ancient Sources

19:1-9	15	21:13	102n.55, 129, 138, 144n.88, 150, 152	23:2-3	159
19:1-12	191n.13			23:3	56, 60, 68n.50
19:3-9	64, 69	21:14	130, 139	23:4	155, 175, 198, 254
19:4	93	21:14-16	120	23:5	155
19:8	195n.24, 201	21:15	131, 137	23:8	173, 176
19:10	69	21:15-16	118, 171	23:8-10	177
19:10-12	184	21:17	137	23:10	174
19:16-22	72, 178	21:18-19	15, 123	23:13	155
19:17	72	21:19	15	23:15	155
19:17-19	62	21:21	141	23:16	132, 143
19:21	72n.58, 178, 184	21:21-22	140	23:16-22	61, 152
19:23	72	21:23	69, 103, 104, 130, 131, 141	23:17	132, 135, 174
19:25	72, 120			23:19	135, 174
19:26	186	21:23-27	114, 116	23:21	132, 143, 144n.88, 148
19:27-30	178	21:26	114, 120		
20:10	135	21:28-32	114, 118	23:22	143
20:17	177	21:31	66, 69, 177	23:23	61, 79, 155, 178
20:17-18	116	21:31-32	119	23:23-28	134, 200
20:18	116	21:32	80, 89n.18, 114, 174	23:24	254
20:19	161n.15	21:33	141, 142	23:25-29	65n.42
20:20-23	15	21:33-46	141	23:28	62n.29
20:25	161n.15	21:41	142	23:29	104, 105, 119
20:25-28	282	21:42-43	104, 152	23:32	228n.2
20:26-28	186	21:43	105, 118	23:34-36	138
20:28	71, 77, 82n.85, 168	21:45	118	23:34-40	15
20:29	117	21:46	120, 165n.22	23:35	88n.16, 102, 132, 143, 152, 167
20:30	71	22–25	142		
20:31	135	22:1-14	118, 142	23:36	98n.47, 119
21–23	115	22:2	142	23:37	103, 109, 119, 120, 125, 145n.89, 165n.21
21–22	120	22:3-7	142		
21	113, 116, 137	22:7	142, 143, 152		
21:1-11	120, 138	22:15-46	118	23:37-39	104, 120, 138, 152, 153
21:1-27	138, 148	22:33	120		
21:1-22:45	90n.22	22:34	120	23:38	103n.60, 119, 122, 129, 144, 150, 161
21:4	140, 228n.2	22:34-35	120		
21:5	109	22:34-40	79	23:39	102, 103, 104, 106, 125, 126, 146
21:8-11	165n.22	22:36-40	62, 65n.40, 69n.51		
21:9	71, 104, 117, 125, 137, 162, 171			24–25	122, 170
		22:40	64, 67n.44, 178	24	105, 147
21:10	104, 114, 116, 120	22:42	71	24:1	103, 131
21:10-11	117	22:44	93	24:1-2	148
21:10-17	15	23	102n.58, 118, 132, 143, 155, 156, 157, 158, 159, 161, 163	24:1-3	122
21:12	59, 69, 104, 131, 138, 139			24:1-51	104
				24:2	119, 122, 129, 131, 146
21:12-13	123, 139	23:1	104		
21:12-17	90n.22	23:1-12	120	24:3	147
21:12–26:14	89n.18	23:2	60, 62, 79	24:3-25:46	146

325

24:5	162n.17	26:5	120, 165n.22
24:9	161n.15, 165n.21	26:6-13	15
24:12	62n.29	26:13	170
24:14	161n.15, 170, 171	26:17	59
24:15	147, 174	26:26	225n.30
24:15-28	183	26:26-29	70n.51, 168
24:16	183	26:28	71, 82n.85, 106, 168
24:17	131	26:29	104, 105, 106
24:19	106n.67	26:31	168
24:20	61	26:31-32	15
24:21	93, 102, 144	26:32	112
24:22	106n.67	26:38	77
24:23-25	15	26:41	185
24:26	178	26:42	77
24:27	162n.17	26:47	121
24:29-31	122, 124	26:52	160
24:30	104, 162n.17, 191	26:53	149
24:31	191	26:54	71, 75, 77, 228n.2
24:35	82, 176	26:55	121, 130, 131, 147
24:36	106n.67	26:56	71, 75, 77, 168, 228n.2
24:37	162n.17		
24:38	106n.67	26:58	168n.28
24:39	162n.17	26:59	118
24:42	15, 162n.17	26:59-60	148
24:43	131, 147, 191	26:59-63	15
24:44	93, 162n.17, 191	26:60	148
24:45	147	26:61	132, 136, 148
24:45-47	104	26:61-63	124
24:46-51	147	26:63	71
24:50	100n.49, 162n.17	26:64	124, 126, 162n.17
25	105	26:66	167
25:1-13	192	26:69	113
25:10	72, 162n.17	26:69-75	168
25:14-19	104	27	113, 155
25:21	72	27:1-2	152
25:23	72	27:2	149
25:29	80	27:3-5	168
25:31	93, 162n.17	27:3-10	149
25:31-46	56, 57, 69n.51	27:4	168
25:32	161n.15	27:5	132, 144, 149
25:34	93	27:6	167
25:40	178	27:6-7	168
25:45	178	27:7	150
25:46	72	27:9	71, 228n.2
26–28	147	27:12-14	165
26:1	100, 111	27:14-16	168
26:4	168	27:15	164

27:15-18	164
27:15-21	164
27:15-23	121
27:16	165n.23
27:18	165, 165n.22
27:19	81, 165, 167n.26
27:20	121, 166, 168
27:21	166
27:22-23	117
27:22-24	166
27:24	165, 166, 167n.26, 168
27:24-25	121, 164
27:25	122, 145n.97, 155, 163, 164, 167, 168, 169
27:27-31	15
27:30	225n.30
27:39-44	121
27:40	124, 132, 136, 151
27:40-42	149
27:42	71, 114
27:43	71, 149
27:45	88n.16
27:46-48	15
27:47-50	168
27:51	151
27:51-54	198
27:52	174
27:53	108, 109, 147
27:54	71
27:55-56	168
27:63	71n.55
28:5	71n.55
28:7	112
28:10	112
28:11-15	112, 126
28:15	109, 114
28:16-20	101, 112
28:18	104, 112
28:19	79, 161, 182
28:19-20	97
28:20	61, 70n.51, 93, 94, 105, 106, 173, 174, 176, 179, 181, 241

Index of Ancient Sources

Mark		11:23	141	6:21	196n.28
1:4	71	11:25	133	6:27	193
1:14	196	11:27	110, 141	6:28	193
1:16-20	15	12:28-31	15	6:45	181
1:29-45	39	12:28-34	120	7:28	95n.36
1:40-45	133	12:32-35	152	7:34	224
1:42	133	12:33	136	8:22-39	39
1:44	133, 136	13:1	146	9:1-6	189
1:44-45	133	13:1-2	152	10:1-16	189
2:17	134	13:14	147	10:7	190
2:23-28	134	13:21-23	15	11:49	144
2:23-3:6	135	13:33-37	15	11:51	144
2:25	67n.47	14:3-9	15	12:22-32	188n.5
3:22	116	14:27-28	15	12:31	196n.28
4:9	250n.9	14:43	110	12:39	191
4:23	250n.9	14:49	148	12:40	191
4:33-34	15	14:53	110	13:34-35	153
4:35–5:20	39	14:55-61	15	14:16-24	118
4:39-40	49	14:56	148	16:16	98
6:1-6	15	14:57	148	20:1	141
6:7-13	189	14:58	136, 148	21:5	146
6:18-29	15	14:70	111	21:20	147
6:45-52	15	15:1	110, 149	22:16	231, 246
6:53-56	15	15:2	149	22:53	148
7:1-12	15	15:16-20	15	24:44	196
7:24-30	15	15:29	136		
7:31	15	15:29-30	151	**John**	
8:1-10	15	15:34-36	15	1:47-51	99
8:16-21	15			3:2	72
8:22-23	139	**Luke**		3:6	72
8:31	110	1:32	238n.44	4:22	101
8:32-33	15	1:75	174	8:31	177
9:11-13	15	2:24	136	11:51-52	238n.44
9:43-48	15	2:25-35	241n.56	12:3	137
10:1-12	15	2:36-38	241n.56	18:11	160
10:11	195n.24	4:9	133	18:20	148
10:12	195n.24	4:16-30	202, 276		
10:35-40	15	4:17-19	246	**Acts**	
10:46	117, 139	4:21	196, 246	1:9	147
10:49	139	5:12-16	133	1:12	147
10:51	139	5:14	133, 136	1:15-20	149
11:9-10	137	5:15-16	133	1:18	149
11:11	15, 116, 137, 138	6:16	195n.24	5:38	75
11:12-14	15	6:17	195n.24	6:2	69
11:16	152	6:18	195n.24	6:13-14	123
11:19	117	6:20	196n.28	8:39	98n.46
11:20-25	15	6:20-49	193	14:21	177n.13

327

15:1	54n.3
15:5	54n.3
21:20	54n.3
23:6-10	118
24:6	131

Romans

1:16	101
1:17	174, 202
2:13	178
3	203
3:10-18	76n.70
3:19	76n.70, 82
3:21	202, 204
3:31	204
6	203
6:13	203
6:19	203
8:3	205
8:4	205
10:4	62
11:17-26	127
12:14-21	193
13:8-9	205
14:17	204
14:20	198n.30
15:12	225

1 Corinthians

4:12	156
6:9	204
7:3	191n.13
7:4	191n.13
8:9	198n.30
9	190, 191
9:1	190
9:13	131
9:18	190n.11
10:11	234n.30
11:23-25	191
13:1-3	205
14:21	76n.70
15:3-5	191
15:8-11	191n.12
15:58	80n.82

2 Corinthians

1:17	196n.26
1:18	196n.26
1:20	241
3:9	80n.82
8:2	80n.82
8:7	80n.82
11:20	156

Galatians

1	191n.12, 193n.17
2	191n.12, 193n.17
2:7	190n.13
3:16	216n.15
4:25-26	127
5:14	65n.41, 205
6:2	82

Ephesians

4:12	156

Philippians

1:9-11	205
3:12	205

Colossians

1:10	205
3:13	156

1 Thessalonians

1:4	80n.82
1:10	80n.82
3:13	205
4	191
4:1	204n.40
4:10	204n.40
4:15-17	192
4:16-17	191
5	191
5:2	191

2 Timothy

3:8	218n.16

Hebrews

12:18-24	127

James

1:25	178
2:5	194, 196
5:1-2	194
5:12	194, 195

1 Peter

1:15-16	185
2:4-10	127
2:12	194
3:9	193
3:14	175, 194
3:21	234n.31
4:13	194
4:14	194

2 Peter

3:10	192

APOCRYPHA

Sirach

6:23-26	67n.46
6:28-31	67n.46
6:30	67n.46
15:26	67n.46
24:19	198n.29
28:19f	67n.46
33:27	67n.46
50:5	151
51:26	67n.46

Wisdom of Solomon

7:27	132n.16
10:1–11:14	132n.16

Baruch

4:12	145

1 Maccabees

10:84	131n.9
11:4	131n.9

2 Maccabees

2:22	75n.67
4:11	75n.67

Index of Ancient Sources

4 Maccabees
5:33   75n.67

PSEUDEPIGRAPHA

Apocalypse of Elijah
2:41   147
4:21   147

Apocalypse of Moses
41:2-3   212n.7

Epistle of Aristeas
305-6   167

1 Enoch
62:6   162n.18
62:9-10   162n.18
63:1-12   162n.18
89:3   141n.73
89:56   141n.73
89:66b-67   141.73
91:12-17   92, 239n.49
93:1-10   239n.49
93:3-10   92

Joseph and Asenath
29:3-4   160

Lives of the Prophets
2:1   132n.16
3:18   132n.16
6:2   132n.16
7:1-3   132n.16

Martyrdom of Isaiah
5:1-16   132n.16

Psalms of Solomon
3:8   66
17:30   140n.62

Pseudo-Philo, *LAB*
12:3   247
17:3   245n.74
32:1   245n.74
32:16   245n.74
40:2   245n.74
45:2   245n.74
54:2   245n.74
56:1   247n.77

Testaments of the Twelve Patriarchs
T. Asher
7:2-7   145n.91
7:3   222n.21

T. Benj.
9:3   222n.21

T. Dan
5:7-9   145n.91

T. Iss.
6:1-4   145n.91

T. Jud.
23:1-5   145n.91

T. Levi
4:1   222n.21
14:2   222n.21
15:1   145, 147
18:3   222, 225

T. Naph.
4:1-5   145n.91

T. Sol.
22–23   142

T. Zeb.
9:5-8   145n.91

DEAD SEA SCROLLS

CD
7:18-21   221
15:15-17   139n.58

1QM
7:4-6   139n.58
11:5-9   221
12:7-9   139n.58

1QS
9:3-6   146n.95

1QSa
2:5-22   139n.58

4Q161   225

4Q174   216n.13

4Q500   141n.73

APOSTOLIC FATHERS

Barnabas
16:1-2   141n.73
16:4   141n.73
16:5   141n.73

JEWISH AUTHORS

Josephus
Antiquities
2.9.2   220
6.374   131n.9
7.67   109
13.9.1   223n.25
20.166   145
20.200   54n.3

Contra Apionem
2.178   12
1.281   65

Jewish War
2.175   149n.114
5.19   145
5.412-13   145
6.295-300   145
6.300ff   146n.97
6.300-305   123
6.438   109
7.123   131n.9

INDEX OF ANCIENT SOURCES

Philo
Legatio ad Gaium
210   12n.20

Life of Moses
1.92   222
1.276   219n.17

Mishnaic, Talmudic, Rabbinic, and Targumic Writing
'Abodah Zarah
6a   224n.27
6b   224n.27
16b   224n.27
17a   224n.27

'Abot
2.9   7
3.2   145
3.2   173n.7

'Abot de Rabbi Nathan A
14–17   5, 6, 16
14.8-14   17
14.17-31   7

'Abot de Rabbi Nathan B
28–30   5, 6, 16
29.1-10   17
29.18-23   7

Berakot
5b   173n.7

Ecclesiastes Rabbah
3.16   144n.87

'Erubin
67a   9n.15

Exodus Rabbah
12.29   242
31.16   145n.91

Genesis Rabah
20:10   212n.7

Giṭṭin
57b   144n.87

Ḥagigah
1.1   139n.58

Targum Isaiah
5:1b-2   141
5:5   141

Targum Lamentations
1.19   144
2.20   144
5.11   144
5.14   144

Leviticus Rabbah
7.3-21   12n.20

Numbers Rabbah
7.48   242
15.10   146n.95

Targum Neofiti
Gen. 3:19   212n.7
Gen. 32:2   215
Num. 24:17   221
Deut. 26:5   215

Targum Onqelos
Num. 24:17   221
Deut. 26:5   215

Pesiqta Rabbati
31   145n.91
29   145n.91

Targum Pseudo-Jonathan
Gen. 3:19   212n.7
Gen. 32:2-3   214
Gen. 35:18-21   216
Gen. 35:21   217
Gen. 45:27   216
Gen. 46:2-4   218
Gen. 46:4   218
Gen. 46:6   218
Gen. 46:6-7   215
Exod. 1:15   219
Num. 22:5   212
Num. 24:17   221
Num. 31:8   213
Deut. 26:5   215

Sanhedrin
2.7   79n.77
39a   173n.7
43a   224n.27
96a   144n.87
103a   224n.27
105   213
106   214
106b   214
107b   224n.27

b. Shabbat
31a   65n.40
115   211

m. Soṭah
78   223

Sukkah
3.15   141

Ta'anit
4.9   144n.87
27b   224n.27

Yalqut Shimoni
173   219

GREEK AND LATIN WRITINGS

Aristotle
Rhetoric
3.9.3   11n.19

Cicero
De oratore
2.355   10n.18

Index of Ancient Sources

Galen
De compositione medicamentorum per genera
5.10   11n.19

Eusebius
Historia ecclesiastica
1.7.14   245
5.20.5-7   12n.22

Herodotus
Historiae
1.183   131n.12

Jerome
Commentariorum in Matthaeum IV
1.2.23   225n.29
27.9   149

Justin
Dialogus cum Tryphone
16   225
43   229, 242

47.1-5   54n.3
66   229
93   225
95   225
96   225
123   225
133   225

Plato
Phaedrus
267a   11n.19

Pliny the Elder
Natural History
30.11   219n.17

Plutarch
Moralia
407f   11n.11

Polybius
Fragmenta
16.39.4   131n.9

Quintilian
Institutio oratorio
11.2.6   12n.21
11.2.7   13n.24
11.2.10   10n.18
11.2.39   11n.19

Seneca
Controversiae
1   12n.21

Statius
Silvae
5.2.170   240

Tertullian
Adversus Marcionem
4.8.1   225

Xenophon
Apologia Socratis
15   131n.12